From
PARTNERS
to
PARENTS

From
PARTNERS
to
PARENTS

The Second Revolution in Family Law

JUNE CARBONE

COLUMBIA UNIVERSITY PRESS

NEW YORK

Columbia University Press
Publishers Since 1893
New York   Chichester, West Sussex
Copyright © 2000 by Columbia University Press
Library of Congress Cataloging-in-Publication Data
Carbone, June.
      From partners to parents : the second revolution in family law / June Carbone.
         p. cm.
      Includes bibliographical references and index.
      ISBN 0–231–11116–9 (cloth : alk. paper) — ISBN 0–231–11117–7 (pbk. :
alk. paper)
        1. Family — United States. 2. Parent and child — United States.
      3. Domestic relations — United States. 4. Parent and child (Law) — United
States.   I. Title.

HQ535 .C253 2000
306.85′0973—dc21   00–020918

Casebound editions of Columbia University Press books are printed on permanent
and durable acid-free paper.
Printed in the United States of America
c 10 9 8 7 6 5 4 3 2 1
p 10 9 8 7 6 5 4 3 2 1

To Bill, Kenny, Genina, and Galen

Contents

Acknowledgments

I BEGAN the original research for this book while a Visiting Scholar at the Institute for Research on Women and Gender at Stanford University, and the inspiration for its structure came from the rich interdisciplinary exchange at the Institute and the supportive environment provided by Institute scholars. I also greatly benefited from planning a conference on the family with the Markkula Center for Applied Ethics at Santa Clara University. Many of the authors whose work contributes to the first part of the book participated in the conference, with Martha Fineman and Bill Galston providing keynote speeches that framed the conference discussion. The National Endowment for the Humanities provided a grant that made possible the timely completion of the middle section of the book. I would also like to thank Deans Uelman and Player for the financial and research support I received from the Santa Clara University School of Law.

I would particularly like to thank Margalynne Armstrong, Bill Black, Peg Brinig, Naomi Cahn, Bill Galston, Martha Fineman, Bryan Ford, David Friedman, Peter Kwan, Nancy Levit, Barbara Maloney, Mike Meyer, Fred Parrella, Helen Popper, Mitt Regan, Cookie Ridolfi, Margaret Russell, Carol Sanger, Jana Singer, Bill Sundstrom, and Barbara Woodhouse for their comments, support, and assistance with various parts of this manuscript. I am indebted to Wanda Ochoa, who prepared the original charts and graphs, and helped with the planning for all of the illustrations. I am very fortunate as well to have been able to enlist Jessie Bontrager to draw cartoons for the book. I would also like to thank Norman Davidson, Barbara Friedrich, and Rebecca Hill as well as the editors at Columbia University Press, John Michel, Alex Thorp, and Roy Thomas, for their help in preparing the manuscript for publication.

From Partners to Parents

The Second Revolution in Family Law

I N 1990, New York's highest court considered the case of Raquel Marie. Born on May 26, 1988, Raquel had lived since infancy with adoptive parents in New Hampshire. When her birth parents, Louise and Miguel, married three months after Raquel was placed for adoption, her mother joined in her father's efforts to regain custody. Raquel Marie was two when her case reached the New York Court of Appeals.

The legal issue before the court concerned her father's failure to consent to the adoption. New York law provided that, while "an unwed mother's consent is always required—an unwed father's consent to the adoption of his under-six-month-old child is required only where he has openly lived with the child or the mother for six continuous months immediately preceding the child's placement for adoption."[1] The trial court had considered only the issue of whether the adoption could proceed without Miguel's consent (the father had vowed to prevent the adoption throughout the pregnancy and had sought custody even before Raquel was placed with the adoptive parents), and it had concluded that "while Louise and Miguel lived separately in the relevant six-month period before placement—during which he several times assaulted her—they had a sufficiently continuous and ongoing relationship to meet the 'living together' requirement of the statute, loosely construed." The Appellate Division took a different view of the couple's tumultuous relationship, concluding that it was "neither normal nor stable" and therefore insufficient to meet the statutory requirement.[2] Miguel asked New York's highest court to find that the requirement that he live with Louise violated the U.S. Constitution, and the Court of Appeals agreed.

The court recognized that the state had an important interest in determining the father's relationship with the child, but went on to observe that

> the difficulty with the "living together" requirement stems from its focus on the relationship between father and mother, rather than father and child. When the child is surrendered for adoption by the mother at birth . . . the father can qualify for a veto right only if he has continuously lived with the mother for a full six months preceding the birth—in which case it seems unlikely that there would even be a conflict between father and mother on the question of adoption. . . .
>
> Although the State plainly has a significant interest in fostering the well-being of the child, . . . the State's objective cannot be constitutionally accomplished at the sacrifice of the father's protected interest by imposing a test so incidentally related to the father-child relationship as this one, directed as it is principally to the father-mother relationship.[3]

The court remanded the case to determine whether Miguel had established a sufficient relationship with Raquel Marie, and a year later the lower courts decided that three-year-old Raquel could stay with her adoptive parents.[4] The standard the New York court employed shifted from the parents' relationship to each other to their relationship with the child. The court emphasized that Miguel did not establish paternity until after the adoption, he contributed only minimally to the costs of the pregnancy, he did not help the overwhelmed mother care either for the newborn or his older daughter, and he sought custody only to block the adoption rather than immediately after birth. Finally, the court noted that Louise alleged that Raquel's conception was a product of forcible rape, Miguel had violated a restraining order to assault her repeatedly during the pregnancy, and he had pled guilty to the resulting assault charges only two months before Raquel's birth. Miguel's behavior toward Louise remained relevant, but only because it reflected on his fitness for custody.

In the spring of 1995, Santa Clara University's Markkula Center for Applied Ethics hosted a conference on the future of the family.[5] One of the keynote speakers, Columbia law professor Martha Fineman, proposed ending legal recognition of marriage, and providing greater direct public support for children. A faculty discussion group after her talk agreed with the need for the latter, but found the former dangerously radical. Even so, all but the family law professors in the group were astonished to learn that, while greater public support may be a long way off, the elements necessary to end legal recognition of marriage have largely been implemented.

Raquel Marie's case, unlike those of the better-known Baby Richard and Baby Jessica cases, did not end with a tearful exchange of parents, but the New York decision is no less part of a wholesale change in the legal regulation of the family. A generation ago the notion that the father's relationship to the mother could be only "incidentally" related to his interest in the child was inconceivable. Responsible fathers demonstrated concern for their children by marrying the mother, preferably before the child was born, and staying with her for life. Their failure to do so could be taken in itself as disqualification for parenthood, and two centuries of common law rulings gave unmarried fathers no interest in their children. Today, courts and legislatures have largely abolished the definitions of parenthood that depend on marriage, and the law—together with the rest of society—is struggling, one piece at a time, to rebuild the idea of obligation to children.

These changes represent neither the triumph of feminism nor the result of some hidden conspiracy to dismantle the family. Instead, they proceed from two revolutions whose magnitude has become apparent only after the fact. The first began with the elimination of fault as a prerequisite for divorce and went on to abolish most of the distinctions that depend on the parents' marital status. Yet no-fault reform, though chronicled in revolutionary terms, was introduced as a technical correction designed to remove collusion and perjury from the legal process.[6] *Stanley v. Illinois*,[7] the first in the line of Supreme Court cases to recognize the rights of unmarried parents, involved a father's effort, upon the mother's death, to regain custody from the state of children he had helped raise during eighteen years of nonmarital cohabitation. These reforms can be called revolutionary in retrospect only because they interacted with changing marital roles to dismantle the older system of family regulation. No-fault rendered the promise to remain married "until death do us part" illusory during an era in which the divorce rate grew to include one of every two marriages.

The second revolution is the subject of this book. Across the academy, the courts, classrooms, and election campaigns, the code of family responsibility is being rewritten in terms of the only ties left—the ones to children. Just as spousal obligation linked to alimony and fault gave way to a clean break between the adults, so too is the clean break giving way to a new emphasis on parental commitment. Child custody determinations have replaced fault as the most emotionally charged sources of family conflict and, for all but the wealthiest parents, the once neglected issue of child support has become the most important of the financial determinations made at divorce. The most heated public debates on the family, from Dan Quayle's election-year criticism of television's Murphy Brown to Hillary Rodham Clinton's election-year book *It Takes a Village*, involve rethinking family responsibility in terms of obligation toward children. Miguel's claims to his daughter Raquel may no longer depend on his relationship with the mother, Louise, but neither do they rest solely on the fact of paternity. The legal redefinition of parenthood that Raquel Marie's case illustrates requires a new ideal of parental obligation, and the creation of that ideal is the topic of this book.

Legal revolutions, whether shouted from the rooftops or proclaimed in obscure texts, seldom take place in a vacuum. Legislative and judicial change produce revolutionary effects only when they interact with sea changes in public perceptions or mores. So it is with the family. The idealized American family of breadwinners and breadmakers is neither timeless nor enduring. In the United States, the rise of the nuclear family, as we think of it today, coincided with nineteenth-century industrialization, which took men from their farms and shops into offices and factories and left women, once thought unfit to do more than follow the husband's bidding, as mistresses of the home and overseers of their children's upbringing. The divorce system California reformed in 1969, with its emphasis on fault and its conception of alimony, was a nineteenth-century relic that had institutionalized the separate spheres of home and market wrought by early industrialization.

The new family law system is emerging in response to a similar transformation. Women who once worked exclusively at home have followed their partners into the labor force, and job insecurity and an increasingly competitive labor market have undermined the promise of a "family wage." In the nineteenth century, changing economic organization did not just affect the jobs men performed. It interacted with a broader array of historical changes, already well under way in Western Europe, to redefine family roles, contribute to a nascent women's movement, spark alarm over increasing divorce rates, and remake understandings about marital virtue, fatherhood, and what Barbara Welter refers to as "the cult of true womanhood."[8] So, too, today the changes that started with greater job opportunities for women are not just about juggling board meetings with parent-teacher conferences. As women have entered the workforce to stay and men have found their positions in it less secure, the distinctions between family and market, mothers and fathers, married couples and single individuals have been blurred or redrawn. These changes have, in turn, challenged our conceptions of families, of how to define them, provide for them, and live within them.

This book charts the intellectual history that has taken us from partners to parents as the central focus of family regulation. Part one undertakes an intellectual survey that examines the ways in which we think about family. It starts with theorists Gary Becker, who won the 1992 Nobel Prize for extending economics to a realm of romance and altruism, and Susan Moller Okin, who replaces the economists' emphasis on efficiency with justice as the basis for critique. Becker and Okin, taken together, explain the ways in which changing marital roles guarantee the greater instability of the nuclear family. Columbia law professor Martha Fineman and Clinton domestic policy adviser William Galston then frame the alternatives. In the midst of disagreement about everything else, both craft family policies premised on obligation toward children as the only coherent contemporary possibilities.

Part two examines the empirical evidence on which the debate is based. It begins by considering the historical research that links (and sometimes unlinks) family change to industrial organization, reviews the distinctive history of the African-American family, and places modern developments in perspective. It then focuses on what sense can be made of the sociological and psychological research that connects children's well-being to family form, considers the racial and class dynamics involved in family transformation, and weighs the implications for a renewed model of family obligation.

Finally, part three ties the intellectual debate to the legal developments. In many ways, the legal system has already implemented the most radical proposals by deregulating the relationship between husband and wife, eliminating the distinctions between marital and unmarital children, writing a detailed code of parental obligations that extends from child support to joint custody schedules to prohibitions on abuse, and changing the shape of Aid to Families with Dependent Children (AFDC). This section considers whether, taken together, the reforms offer a coherent way of thinking about provision for children. The book concludes that, just as the older system relied on an integration of public regulation and private norms, so too will the success of the new era depend on popular acceptance of responsibility toward children. The unfinished revolution involves remaking the understanding between partners necessary to realize their obligations toward children.

From
PARTNERS
to
PARENTS

PART I

From Partners to Parents

The Philosophical Divide

T HE family is a daunting subject of study. We all know too much about our own families, and sometimes those of our neighbors and presidents. We also know too little about what is possible in family relationships, and about what occupies the growing mountain of books in disciplines other than our own.

This first section of the book tries to cut through the disciplinary maze to establish the parameters of the ongoing debate about the future of the family. I make no attempt to be comprehensive. Nor could I be in the face of an almost endless array of possibilities. Instead, I have picked four representatives — Gary Becker, Susan Moller Okin, Martha Fineman, and William Galston — to define the four corners of the debate. Their disciplines (political theory, economics, and law) are relative latecomers to the family as a major focus of study. Yet their disciplines are central players in every policy debate and are increasingly influential in the discussion of what form future families *should* take, as well as what measures society should adopt to secure those results.

At the end of this section, after a discussion of disciplinary differences and individual perspectives, I conclude that two dimensions are central to the scholars' divisions about the future:

1. Should provision for family caretaking involve egalitarian roles or specialized ones?

2. Should the two-parent family be seen as essential or as an optional element in family well-being?

In this debate, Gary Becker presents an economic defense of the specialized two-parent family, Susan Moller Okin critiques the traditional family's specialized roles as inherently unjust, Martha Fineman rejects Okin's preference for an egalitarian division of responsibility as one that shifts the responsibility for caretaking from parents to economically marginalized nannies and day care workers, and William Galston argues that, whatever the division of responsibility, children need the security of two-parent relationships.

I will argue at the end of the section that while the four do an admirable job of defining the four corners of the debate, they cannot finally resolve it — partly because each perspective is incomplete in itself, and partly because the new structures they would create have already been taken over by events.

1

Economics and the Family
Reformulating the Old Order

Economics, widely referred to as the "dismal science," has long involved the study of commerce, trade, resource allocation, and anything else that can be profitably explained in terms of greed. For equally long a period, its contributions to the realms of love or emotion have been suspect. In the mid-1950s, Gary Becker, a University of Chicago economist, set out to change all that. Imperial economics' leading colonizer, Becker declared that "the economic approach provides a framework applicable to all human behavior" from homicide to filial affection. The centerpiece of his colonizing efforts within the family was his *A Treatise on the Family* (1981);[1] a decade later he was rewarded with the 1992 Nobel Prize in Economics.

Applying economics to the family is controversial, in part because of the assumptions at the core of economic theory. As a discipline, economics acquires its power, its ability to express insights in mathematical form and to predict human behavior with a physics-like appearance of precision, from its use of simplifying assumptions. The most important of these assumptions is the notion that people act rationally to maximize utility or, in other words, that they will do what is necessary to get what they want. If, for example, a suburban homeowner enjoys *Star Trek* reruns more than mowing the lawn, an economist would not be surprised to learn that she spends more time watching TV than cutting grass, or that she is willing to pay more for lawnmowing than her neighbor who enjoys the exercise. In the hands of an economist, such assumptions might be used to analyze the pricing structure of an entire industry.[2]

To be sure, these simplifying assumptions can be controversial even when applied to financial transactions. Law professor Robin West argued in the *Harvard Law Review* that the portrait of human motivation in Franz Kafka's novels presents at least as persuasive an alternative.[3] Kafka, one of the most distinctive of European novelists, delighted in featuring central characters absorbed, for example, by one's metamorphosis into a cockroach. His characters, West emphasizes, are often devoid of rational, let alone profit maximizing, behavior. It would not be hard to imagine a Kafkaesque character who hated mowing the lawn and did it, whether needed or not, several hours a day. Richard Posner, invited by the *Harvard Law Review* to respond, disputed West's interpretation of Kafka,[4] but the classic answer is Milton Friedman's. Friedman argued in the thirties that economics does not depend on people being either rational or selfish. All that matters is that they act as though they are. Friedman maintained that economics was in the business of prediction, not psychology. If, on aggregate, people who hate lawnmowing are willing to pay others to do it for them, it does not matter whether Franz Kafka can find (or imagine) someone who defies prediction.[5]

Gary Becker, who worked with Friedman at Chicago, pioneered the use of economics to explain family behavior. Initially, these efforts were met with ridicule. He describes "giving a paper on economics and population at a conference in 1957 and people laughing at me."[6] Becker nonetheless persisted and, particularly with the enhanced stature that attends a Nobel laureate, he has assumed a role as one of the traditional family's leading theorists. His work, in a fashion characteristic of the economic approach, attempts to explain the family in terms of "grand theory," that is, to reduce a large number of complex and sometimes seemingly inconsistent events to a single conceptual framework, and then to use that framework to explain how the existing system came to be and the form future changes are likely to take. What Becker discovers, repackaged in economic terms, is the rise and fall of the nuclear family.

Becker's *Treatise on the Family* exalts, as the central feature of family life, the sexual division of labor, and the evolution of a marriage as a long-term contract designed to promote and protect this division. Becker's idea of specialization will be familiar to anyone who has ever taken an undergraduate course in economics. Imagine two islands, X and Y, that produce two goods — guns and butter — or more realistically, coconuts and eggs. The two islands can increase their joint production of the goods, the economic account maintains, if X specializes in one, Y specializes in the other, and they trade. Even if Island X is better at producing both coconuts *and* eggs, it can increase its overall wealth by specializing in the form of production in which it has the greater comparative advantage over Y, and encouraging Y to invest in production of the other good.

Becker uses the same approach to describe the advantages of the family. In chapter 2 of his *Treatise* he posits two types of human activity, H1, defined in terms of market activity, and H2, household production. He observes that within families "[t]he most pervasive division is between married women, who traditionally have devoted most of their time to childbearing and other domestic activities, and married men, who have hunted, soldiered, farmed and engaged in other 'market' activities."[7] With scientific precision, he then advances a series of theorems, along with supporting equations. Theorems 2.1 and 2.4, for example, provide that:

Theorem 2.1 If all members of an efficient household have different comparative advantages, no more than one member would allocate time to both the market and the household sectors (17).

Theorem 2.4 If commodity production functions have constant or increasing returns to scale, *all* members of efficient households would specialize completely in the market or household sectors and would invest only in market or household capital (19).

The corresponding equation,[8] which defines the comparative advantage of each household member in terms of the relation between the ratio of his or her marginal products in the market and household sectors and the ratios of other family members, looks like this:

$$\frac{(\partial Z)/(\partial t_{w_i})}{(\partial Z)/(\partial t_{w_j})} = \frac{\hat{H}_i^1}{\hat{H}_j^1} > \frac{(\partial Z)/(\partial t_{h_i})}{(\partial Z)/(\partial t_{h_j})} = \frac{\psi(\hat{H}_i^2)}{\psi(\hat{H}_j^2)}.$$

Equation 1.1

While Becker's defense of specialization is economic orthodoxy, his application to the family is both innovative and controversial. It is difficult, for example, to visualize what "commodity production functions with constant or increasing returns to scale" would mean in the context of the family: the increasing marginal productivity of childrearing (because five children do *not* cost five times as much to raise as one)? Or of cookie-baking (because thirty batches of chocolate chip cookies can be more efficiently produced than twenty-nine)? Or of lawn-mowing (because larger lawns take less time to mow per square foot than smaller ones)? Even the weaker assumptions of Theorem 2.1 result in the conclusion that to reap the greatest benefits only one parent should concentrate on a career; the other would be better off with no more than a part-time job. In Becker's world the most efficient families will be those in which Dad brings home the bacon and Mom cooks it.

Becker maintains that the advantages that proceed from this division of labor do not depend on testosterone or any other inherent differences between men and women. Gay or lesbian couples, for example, could also reap advantages from having one partner concentrate on the home and the other on the market. Nonetheless, in one of the most controversial parts of the book, Becker uses biology to explain why the intrafamily division is a sexual one.

> Although the sharp sexual division of labor in all societies between the market and household sectors is partly due to the gains from specialized investments, it is also partly due to intrinsic differences between the sexes. . . .
>
> [B]iological differences in comparative advantage explain not only why households typically have both sexes, but also why women have usually spent their time bearing and rearing children and engaging in other household activities, whereas men have spent their time in market activities. This sexual division of labor has been found in virtually all human societies, and in most other biological species that fertilize eggs within the body of the female (23).

Becker acknowledges the societal role in promoting gender stereotypes, and explains how this, too, is efficient. He reasons that "deviant investments [medical education for women?] would presumably be more common if deviant biology [women unable to have children, women unwilling to be homemakers, or women more likely than their husbands to succeed in the medical profession?] were more common — or if it were revealed at younger ages."[9] Given the inability to predict these matters from childhood, it is easier to advise girls to take home economics while boys study auto mechanics. Different comparative advantages (those trained to be doctors — or auto mechanics — will find, upon marriage, that they can earn more than spouses trained to be homemakers) then produce a self-fulfilling prophecy.

If, as Becker claims, the sexual division of labor is universal and the central advantage of family organization, why do so many scholars believe it is imperiled? Becker emphasizes that arranging an efficient division of labor is far from automatic, and that much of the development of the family as an institution is designed to encourage the desired specialization.

> Specialization of tasks, such as the division of labor between men and women, implies a dependence on others for certain tasks. Women have traditionally relied on men for provision of food, shelter, and protection, and men have traditionally relied on women for the bearing and rearing of children and the maintenance of the home. Consequently, both men and women have been made better off by a "marriage," the term for a written, oral, or customary long-term contract between a man and a woman to produce children, food and other commodities in a common household (27).

Although this paragraph treats the relationship between men and women as symmetrical, elsewhere Becker writes that "[s]ince married women have been specialized to childbearing and other domestic activities, they have demanded long-term 'contracts' from their husbands to protect them against abandonment and other adversities. Virtually all societies have developed long-term protection for married women" (14). Marriage, and the traditional family, served as a guarantee necessary to persuade women to undertake their domestic tasks.

Lloyd Cohen puts it more bluntly. In an article subtitled, "I Gave Him the Best Years of My Life," Cohen notes that the investments men and women make in their respective spheres are not parallel.[10] Investment in market capital is portable; a man with a good job can take it with him to another marriage. Investment in household activities, on the other hand, is "marriage specific"; the children from a first marriage are a liability to a second. In the marriage market Becker and Cohen describe, those commanding the greatest value are young women and wealthy men.[11]

Cohen argues that this asymmetry in marital contributions creates the risk of what economists call "opportunistic behavior," and what others have referred to as "wife-stuffing." *Doonesbury*, though, almost certainly does a better job than the economists in depicting the phenomenon. Several years ago, Gary Trudeau, *Doonesbury*'s creator, ran a series of comic strips in which Mark Slackmeyer's middle-aged father divorces his wife of many years. Mark's mother, wrinkled, graying, and middle-aged, is drawn as the personification of Cohen's subtitle. In the final set of the series, Philip Slackmeyer, short, balding, and just as middle-aged as the wife he left behind, is shown walking down the aisle with a stunningly attractive young professional. Slackmeyer, portrayed in the strip as a wealthy executive, has successfully "traded in" his wife of many years for a new model.

Picking up Becker's mantle of economic analysis and applying it to family law, Allen Parkman, the Regents Professor of Management at the University of New Mexico, maintains that this scenario illustrates the answer to the question in the title of his book, *No-Fault Divorce: What Went Wrong?*.[12] Realization of the gains from specialization and trade require enforcement of the bargain, Parkman argues. If one party lives up to her end of the deal, becoming more vulnerable because of it, and the other party is free to walk away at any time — and can benefit from doing so — then the gains that occur from specialization will not be realized. Parkman uses this analysis to argue that no-fault divorce is dangerously misguided. If Becker is right that the foundation of the family is specialization, and Cohen is right that the exchange that follows is asymmetrical, then treating marriage as no more than a voluntary relationship that either party can end at will discourages the enterprise. Parkman predicts that women will reject the path of efficiency, and refuse to stay home and take care of the children.

Becker, skeptical about the impact of legal rules,[13] identifies an alternative culprit to explain higher divorce rates, falling fertility, and other signs of decreasing domestic productivity. "I believe," he writes, "that the major cause of these changes is the growth of the earning power of women as the American economy has developed. . . . The gain from marriage is reduced by a rise in the earnings and labor force participation of women and by a fall in fertility because a sexual division of labor becomes less advantageous. . . . And divorce becomes more attractive when the gain from marriage is reduced" (245, 248). At the margin where economists conduct their calculations, women enjoy more attractive alternatives to marriage and homemaking than they once did, and thus the price it takes to persuade them to marry, and stay married, has risen.

Becker himself, in a manner typical of economists, limits his analysis to description, reserving judgment about whether these changes in the family are for better or ill. Indeed, his last chapter has the feel of a Greek tragedy in which what happens to the central characters (at least to the extent it is tied to women's workforce participation) is the product of ineluctable forces beyond hope of control. Those using economic analysis in other disciplines, however, recognize no such limitations. Within law, which as a discipline addresses what the law *ought* to be as much it describes what the law *is*, the type of analysis Becker pioneered has been used to prescribe a more traditional family code. The law should encourage family stability, Ira Ellman argues, by protecting the exchange upon which the traditional family is based.[14] Eliminating fault from the system eliminated the traditional obligation to stay married in ways that work systematically to the disadvantage of women who devote their energies to the home. Reintroducing mutual consent as a prerequisite for divorce, which Parkman champions, or redefining alimony in terms of lost career opportunities, which Ellman advocates, should eliminate some of the "distorting incentives" that discourage women from devoting themselves to a domestic role and that undermine the benefits of family life.

This legal analysis, which at its best explains why family law may have accelerated the pace of family change, ultimately fails, however, to provide a comprehensive picture of how specialization within the family will coexist with the larger changes occurring in the world outside, and to account for the fact that, with the advent of no-fault divorce, women, not men like Philip Slackmeyer, are the ones most likely to initiate divorce.[15]

Figure 1.1

2

Feminism and Political Theory
The Traditional Family and Its Discontents

I F Becker is a seminal figure in the extension of economic analysis to the family, then Susan Moller Okin is an ovular one in applying principles of justice to the domestic sphere. Okin, a professor of political science at Stanford, provides what Michael Walzer describes as "the first sustained feminist account of distributive justice."[1] Okin's thesis, developed philosopher by philosopher, is that, however justice is measured, if the same principles were applied to the family, the family could not pass muster. What is so startling about Okin's work is that, until the 1989 publication of her book *Justice, Gender, and the Family*, no one seemed to notice.

Okin's introduction explains:

> Political theory, which had been sparse for a period before the late 1960's . . . has become a flourishing field, with social justice as its central concern. Yet, remarkably, major contemporary theorists of justice have almost without exception ignored the [family]. . . . They have displayed little interest in or knowledge of the findings of feminism. They have largely bypassed the fact that the society to which their theories are supposed to pertain is heavily and deeply affected by gender, and faces difficult issues of justice stemming from its gendered past and present assumptions. Since theories of justice are centrally concerned with whether, how and why persons should be treated differently from one another, this neglect seems inexplicable.[2]

Okin then reviews the work of the leading contemporary political theorists — Michael Sandel, Allan Bloom, Carl MacIntyre, Robert Nozick, John Rawls, and Michael Walzer — and demonstrates how their conceptions of justice cannot be reconciled with the operation of the family. Her consideration of John Rawls occupies the literal and intellectual center of the book.

Okin begins her discussion of Rawls by noting that his *A Theory of Justice* "has had the most powerful influence of any work of contemporary moral and political theory" (89). Indeed, Rawls has been credited with single-handedly bringing about the revival of political theory Okin describes in her introduction. Rawls's work champions the idea of "justice as fairness" and, in determining what is fair, Rawls uses what Okin terms "a construct, or heuristic device, that is both his single most important contribution to moral and political theory and the focus of most of the controversy his theory still attracts, nearly twenty years after its publication" (90). Rawls's construct involves imagining an "original position" in which parties deliberate through a "veil of ignorance" in which they do not know the personal characteristics — wealth, class, intelligence, race, gender — they will have in the world governed by the principles they devise. He then assumes, among other things, that his representatives are risk averse, that is, that they fear loss of the basic necessities of life more than they value the opportunity for extraordinary gain. From these assumptions Rawls derives two principles to which those in the original position would presumably agree: the principle of equal basic liberty for all individuals, and the "difference principle," which provides that for differences in authority, wealth, and other benefits to be justified, they must work to the greatest benefit of the least advantaged and must be attached to positions accessible to all under conditions of fair equal opportunity.[3]

Rawls makes no attempt to apply this construct to the family. Indeed, he makes the parties in the original position *heads* of families, rendering, as Jane English observes, "the family opaque to claims of justice."[4] Nonetheless, Okin argues, not only is there no reason in theory why Rawlsian principles should not be applied to gender, but the idea of the original position seems particularly well suited to testing the fairness of the consequences that flow from sexual difference. Okin then systematically critiques the ways in which a gendered society cannot meet the criteria of *A Theory of Justice*. The most important of her claims concerns the gendered operation of the family.

The family Okin describes should be immediately recognizable to anyone who has studied Gary Becker. Its central features are a sexual division of labor, and concomitant dependency and restricted opportunities for women. Whereas Becker addressed rational choice and efficiency, however, Okin's concern is power, and she invokes the work of another economist,

Albert O. Hirschman, to explain the traditional family's power dynamics. Hirschman's *Exit, Voice, and Loyalty* (1970)[5] offered a classic exposition of the role of asymmetry in relationships and, like Becker and Allen Parkman, Hirschman used analogies drawn from international trade to illustrate his ideas. Imagine, Hirschman posited, two islands, A and B, which specialize in different goods (eggs and coconuts? H1 and H2?) and trade. Imagine further that B, which has fewer outlets for its products, is more dependent on the trading relationship than A. While both parties benefit from their continuing trade, A has the greater ability to leave unharmed and, Hirschman concludes, this threat gives A greater ability to dictate the terms of the relationship.

Okin spends the last several chapters of her book demonstrating how such asymmetries systematically disadvantage women. She emphasizes studies of power within the family showing that, for all but lesbian couples, "the amount of money a person earns — in comparison with a partner's income — establishes relative power"; thus, the housewife with preschool children is at the least powerful point in her marriage, and her power is likely to decrease further with the birth of additional children. Okin notes with some irony that the *more* a woman contributes in the form of domestic services (i.e., the more she specializes in the production of a product of value to her husband alone), the *less* her influence is likely to be within the relationship.[6]

Although Okin entitles her analysis "Vulnerability by Marriage," she take pains to show, in a manner strikingly similar to Becker's, the interactions between women's domestic role in marriage, their premarital education and socialization, their limited opportunities within the workplace, and their vulnerability by separation and divorce. Okin echoes Becker's conclusion that while no-fault divorce has probably not had much impact on the divorce rate itself, it has affected the allocation of resources contributing to the impoverishment of divorced women and their children.[7]

Okin's ultimate conclusion is that women's systematic vulnerability because of, and within, marriage cannot be reconciled with any of the accepted accounts of justice in our society, and that "any just and fair solution to the urgent problem of women's and children's vulnerability must encourage and facilitate the equal sharing by men and women of paid and unpaid work, of productive and reproductive labor. We must work toward a future in which all will be likely to choose this mode of life. A just future would be one without gender" (171).

Okin's call for more egalitarian families resonates with the conclusions of scholars in other disciplines. Rhona Mahony's *Kidding Ourselves: Bread-winning, Babies, and Bargaining Power* (1995) amplifies Okin's discussion of power. Mahony draws on game theory to design strategies intended to implement the egalitarian future Okin advocates. Mahony advises women to (1) "train up," that is, to acquire the education and skills necessary for well-paying jobs; (2) "marry down," that is, marry otherwise desirable men likely to earn less than they will; (3) increase their BATNAs (best alternative to negotiated agreement) by refusing to cut back disproportionately on their labor market activity or to assume the major share of childrearing; and (4) revalue homemaking to make it more attractive for men as well as women. Mahony acknowledges, however, in a way that Okin does not, the tension between gains from specialization within marriage, on the one hand, and egalitarian roles, on the other. Her solution is to focus on the elimination of the *sexual* division of labor in the belief that "when men are doing half the child care, more couples will choose to reap the gains of specialization that a homemaker gives his or her family. Breadwinner-homemaker couples will outnumber the oddballs who try to share parenting fifty-fifty."[8] In the meantime, however, women should avoid making the choices that consign them to a domestic role.

Mahony is sensitive to the charge that family life should be about more than maneuvering for personal advantage; she responds that the existing division of household labor is already the product of negotiation, and her book simply points out how women can become better at it. In similar fashion, movement toward the more egalitarian roles Okin and Mahony advocate has occurred more through individual decisions than from invocation of abstract principles or self-conscious gender reform. Consider two popular accounts of the very different sets of choices made by two famous American women.

> In the fall of 1919, [Rose Kennedy] . . . became pregnant for the fourth time in four years. Sick of Joe's philandering and his absences, she declared she'd had enough. Early in January 1920 Rose left her children and her husband and returned to her parents in Dorcester.
>
> The separation lasted three weeks. But if Rose hoped her errant, perpetually absent husband would come crawling for forgiveness, she was to be disappointed. Joe did not come at all. It was thus left to her father, John F. Fitzgerald, to tell Rose her Irish-Catholic duty. . . . Rose [who had married Joe over her parents' objections], he felt, had made her own bed and she must lie in it. "What is past is past. The old days are

gone. . . . You've made your commitment, Rosie, and you must honor it now."

To her credit, Rose Kennedy did. She returned to Beals Street, her three children, and her husband. A few weeks later, on February 20, 1920, she gave birth to her fourth child, a second daughter, whom they christened Kathleen. Rose never again broke down or even complained. For good or ill, she would become the archetypal, stoic Irish-Catholic mother.[9]

By now [the time of the Whitewater investment], it must . . . have been obvious that Hillary couldn't count much on financial contributions from her husband, given his earning prospects and lack of interest in making money. . . .

According to friends of the couple, it was also at this time that Hillary expressed doubts about the future of her marriage, and, as a result, whether she could count on Bill to support her and a child. Their marriage, now in its third year, was at a low point. If Gennifer Flowers's account can be believed, she and Bill were in the passionate early stages of their affair that summer. People close to the Clintons were aware of other women in Bill's life, too. . . .

Bill and Hillary's move to the governor's mansion in January 1979 did little to ease these anxieties. If anything, Bill's greater celebrity status opened up more opportunities. He confided in Susan McDougal that he loved being governor: "This is fun. Women are throwing themselves at me. All the while I was growing up, I was the fat boy in the Big Boy jeans."[10]

However much one might discount the popular versions of their lives, Rose Fitzgerald Kennedy and Hillary Rodham Clinton clearly responded differently to their husbands' infidelity based on their perceptions of the alternatives available to them. Rose "specialized" in the family (while her absent husband made millions) in almost precisely the way Gary Becker describes. Hillary became a partner in the most prestigious and lucrative firm in Little Rock — and invested in Whitewater, James Stewart believes — because of the type of reasoning Rhona Mahony advocates. While Stewart reports that, with Chelsea's birth, Hillary's "thoughts of leaving Bill were banished" (82), she appears to have fashioned a more independent and certainly more influential role than Rose. Indeed, when First Daughter Chelsea needed permission at school to take some aspirin, she is widely re-

ported to have told the school nurse, "Call my dad, my mom's too busy."[11]
Gary Becker would have nonetheless predicted the other striking difference
between the two couples: Rose had nine children while Hillary has one.

Figure 2.1

3

Feminism *and* Economics

Becker Meets Okin

DESPITE differences in discipline and perspective, Gary Becker and Susan Moller Okin describe the same family — the nuclear family at midcentury. And despite occasional pretensions to universality (Becker: "the sharp sexual division of labor in all societies between the market and household sectors")[1] and diversity (Okin: "there are no shared meanings . . . about the appropriate roles of men and women, and about which family forms and divisions of labor are most beneficial for partners, parents and children"),[2] they could both take as their starting point the sitcom couples of the fifties: the Nelsons (*The Adventures of Ozzie and Harriet*), the Reeds (*The Donna Reed Show*), even the Ricardos (*I Love Lucy*). These shows played out the sexual division of labor Becker and Okin describe with successful breadwinners, full-time homemakers, tensions that build to successful resolution, and only occasional yearnings for something more.

Becker and Okin achieve their greatest resonance, however, when they describe the changes that take us away from the idealized families of the 1950s. Becker, although he uses dramatic language ("the family in the United States changes more rapidly [from 1950 to 1977] than during any equivalent period since the founding of the colonies"),[3] concentrates most of his analysis, in proper economic focus, at the margin — that is, on the incremental changes that affect family decision-making. Becker believes that the major cause of increasing divorce, declining fertility, delayed childbearing, and increased illegitimacy is "the growth in the earning power of women as the American economy developed."[4] In short, with increasing pay for women's services, women work more. As a result, Becker argues, specialization within the family lessens, the gains from marriage drop, and divorce rates jump. Welfare state programs that subsidize the cost of chil-drearing increase the effect.

What is curious about Becker's analysis is that he could have described exactly the same developments in terms of *increased* specialization, and had he done so, the analysis would have been more accurate. Economist David Friedman explains that the increased workforce participation Becker em-phasizes produces greater, not less, specialization as women trade in the largely undifferentiated role of wife and mother for a more complex array of activities.[5] In the sitcom families of old, Lucy Ricardo's activities differed only slightly from Donna Reed's. In the real world, Lucille Ball was a suc-cessful executive and Donna Reed a recognized actress (and by the 1980s her TV character might have been a medical professional) in addition to their activities as wives and mothers. Moreover, while women's productiv-ity gains as they become doctors, lawyers, day care providers, office work-ers, fast food servers, and medical technicians are dramatic, any correspon-ding decrease in specialization between men and women has been minimal. Barbara Bergman reported in the mid-eighties that "husbands of wives with full-time jobs averaged about two minutes more housework per day than did husbands in housewife-maintaining families, hardly enough addi-tional time to prepare a soft-boiled egg."[6] Women's increased specialization accordingly dwarfs any reallocation of responsibilities within the family. How then can decreased specialization explain Becker's parade of horribles? Becker's analysis requires translation, and Okin supplies the vocabulary.

Simply stated, Okin's book explains just how bad a deal traditional mar-riage has been for women. Surveys consistently show that married men are happier than single men, and single women are happier than married women.[7] Unhappily married women remain married, Okin maintains, be-cause the very things that Becker identifies with marriage — children, fi-nancial dependence — make women less able to leave or to credibly threaten to do so. Without the possibility of "exit," therefore, "voice" — and the abil-ity to reallocate the burden of changing diapers or making school lunches — diminishes as well.[8]

Becker acknowledges the circular reinforcement of women's domestic role as employers discriminate against women on the basis of their stereo-typical expectations that women will devote more energy to home than market, girls invest less in education and training in response to such ex-pectations, and women then choose to spend more time at home because of the lack of alternatives. What he does not acknowledge is that the same forces reinforce patterns of power and satisfaction within marriage. Joe Kennedy could get away with flagrant adultery and a highly visible affair with Gloria Swanson at least in part because Rose had no where to go.

Restated in terms of Okin's analysis of power, Becker's reference to "reduced gains from marriage" becomes an explanation of the increasing attractiveness of the alternatives.[9] Consider again the powerless mother with young children in Okin's book. If she works full time and hires a babysitter, the family may gain more from the extra income than it would from her domestic efforts. If, however, her husband drinks too much, stays out too late, or emotionally abuses her or the children, divorce becomes a more realistic option than it would be for her homemaker counterpart. The overall well-being of this couple may well be greater than if she remained a homemaker, but the resources in their marriage will be distributed differently and the relative advantages to remaining married may be accordingly less. Proud, ambitious, college-educated Rose Fitzgerald, were she a young woman today, would almost certainly leave Joe Kennedy even if the potential benefits from staying were no less.

It is tempting at this point to conclude that Becker is right — women's new jobs cause family breakdown; it is just that Okin better states the reasons: once women acquire a measure of independence, they become unwilling to put up with the louts they married. Indeed, Okin's insights are easily translated into economics terms. Becker himself might note that as the gains women make from trading with each other increase, their price for continued participation in marriage rises, and fewer men are willing or able to pay. Shoshana Grossbard-Shechtman, who studied under Becker in Chicago, proposes a general theory of marriage in almost exactly such terms,[10] and empirical research confirms that women, particularly younger women, are more likely to initiate divorce than men.[11] Lenore Weitzman's *The Divorce Revolution*, in the midst of pessimism about everything else liberalized divorce has wrought, reports that "even the longer-married housewives who suffer the greatest financial hardships after divorce (and who feel the most economically deprived, most angry, and most 'cheated' by the divorce settlement) say they are 'personally' better off than they were during the marriage."[12]

If this were happening in isolation, however, the result would not necessarily have to be more divorce. Instead, with time, the terms on which marriages were conducted would change, women would acquire a greater measure of influence, society would shift toward the more egalitarian future Okin advocates, and the divorce rate would increase only temporarily until couples adjusted to the new power structure, and men became more willing to wash the dishes. Okin's book would become not only prescriptive but predictive, driven by the forces Becker identified. The real world, however, is more complicated.

To begin with, relative power within marriage is not the only thing that shapes attitudes. Polls show that men and women have different expectations about the roles they and their spouses will play during marriage, and that the size of the gender gap varies over time, race, and class.[13] Income and employment differences between African-American men and women, for example, are smaller than those between white men and women without necessarily resulting in more egalitarian attitudes or gender roles.[14] While the reasons for the racial differences are complex, the result of women's greater independence can be less marriage rather than renegotiation of its terms.[15] Joe Kennedy, after all, might find it harder to continue his affairs on the side, but he would also find it easier to divorce Rose and marry Gloria Swanson.

In addition, any decline in specialization between men and women is *only* at the margin. Despite women's relatively greater independence, they still bear the overwhelming responsibility for childrearing whether they do it themselves or hire other women to help them. Okin requires dismantling the sexual division of labor, but while she puts forward a number of proposals that would make the childrearing role less perilous, she does not persuasively explain how the elimination of gender differences is to occur. Victor Fuchs sounds a cautionary note. He argues that it is not the fact that women take care of children that is the source of their disadvantage, but the fact that women care more about children.[16] If Fuchs is right, women's increased employment may result in greater autonomy, but it is unlikely to produce equality. The problem is one of how to get there from here.

Figure 3.1

4

Law, Public Policy, and the
Feminism of Difference

B ECKER and Okin are characteristic of the family scholars of the 1980s. They focus on the relationship between spouses; their concerns involve equality, complementarity, exchange. Martha Albertson Fineman, though she began to write before Okin published her book or Becker won the Nobel Prize, could be considered the first family scholar of the 1990s — and she is very much focused on how to get there from here.

Fineman differs from other scholars of the family by any standard. The Maurice T. Moore Professor of Law at Columbia University, Fineman is one of what remains a small number of women holding endowed chairs at national law schools. The first generation of women to achieve such distinction did so largely on male terms, that is, not only in accordance with male standards but in mimicking male lifestyles. A colleague of mine who spent a year visiting at a major law school in the late eighties describes attending a women's faculty lunch. She reports discovering that not only was she the only woman in the room with three children but one of the few who had any children. Women with children and supportive partners have only recently achieved academic prominence. Fineman is virtually alone among the ranks of nationally recognized legal scholars to have raised four children on her own.

Fineman's experiences — she made it through the University of Chicago Law School as a divorced single parent with young children — undoubtedly contributes to her wariness of the scholarly approaches penned by conventionally married authors. This skepticism, at least in its scholarly form, began with her ringside observations of divorce reform in Wisconsin.[1] By the time Wisconsin took up its consideration of no-fault divorce in the mid-1970s, the reformers were already convinced that no-fault operated as a "wife-stuffing" measure that allowed husbands to trade in their wives without provision or penalty.[2] Fineman, then at the University of Wisconsin, chronicled the role of a small group of politically active women determined to avoid such results. In 1975 these women contributed to the narrow defeat of a bill that would simply have added no-fault grounds to Wisconsin's existing divorce legislation.[3] The reformers circulated "horror stories" that featured men like *Doonesbury*'s Philip Slackmeyer, who deserted their homemaker wives, as the villains, and "a legal system which closed not only the eyes but the ears of justice in the name of property rights, leaving the wife and children destitute and abandoned."[4] The Wisconsin "solution" to this victimization, Fineman observes, was "equality," that is, recognition of the housewife's contributions to the family and a corresponding right to equal division of the property acquired over the course of the marriage. With amendment of the property provisions in 1977, Wisconsin joined the growing ranks of no-fault states.

Fineman notes with considerable irony that the Wisconsin reformers, consciously attempting to correct the inadequacies of earlier no-fault efforts, advanced proposals nearly identical to the provisions that California had adopted nearly a decade earlier. California, a community property state, had long recognized equal spousal claims to property accumulated during marriage. Yet equal division had done little to redress the postdivorce income disparities between women and men, custodial and noncustodial parents. Indeed, there is evidence in both states that equal property divisions have left many women worse off than prereform judgments that recognized custodial mothers' interest in the family home. Fineman's conclusion was that the rhetoric of equality had proved to be a straitjacket. Even when advanced by and supposedly for women, it "actually reinforced men's control within the family before and after divorce."[5]

With hindsight, Fineman's disaffection with divorce reform appears unremarkable. For women legal scholars in 1983 (the year Fineman published her Wisconsin account), it was heretical. No fault, in the public and academic mind, was associated with a generation of liberal women, and other women were hesitant to break ranks.[6] Moreover, Fineman's criticism departs from other feminist analysis not only in its approach to divorce but in its willingness to acknowledge the contradictions at the core of feminism itself. For the generation of women who came of age in the 1960s and the 1970s, "equality" was a mantra — and a crowbar that had pried open schools, jobs, and activities previously closed to women. The feminist challenge was to dismantle the institutions that perpetuated male dominance and, for legal scholars in particular, equality supplied a standard that could be used to identify the institutions to be condemned not in the name of feminism alone, but in terms of basic considerations of justice. Susan Moller Okin, although writing in political theory rather than law, invoked time-honored feminist method[7] when she made the inequality between husbands and wives the focal point of her family critique.

By 1991, Fineman, in contrast, had issued a call "to abandon equality."[8] In *The Illusion of Equality* she explains that "market and political access appear to be the primary ideological goals of the [women's] movement," and equality within the family has accordingly been understood "to provide *relief* to women from the burdens of domestic life. . . . Women were no longer to be formally designated and identified as caretakers of children, a role that would impede equal market involvement."[9] Hillary Rodham (belatedly) Clinton, who refused to "stay home and bake cookies"[10] and who was mistakenly believed during the presidential campaign not to have any children, represented the new ideal. Fineman's disavowal results not so much from consideration of equality in the abstract (nor from any personal criticism of Hillary), but from the consequences she attributes to the rhetoric. She believes that treating divorcing fathers and mothers as equally capable of self-support renders invisible the costs of childrearing and contributes to the impoverishment of children and the great majority of caretakers who are not corporate law firm partners. She maintains that gender-neutral custody standards "trivialize women's emotional investment in their primary caretaking relationship with their children."[11] True equality, for Fineman, requires explicit consideration of the needs of children and of their gendered relationship with those who care for them.

Fineman's *The Neutered Mother, the Sexual Family, and Other Twentieth-Century Tragedies* (1995) moves from critique to prescription in an effort to provide such an approach. It is among the most distinctive — and provocative — pieces in the family law literature. Her starting point, though different in vocabulary and perspective, echoes Becker. Fineman believes that "dependency," both the dependence of the young, the old, and the infirm on their caretakers, and the dependence that makes unpaid caretakers incapable of self-support, is an inevitable part of life.[12] She is intensely critical of those who believe that an equal sharing of responsibility for caretaking is either possible or likely to eliminate dependence. At the same time, her analysis of the consequences of caretaking shares much in common with Okin. For Fineman agrees that the social structure designed to support caretaking — the nuclear family and the sexual division of labor at its core — works to the systematic disadvantage of women. Fineman, however, departs from the other scholars in locating the source of women's disadvantage not just in the inequalities within marriage, but in the insistence that nuclear families assume responsibility for caretaking entirely on their own. The traditional "solution" to the issues of caretaking, Fineman observes, has been to link the dependent to the independent, and that has overwhelmingly meant subjecting women to male supervision and control.

The Neutered Mother relentlessly documents the ways in which "unsupervised women" are subject to marginalization or domination as the price of their caretaking activities. Historically, young women have been cloistered, chaperoned, or stigmatized (one need only consider the modern Islamic emphasis on the veil) in an effort to lock their childbearing activities securely within marriage. Divorced women, who today may succeed in breaking free of marital bonds, are, Fineman observes, reconnected to their former mates through provisions that threaten them with loss of custody for a catalogue of sins that range from working too much (e.g., full time) to not earning enough. Never-married mothers are labeled "deviant."[13] If they seek public assistance, a system of bureaucratic oversight replaces marital supervision. If, like TV's Murphy Brown, they are highly paid professionals able to remain independent, then they do so by hiring nannies to do much of the actual caretaking. Murphy Brown manages motherhood without marginalization by shifting the caretaking — and the marginalization — to someone else.

Fineman ends the book with a call to reconstruct family law around a revitalized image of mother. She identifies terms such as "caretaking" or "nurturance" with "mothering," and while she believes that men can "mother," she insists on recognition that mothering is a gendered activity that is qualitatively different from fathering. She reserves greatest disdain for liberal feminists, who would, in the name of the egalitarian family, equate mothering with fathering, and substitute the term "parenting" for both activities. Fineman describes this conflation as the "neutering" of mother, erasing her — and the distinctive activities with which she is associated — from view. The result contributes, for the middle class, to the creation of the two-parent family as an "institution with potentially NO available caretakers,"[14] and for the poor, to the demonization of single mothers — and the determination to reduce their numbers — at the heart of modern welfare reform.

Fineman proposes revaluing motherhood, considering the ways in which caretaking benefits society as a whole, not just the families of the ones receiving the care. She wishes to celebrate, rather than punish, those who assist others unable to care for themselves. In the process, she asks: What would unsubjugated motherhood look like? Unsupervised motherhood, as a social institution, recognized as performing a valuable societal role, would be given privacy (without paternity), subsidy (without strings), space (to make mistakes).[15] To accomplish this, Fineman suggests two objectives: first, ending marriage as a legal category, and with it the pretense that the traditional family alone can solve the problems of dependency, and, second, securing protection for those who mother, with the mother/child dyad rather than the husband/wife union recognized as central to the definition of family and deserving of support in its own right.

5

Liberal Feminism vs. the Feminism of Difference

Or, The Huxtables vs. Grace Under Fire

I T is tempting, and perhaps all too easy, to characterize the differences between Okin and Fineman in terms of the conflict between liberal feminism, which seeks equality for women on the same terms as men, and the
feminism of difference, which seeks to acknowledge and protect the ways
in which women differ from men.[1] Okin's book represents the high-water
mark of liberal feminism. It persuasively extends the ideal of equality to an
arena in which it had been previously thought not to apply. In the opposing corner, Fineman's work marks the emergence of the feminism of difference within family law. Fineman's 1983 Wisconsin article appeared only a
year after publication of Carol Gilligan's book *In a Different Voice: Psychological Theory and Women's Development*, the work that challenged male
norms for moral development, and it resonates with efforts to revalue the
feminine across the academy.

If the tensions between Okin and Fineman were no more than an ideological conflict between sameness and difference, however, this chapter
could be limited to a declaration of victory for the difference perspective.
By the time Fineman published *The Neutered Mother* in 1995, the feminism
of difference ruled the day. Feminist anthologies of the 1990s are hard-
pressed to find representatives of the sameness perspective, and women's efforts to gain entrance to the Citadel and VMI, the publicly supported military academies in South Carolina and Virginia, were among the few issues
still framed in terms of equal access.[2] Feminism has come almost to be defined in terms of the discovery and celebration of difference. This triumph,
however, represents as much a changing of the subject (What does entry to
the Citadel have to do with the appropriate amount of child support?) as an
ideological resolution.[3]

At least part of the difference between Okin and Fineman is, after all, a matter of disciplinarity, a literal changing of the subject. Okin's *Justice, Gender, and the Family* constitutes the rediscovery by a mature field — political theory — of the ancient but neglected subject of the family. While older political theorists — Plato, Locke, Kant — considered the family in their efforts to prescribe the ideal society, modern theorists have tended to assume it as a given, rendering it invisible as a subject of study. Okin's major contribution involved her ability to invoke the philosophers of her day and prove their applicability to the family. Equality was the medium that permitted the translation.

Fineman's work, in contrast, corresponds with the coming of age of the relatively young field of family law scholarship. Compared with the rest of the academy, law professors have historically written little. Even at the best schools, law professors once spoke of "a tenure piece" (a single substantial law review article was sufficient to secure tenure at many schools), while their university colleagues wrote books. The scholarly literature addressing family law was particularly thin. Like many areas of primary concern to women, family law was an intellectual backwater characterized by at least one dean as "the soft underbelly of the law."[4] Despite the fact that the law has been interested in domestic relations at least as long as economics, it would be hard to find a legal counterpart to Gary Becker's economic account of the traditional family.

By of the end of the 1980s, however, this all began to change. A flood of law school graduates in the seventies, though often attributed to the baby boom, more accurately reflected the large-scale entrance of women into the profession.[5] With more lawyers — and much more intense competition for tenured positions — the growth in the family law literature has been dramatic, and much of it has been by and about women. Despite this, it was the work of a sociologist employing social science methodology that focused feminist attention on family law. Lenore Weitzman's *The Divorce Revolution: The Unexpected Social and Economic Consequences for Women in America* (1985), published two years after Fineman's Wisconsin account, galvanized dissatisfaction with no-fault divorce.[6] Legal feminists sought to increase the resources available for women and children at divorce. In her critique of equality, Fineman nonetheless found that the growing ranks of feminist scholars replicated the contradictions underlying the Wisconsin reforms. Either, as in Becker's work,[7] women were "victims," impaired by their inability to participate in the market on male terms and entitled to compensation in accordance with their relationship to a particular man, or, as in Okin's work, women were equals, to be dissuaded from sacrificing their own interests for their children. With the dismantling of the fault system that had championed the sexual division of marital labor, neither law nor feminism supplied what should be the core of family regulation — the identification of distinctive *family* values for the law to promote and protect. *The Neutered Mother* constituted a feminist effort to fill the family law void.

Applying Okin and Fineman to the same topics sharpens — and narrows — their differences. To the extent that the subject is justice, the preoccupation of Okin's discipline, then equality provides an appropriate measure. Okin's thesis, stated briefly, is that the traditional family involves two unequal roles — breadwinner and homemaker — assigned by gender. The systematic assignment of the subordinate role to women violates principles of justice.[8] When the topic changes to provision for the family, Fineman's subject, ending the assignment by gender is insufficient so long as the caretaking role, a role of central family importance, remains a subordinate one. Fineman does not dispute Okin's conclusions about the justice of the gendered family, and Okin embraces the need to provide greater support for caretaking.[9] The larger differences between them are not so much about theory as about men.

In a fundamental sense, when Okin and Fineman discuss "the family," they are not talking about the same families at all. Okin's work sometimes reads as though the objective is to replace Ozzie and Harriet with the Huxtables. *The Cosby Show*, in which a doctor and lawyer jointly take responsibility for their children's upbringing, comes close to the egalitarian ideal. Okin writes that it "seems reasonable to expect that children after divorce would still have two actively involved parents, and two working adults economically responsible for them,"[10] and it is not difficult to believe that, in the unlikely event that Hollywood producers allowed the Huxtables to divorce, they would portray them in exactly that way. Of course, much of what makes it possible to envision a satisfactory divorce are traits likely to keep the parents together. Dr. Huxtable is a role model to which many fathers might aspire.[11]

Were Fineman to illustrate her work, in contrast, she might select Roseanne (perhaps after her divorce from Tom Arnold) or the star of *Grace Under Fire*. Grace, a more recent addition to the world of TV sitcoms, is the divorced mother of three. Jimmy, her abusive, alcoholic ex-husband, who deserted the family, has come back into the picture, and he has little in common with Bill Cosby's Dr. Huxtable. His presence is a mixed blessing. The trips to the fair and his appearances at the children's birthday parties are a definite plus, but the children haven't overcome their earlier resentment, and their father can be intrusive as well as helpful. There is no confusing, however, Jimmy's occasional contributions with Grace's financial and emotional support of the family. Fineman is dismissive of what she terms the "family values" perspective that "disingenuously compares idealized nuclear families with those of single mothers already in trouble."[12]

Okin's and Fineman's unspoken choice of paradigmatic families has much to do with another major difference between them — the attention they pay to the role of the state. Okin focuses overwhelmingly on the private relationship between couples. While she favors increased state support when the issue arises, she minimizes the need for direct intervention. The last page of her book concludes:

> Some of what I have suggested would not cost anything, in terms of public spending, though it would redistribute the costs and responsibilities of rearing children more evenly between men and women. Some policies I have endorsed, such as adequate public support for children whose fathers cannot contribute, may cost more than present policies, but may not, depending on how well they work. Some, such as subsidized high-quality day care, would be expensive in themselves, but also might soon be offset by other savings, since they would enable those who would otherwise be full-time child carers to be at least part-time workers.[13]

Fineman's critique, in contrast, is as concerned with the relationship between family and society as it is with the relationships within. Fineman believes that the equality Okin seeks will come only with greater societal support for caretaking itself, "for the dependents who need protection." She explains: "If marriage has no legal significance and the traditional family is not state subsidized and supported, these dependencies will be more visible. Hopefully, they will also become the object of generalized societal concern."[14] Fineman insists on recognition that we all lead "subsidized lives," and she advances her most radical proposal — the call to end marriage as a legal category — in an effort to make "dependencies" more visible, and to shift subsidization from the traditional family to those providing the care. Where Okin sometimes seems to envision paid nannies as the only full-time caretakers, Fineman insists on support for anyone who would undertake the task.

The divide between these two approaches becomes a chasm when it addresses the role of fathers, and the contrast between the men on *The Cosby Show* and those in *Grace Under Fire* has much to do with the authors' differences. When Okin says that some of her proposals "would not cost anything," she is thinking of the Huxtables, who, with two incomes and greater productivity, almost certainly generate more wealth than the Nelsons (or even the doctor in *The Donna Reed Show*). When she speculates that adequate public support for children whose fathers cannot contribute may not cost more, she depends (as she explains in a note) on the prospects for collecting more from delinquent fathers than the fathers might otherwise contribute — or on using the financial assessments to persuade them to avoid paternity in the first place.[15] Only when she discusses state subsidies for child care does she endorse state provision for caretaking independently of family structure.

Okin's model of equality is impossible without the continued involvement of both mothers and fathers in their children's upbringing; Fineman locates much of the oppression she condemns in the efforts to insure the link between them. Jimmy's renewed relationship with his children, even in Hollywood, does not result in a Hollywood ending, much less Okin-defined equality, and Fineman fears that the emphasis on equal roles for mothers and fathers can only complicate Grace's efforts to care for her family. Fineman might well join the rest of the country in preferring the Huxtables to Grace and Jimmy as role models, but, for Fineman, that judgment has little to do with custody, support, or the needs of Grace and Jimmy's children.

Figure 5.1

6

Fineman and Becker

Feminism vs. Economics

I f the differences between Okin and Fineman are a matter of disciplines, assumptions, and sitcom characters (or, more formally, paradigmatic illustrations) that complicate charting their precise divergences, the differences between Fineman and Becker involve a head-on collision, however measured.

The conflicts between them start with, rather than are assuaged by, disciplinarity. Fineman is among a number of feminists who suspect that economists' emphasis on "efficiency" is no more than a rationalization of existing patterns that perpetuate the subordination of women.

> The University of Chicago's Gary Becker . . . analyzes role divisions that systematically disadvantage women in the public sphere and concludes that they are "efficient." . . . Pay differentials for women's work outside the home become the justification for a continued unequal division of labor within the family and for the maintenance of rigid gender roles. This version of economics is bolstered by sociobiology establishing that women have a stronger "preference" for children. It is their preference and the choices based upon it which contribute to their ultimate status as unequal. Woman, so cast, need and want men just as they need and want the nuclear family, and they get what they want (and deserve): inequality.[1]

Fineman, like much of the left, is critical of any discipline that enshrines "choice" without examining the societal factors that limit the alternatives.

Becker, on the other hand, is likely to view such arguments as rationalizations designed to avoid acknowledging inevitable trade-offs (e.g., dieting versus weight gain) or what Guido Calabresi called in a Yale Law School class "tragic choices." Becker couches his formal work in positive rather than normative terms (he purports to describe what is, not what should be), and insists that well-meaning government initiatives often produce disastrous results because of refusal to recognize the "perverse" incentives such programs create. He has been particularly critical of government intervention in the family and would almost certainly regard Fineman's call for giving motherhood "subsidy (without strings)" as an invitation to "moral hazard," without any necessary reference to sexual morality implied or intended.[2]

When the argument between economics and feminism is put aside, however, the substantive dispute between Becker and Fineman remains, and their terms of disengagement can be translated into each other's vocabulary. For Becker, a major advantage of the nuclear family is that it internalizes decisions about children. Parents, who reap the greatest benefits and bear the major costs associated with children, decide how many children to have, how to arrange their lives to combine caretaking with other activities, whether to emphasize music or athletics, and how many toys to buy. If the parents cannot afford or do not value oboe lessons, the children do without. Parental decision-making need not be perfect to be better than most of the alternatives in balancing costs and benefits.

Fineman is, of course, intensely critical of just such decision-making and, if she chose, she could express the critique in the language of economics. Caretaking, Fineman might argue, generates externalities. Society as a whole has an interest in providing for its children, as well as for the elderly and infirm. To the extent that society benefits from private efforts (a child given music lessons might someday become an internationally acclaimed violinist), the externalities are positive; to the extent that private decisions impose costs on society (a child given a drum set might disturb neighbors), the externalities are negative. If no reason exists to believe that private decision-making will reflect the societal costs and benefits, the decision-making will be inefficient (hence the importance of public education, state-subsidized vaccinations, and noise restrictions). If, in addition, private decision-making about the family systematically subordinates women to men (Okin) or those who perform the societally beneficial caretaking role to those who don't (Fineman), it may also be unjust. And either inefficiency or injustice may justify government action.

Becker need not dispute this account directly; he need only argue that the alternatives are worse. Indeed, the easiest way to distinguish liberal and conservative economists is precisely in such terms. Liberals carefully select examples of market failure (e.g., in a purely private system, some people will die because they cannot afford medical care even though the cost of emergency care may be less than the costs their deaths impose on society) and posit unexamined government intervention as the solution. Conservatives carefully select examples of government inefficiency (e.g., free emergency care, which encourages those without health insurance to seek relatively more expensive emergency room treatment for minor ailments) and posit the market as the unexamined solution.

Becker, true to conservative form, trains his guns on the welfare state. In a set of sweeping generalizations, he observes:

> Payments to mothers with dependent children are reduced when the earnings of parents increase, and are raised when additional children are born or when fathers do not support their children. It is a program, then, that raises the fertility of eligible women, including single women, and also encourages divorce and discourages marriage (the financial well-being of recipients is increased by children and decreased by marriage). In effect, welfare is the poor woman's alimony, which substitutes for husband's earnings. The expansion of welfare, along with the general decline in the gain from marriage, explains the sizable growth in the ratio of illegitimate to legitimate birth rates despite the introduction of the pill and other effective contraceptives.[3]

Becker thus reduces a complex development — increasing nonmarital birthrates — to a single primary cause: aid for families with dependent children. He cites no support for his observations, and his empirical claims are controversial. Some studies, for example, show no correlation between fertility and the generosity of welfare benefits. Other studies, which use the combined value of direct payments, Medicaid, and food stamps, show mixed or modest correlations.[4] For Becker, at least in his *Treatise on the Family*, it is a matter of faith. Identify the incentives and they will come — or at least have children.

Fineman could thus dispute Becker's attribution of cause. Many feminists insist, with some empirical support, that women do not have children for welfare benefits, and Fineman cites studies indicating that the picture Becker draws conceals more complexity than it recognizes.[5] Instead, however, Fineman translates Becker's observations into feminist terms and critiques their ideological implications. She begins:

The process of reformulating and reinforcing the historic control of fathers over children and in families hinges on casting the practice of single motherhood as "deviant." The impetus for this designation seems to be that the existence of unstigmatized mothers successfully mothering outside of the traditional heterosexual family calls into question some of the basic components of patriarchal ideology. The very fact of their singleness is central to the construction of deviant mothers.   *(101)*

Fineman then catalogues the ways in which single mothers are blamed for much of society's ills. She cites Charles Murray ("illegitimacy is the single most important social problem of our time — more important than crime, drugs, poverty, illiteracy, welfare, or homelessness, because it drives everything else"), Sen. Daniel Patrick Moynihan ("We talk about the drug crisis, the education crisis, and the problems of teen pregnancy and juvenile crime. But all these ills trace back predominantly to one source: broken families"), and Barbara Defoe Whitehead ("Dan Quayle was Right") (113-14, 125). She ridicules those using Becker-like language to argue that welfare benefits could trigger "perverse effects" that permit a "welfare mother . . . to have a child every two years and never have to work at all" and concludes that "[t]his casts the single mother not as a victim but as a calculating individual who lives lavishly off the poor, victimized taxpayer. She is demonized into the 'bad' mother" (117).

Fineman could similarly recast Becker's analysis. Where Becker sees welfare as a program that raises the fertility of single women, Fineman might see a program that gives women the choice of maternity without an improvident marriage. Where Becker sees a program that encourages divorce, Fineman might see support for women who would otherwise be trapped in abusive relationships. Where Becker describes public aid as the "poor woman's alimony, which substitutes for husband's earnings," Fineman would question the need for women's dependence on their husband's earnings in the first place. Becker's parade of horribles, his list of "perverse incentives" is, in Fineman's terms, a description of women mothering outside of male control.

Were this debate cast in dramatic terms, Fineman might choose Emma Mae Martin, Supreme Court Justice Clarence Thomas's sister, as her heroine. Thomas, then the head of the Equal Employment Opportunity Commission, gave a speech in 1983 that criticized his sister's welfare dependence.[6] His sister (unrepresented, of course, in Thomas's account) later told newspaper reporters of going on welfare, while the pregnant mother of two, to escape a husband who gambled, went around with other women, and abused her. She describes getting off public assistance before Thomas gave the speech by working double shifts at a minimum wage job,[7] and of later going back on welfare when the aunt who raised her suffered a stroke and needed assistance.[8] To the extent that welfare encouraged Martin's divorce or permitted her to care for her aunt, Fineman would suggest that applause, not vilification, is in order. Fineman would also cast Thomas's misuse of his sister's story, along with Becker's *Treatise on the Family*, as part of the campaign of demonization she decries.

The head-on collision between Fineman and Becker ends here, without resolution. Were the exchange to continue, Becker would undoubtedly criticize Fineman's assumption that the government *can* provide a solution. The exchange cannot proceed further, however, because Fineman's thin last chapter sketches what she calls "an alternative vision" rather than a program for implementation. In doing so, Fineman is not unmindful of the limitations of government programs; she can be as scathing as Becker in describing the substitution of state for husband as an instrument of supervision and control. Nonetheless, by the end of *The Neutered Mother*, Fineman has reached the boundary of her discipline. Both law and feminism are more comfortable with critique than prescription, and developing a fully detailed program of government provision for the family crosses the line into public policy. Such an enterprise requires at least some consideration of economics and, more critically, of the interaction between provision for the family and other social objectives. Sylvia Law, a professor of law at New York University and longtime welfare scholar, and Carol Stack, a University of California (Berkeley) sociologist and scholar of the African-American family, have reminded me that welfare critiques are not solely the province of the right. The left has also challenged the wisdom of subsidizing poor women's role as mothers without also investing in their — and their potential partners' — education and employment. Fineman and Becker will never weigh the advantages and disadvantages of government intervention on the same scale. If there is any area of potential agreement, however, it may be on the importance of the ways in which choices are framed, and of encouraging the well-being of existing children without persuading women to choose motherhood on terms that work to their — and society's — disadvantage.

7

Morality, Family, and the State

I is in many ways remarkable to have reached the seventh chapter of a book on the family without having mentioned the subject of sex. Were this book written a century ago, reticence might have kept the word off the page, but the subject would be written into the interstices of every chapter. Today, the absence of more explicit references conveys no hidden meanings, and no understanding about the role of sexuality in the family can be assumed.[1]

This omission is notable if only because for so long the Anglo-American family has been defined by marriage, and marriage defined by sex. Laws still on the books declare that marriage is the sexually exclusive union of one man and one woman for life.[2] English law regarded the child of an illicit union as "*filius nullius*" (literally, the child of no one — particularly for purposes of inheritance), and the first two centuries of American law drew clear distinctions in family membership between marital and nonmarital children.[3] History and literature are replete with drama playing out the importance of sexual morality. Henry VIII founded the Church of England in order to secure legal recognition of his prospective union with Anne Boleyn after the Pope refused to annul his marriage to Catherine of Aragon (and Catherine failed to produce a male heir).[4] Hester Prynne, American literature's most notable single mother, would have found her daughter's conception in her husband's absence a public advertisement of adultery even without the scarlet letter that serves as the title of Hawthorne's book.[5] Historian Michael Grossberg writes, in tracing the nineteenth-century regulation of marriage, that "[i]rregular or clandestine marriages faced an uncertain reception because, as American legal authority David Hoffman suggested in 1836, the end of marriage could not be achieved 'unless promiscuous intercourse be restrained.'"[6] A prominent raison d'être for the legal regulation of the family was to reinforce and police sexual morality.

Although the idea of reviving the scarlet letter generates occasional enthusiasm from politicians or the pulpit,[7] the thrust of modern family law has been the moral deregulation of the family. University of Michigan law professor Carl Schneider, in a thoughtful series of articles, has argued that not only has family law eschewed policing sexual behavior, it has renounced any claim to regulate the family in the name of morality, sexual or otherwise.[8] Schneider tests the social attitudes that underlie the new system[9] by recounting his Michigan law school classes' reaction to the story of Mr. and Mrs. Appleby, of Milan, Michigan.

> He is fifty-eight; she is fifty-six; they have been married for thirty-five years. He has been a salesman all his life, she is a housewife. Their only child, Meg, is now thirty-two and living in New Mexico. Mrs. Appleby has always spent most of her time at home, in large part because her husband has always insisted on it and because he becomes angry when she does not. Mrs. Appleby consequently has few friends of her own, and what social life the couple has revolves around Mr. Appleby's friends. Mr. Appleby has been spending less and less time at home, and Mrs. Appleby has become more and more distressed. One evening, he tells her that he has fallen in love with his nineteen-year-old secretary and wants a divorce so that he can marry her. . . . Mr. Appleby has never earned much, and they have never saved much. If they are divorced, all his modest income will be consumed supporting his new wife and her twin sons. Mrs. Appleby has a high school education and hasn't been on the job market for thirty-five years.[10]

Schneider then stipulates that "legally Mr. Appleby could undoubtedly have a divorce if he wanted one," but asks his class to discuss what he terms a "prior" question: Was Mr. Appleby *morally* entitled to a divorce? The students had difficulty with the question and, indeed, with the idea of morality itself. When Schneider explained that "moral questions are questions about right and wrong," an editor of the law review objected that this definition would "make murder a moral issue, which it clearly wasn't." Schneider could only speculate that, for some students, morality has come to be identified exclusively with sexual issues. He characterizes the students' responses:

> In sum, the preponderant view in class after class was that Mr. Appleby was morally entitled to a divorce. The grounds were multiple and in-

cluded a narrowed definition of "morality," various versions of moral rel-
ativism, the theory that morality has proved socially dangerous and
hence should not be relied on, the position that Mrs. Appleby was
wrong to oppose a divorce, the belief that marriage is not forever, the
feeling that Mr. Appleby was entitled to be happy, a distaste for the
"punitive" quality of any other conclusion, an underlying commitment
to personal autonomy, and an aversion to social constraint.[11]

Schneider reports that, in other parts of the country, the students he queried
were somewhat more willing to question the moral basis of Mr. Appleby's
actions, but that the reluctance to pass moral judgment was deeply imbedded in all the groups he addressed.[12]

Schneider attributes at least part of this reluctance to liberalism. The liberal tradition, he observes, "holds that the state should be neutral among
conceptions of the good." This neutrality deprives the state of any legitimate way of choosing standards for evaluating whether a couple ought to
stay married. Seen in this light, "the problem with traditional divorce law
was exactly that it required moral discourse; no-fault divorce was necessary
precisely to excise moral discourse from the law."[13] Schneider acknowledges
that the shift to no-fault also involved a change in the mores of marriage
and divorce, and that the legislation itself was seen as no more than a technical correction. Nonetheless, he identifies no-fault divorce as part of a
broader movement of moral deregulation that refuses to pass judgment on
family matters, particularly those family matters that historically have been
the focus of government regulation.[14]

William Galston, Clinton's domestic policy adviser at the beginning of
his first term in office and a major architect of the president's welfare reform
plan, wrote a book objecting to this view of liberalism. At the time, he was
a professor at the University of Maryland's School of Public Affairs and Institute for Philosophy and Public Policy. His book, like Susan Okin's, is an
exercise in political theory, and a primary target is the concept of liberalism
Carl Schneider attributes to his students. Galston begins by rejecting the
view that "the liberal state can be understood as 'neutral' in any of the senses
in which that term is currently employed. Like every other political community, it embraces a view of the human good that favors certain ways of
life and tilts against others."[15]

With this introduction, Galston challenges the conventional accounts
of liberalism. Classic liberalism, articulated by theorists such as John Locke
or John Stuart Mill, arose in a post-Reformation Europe beset with religious wars. Its central tenet was toleration; its greatest accomplishment the

creation of a limited state that did not require any particular creed of its citizens. Initially, liberalism's embrace of toleration may have reflected the conviction that the cost of coercion was just too high, whether measured in terms of loss of individual freedom or the destruction visited by religious wars and inquisitions.[16] Contemporary theorists (liberalism's critics most prominent among them) began more recently, however, to treat neutrality as the centerpiece of liberal theory, and to extend this neutrality not only toward religion but toward all conceptions of the good life.[17] Carl MacIntyre writes that liberalism and its attendant emphasis on government neutrality and toleration are inevitable responses to the loss of faith in a human telos and objective ethical truths.[18] If the truth is unknowable, it is harder to impose it with conviction.

Mary Ann Glendon, who like Galston objects to this account, terms it "a skimpy view of liberalism," with the state as traffic cop, "permitting individuals to pursue their diverse ideas of the good life with as few collisions as possible."[19] Beliefs, values, and character develop offstage as the state insures only that the conflicts between different groups and ideals do not threaten to derail the enterprise. Critics argue, however, that the source of those beliefs, values, and character are the very religious and cultural institutions that the liberal state refuses to promote, and may inadvertently undermine. Galston observes, "In the past generation, thinkers along the political spectrum from Irving Kristol to Jurgen Habermas have contended that liberalism is dependent on — and has depleted — the accumulated moral capital of revealed religion and premodern moral philosophy."[20] The fear is that people will not work hard, live moderately, or attend to their families without promotion of the religious and community associations with which such values are associated, and that liberal society is incapable of such promotion.

Galston rejects this critique arguing that "[l]iberalism contains *within itself* the resources it needs to declare and to defend a conception of the good and virtuous life that is no way truncated or contemptible."[21] He begins by noting that no form of political life can be justified without some view of what is good for individuals. Liberalism, for example, has no difficulty banning the violent overthrow of the government, or preferring tolerance to bigotry.[22] At a minimum Galston argues, liberalism embraces the worth of human existence, the value of the fulfillment of human purposes, and the commitment to rationality as the chief guide to both individual purposiveness and collective undertakings. "What is distinctive about liberalism is not the absence of a substantive conception of the good," he concludes, "but rather a reluctance to move from this conception to full-blown public coercion of individuals."[23]

Galston spends the last part of the book describing a liberal conception of the good, and the means of accomplishing it with a minimum of coercion. Central to his efforts is an articulation of liberal virtues. Outside of philosophy, the term "virtue" sounds archaic. Contemporary discussion of the classical virtues of "prudence" or "temperance" is rare, however admirable the traits remain, and mention of "piety" or "chastity" would be greeted with laughter in many circles. Moreover, contemporary discussion of virtues risks partisanship; William Bennett's *A Book of Virtues*, the most successful recent effort to discuss virtue, is associated in the minds of many with the Republican right's efforts to emphasize personal responsibility at the expense of public support. Nonetheless, in philosophical circles, virtue is enjoying a comeback. Ethical obligations are more powerfully presented in aspirational terms, and the inability to agree on a hierarchy of virtues does not necessarily defeat the usefulness of the exercise.

Galston's list of liberal virtues, like most such lists, is unobjectionable, if not bland. He identifies virtues associated with liberal society (independence, tolerance), liberal economy (industry, delay of gratification, adaptability), liberal politics (citizenship, leadership, courage, law-abidedness, loyalty), and individual excellence, and connects them to a societal obligation to promote both the virtues themselves and the institutions, such as families, schools, churches, the legal system, political leaders, and the media, that foster them. The family receives special attention. He observes:

> From the standpoint of the economic well-being and sound psychological development, the evidence indicates that the intact two-parent family is generally preferable to the available alternatives. It follows that a prime purpose of sound family policy is to strengthen such families by promoting their formation, assisting their efforts to cope with contemporary economic and social stress, and retarding their breakdown whenever possible. This is of course not the only purpose: Family policy must also seek to ameliorate the consequences of family breakdown for children while recognizing that some negative effects cannot be undone.[24]

Galston's embrace of the two-parent family, although he takes pains to keep it within a liberal (and Democratic) tradition, echoes the emphasis on the family within communitarian circles. The resonance is not accidental. Galston is one of the founders of the American communitarian movement.

He initially set forth his case in the lead article of the first edition of *The Responsive Community*, the leading voice of communitarian thinking in the United States, and his proposals owe much to Mary Ann Glendon, a Harvard law professor and comparative family law scholar, who serves with Galston as a coeditor of the journal. To reinforce the two-parent family, and the importance of keeping both parents involved in their children's upbringing, Galston advocates "braking" mechanisms that would require divorcing parents to pause for reflection, and more effective child support enforcement, with the state insuring the identification of every child's parents and requiring all absent parents to pay a percentage of their income to the child's support.[25] Moreover, as Clinton's domestic policy adviser, Galston has been identified with the president's early welfare reform efforts, designed, in part, to underscore objection to the growing number of nonmarital births. Communitarians believe that individual action can be circumscribed for the good of the community; Galston seeks to demonstrate that such proposals can be reconciled with liberalism as well. Liberals need not hesitate in passing judgment on Carl Schneider's Mr. Appleby.

Closely reading *Liberal Purposes* for a standard to apply, however, is another matter. Galston's discussion of liberal virtues barely mentions family matters. Rather, he discusses family structure as a means to an end, as the best way to instill virtue in the next generation, and as a matter of concern for public policy. Within this scheme, the Applebys are not of central importance. Their only child is now an adult, and Galston recognizes "a deep difference between families with children and those without them." He acknowleges that in families like the Applebys where children are not at issue, "principles of individual freedom and choice may be most appropriate," but, in families with children, "moral categories such as duty, continuing responsibility, and basic interests come into play."[26] He thus limits his call for a braking mechanism at divorce to families with children. The issue of what kind of duty, continuing responsbility, and basic interests might apply between adults is left to family law scholars — or to William Bennett.[27]

In this sense, Galston has come full circle from the days of the scarlet letter. The older ideal of sexual morality permitted sex only in the context of the Kantian ideal of a relationship built on the exchange of mutual promises of lifelong union.[28] The law enforced the promises the couple made to each other and, indeed, viewed marital infidelity as an indicia of character that could affect custody, employment, and presidential bids. In the new order, such promises are to be reconciled with "principles of individual freedom and choice." It is the couple's obligations to the child that stand in their place. All of Galston's proposals — the braking mechanism, child support, Clinton-style welfare reform — involve the use of the state to police parental responsibility toward children. Within the family, parenthood, not partnership, is the foundation of Galston's moral order.

8

What *Is* the Purpose of Family Policy?

Galston vs. Fineman — with the Others Watching from the Sidelines

I N many ways, Galston has little in common with other scholars of the family. He is a political theorist. His subject is the state. His book on liberalism devotes only a few pages to the family. Yet the questions he asks are fundamental. What is the role of the family within society, and what is the purpose of state policy? His answers are unequivocal: a primary purpose of the family is to raise children, and for this purpose families with stably married parents are best.[1] Thus, questions of family structure are not purely private, but important matters of public policy. The difficulty is that Galston's project requires linking public policy concerns to individual behavior at a time when older norms have given way, and there is no consensus on their replacement.

Comparing Galston to Gary Becker and Susan Okin underscores the difficulties. Becker and Okin largely share Galston's preference for two-parent families, but the sources of family obligation they identify lie with the parents' obligation to each other. Becker believes that the central advantage of the traditional family is not just the presence of two parents but the division of labor their union permits. Unlike Galston, therefore, he describes family commitment in terms of the spousal exchange necessary to promote and protect specialization.[2] For Becker, Mr. Appleby's decision to leave Mrs. Appleby is exactly the type of event traditional marriage, and the conventional norms associated with it, were designed to prevent.

Okin, who chronicles the ways in which the two-parent family has worked to the detriment of women, places more emphasis than Galston on encouraging fathers to accept an equal share of the responsibility for children, and less on keeping the family together. She identifies women's inability to leave unhappy marriages as a critical element in their disadvantage, and one would therefore expect Okin to be wary of efforts to discourage divorce, particularly in abusive families. While Okin identifies the well-being of women *and* children with a reformed family that requires two parents to share childrearing, she combines obligation to children with obligation to protect those made vulnerable by domestic responsibilities. She would thus insist on recognition of Mr. Appleby's duty to support Mrs. Appleby, not because of the circumstances of their divorce but because of the division of responsibility within the marriage.

Only Fineman shares Galston's emphasis on the centrality of provision for children, and only Fineman challenges Galston directly. She agrees that the primary purpose of the family is to provide for children, but she argues that the association between children's well-being and the two-parent family is at least in part circular. Children need food, clothing, shelter, love, and affection. The nuclear family meets those needs by dividing responsibility between homemaking mothers and breadwinning fathers, but it is not the only way to insure children's well-being. Many societies recognize nurturing roles for a host of adults (godparents, grandparents, aunts, uncles, and the masters of apprentices),[3] or provide for families' material needs in ways that are not so dependent on a single breadwinner. Fineman argues that the only constant is children's need for nurturance and their caretakers' need for support. Efforts to promote the two-parent family, whether in the form of joint custody or welfare cuts, often work to children's detriment. During an age in which even Galston concedes that the state can have only a marginal effect on the increase in the number of single-parent families, Fineman argues that children's interests lie in making two biological parents less, rather than more, critical to their well-being.

At this point, the dispute between Galston and Fineman becomes an empirical one. Galston cites "a mountain of evidence" linking the drug crisis, the education crisis, and the problems of teen pregnancy and juvenile crime to broken families; Fineman challenges the studies' validity and their ability to establish a causal relationship. Galston claims that government action can strengthen the two-parent family to the benefit of children; Fineman argues that such intervention is more likely to worsen their lot. Neither attempts a full evaluation of the growing, and sometimes conflicting, body of social science data, and, even if they did, it could not fully resolve their conflict over the efficacy of alternative approaches.

Nonetheless, it is important to emphasize that the dispute between them *is* to an important degree empirical, in part, because Galston's liberal defense of the two-parent family does not appeal to overarching ethical or moral claims. In *Liberal Purposes*, Galston emphasizes a distinction between what he calls "intrinsic traditionalism" and "functional traditionalism." He explains:

> [Intrinsic traditionalism] . . . is crystallized in sentiments in the form "X is unnatural, disgusting, ungodly (or whatever)" and moves directly to the proposition that anything judged innately unacceptable by such standards may be legally prohibited. The second form of traditionalism, which I call *functional*, rests its case on the asserted links between certain moral principles and public virtues or institutions needed for the successful functioning of a liberal community. So, for example, an intrinsic traditionalist might deplore divorce as a violation of divine law, whereas a functional traditionalist might object to it on the grounds (for which considerable empirical evidence can be adduced) that children in divorced families tend to suffer kinds of economic and psychological damage that reduce their capacity to become independent and contributing members of the community.[4]

Galston's ethical rationale, at least as it applies to his defense of the two-parent family, is utilitarian (public policy should promote the greatest good for the greatest number) rather than Kantian.[5]

This distinction separates Galston from the older order of sexual morality that Carl Schneider's students so distrusted. But it also creates its own complications. Consider Dan Quayle's election-year criticism of sitcom character Murphy Brown's nonmarital pregnancy. Surely Galston, with his invocation of the importance of the two-parent family, would join Quayle in his criticism of TV morals. But as Quayle found, establishing the precise grounds for criticism is not so easy. An intrinsic traditionalist — or any old-time moralist — would have no difficulty. An unmarried woman, whatever her age, had no business having sex, even with her ex-husband. Not only would New England preachers spouting fire and brimstone condemn her, but Immanuel Kant, in his *Philosophy of Law*, maintained that sexual relations were permissible only in an exclusive lifelong union. The immoral act of conception would be, in itself, grounds for condemnation. She could escape public censure only by marrying the father in time to avoid embarrassing questions.

Galston, however, along with a majority of the American public, takes no position on sexuality itself.[6] Indeed, a poll taken by the Gallup organization after Quayle's speech indicated that Murphy Brown enjoyed more support than Dan Quayle. A sampling of the results:

Were you offended by Murphy Brown's decision to have a baby as a single parent?

Yes: 17% No: 76% Don't know: 7%

Does Murphy Brown set a bad example?

Yes: 27% No: 65% Don't know: 8%

Only 31% of married people frown on Murphy's example of unwed motherhood; that figure drops to 21% for singles.[7]

A larger percentage of the sample (40 percent) thought that Dan Quayle set a bad example.

If the sexual act itself is unproblematic for a majority of Americans, then what is? The Murphy Brown character did not plan to get pregnant, so she can presumably be criticized for a negligent failure to prevent conception. It is difficult to imagine, however, a public policy that distinguishes between planned, negligent, and unavoidable births. The problem must therefore be with her decision to keep the child and raise him on her own. Diane English, *Murphy Brown*'s creator, is said to have responded that if Quayle thought it was "disgraceful for an unmarried woman to bear a child, he'd better make sure abortion remains safe and legal."[8] The Bush White House, which had initially supported Quayle, backtracked when the issue of abortion was raised, but at least some of those who share Galston's concern for the two-parent family would urge that abortion — or adoption at the mother's election — represents the better course.

Quayle himself stated that Murphy Brown "epitomizes today's intelligent, highly paid, professional woman," and her bearing of a child alone amounts to "mocking the importance of fathers."[9] A large part of the response to Quayle's attack, however, asked what was wrong with an intelligent, highly paid professional, prepared to devote herself to her child's welfare, electing single parenthood over abortion or adoption. The fictional Brown's decision was not lightly taken, and it is difficult to imagine anything short of draconian state intervention or the return of the scarlet letter changing the outcome. Declaring Murphy ineligible for welfare, requiring that she acknowledge the father, and requiring him to pay child support are unlikely to have more than a marginal effect on either her decision or the child's welfare (not to mention the plotline).

Galston is not Dan Quayle. He doesn't mention either abortion or adoption in his discussion of the family and, indeed, he is not on the record with respect to Murphy Brown.[10] The virtues he advocates include a conception of individual excellence defined in terms of a Lockean sense of rational liberty or self-discipline, a Kantian account of rational morality and mutual respect for oneself and others, and a Romantic notion of the full flowering of individuality.[11] Murphy Brown's actions might well be reconciled with this definition of virtue. She considered abortion and reached a reasoned decision that she was willing to make the commitment necessary to raise a child on her own. She was concerned about the importance of male role models and resolved to include father figures in the child's upbringing. It is difficult to conclude, as Dan Quayle found, that Brown was wrong without specifying the alternatives. If sex does not imply a promise to marry, and contraception is imperfect, then decrying single parenthood does not resolve Brown's dilemma.

Galston's problem is that it is difficult to link statistics on the negative outcomes associated with nonmarital births to moral exhortation. Rule utilitarian reasoning (society would be better off generally if all children were born to stable two-parent families) does not translate neatly into individual morality (Murphy Brown should have elected abortion or adoption). This, of course, does not mean that Galston is wrong; only that his project is both controversial and incomplete.

To test my students' moral reasoning on this issue, I often use the case of Crystal Chambers.[12] Chambers, in her early twenties, was an arts and crafts instructor with Girls Club of Omaha. Girls Club insisted that all its employees act as role models for the participants, and when Chambers, who was unmarried, became pregnant, she was fired. Chambers sued, alleging discrimination on the basis of pregnancy status and race (both she and 90 percent of the Girls Club participants were African-American, and nonmarital births are more common and more accepted in the black community).[13] The court sided with Girls Club, deciding that its role model requirements were bona fide occupational qualifications that justified the discharge.

My Feminist Jurisprudence class tends to identify with Chambers. They are about the same age and a majority of the students are women. They find the emphasis on Chambers's marital status inappropriate. Rather, they emphasize that she is different from her teenage charges because she is an adult. They note with some irony that she is financially able to support a child, but only because of the job that is imperiled by the pregnancy. Unlike the reaction of Carl Schneider's students to the Appleby hypothetical, my students do express a degree of moral judgment with respect to Chambers's decision to bear the child. But it tends to be tied to her ability to provide for the baby, emotionally and materially, rather than to her status as an unmarried parent.

This reasoning is surprisingly close to Galston's, even as it reaches a different conclusion. Both premise parental responsibility, and moral decision-making, on ability to care for the child. They disagree on what that requires, and the single greatest element of disagreement is on the importance of fathers. When Dan Quayle accused Murphy Brown of "mocking the importance of fathers," he implied no disrespect toward Murphy's ex-husband. Rather, he was affronted by the conviction that a mother could adequately raise a child without first insuring a father's participation. Galston's emphasis on the two-parent family (independently of Becker-style gender roles, sexual morality, financial security, or emotional maturity) ultimately rests on the same conclusion. My students disagree, both because they place less importance on fathers and because they place greater value on their — and Crystal Chambers's — ability to reach their own decisions. Galston, by the end of *Liberal Purposes*, has not bridged the cultural divide. The question we are left with is whether it is possible to use the idea of commitment to children, which Galston shares with the students, to rewrite a code of parental conduct capable of bridging their deep disagreements.

9

Conclusion

Iɴ the twenty years since Gary Becker began work on his treatise, there is very little about the family that has not changed, and few verities that remain unchallenged. Nonetheless, while Becker's description of specialization between breadwinners and homemakers has been overtaken by events, the type of economic analysis he championed suggests a new model. This model would hold, at a minimum, that

1. the single biggest change resulting from women's greater workforce participation is not less specialization between men and women but more specialization among women as women assume a greater variety of roles and pay others (from nannies to McDonald's) to help with child care, food preparation, and other domestic chores;

2. the greater specialization among women increases societal productivity and wealth and gives women both a greater share of that wealth and greater independence in deciding how to live their lives;

3. women's increased status and earnings, all other things remaining equal, increase their ability to remain single, to elect divorce or single parenthood, or to demand more from partners or potential partners;

4. the net effect of women's increased status and earnings depends on a variety of factors, including societal attitudes and relative changes in men's income, adaptability, and alternatives to marriage.

At a theoretical level, this analysis ends with item number four because the interaction between women's workforce participation, male attitudes, and changing mores toward sexuality and divorce is impossible to predict. At an empirical level, however, the story continues apace, and there are two empirical conclusions that brook no dissent. The first is that the structure of the family has changed, and changed in the direction of greater instability, with divorces leveling off at one of every two marriages, and nonmarital births reaching one-third of the total.[1] The second is that children are worse off, and they are worse off at least in part because of the change in family structure.

While many of the claims that single-parent families *cause* children's problems are controversial, a significant portion of these claims is axiomatic. The older system linked children to the nuclear family, and the nuclear family to the specialized division of labor Gary Becker describes. Married couples within this system were self-sufficient to the extent that fathers could earn a "family wage." Schools could end at three o'clock in the afternoon with gymnastics practice a mile away at four because mothers did the driving. The new system depends to a much greater degree on two-income families at the same time that mothers' traditional responsibilities remain difficult to reconcile with the demands of employment. And when, in response to the changes of modern life, partners do not stay together, single parents' difficulties multiply. So long as society continues to provide adequate support for children only in the context of traditional families, the declining number of traditional families must necessarily work to children's detriment.

To improve the lot of children therefore requires rebuilding the societal infrastructure that supports them. Becker, Okin, Fineman, and Galston frame the alternatives, and the relationship between their approaches can be expressed in terms of figure 9.1.

	Two-Parent Family *Favor*	Two-Parent Family *Neutral*
Specialization *Favor*	*Becker:* Specialization linked to traditional family	*Fineman:* Specialization irrespective of family structure
Specialization *Neutral or Oppose*	*Galston:* Two-parent family irrespective of specialization	*Okin:* Egalitarian roles irrespective of family structure

Figure 9.1

The key to their differences lies in the relationship between the two-parent family and specialized roles, and the changes in the nature of family commitment that the alternatives require. Becker the traditionalist describes specialization as the two-parent family's reason for being. He argues that the gendered division of labor, given the dependence it produces in women, will not occur without the couple's commitment to each other. Once the commitment is made, however, the parents can be expected to act in the interests of their children — at least so long as the family remains together.[2] Thus, the traditional family's central obligations were the ones the spouses undertook toward each other.

Fineman agrees with Becker that caretaking is a specialized task that requires a complementary provision of material goods, but she identifies the universality of the nuclear family less with the exchange of marital vows than with the coercion and subordination that insured women's participation. She seeks to rebuild the idea of family directly on the caretaker's provision of care, while treating the provision of resources as the responsibility of the state. She thus envisions two parallel — and specialized — systems of obligation replacing the relationship between the adults: one within the family from caretaker to child, and one without from society to family.[3]

Galston believes that the key to children's well-being lies with the two-parent family, without identifying the advantages with any particular assignment of roles. Unlike Becker, therefore, he does not emphasize the parents' obligations to each other, but rather their responsibility to stay together for the well-being of their children. His divorce and welfare proposals track the normative assessment; it is parents, not partners, whose responsibilities are at issue. Thus, despite his embrace of the two-parent family, his idea of obligation is closer to Fineman's emphasis on commitment to children than to Becker's focus on the relationship between the adults.

Okin's objective is egalitarian roles, and she emphasizes ways to encourage shared responsibility for childrearing irrespective of family structure. She gives greatest priority to workplace reforms such as subsidized child care that would ease the relationship between home and family, and favors measures such as joint custody and child support that keep both parents involved with their children whether they themselves are together or apart. While her goal is a reformed relationship between men and women in which egalitarian partnerships may be the ideal, provision for children independently of marriage is necessary to her success.

With the end of the conditions that produced the traditional family, the authors agree that parental interests can no longer serve as a proxy for those of their children. Yet, whether or not they have wage-earning fathers and caretaking mothers, children still require both the material things that money can buy as well as love and attention, supervision and support. Modern society has broken the link between the resources of the current generation and the well-being of the next. The theorists, despite their differences, focus on provision for children as central to reforging the link. What all four leave out is Murphy Brown — the economically self-sufficient mature adult who can realistically choose to raise a child on her own.

Nevertheless, all four would reject her. Only Fineman's inferred rejection is surprising, but her reasons underscore the difficulties a Murphy Brown poses for the others. The critical factor for Fineman is that Brown can be a self-sufficient single parent only because she can afford to hire someone else to perform the bulk of the actual care. Brown's relation with her nanny replicates the specialization — and the subordination — of the traditional family. Murphy Brown, in Becker-like fashion, "specializes" in the market, while hiring another (necessarily less well-paid) specialist to care for her son. Caretaking, the quintessential family activity, has been commercialized. Becker, who objects to the distorting incentives of welfare and no-fault divorce in needlessly encouraging family instability, has no basis on which to object to Brown's presumably utility-maximizing choice. Yet Brown's full-time-employee nanny challenges the distinction between family and market at the core of Becker's analysis, and suggests that the market may supply a continuum of family arrangements in the future. Okin, a feminist who in other contexts might be expected to celebrate women's greater autonomy, cannot be happy with the very different positions of father and mother in Murphy's son's life. She does not go so far as to argue that single women need secure a father's commitment as the price of parenthood, but it is hard to imagine an egalitarian commitment to childrearing without one. Galston would like to impose just such a requirement, but his reasons for doing so ultimately rest on the question of which comes first, the chicken or the egg? Should society support two-parent families because they are better for children or is it the societal support for the two-parent family that makes them so important in the first place?

Murphy Brown destabilizes the categories. The four theorists recognize that contemporary families challenge conventional notions of family form, and reconceive the alternatives. Yet they do so by adjusting the relationship between the adults (or, in Fineman's case, between society and caretakers), and then providing for children within the revised adult framework. Murphy Brown suggests that these efforts are futile, that the altered boundaries between home and market will produce too varied a set of adult relationships to provide for everyone, and that the norms governing adult relationships will not necessarily take children's interests into account. The challenge then becomes the systematic reconnection of one generation to the next in a context supplied by history and the larger forces of family change.

PART II

From Partners to Parents

The Empirical Debate

THIS century is not the first to witness family instability. Library shelves are filled with volumes documenting nineteenth-century concerns that divorce rates were rising too rapidly, women had become too independent, men too unreliable, and children were suffering. One hundred years later, the judgment of history is that yes, the family did change, and we have so internalized what were once "new" family values that we have long since stopped asking whether the changes were good ones. At some point, it simply becomes impossible to go back.

We are now in the midst of a similar transformation. The philosophical divisions about the future of the family, for all their appeal to truth and justice, ultimately rest on empirical assumptions about the effect of family forms on men, women, and children, and the possibilities of restructuring family life in more efficient, more just, or more compassionate ways. If I were to approach this section as I did the last, it would feature two opponents: (1) Karl Marx, whose scientific materialism maintained that history is the inevitable product of impersonal forces, and (2) his descendants, who see the world as a social construct and therefore attribute its failings to a lack of imagination and will. Instead, I believe that almost everything of interest lies between.

First, I think it is important to see that the family *is* a product of historical forces, however much we continue to debate just which historical forces. The families most of us remember fondly from our youth (and some of us remember more fondly from TV sitcoms) were once themselves viewed as radical harbingers of family instability. The idea that partners could choose their mates, for love rather than family obligation, and with or without parental approval was so earth-shattering a concept that it produced many a sermon in the eighteenth century, literary preoccupation in the nineteenth, and an entire musical (*Fiddler on the Roof*) in the twentieth. Conventional historical wisdom (however much historians deny that there is any such thing) even provides a modicum of agreement about the axes along which family change occurred, suggesting that we consider

- the relationship between family and community (are the neighbors *supposed* to snoop?);

- the nature of marriage (are women *really* supposed to obey?);

- the importance of children (the "banal" or the center of existence?);

- the purpose of sexuality (duty, honor, or pleasure, with speculation about the importance of bathing).

These measures, moved from their eighteenth- and nineteenth-century contexts to the twentieth, indicate that the family is undergoing as significant a transformation today as it did during the early days of industrialization. While this part of the book cannot pretend to chart every empirical controversy that attends family studies, it identifies the markers of family change that inform the debates about their wisdom.

Second, I think that it is also important to recognize that these changes do not play out evenly over time, class, race, gender, geography, or age. The family is part of the process of change itself, contributing to group identity in some eras, exacerbating inequalities in others, and, at the very least, altering the vantage point of the commentators. The empirical "debate" that is the subject of this section thus becomes one of contrasting perspectives rather than opposing positions. Chapter 10 will examine these changes from the perspective of history; chapter 11 in terms of the racial divisions in the United States. Chapter 12 will return to microeconomics and the greater convergence over the last decade of black and white family patterns while chapter 13 returns to Lawrence Stone's historical analysis of "sentiment," and the perspective of class. Chapter 14 asks, "And What About the Children?"

History and the Making of the Modern Family

(with Apologies to Edward Shorter)

T HE answers to the riddles of Murphy Brown — where do our mores about childrearing come from, and how enduring are they — are properly the subject of history. Yet history, as a discipline, seems determined to muddle as much as to clarify, "to cleanse the story of mankind from the deceiving visions of a purposeful past."[1] If there are answers to be found, they must be disinterred from the mass of data (often perversely conflicting) that historians have supplied.

In making sense of their field, family historians begin by emphasizing the relative youth of the enterprise. While history itself is an ancient subject, and although it has addressed lineage from the recently decoded Mayan hieroglyphics to the "begat" clauses of the Bible ("Abraham begat Isaac . . ."), the systematic study of family form and function took longer to emerge. Friedrich Engels wrote in 1891:

> Before the beginning of the 'sixties [1860s], one cannot speak of a history of the family. In this field, the science of history was still completely under the influence of the five books of Moses. The patriarchal form of the family, which was there described in greater detail than anywhere else, was not only assumed without question to be the oldest form, but it was also identified — minus its polygamy — with the bourgeois family of today, so that the family had really experienced no historical development at all; at most it was admitted that in primitive times there might have been a period of sexual promiscuity.[2]

It took the nineteenth-century realization that not all cultures shared the European preference for patriarchy for the history of the family to become a proper subject of inquiry.[3] Even then, Edward Shorter could still comment a century later that "[t]he 'history of the family' has only recently become a recognized field of research and the few books about it are not very good." It has only been in the brief period since Shorter that family history has become a field of its own.

The other key to navigating the shoals of historical research is to recognize that the historiography of the family has been characterized as much by dissension as to what constitutes good history as by competing accounts of the family. Indeed, each generation of family historians has seemed determined not just to question their predecessors but to reinvent the field. Within this process, the most definitive answers have been the most thoroughly discredited.

The first generation of family historians, writing in the era of Darwin, were evolutionists, and their subject was the rise of the patriarchal family. Engels' work was among the more ambitious. Influenced by Bachofen's *Mutterrecht*,[4] to which he credits the beginning of the field, and Lewis Morgan's work among the Iroquois in nineteenth-century New York,[5] Engels sought to link domestic developments to mankind's material progress. In *The Origin of the Family, Private Property, and the State*, he set forth three distinct periods of human development:

1. The first linked "savagery," or the hunter-gatherer stage of human existence, with group marriage. During this period, promiscuity was the norm as each member of the group had a right of sexual intercourse with others of the group, and descent was traced exclusively through the female line.[6]

2. The second stage associated "barbarism," or the early stages of herding and farming, with pair-bonding. In the pairing family, one man lived with one woman, occasionally tolerating polygamy and the man's (but not the woman's) sexual infidelity. The marriage tie could, however, be readily severed by either party, with the children remaining with the mother.

3. The third stage produced "civilization," the period of industry, art, the accumulation of wealth — and monogamy. Monogamy differed from pair-bonding in its insistence on lifelong family ties and the shift from maternal to paternal lines of descent. Engels observed that "the sole exclusive aims of monogamous marriage were to make the man supreme in the family, and to propagate, as the future heirs to his wealth, children indisputably his own."[7] Echoing Marx (and sounding very much like Susan Moller Okin), he concluded that "it will be plain that the first condition for the liberation of the wife is to bring the whole female sex back into public industry, and that this in turn demands the abolition of the monogamous family as the economic unit of society."[8]

While Engels' work remains influential as a commentary on patriarchy,[9] and while it is in some ways prophetic, it has been largely dismissed as reputable history or anthropology.[10] Engels rested his case on the best ethnological work of his era, but not even Morgan's field research, singular in its time, would meet modern standards, and any number of the particulars equating Native American and Asian kinship systems as equivalent levels of "barbarism" have proven to be mistaken.[11] Nonetheless, it is the claim to the universal (along with its Eurocentric moralism) rather than any error in the details that most dates Engels' claims. The scholars of Engels' time sought to outdo each other in the discovery — and proclamation — of grand theory. Thus, Engels examined the family within a tradition influenced by Marx's scientific materialism and aptly represented by Sir Henry Maine's declaration in 1861 that

> The movement of the progressive societies has been uniform in one respect. Through all its course it has been distinguished by the gradual dissolution of family dependency, and the growth of individual obligation in its place. . . .
> [T]he movement of progressive societies has hitherto been a movement from *Status* to Contract.[12]

While Maine continues to be among the most quoted historians of his time, modern scholars cringe at the grandiosity of his claims. Stephanie Coontz could be writing with Maine, Morgan, or Engels in mind when she explains in more respectable modern fashion that

> In focusing attention on the different ways that families are embedded in the specific social relations of society, we may be able to avoid grand historical pronouncements about the relationship of family history to industrialization or "modernization." . . . Nor need we postulate unilinear theories of social change whereby some grand historical family transformation begins in one sector of society and trickles down or seeps up to the rest. For the "modernization" of one sector, at least in a competitive economy or polity, often involves the devolution of another . . . , while the same forces that impel one class to restrict its household size and family interactions may stimulate another to expand its household or extend contracts with kin.[13]

In short, generalizations are suspect; emphasis on the particular and recognition of differences across time, race, and class are the hallmarks of rigor in modern historical scholarship.[14]

With this shift, the issue arises whether historians can say anything with certainty (particularly, as Coontz's prose suggests, to a popular audience).[15] One answer, provided by French and English demographers, was to replace grand theory with statistics. Peter Laslett and the Cambridge Group for the History of Population and Social Structure, influenced by the earlier efforts of the French, drew on the voluminous records of births, deaths, and marriages kept by local churches to create of a picture of English family life since the sixteenth century. Laslett's original work sought to debunk the enduring belief that the nuclear family was a product of industrialization, that extended families gave way to more democratic, nuclear ones only with the Industrial Revolution.[16] He and the researchers identified with him produced data demonstrating that, from the sixteenth through the nineteenth centuries, average household size remained fairly constant at about 4.75, and the proportion of extended families *increased* in industrial towns during the mid-nineteenth century.[17] Sounding perilously like the theoreticians who preceded them, one of the researchers was so bold as to declare: "It is simply untrue, as far as we can yet tell, that there was ever a time or place when the complex family was the universal background to the ordinary lives of ordinary people," and Laslett himself speculated that "the human family, if not necessarily the household, must always have been small and almost always nuclear."[18]

Such declarations could not go without challenge, and other authors have documented the widespread presence of extended families in southern and eastern Europe and the ancient Mediterranean. By 1977, Laslett properly qualified his conclusions, noting only "the extent to which the single family household prevails in England, the Low Countries, and northern France."[19] For modern historians, however, Laslett's retreat made his work of greater, rather than lesser, interest as it moved away from universal claims to documentation of the distinctive development of the English family. A decade later, historians would summarize the contributions of the group with which Laslett was associated in terms of the particular, concluding that

> These "new" social historians have found that from an early date, long before industrialization, most Western European families lived in nuclear households and differed from families elsewhere in the late age at which women married; the large proportion of men and women who never married or bore children; the emphasis placed on the conjugal tie between husband and wife; the religious emphasis placed on free and mutual consent in marriage and hostility toward endogamous mar-

riages, polygamy, and concubinage; and the early adoption, beginning in the eighteenth century, of effective methods of contraception.[20]

Historians rediscovered the monogamous, nuclear family as a distinctive feature of northwestern Europe, while disavowing the conclusion that family form was an inevitable by-product of industrialization. For more traditional historians, this raised anew the question of the family strategies producing such results.

Lawrence Stone provides over a thousand pages of answers.[21] If there remains dissension as to the proper field in which to place Morgan or Engels or even Laslett, there is none with Stone. Stone is indubitably an historian, using the most conventional of historical methods. He attempts "to chart and document, to analyse and explain" the vast and elusive cultural changes that affected the English family over a three-hundred-year period and forged what Shorter terms the "modern" family and Becker and Okin regard as the "traditional" one. In doing so, he charts something of a middle course. He is sufficiently removed from Engels and Maine that he makes no attempt at grand theory. Instead, he places his greatest reliance on the type of personal documents, diaries, autobiographies, memoirs, domestic correspondence, popular handbooks, literature, art, and legal documents that supply detail and nuance and constitute the traditional stuff of historical research. He is nonetheless of a different generation from the more contemporary historians who focus only on the partial or the stories overlooked because of class or race or gender. He is willing to generalize enough to create a coherent composite picture, but his project — the change from distance, deference, and patriarchy to affective individualism — is one that defies precision or quantification. He does not entirely avoid incautious asides, describing his topic as "perhaps the most important change in *mentalité* to have occurred in the Early Modern period, indeed possibly in the last thousand years of Western history."[22] Yet he also acknowledges the limitations of even his massive study: the ways in which the nature of the surviving evidence inexorably biases the work toward the study of the small minority consisting of the literate and articulate classes, and the inevitable objection "that any behavioural model of change over time imposes an artificial schematization on a chaotic and ambiguous reality" (at 26). Subsequent historians have quarreled with some of Stone's conclusions, but the value of his efforts lies with his willingness to chart the rise in the West "of the individualistic, nuclear, child-oriented family . . . [as] the sole outlet of both sexual and affective bonding" in ways that have shaped the debate ever since.

Stone begins with one of the most distinctive parts of English family history — the high percentage of adults who never married and the relatively late age of marriage for those who did. The first chapter is designed as much as anything else to explain the data produced by the demographers. Stone reports that, in the late seventeenth and eighteenth centuries, bachelordom became more fashionable for the owners of medium to large country houses. The rates of peers' children never marrying rose for males from 15 percent in the early part of the seventeenth century to over 20 percent by the end of the century. Female rates rose even more dramatically from 10 percent in the sixteenth century to 15 percent in the early part of the next century to 25 percent in the years between 1675 and 1799.[23] In contrast, in the United States, the percentage of women who never marry has stayed below 10 percent for most of this century.

Complementing the increase in the number who never married was a later age of marriage for those who did. For the "heirs" — that is, the eldest sons who lived long enough to inherit — the median age of marriage rose from twenty-one in the early sixteenth century to twenty-two toward the end of the century to twenty-four to twenty-six in the seventeenth century and twenty-seven to twenty-nine a century later (at 41–43). The average age of marriage followed different patterns for other males, but Stone concludes that elite younger sons often married even later, if they married at all, and both men and women from the middle and lower classes married remarkably late from the fifteenth century on.[24]

While Stone characterizes the delayed marriages of the population as a whole as an "extraordinary and unique feature of north-west European civilization" (at 44), he is careful, in attempting to explain the phenomenon, to distinguish between the upper classes and what he terms the "plebeian" ones. The pattern he presents for the landed classes reforges Engels' connections between family and property[25] recast, however, in terms of the particular circumstances of English elite. For these classes, Stone argues, the "three objectives of family planning were the continuity of the male line, the preservation intact of the inherited property, and the acquisition through marriage of further property or useful political alliances" (at 37–38).

These objectives, however, were often at odds. Given the very uncertain prospects for survival, procreation of the largest possible number of children was the most effective way to ensure that at least one male heir would live to a marriageable age. At the same time, preservation of the family patrimony required restricting the claims of the other children through primogeniture, and favorable marriages meant a major financial commitment. Stone concludes: "The second objective [preserving the family patrimony] thus directly clashed with the third [advantageous marriages], and if the former were given priority, as it often was, it meant the sacrifice of daughters by putting them into nunneries, and the extrusion of younger sons to fend for themselves as military adventurers or clergy or otherwise" (at 37–38). Those younger sons who married at all did so at later ages than their siblings; earlier marriage "would have meant a socially inferior partner and a severe economic handicap in the struggle for reintegration into the elite world of their childhood" (at 42).

If the upper classes limited marriage as part of conscious family strategy, the lower classes displayed similar patterns as a result of more externally imposed constraints. Stone cites the widespread practice of apprenticing children through age twenty-one, and the need to set up an independent household as factors in the delay. In other parts of the world, newlyweds moved in with mom and dad; in England, they were on their own. Moreover, in the rural communities and small towns of pre-Reformation England, couples beyond the authority of their parents never escaped the scrutiny of neighbors. The community controlled the common fields available for planting and grazing, and Church and village policed the personal morality of town inhabitants. Delayed marriage was accompanied by low rates of nonmarital fertility for rich and poor alike (at 45, 76). Stone cannot resist speculating that "the sublimation of sex among male adults may well account for the extraordinary military aggressiveness, the thrift, the passion for hard work, and the entrepreneurial and intellectual enterprise of Western man" (at 408).

Stone's larger point, however, even as he engages in class analysis of his own, is to refute the type of economic determinism that Engels championed. "What needs explaining," he observes, "is not a change of structure, or of economics, or of social organization, but of sentiment" (at 414). People within the nuclear families of the 1780s treated each other differently from the way their great-grandparents had treated each other within the nuclear families of the 1600s. The authoritarian relationships between family members of the sixteenth century were replaced by a warmer and more equal partnership between spouses, greater freedom and affection for children, less interference or support from kin, and greater privacy from the surrounding community. Stone argues that the rise of this "affective individualism" predated industrialization and that "the early and erratic chronology and social specificity of these developments make it impossible to accept" any general theory of modernization.[26]

To the extent that Stone is persuasive, it is partly because he has chosen his topic well — it is much harder to link changes in sentiment to economic factors than more discrete changes such as the decline of primogeniture — and partly because he does not reject the links to economic development or modernization altogether. Instead, the key phrase in his dissent is "social specificity." If the topic is sufficiently discrete — e.g., fertility — and the class and time determined with some precision, economic analysis is welcomed. Thus, in explaining a striking decline in the fertility of the nobility, Stone, after noting with some irony that "[s]o long as the futures of younger sons and of daughters are not of primary concern for their parents, it does not matter too much how many there are," observes that

> the decision to limit births is thus partly the result of a cost-benefit analysis, a trade-off between known parental resources and anticipated costs in both time spent by the mother in rearing and money spent by the father on education. . . . Contraception is therefore only likely to happen in a child-oriented society in which bringing up the child and launching him into the world is becoming so burdensome in its demands for love, time, effort and money, that some reduction in numbers is highly desirable.   *(Stone,* The Family, *at 263)*

Stone uses this analysis to explain how the English upper classes, who historically had larger numbers of children than the poor, were the first to practice effective contraception as they became less dependent on their children's income and burdened from an earlier date by the rising costs of education and marriage. Even with this use of economics, however, Stone is careful to conclude that moral theology, affect between spouses, and care for children were all involved in the growth of contraception among the elite.

By the end of the book, Stone, despite his disclaimers, has created a remarkable portrait of family change. He charts, in particular, four areas of transformation that lay the foundation for the modern family. What is striking about his categories and conclusions, however, is not their originality; they replicate, sometimes in the same language, the findings of almost every other recent historian. Indeed, the terms have become so commonplace, they may be said to be part of the definition of modernity itself.

FAMILIES   While northwestern European *households* may have been primarily nuclear in form, the families within them were part of an extended web of relationships that do not exist today. The English feudal elite depended for their well-being not just on landed estates, but on an extended network of kinship ties, lineage loyalties, and lordship arrangements critical to status and wealth. Stone emphasizes that "[i]t was the relation of the individual to his lineage (relatives by blood or marriage, dead, living or yet to be born) which provided a man of the upper classes in a traditional society with his identity, without which he was a mere atom floating in a void of social space" (at 29). Poorer families, in turn, were subject to the intervention of lord or community.

With the rise in the power of the state, the growth of a market economy, greater urbanization, and increasing geographical mobility, the network of kin, neighbors, and patronage that had surrounded and supported the loosely bound family weakened, leaving a much more isolated nuclear family at its core. By the end of the eighteenth century, the result was "a family serving fewer practical functions, but carrying a much greater load of emotional and sexual commitment."[27]

MARRIAGE   With the attenuation of kinship and community ties, marriage changed from an arranged affair designed to advance the interests of the family as a whole to a relationship based on mutual love and affection, with the continued interest and cooperation of the spouses necessary to hold the institution together. Paralleling the rise of "separate spheres" in the United States, middle-class women withdrew from family economic production, and although their economic dependence increased, "they were granted greater status and decision-making power within the family, and they became increasingly preoccupied with the nurturing and raising of their children."[28]

CHILDREN   Children became much more central to family life, and families became better at raising them. High levels of infant mortality had encouraged English parents to invest little in young children, and practices such as fostering out — that is, sending infants to be nursed by other women — had raised mortality rates higher still.[29] Beginning with the middle classes, which Stone describes as "neither so high to be too preoccupied with pleasure or politics to bother with children, nor so low as to be too preoccupied with sheer survival to be able to afford the luxury of sentimental concern for them," parents traded quantity for quality. The middle classes, in particular, began to invest more in each child in terms of love, affection, training, and education, and the historical relationship between higher birthrates and class standing was reversed.[30]

SEX   In the earliest period Stone documents, nonmarital pregnancy was rare, relatively large portions of the population married late or not at all, and within marriage, the idea that sexual intercourse was legitimate only so long as it led to procreation was so deeply imbedded that contraception was unthinkable. (Stone speculates that there was simply less sexual activity than there is today and identifies the English refusal to bathe as a major factor.) By the beginning of the nineteenth century, all indicators of sexual activity except for legitimate births had increased dramatically. Within marriage, contraception became the norm, and pleasure joined procreation as an accepted purpose of the activity (though at an earlier date in the middle classes than the plebeian ones).[31]

Figure 10.1 Stone's Depiction of Class in Late Eighteenth-Century England: Stone recaptioned Rowlandson's "Charity Covereth a Multitude of Sins" as "A brothel for the upper classes." (Illustration 27 from *The Family, Sex, and Marriage in England, 1500–1800* [insert between pages 216 and 217 of Stone's text].) By T. Rowlandson, 1781. Copyright (c) The British Museum. Reprinted by permission.

Stone speculates that the eighteenth-century rise in prenuptial conceptions and illegitimate births (from one-half of one percent for the latter in
1651 to over 6 percent by 1780) was

> not cultural but economic. Anthropologists tell us that the value at-
> tached to chastity is directly related to the degree of social hierarchy and
> the degree of property ownership. . . . Pre-marital female repression
> is thus built into the social system, since male and female are bargaining
> on the marriage market with different goods, the one social and eco-
> nomic, the other sexual. The withholding of sexual favours is a woman's

BLACK BROWN & FAIR.

Figure 10.2 Stone's Depiction of Class in Late Eighteenth-Century England: Stone recaptioned Rowlandson's "Black, Brown, & Fair" as "A brothel for the lower classes." (Illustration 28 from *The Family, Sex, and Marriage in England, 1500–1800* [insert between
pages 216 and 217 of Stone's text].) By T. Rowlandson, 1807. Courtesy the Metropolitan
Museum of Art, The Elisha Whittelsey Collection, The Elisha Whittelsey Fund, 1959
(59.533.1386). Reprinted by permission.

only source of power over men. . . . The system serves the interests of both parties, since the male is guaranteed that he is purchasing new and not second-hand goods, while the female has a powerful lever to obtain marriage. Both the principle of pre-marital female chastity and the double standard after marriage are, therefore, functional to a society of property owners, especially small property owners. It follows that the most sexually inhibited class in the population is likely to be the lower-middle class of small property owners, among whom rigid ideas of patriarchy, extreme loyalty to the authoritarian state, and extreme sexual inhibitions tend to be the norm, among both husbands and wives. The poor were under no such constraints, and the rise of a class of landless rural labourers without property or status meant the rise of a class to whom virginity was not important, and foresight, prudence and planning were irrelevant to their dismal economic future.

(Stone, The Family, *at 401–402)*

The middle class thus exchanged one reproductive strategy for another — both emphasizing birth within marriage. The poor lost the supervision (and for servant women the protection) of the community without acquiring any greater internal constraints.

Stone ultimately, then, departs most from Engels, not in his use of economics but in his attitude toward sex and class. Engels reasoned that only marriage removed from the type of economic considerations Stone describes can be considered "free," and it is only the laboring classes therefore who can be said to marry for love.[32] Stone insists that Engels' class analysis is wrong, that it is the landed, professional, and upper bourgeois classes, not the propertyless industrial poor, who were the first to embrace the ideology of individualism necessary to an ideal of married love (at 417). What Engels describes as a woman's refusal to give herself to her lover for economic considerations, Stone describes as prudence. What Engels terms love, Stone sees as lust.[33]

Race, Class, and Controversy

I F Stone is circumspect in comparison with Engels, the historians who follow Stone are more cautious still. Engels engendered controversy by staking out a bold thesis and defending it; the controversial aspects of Stone's work come more from his asides and omissions than his organizing principles. The historians of the last two decades have strived to avoid incautious speculation altogether. Their controversies, laments a recent president of the American Historical Association, are technical ones. The history of the African-American family stands in stark contrast. There are few aspects of its history, historiography, or sociology that are not fraught with controversy, and one of the fault lines in those controversies is the issue that divided Stone and Engels: the importance of class.

Study of the African-American family dates back to Engels' time, and the scholarly work that endures is that of the first African-American sociologists. The early scholars of color struggled, and to a remarkable degree succeeded, in wresting the field from the racist sociology of their day. While Engels' references to "savagery" and "barbarism" and Stone's description of the lowest English social classes as "a bastardy-prone minority group" today provoke wry amusement that dates — or discredits — their work, the comparable American references to the "primitive social organization" or natural "licentiousness" of the African race continue to wound. Within this context of racial and scholarly essentialism, the family studies of W. E. B. Du Bois, the preeminent African-American intellectual of his era, and E. Franklin Frazier, one of the most important family sociologists of the first half of the twentieth century, stand as powerful antidotes.

Du Bois wrote *The Negro American Family* to counter white turn-of-the-century scholarship that associated African-American family patterns with racial inferiority.[2] Du Bois attempted to "show greater internal differentiation of social conditions" among blacks than white authors had been willing to recognize, and to demonstrate that this failure to recognize the effect of class differences was the "cause of much confusion."[3] While Du Bois concluded that African-American family life was "less efficient for its onerous social duties," he laid the cause in class, not race; history, not genes; and oppression rather than choice. Du Bois concluded that African-Americans emerged from slavery with families weakened by the experience and a dual set of sexual mores, distinguishing between the descendants of house servants, who had a more "monogamic" family structure, and the descendants of field hands, whose family lives had been more disrupted.[4] While subsequent historians have questioned the precise relationship between slavery and later family patterns, Du Bois's work mandated recognition of class differences as the hallmark of rigorous consideration of the African-American family — and of rigorous sociology.

Sociologist Franklin Frazier's midcentury work on black family life so dominated the field that when Gunnar Myrdal and Daniel Patrick Moynihan sought to examine the African-American family decades later, they simply cited Frazier. Like Du Bois, Frazier sought to present a more nuanced view of the black community than that which prevailed in the white scholarship of his day. Referring to a work entitled "Sketches of the Higher Classes of Colored Society in Philadelphia," he felt compelled to note that "[t]he prejudiced reader, I feel well assured, will smile at the designation 'higher classes of colored society.' The public — or at least the great body, who have not been at the pains to make an examination — have long been accustomed to regard the people of color as one consolidated mass, all huddled togther, without any particular or general distinctions, social or otherwise."[5] He then selected free black families before the Civil War as an initial subject of study because of his conviction that "[e]conomic competency, culture, and achievement gave these families a special status and became the source of a tradition which has been transmitted to succeeding generations. These families have been the chief bearers of the first economic and cultural gains of the race, and have constituted a leavening element in the Negro population wherever they have been found."[6] Given the opportunity, Frazier concluded, African-Americans demonstrated the same marital mores of the rest of society.

Frazier's classic work, *The Negro Family in the United States*, published in 1939, undertook a comprehensive look at the African-American family in the United States. His thesis was one of material challenge and social renewal. Slavery shattered African cultural patterns and laid the basis for the dominant role of the mother in family groupings. Emancipation created greater opportunities for father-centered families with access to land and the better occupations, but it also reinforced the role of the matriarchy among the rural poor.[7] The move to the urban North tore African-Americans from their cultural moorings, increasing the size of the middle class, occupational differentiation within the community as a whole, and the social disorganization of the poorest of the urban migrants. Wholesale improvement would come, Frazier concluded, only with full integration into the country's economic and social life.

By the 1960s, the main body of Frazier's work was thirty years old and ripe for reexamination. Donna Franklin, part of a new generation of African-American women taking up the mantle of sociological research, documents the subsequent scholarship that has questioned (and sometimes refined or reaffirmed) almost every element of Frazier's account. Yet the process has not been the ordinary scholarly one of revision and reconsideration. Instead, there is a decades-long gulf between Frazier's work and its systematic reexamination — and in the center of that gulf is the 1965 publication of the Moynihan report.

The Moynihan report, formally titled *The Negro Family: The Case for National Action*,[8] most scholars agree, contained "nothing new." It relied heavily on government statistics and the conclusions of Franklin Frazier. What attracted attention was the report's emphasis and its public prominence. Moynihan stated that "at the heart of the deterioration of the fabric of Negro society is the deterioration of the Negro family." He observed that (1) nearly a quarter of urban black marriages end in divorce, (2) nearly one quarter of African-American births are illegitimate, so that (3) as a consequence, almost one fourth of African-American families are headed by females, and (4) this breakdown of the family has led to a startling increase in welfare dependency. Asking "Why should this be so?" Moynihan found "the roots of the problem" in slavery, in the effects of reconstruction on the family and, particularly, on the position of the black man, in urbanization, in unemployment and poverty, and in the wage system that often does not provide a family wage.[9] He then went on to propose public works programs that would guarantee employment for African-American men — programs that were never adopted.[10]

Thirty years later, the report remains a potent symbol of racial division. Donna Franklin describes attending a family conference in 1989 and having references to the report provoke the strongest response among conference attendees. Her impression of their reactions: blacks strongly disagreed with its contents while whites seemed to think that Moynihan was right.[11] Robert Staples and Leanor Boulin Johnson explained in 1993 that the reasons for the report's critical reception "are obvious":

> In effect, Moynihan made a generalized indictment of all Black families. And, although he cited the antecedents of slavery and high employment as important variables historically, he shifted the burden of Black deprivation onto the Black family rather than indicting the American social structure. . . . The conclusion drawn by most people was that whatever his solution, it would focus on strengthening the Black family rather than dealing with the more relevant problems of racial segregation and discrimination.[12]

They contrast the Moynihan report with research from a "Black nationalist perspective" that "not only considers Black families nonpathological but delineates their strengths as well."[13] Moynihan, like many of the white scholars with whom Du Bois and Frazier had taken issue, had failed to emphasize the class distinctions within the African-American community, and the fact that the social circumstances that aggravated black family instability affected everyone.

Despite, or perhaps because of, dissatisfaction with the report and its reception, Donna Franklin writes that it has had "a colossal impact on the generation of scholars who were emerging at the time."[14] As with other areas of family study, the literature was thin before the mid-1960s, but between 1970 and 1990, more than one hundred books and over one thousand articles were published on the African-American family.[15] While William Julius Wilson describes serious research on the ghetto as coming to "an abrupt halt" in the early seventies — in large part because of the response to Moynihan's efforts[16] — other research reexamined, one strand at a time, the traditional assumptions about the African-American family.

Herbert Gutman mounted the most immediate challenge, questioning the link between slavery, reconstruction, and family structure in the urban ghettos of the 1960s. Gutman attributed Moynihan's shortcomings to the scholarly consensus of the time, a consensus resting on the work of Frazier and Du Bois. According to Gutman:

> Scattered evidence convinced Mr. Frazier that enslavement destroyed all African family and kinship beliefs and that only privileged slaves ("the

favored few") could sustain "normal" family life. For the rest — mostly field hands and common laborers — the "matriarchal family" prevailed, accompanied them into freedom and rural poverty, and traveled with their migrant children to Northern cities and urban poverty.[17]

Drawing on data from 1725 to 1925, Gutman disputed Frazier's portrait of life under slavery, concluding that right up until the eve of the Great Depression, African-Americans lived in nuclear families and bore the majority of their children within two-parent relationships. He cites Reconstruction-era evidence and census data to show that between three-fourths and five-sixths of ex-slave households contained two parents and their children; that one in four ex-slaves registering their marriage after the Civil War had lived with the same mate for ten to nineteen years, and another one in five for twenty or more years; that in Central Harlem in 1880, 85 percent of black households had at their core either a husband and wife or two parents and their children; that only 3 percent of the New York households were headed by women; and that five of six children under the age of six lived with both parents.[18] To the extent that instability characterizes African-American families, the instability arose not with slavery but in the relatively recent past.[19]

With recognition that slavery had not obliterated slave family practices, African-American scholars expressed renewed interest in the connection to Africa. Europeans of the nineteenth century had been startled to discover that the monogamous patriarchal family was neither timeless nor universal; by the time of Laslett and Stone, scholars were ready to affirm the distinctiveness of the Anglo-American family. African-Americans were heirs to a different tradition. Du Bois had written in 1908 that although African-Americans cannot "trace an unbroken social history from Africa, . . . there is a distinct nexus between Africa and America which, though broken and perverted, is nevertheless not to be neglected by the careful student."[20] Serious exploration of the connections began with Carter Woodson and Melville Herskovits in the thirties and forties, but even with much greater interest today, the literature remains limited.[21] Niara Sudarkasa, in a short chapter in a collection on black families, provides one of the better overviews.[22] She explains, in anthropological terms that would have been familiar to Morgan or Engels, that while Western Europeans have defined family membership in terms of *conjugality* (i.e., marriage and the relationship between the spouses) since at least the Middle Ages, African families were organized by *consanguinity*.

In a consanguineal family, family membership is defined by the relationship between blood relatives, typically a core group of brothers or sisters.[23] When one of the core group marries, the spouse joins the family compound. The extended family owns and manages whatever property the family has, and these property rights pass to the next generation of blood kin; spouses do not inherit. Children are treated as children of the extended family, not just of their conjugal unit within it. Sudarkasa explains that since "for many purposes and for many occasions, *all* the children of the same generation within the compound regarded themselves as brothers and sisters (rather than dividing into siblings versus 'cousins'), and since the adults assumed certain responsibilities toward their 'nephews' and 'nieces' (whom they termed sons and daughters) as well as toward their own offspring, African conjugal families did not have the rigid boundaries characteristic of nuclear families in the West."[24]

Sudarkasa concludes that African families emphasized "respect, restraint, responsibility, and reciprocity. Common to all these principles was a notion of commitment to the collectivity."[25] Within such a system, blood ties formed the basis for enduring family relationships; marriages were largely a matter of contract. By modern standards, these contracts were long-lasting (particularly within patrilinear societies, Sudarkasa adds), but it mattered less than it did in a nuclear family system when marriages dissolved. Divorced spouses were expected to remarry, with the children remaining in their natal compounds (perhaps explaining why divorce was more common in matrilinear families).[26] While polygamy was widely practiced, Sudarkasa observes that "in the context of polygamy women as well as men had sexual liaisons with more than one partner." The husband ordinarily treated all of his wife's children as his own; "in the context of the lineage (especially the patrilineage), all men desired to have as many children as possible."[27] In a collective property system, the most successful reproductive strategy depends not on the survival of a single heir, but on siring as many members of the next generation as possible.

History — the history of slavery and the longer history that reaches back to Africa — provides an interesting detour; modern researchers have nonetheless asked with some vehemence, "What bearing does this rewriting of black history have for social policy today?."[28] The short answer is: nothing. The stable two-parent families that Gutman reports, and the traditional, largely patrilinear, compounds that Sudarkasa elucidates, do not exist for much of today's African-American population. The statistics that Moynihan reported with alarm in 1965 — a quarter of marriages dissolved, a quarter of births outside of marriage — now more accurately describe whites. By the mid-1990s, two-thirds of all African-American births were nonmarital, divorce rates for the population as a whole had reached one of two marriages and were higher still for blacks, almost 60 percent of African-American children lived in single-parent families, and half of those families were below the poverty line.[29] The question Nathan Glazer asked in 1976 ("What happened?") has become even more salient, and as Sudarkasa herself observes: "It is as erroneous to try to attribute what developed . . . solely to slavery as it is to attribute it solely to the African background." She is even more emphatic in declaring that "on the question of the origin of female-headed households among Blacks in America, Herskovits was wrong, and Frazier was right in attributing this development to conditions that arose during slavery and in the context of urbanization in later periods."[30]

The longer answer to Glazer's question, then, requires linking existing conditions to their historical roots, ancient and modern, and Donna Franklin provides one of the more comprehensive efforts to do so. A sociologist who has been closely associated for more than a decade with William Julius Wilson and his study of inner-city poverty, Franklin entitles her book *Ensuring Inequality: The Structural Transformation of the African-American Family*. Like Wilson, she draws sharp distinctions between the conditions of the African-American middle class and those of the urban poor. Like Wilson as well, she does not hesitate to associate the overwhelming decline in the marriage rates of inner-city African-Americans with the characteristics of the underclass. She attributes the transformation in family structure to a complex mix of history, economics, culture, and oppression, and advocates policies that assist, rather than punish, single parents. She begins her account by reexamining what is known about slavery.

Franklin emphasizes that just as it misleading to generalize about the African-American family today without acknowledging differences in social class, so too is it misleading to generalize about slaves. Du Bois and Frazier found "class" differences there, too, and attempted to attribute them to the distinctions planters drew between field hands and house servants. Franklin draws on more recent econometric studies to argue that the more critical distinction is between large and small plantations. Gutman, in his detailed portrait of slave families, relied on the records of six large slaveholdings in primarily black counties because they had the best records. It is not surprising, Franklin observes, that he found some of the strongest evidence of stable family patterns. The econometric studies demonstrate that single-parent families were 50 percent more prevalent on plantations with fifteen or fewer slaves than on larger ones; that the proportion of slave children who were mulatto (one in ten overall) was seven times higher on a small plantation engaged in mixed farming than on a large cotton plantation in the deep South; and that the number of women on large plantations who lived through their childbearing years without bearing a child was almost double the percentage on small plantations (19 percent compared to 10 percent).[31] Orville Burton observes, on the basis of his examination of nineteenth-century narratives from South Carolina, that on large plantations "the slave communities served as a buffer against white oppression."[32] Franklin concludes that the fact that the majority of slaves were held on large plantations contributes to the idea that "the black family emerged from slavery with remarkable stability."[33]

Stable slave families were, however, not necessarily identical to white families of the period. Owners had an economic interest in promoting slave births, and slave women had more children, starting at younger ages than did their white counterparts.[34] Marriage, whether legally recognized or not, was the norm, and monogamy and fidelity important virtues, but virginity was decidedly less so. Franklin refers to a Georgia plantation owner who is said to have observed: "The Negroes had their own ideals of morality, and held to them very strictly; they did not consider it wrong for a girl to have a child before she married, but afterwards were extremely severe upon anything like infidelity on her."[35] Eugene Genovese observes that virginity at marriage carried only small prestige, and that a "slave girl's chances to get the man she wanted did not slip much because she had an illegitimate child."[36] She and the child continued to live with her parents until she married and set up a residence of her own. On small plantations, however, single-parent families were more common as spouses were more likely to be involuntarily separated (either because of sale or different owners) and slave women were more likely to have sexual relations with their owners. Franklin concludes that, despite the overall stability of slave families, African-Americans did emerge from slavery with two distinct types of families: two-parent and single-parent ones. These single-parent families, which Sudarkasa observes were almost unheard of in Africa,[37] were a product of slavery, while the continued importance of extended kin for families of all types was of more direct African lineage.[38]

Reconstruction, and the sharecropping system that followed, reinforced many of these patterns. At the end of the nineteenth century, 80 percent of American blacks resided in rural areas, primarily in the Cotton Belt, and by

1910, 90 percent of all black southerners who made a living from the soil worked as tenant farmers, sharecroppers, or contract laborers.[39] Sharecropping, which placed a premium on a flexible labor supply able to expand rapidly at harvest time, encouraged large families and, to a lesser degree, nearby kin. Charles Johnson, another University of Chicago sociologist who conducted one of the first in-depth analyses of family formation patterns, found that, compared to whites, blacks had earlier marriages, higher fertility rates, and larger families, in part because of the importance of children to agricultural production.[40]

The relationship between children and marriage also followed many of the patterns established during slavery, although, Franklin emphasizes, with growing class distinctions. Thus, while Johnson reported that "elite" African-Americans in the Black Belt during the 1930s "accepted rigid standards of chastity" for both men and women, he found in rural Alabama that

> The active passions of youth and late adolescence are present but without the unusual formal constraints. Social behavior rooted in this situation, even when its consequences are understood, is lightly censured or excused entirely. . . . When pregnancy follows, pressure is not strong enough to compel the father to either marry the mother or support the child. The girl does not lose her status, perceptibly, nor are her chances for marrying seriously threatened. . . . There is, in a sense, no such thing as illegitimacy in this community.[41]

Gutman, reviewing 1900 census figures, also reports a significant number of nonmarital conceptions and births, particularly in rural areas, but adds that by their mid-thirties, over 90 percent of African-American women had married (though not necessarily to the father of their first child). With Johnson's data mirroring Gutman's and showing that fewer than 6 percent of the 612 couples that he studied had not married, it appears that marriage in the rural South, whether it preceded or followed childbirth, was the norm.[42]

Scholars nonetheless differ in their characterization of the stability of these marriages. Franklin argues that, at the same time that the sharecropping system increased the importance of families, it also planted the seeds of tension between men and women. Compared with slavery, African-American men now had formal recognition as heads of households and, in accordance with the patriarchal system of the time, the Freedman's Bureau gave them greater access to land, higher wages, and the authority to act on behalf of the entire family. With white planters reasserting control, however, greater authority within their own families did not correspond to any greater status in the larger society, and Franklin argues that it increased the dissatisfaction of women who shared largely egalitarian working conditions. Even in a period characterized by high rates of marriage, Johnson found skepticism, particularly among women, that "[m]arried life imposes certain obligations which are, in the feeling of this element of the community, more binding than necessary or practical. It gives license to mistreatment; it imposes the risk of unprofitable husbands; and it places an impossible tax upon freedom in the form of a divorce."[43] The picture of marriage in the rural South is thus a mixed one, with modern demographers concluding that

> Frazier's account of more fluid and less formal marital arrangements in the rural south at the turn of the century, based on ethnographic observations and a skeptical use of census and other data is more accurate [than Gutman's]. Accordingly the role of slavery and its aftermath, and perhaps also the legacy of West African family traditions, deserve more than a footnote in histories of the evolution of the black family.[44]

There is no dispute, however, that the transformation of the African-American family occurred with the move North. Franklin argues that "in trying to refashion their family economies by seeking better opportunities in the North, black families paradoxically weakened a family structure that was already breaking down, and set the stage for the exponential increase in black mother-only families that was 'discovered' by social scientists after World War II."[45] The chief culprit that Franklin identifies is the disproportion between the opportunities open to women and those available to men. She argues that women, not men, led the move from farm to city and cites Kelly Miller, a Howard University professor writing in 1910, to the effect that "Negro women rush to the city in disproportionate numbers, because in the country there is little demand for such services as they can render." The black men then follow the women into the cities, but when the black man arrives he "has no fixed industrial status . . . and loiters around the ragged edge of industry, and is confined to the more onerous and less attractive mode of toil" while black women "find an unlimited field of employment in the domestic and household industries."[46] David Katzman confirmed that from 1870 to 1910 the number of female domestic servants rose from 960,000 to 1,830,000, and that observers at the time agreed that "the number of domestics was limited not by the demand, but by the adequacy of the supply."[47] In New York at the turn of the century, 90 percent of black women workers were in domestic and personal service; 84.3 percent of the employed black women in Philadelphia were servants or laundresses.[48] Although the majority of African-American wives did not work outside the home, they were more likely to be in the labor market than their white counterparts, even controlling for class and income.[49]

The prospects for men were not so promising. While African-American men often earned more in a wider variety of occupations than did the women, the work available was less dependable. Given pervasive discrimination, African-Americans served as a reserve army available to take the jobs no one else wanted. With domestic service, black women faced fewer competitors, particularly with the restriction of immigration in the 1920s. The opportunities for black men were more variable. Industrial jobs were often dirty and dangerous, and they contributed to African-American men's higher rates of mortality and disability. Black men were more likely than the women to work out-of-doors and were subject to seasonal layoffs. Industrial opportunities that expanded with each war contracted with the return of the soldiers. The Depression hit African-Americans particularly hard as there were few remaining jobs whites were unwilling to fill. Between 1930 and 1940, for example, the proportion of African-American meat workers in Chicago dropped from 31 to 20 percent, and black unemployment in the city rose to between 40 and 50 percent.[50] St. Clair Drake and Horace Cayton observed that, by the 1940s, "roving masses of Negro men" were "an important factor . . . in preventing the formation of stable, conventional family units" among lower-class blacks.[51]

The changes that corresponded with the move north had a long-term impact on the structure of the African-American family. Between 1880 and 1940, the birthrates for black women in the United States fell by more than one half — "a decline that was much sharper, both absolutely and relatively, than the decline for whites."[52] By 1910, African-American city dwellers were having fewer, and even better educated, children than their white counterparts of comparable social standing.[53] The number of female-headed black households increased steadily over the course of the century, but the 33 percent increase in the Depression-era thirties was the most dramatic.[54] Increasing desertions were the major cause. Among black families, the father's rate of absence (with or without — usually without — divorce) ran several times higher than the comparable white rates, spiking sharply for both races at the height of World War II.[55] Nonmarital births increased more gradually, but the rates were particularly high among the poorest social classes, in urban as opposed to rural areas, and, Frazier observed, among those who had been in the city the shortest amount of time.[56]

Franklin reports that

The response to weakened marital ties among poor African-Americans was a family pattern characterized by strong ties between mothers and children, and marginalized relationships with the biological fathers. With black fathers' increasing desertion of their families, the most economically disadvantaged single black mothers became more reliant on assistance from welfare. And although these families represented a minority of the black poor during this period, these nascent family patterns would contribute not only to the proliferation of single black mothers but to a new urban "underclass" after World War II.[57]

All the trends that began with the initial movement north accelerated after World War II. The war itself and the increasing employment opportunities created by industrial expansion spurred a new wave of migration north that ultimately dwarfed the first. African-American income doubled during the war, with black men benefiting more than the women, but the increase leveled off when the war ended. By the early 1960s, African-Americans had lost ground, and in the poorest areas in the North, high unemployment was endemic, even in relatively prosperous times.[58] As with whites, marriage rates increased during the war and peaked with the return of the soldiers in 1946. Divorce rates, however, also rose during the war — and peaked with the return of the soldiers. While white divorce rates declined steadily through the remainder of the forties, however, African-American rates remained high.[59] By the 1970s, 37 percent of black men were divorced compared to 22 percent of whites, and 42 percent of black women compared to 23 percent of white women.[60]

The most dramatic change, however, involved declining rates of marriage. African-Americans had married more frequently and at earlier ages than whites for almost as long as records have been available. In 1950 the percentage of never-married African-American women in the twenty to twenty-four-year-old age range exceeded that of whites for the first time and climbed steadily thereafter.[61] The change would be less significant if it were simply an indication of delayed marriage or childbearing. Instead, it was a move away from marriage altogether. Forty-four percent of the African-

American women born between 1946 and 1950 would still be unmarried in their forties compared to 23.6 percent of whites in the same age group.[62] By 1996 the marriage gap would become significant for all age groups.

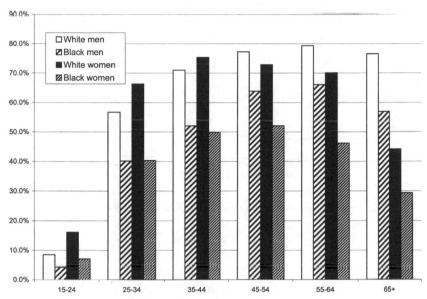

Figure 11.1 Percent of Americans married in each age group, by race and gender, 1998. Author's depiction of data from U.S. Bureau of the Census, "Unpublished Tables — Marital Status and Living Arrangements: March 1998" (update), found at www.census.gov/prod/99pubs/p20–514u.pdf (visited June 28, 1999).

Declining marriage rates did not necessarily correspond to lower fertility. Franklin reports that, from 1940 to 1960, both blacks and whites experienced an exponential increase in rates of nonmarital childrearing. But while as many as 70 percent of white children born to unmarried mothers were placed for adoption, only 3 to 5 percent of African-American children were. David Fanshel attributed the difference to a "seller's market" for white babies, in which supply could not keep up with demand, and a "buyer's market" for African-Americans in which it was difficult to secure appropriate placements owing to the indifference, if not outright hostility, of adoption and social service agencies.[63] Moreover, while in earlier times adolescent single mothers would have stayed with their parents until they married at a later age, increasing percentages of young mothers did not marry at all.

By the 1970s and 1980s, these changes had transformed the African-American family. At the time of the Moynihan report, approximately a quarter of African-American births were nonmarital, with the percentages having increased slowly over the course of the century. In the years following issuance of the report, rates skyrocketed, exceeding 60 percent of all African-American births by 1985 and leveling off by the early 1990s after reaching two-thirds of total births.[64] (See figures 11.2 and 11.3.)

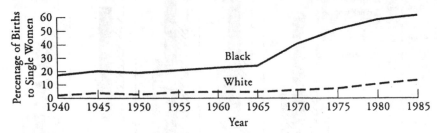

Figure 11.2 Trends in percentage of total births delivered to single women by race, 1940–1984.

Given the high nonmarital birthrate, declining rates of marriage, and high divorce rates, almost 60 percent of African-American children live in single-parent families. Moreover, while in earlier eras the majority of single-parent families would have been the product of divorce, widowhood, or separation, by 1993 58 percent of the African-American children living in single-parent families were living with never-married mothers.[65]

Franklin describes these results as the culmination of several trends:

1. African-Americans have "bifurcated" fertility rates, with significant declines in fertility for the well-educated, the middle class, and married couples, increasing the proportion of births to the unmarried and the poor.[66] The movement of African-Americans into the middle class has therefore accelerated the decline in overall fertility rates and increased the percentage (but not the number) of African-American children who experience poverty.

2. While conditions improved for middle-class African-Americans after the civil rights era of the 1960s, they worsened appreciably for the urban poor owing to the stagnation of the economy in the 1970s, the disappearance of high-paid manufacturing jobs, increasing competition with immigrants, and deepening poverty and isolation in black inner-city neighborhoods.[67] The African-American percentage of the poor in the last quar-

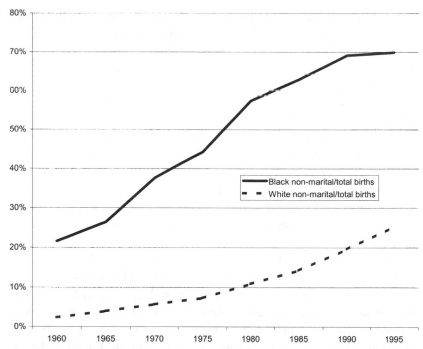

Figure 11.3 Nonmarital births as a percentage of total births by race, 1960–1995. Author's depiction of data from U.S. National Center for Health Statistics, *Vital Statistics of the United States* (annual), and Federal Interagency Forum on Child and Family Statistics, *America's Children: Key National Indicators of Well-Being, 1998* (Washington, D.C.: GPO, 1998).

ter-century increased from a quarter to a third, and approximately half of all African-American children fall below the poverty line.[68]

3. Within poor communities, the disparities between men and women that began with the move north have increased. William Julius Wilson estimated that for every one hundred African-American women, there are fifty marriageable black men. Staples and Johnson break down the numbers further, indicating that (*a*) higher male mortality rates between the ages twenty-five and sixty-four reduce the sex ratio to eighty-five black men for every one hundred black women; (*b*) one in four African-American males between the ages of twenty and thirty is in jail, and the number grows to one in three with the inclusion of those on probation and parole;[69] (*c*) 46 percent of working-age African-American males are not in the labor force, and those who are are disproportionately unemployed or underemployed;

and (*d*) a significantly higher percentage of African-American males than the general population have drug and mental health problems, with as many as one-third of inner-city males estimated to have a serious drug problem.[70] The odds are against those women who would like to marry, and marry well.

4. While better-educated African-American women have responded by having fewer children, the urban poor have had them on their own. Franklin compares never-married African-American mothers with divorced, widowed, and separated black mothers and finds that the never-married group is younger, less educated, more likely to have four or more children, to live in central cities, to have become pregnant as a teenager, to have a relatively weak attachment to the labor force, and to be receiving welfare. She describes these characteristics as the "traits generally associated with the so-called underclass," and observes that "while the young women may dream of marriage, the reality is that AFDC has replaced a husband as the primary means of financial support in the poorest black neighborhoods."[71]

5. The increase in single-parent families, and particularly the exponential increase in the percentage of African-American births to young unmarried women, has helped fuel the feminization of poverty. African-American families are disproportionately poor, and black families headed by women with children tend to be the poorest of all. Moreover, the creation of "age condensed" families in which relatively young grandmothers care for the children of their teenage daughters exacerbates the tensions between mother and daughter, works to the detriment of the children, and contributes to the perpetuation of poverty and disadvantage in the next generation.[72]

The portrait that Franklin presents is at once familiar in its broad outline and nuanced and original in its details. As recently as 1964, mainstream sociologists such as Charles Silberman were writing that

> Slavery had emasculated the Negro males, had made them shiftless and irresponsible and promiscuous by preventing them from asserting responsibility, negating their role as husband and father, and making them totally dependent on the will of another. There was [after emancipation] no stable family structure to offer support to men or women or children in this strange new world. With no history of stable families, no knowledge of even what stability might mean, huge numbers of Negro men took to the roads as soon as freedom was proclaimed. . . . Thus there developed a pattern of drifting from place to place and woman to woman that has persisted (in lesser degrees, of course) to the present day.[73]

Franklin, who also documents the negative images of African-American families popularized by the more contemporary press, counters these stereotypes by paying careful attention to class, time, and place, and distinguishing the circumstances of the urban poor from those of African-Americans more generally. She avoids unilinear explanations, emphasizing the interactions between "slavery; the northern migration (especially the loss of communal institutions); welfare policies; declining job opportunities for black men; and isolation in neighborhoods of concentrated poverty." She brings a feminist consciousness to her prescriptions, acknowledging "the irreversibility of high rates of non-marriage" and the need for major government intervention to assist poor families.[74] Her conclusions nonetheless venture onto contested terrain.

In the wake of the Moynihan report, the greatest divide involved the willingness to reach judgments about family form. William Julius Wilson summarized the African-American opposition:

> These scholars were highly critical of the Moynihan report's emphasis on social pathologies within ghetto neighborhoods not simply because of its potential for embarrassment but also because it conflicted with their claim that blacks were developing a community power base that could become a major force in American society. This power base, they argued, reflected the strength and vitality of the black community. These African-American scholars emphasized the positive aspects of the black experience. In fact, those elements of ghetto behavior described as pathological in the late 1960's studies of the inner city were seen as functional in this new interpretation because, it was argued, inner-city blacks, and especially the black family, were resilient, able to survive and even flourish in a racist environment. These revisionist arguments shifted the focus from the consequences of racial isolation and economic class subordination to inner city black achievement. In short, as in *The Bell Curve*, but of course for entirely different reasons, the devastating effects of the inner-city environment were ignored, played down or denied.[75]

Wilson accuses his critics of ceding the floor to the conservatives who now dominate modern debate. More radical scholars have been equally dismissive of Wilson. Staples and Johnson describe Wilson's work as assuming

> the dominant position in Black family studies once occupied by the Moynihan report and, in some circles, is almost as controversial. . . . While Wilson acknowledges that the cause of Black family destabiliza-

tion is the high rate of unemployment among Black males, he only sees economic forces as a contributing factor; he fails to emphasize the combination of racial and economic forces that have placed Blacks in such a high risk position in the American economy from the outset. When he deals with noneconomic variables, it is to depict the culture of inner-city Blacks as dysfunctional in meeting the requirements of American industry.[76]

In short, Staples and Johnson suggest that Wilson is giving aid and comfort to those who would disparage African-Americans.

Franklin attempts to forge something of a middle ground. She certainly addresses the "combination of racial and economic forces that have placed Blacks in such a high risk position in the American economy," and she takes her former colleague Wilson to task for overemphasizing the effects of male employment on family structure and failing to give sufficient consideration to the interests of "poor black women who may remain single."[77] To the extent that "conservatives believe that most poor people are undeserving because it is their own fault that they are poor" and liberals believe that "virtually all poor people are deserving because poverty is an institutional and political problem, not a personal one," she is clearly a liberal.[78] She nonetheless does not confuse empathy for the urban poor, or an understanding that changing family structure has been an adaptive response to oppressive conditions, with approval for the changes that have been wrought. She writes within a social work tradition that emphasizes assistance for the disadvantaged, and a scholarly tradition that requires acknowledging "that increased childbearing among younger black women has widened the social and economic divisions within the black community by generating an ever-larger proportion of black children born into poverty."[79] The result, proclaims the title of her book, is "ensuring inequality."

12

What *Did* Happen?

Economics Revisited

Almost no scholar of the African-American family can resist commenting that the statistics that Moynihan viewed with so much alarm in 1965 — that one in four births occur outside of marriage, one in four marriages end in divorce, one of four children are raised in a single-parent family — now more accurately describe nonminority families, and that the academy may be even farther from understanding changing family patterns among whites than among blacks.[1] Part of the reason is that some of the most dramatic changes are relatively recent. For African-Americans, the 1930s gave witness to the greatest increase in single-parent families, with the comparable growth in nonmarital births occurring during the 1970s. For whites, the "divorce revolution" occurred during the sixties and the seventies, with the most dramatic increase in nonmarital births beginning in 1988 and leveling off by 1994. Scholars are only just beginning to recognize the magnitude of the change, and it is still too early to assess its full significance.

In a larger sense, however, the explanation for these trends begins where Lawrence Stone left off — with the forces of modernity. The premodern family Stone describes, whether in Europe or in Africa, was deeply embedded in a web of relationships that left little room for privacy or for individual expression. As Edward Shorter observes:

> [I]n the Bad Old Days — let us say the sixteenth and seventeenth centuries — the family too was firmly held to a larger social order. One set of ties bound it to the surrounding kin. . . . Another set fastened it to the wider community, and gaping holes in the shield of privacy permit-

ted others to enter the household freely and, if necessary, preserve order. A final set of ties held this elementary family to generations past and future. . . . In its journey into the modern world the family has broken all these ties.[2]

Stone, Shorter, Deglar, and the other chroniclers of the modern family conclude that, beginning with the middle class, the family responded to the loss of these larger ties with a much more intense — and central — relationship between husband and wife. Spousal ties, observes Stone, were to carry "a much greater load of emotional and sexual commitment," and they were premised to a much greater degree than in "traditional" families on the advantages of a sexual division of labor "with the female as full-time housewife and the male as primary provider and ultimate authority."[3] These historians not only dispute Becker's claim that the sexual division of labor is universal, they also find that the highly specialized modern family that Becker identifies with family stability was more fragile than its less specialized predecessor. Divorces in the United States rose steadily over the course of the nineteenth century, generating cries of alarm by the turn of the century. William O'Neill, in his study of divorce during the progressive era, tied the trends to the intensifying demands placed on marriage. He explained that "when families become the center of social organization, their intimacy can become suffocating, their demands unbearable, and their expectations too high to be easily realizable." Divorce then becomes "the safety valve that makes the system workable."[4]

If greater instability is a permanent feature of the modern family, the level of instability has nonetheless changed both incrementally and dramatically over time — raising the question of whether, at some point, historians will conclude that the "modern" family gave way to a new institution just as the early modern family gave way to the modern one. Assessing any change while in the middle of the process is a risky enterprise; with the family, part of the problem is deciding what time period provides the proper perspective. The following charts illustrate the difficulty. Figure 12.1[5] shows divorce rates by the year in which the divorce occurred. In this chart, the spike in divorce rates following World War II appears to be an anomaly, and the more permanent increase in the 1970s and 1980s a harbinger of a new family order. If the data is arranged by the couples' date of marriage, however, a different picture emerges. From the perspective of figure 12.2,[6] divorce rates rise linearly over a century and a half of continuously increasing family instability, and the discordant lines show the *drops* in divorce rates for marriages in the 1950s and 1980s. (See also Appendix, figure A.6.)

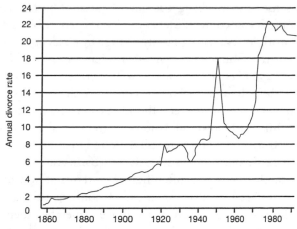

Figure 12.1 Annual divorce rate, United States, for 1920–1988: divorces per 1,000 married women aged 15 and over: divorces per 1,000 existing marriages.

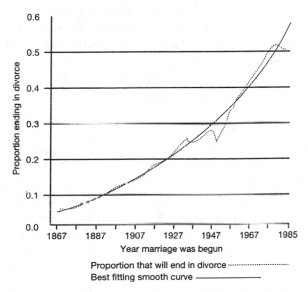

Figure 12.2 Proportion of marriages begun in each year that will end in divorce, 1867 to 1985.

Making sense of these changes is thus a matter of both long-term perspective *and* particular context. Stephanie Coontz contributes enormously to our framework for evaluating family change by challenging our misconceptions about the families we remember. Her book, *The Way We Never Were: American Families and the Nostalgia Trap*, takes particular aim at the 1950s. For the baby boomers who now constitute the largest group of academic and policy decision-makers, the fifties were the golden era of our childhood. "Our most powerful visions of traditional families," Coontz writes, "derive from images that are still delivered to our homes in countless reruns of 1950's sitcoms. When liberals and conservatives debate family policy, for example, the issue is often framed in terms of how many "Ozzie and Harriet" families are left in America."[7] Coontz questions whether the families of the fifties really were the way we remember them, and even when they were, the extent to which those families reflected "traditional" American family patterns. She observes:

> In fact, the "traditional" family of the 1950's was a qualitatively new phenomenon. At the end of the 1940's, all the trends characterizing the rest of the twentieth century suddenly reversed themselves. For the first time in more than one hundred years, the age for marriage and motherhood fell, fertility increased, divorce rates declined, and women's degree of educational parity with men dropped sharply. In a period of less than ten years, the proportion of never-married persons declined as much as it had during the entire previous half century.

The family of the 1950s, Coontz concludes, was "a new invention," the declining rates of marriage and childbearing in the sixties and seventies a return to historical patterns.[8]

The distinctive families of the 1950s were not, however, just a historical anomaly. They also shaped what was to come. The defining element of the fifties was the very centrality of family life. The decade witnessed the height of the baby boom. Fertility rates for every social class reached levels that have not been exceeded since. Most striking, perhaps, was the explosion in teenage pregnancies. Coontz reports that, in 1957, 97 out of every one thousand girls between the ages of fifteen and nineteen gave birth, compared with only 52 of every one thousand in 1983. The most notable difference: in 1960 only 15 percent of all teen births were to unmarried mothers; by 1986 the majority of teen births would be outside of marriage.[9]

Increasing teen births were not just a function of earlier marriages. The

1950s, Coontz concludes, were the unheralded start of the modern sexual revolution. Along with the rise in marital births came an 80 percent increase in the number of babies placed for adoption, and a doubling of the white brides who were pregnant at the altar.[10] She cites Elaine May Taylor's argument that sexual repression gave way to "sexual containment," with the new practice of "going steady" widening "the boundaries of permissible sexual activity," creating a "sexual brinkmanship" in which women bore the burden of "drawing the line," a line that was constantly changing. When the line was crossed, young people were not taught to say "no"; they were handed wedding rings.[11] These young couples were then locked into a gendered division of roles with the mothers consumed by the care of their newborns, and the fathers by the need to support them.

The families of the 1950s set the stage for the accelerating divorce rates of the sixties and seventies. With more — and less voluntary — marriages, at younger ages, increased marital tensions were inevitable. These tensions coincided, moreover, with a series of longer-term trends that promoted family instability. Coontz identifies, as "[p]erhaps the most significant component of the early increase in divorce," "the rising rate among 1950s parents whose children had left home."[12] The concentrated increase in fertility in the 1950s had, by the 1970s, given rise to a concentrated increase in the number of couples experiencing "empty nests." The temporary wave crested, moreover, in the midst of longer-term currents producing greater longevity, declining fertility (with the exception of the 1950s), and closer spacing of children (particularly during the 1950s) — in sum, longer periods in which adults freed from the responsibilities of childrearing might divorce.

The initial increase in divorce was then sustained by changing attitudes and ideology. Underlying these changes was a wholesale reorganization of work and family. Coontz introduces the topic by noting how long delayed — and long in coming — married women's greater workforce participation was. In the nineteenth century, she begins, the value of a woman's household labor generally outweighed her potential earnings for the middle class and working class alike; by 1900, "the relative value of home work and paid work had begun to be reversed."[13] Women increased their labor force participation in every decade after 1880; nonetheless, the Depression, two world wars, and their aftermath had slowed the wholesale entry of married women into the labor market until the 1960s and 1970s. Once women entered the labor market to stay, however, the interaction with family roles was far-reaching. In carefully measured language, she notes that

As women gained experience and self-confidence, they won benefits that made work more attractive and rewarding; with longer work experience and greater educational equalization, they became freer to leave an unhappy marriage; and as divorce became more of a possibility, women tended to hedge their bets by insisting on the right to work. Although very few researchers believe that women's employment has been a direct cause of the rising divorce rate, most agree that women's new employment options have made it easier for couples to separate if they are dissatisfied for other reasons. In turn, the fragility of marriage has joined economic pressures, income incentives, educational preparation, and dissatisfaction with domestic isolation as one of the reasons that modern women choose to work.[14]

Coontz emphasizes that changes in behavior preceded the changes in attitudes. Women's workforce participation increased dramatically *before* the rise of modern feminism, and divorce rates skyrocketed *before* polls registered greater acceptance of the practice. While the liberalization of divorce laws that occurred between 1965 and 1985 facilitated the accelerating divorce tide that did not level off until it had reached one of every two marriages, the "divorce revolution" that Lenore Weitzman heralded in the 1980s was at least a century in the making.[15]

If Coontz is able to present something approaching a consensus view on divorce, there is less agreement on the more recent increase in nonmarital births. Kristin Luker, in her comprehensive account of the politics of teen pregnancy, repeatedly states that the reasons for the increase, which are international in scope, are "something of a mystery."[16] George Akerloff, Janet Yellin, and Michael Katz undertake one of the more ambitious efforts at explanation.[17] The three are economists. They were associated, at the time of their research, with the University of California at Berkeley. Yellin, a business school professor, left Berkeley for the Federal Reserve Board and later headed the President's Council of Economic Advisors. Akerloff has long been a mainstay of Berkeley's Economics Department and, with his wife's move to Washington, he accepted a position at the Brookings Institution. Like Gary Becker, he has brought economic analysis to a wide variety of traditional and not-so-traditional subjects, but unlike Becker he is more sanguine about the product of markets.

As economists, the three are less interested than the historians in nuance and context. They seek to provide answers, precise and qualified to be sure, but answers nonetheless, and that is exactly what their article does. They attribute the increasing nonmarital birthrate (to be precise, three-quarters of the white increase and two-fifths of the increase for African-Americans) to the declining practice of "shotgun marriage." Like Coontz, they note that shotgun marriages were the preferred solution to the accidental pregnancies of the 1950s and 1960s. They cite a study of working-class San Francisco whites to the effect that courtship was likely to be brief and sexual. (Quoting one of the subjects: "If a girl gets pregnant you married her. There wasn't no choice. So I married her.") They then attribute the practice's decline to "the advent of female contraception for unmarried women and the legalization of abortion" (at 279).

To explain the link, the economists draw an analogy to technological change, observing that a "cost-saving innovation almost invariably penalizes producers who, for whatever reason, fail to adopt it." They posit that

> a decline in the cost of abortion (or increased availability of contraception) decreases the incentives to obtain a promise of marriage if premarital sexual activity results in pregnancy. Those women who will obtain an abortion or who will reliably use contraception no longer find it necessary to condition sexual relations on such promises. Those women who want children, who do not want an abortion for moral or religious reasons, or who are unreliable in their use of contraception, may want marriage guarantees but find themselves pressured to participate in premarital sexual relations without any such assurance. They have been placed at a competitive disadvantage: in this case analogous to wheat farmers who do not switch to the new varieties of wheat. Sexual activity without commitment is increasingly expected in premarital relationships, immiserizing at least some women, since their male partners do not have to assume parental responsibility in order to engage in sexual relations. *(Akerloff, Yellin, and Katz, at 280)*

If Akerloff, Yellin, and Katz were historians, they would come to such conclusions through a very different route. They would describe, as Stephanie Coontz did, the practice of shotgun marriage across race and class lines in the 1950s. They would then detail, over the course of a chapter or so on each topic, the changing mores of the 1960s as women postponed marriage, increased their use of contraception, and experimented more freely with sexual relationships; of the 1970s as they became more likely to elect abortion over marriage or adoption; and of the 1980s as women became more likely to keep the children who resulted from unplanned pregnancies. They would add another chapter on the men who contributed to these results and describe how they ceded decision-making authority — and ultimate responsibility — to the women alone (paying even greater scholarly attention to the fathers' rights groups on the Internet, already cited in the article, who insist that "[s]ince the decision to have the child is solely up to the mother, I don't see how both parents have responsibility to that child"). Finally, they would conclude that the increase in nonmarital births resulted from the complex interaction of all of these factors. Instead, as economists, Akerloff, Yellin, and Katz use equations.

The economists begin with the following "decision tree" (figure 12.3)[18] charting the sequence of decisions and their payoffs for a couple deciding whether to initiate a sexual relationship.

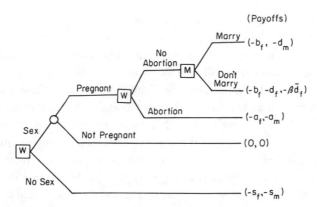

Figure 12.3 The "decision tree": sequence of decisions and payoffs confronting a couple initiating a sexual relationship.

The "payoffs" represent the expected value of a given course of action. Thus, "$-s_f$," expressed as a negative number, is the payoff from a woman's ("f") decision not to engage in a sexual relationship, while "$-a_m$" is the negative payoff to a male ("m") of his partner's decision to have an abortion, and so forth. Akerloff, Yellin, and Katz then use the payoffs in the "decision tree" analysis ("d_m" is male disutility from marriage; "D_m" is maximum male disutility; "$-b_f$" is female utility from married parenthood; "$-d_f$" is female disutility from single parenthood; and so on) to construct a series of equations, centered on the following (equation 12.1),[19] which describes a woman's decision to abort in terms of "her perceived probability that the man will marry her if she carries the baby to term" (301):

$$\frac{b_f \beta \overline{d}_f}{D_m} + (b_f + d_f^{\text{crit}}) \left(\frac{D_m - \beta \overline{d}_f}{D_m} \right) = a_f$$

Equation 12.1

The assumptions built into the equations (e.g., that "men have no information concerning the actual d/f of their partner but . . . do have an accurate assessment of the mean value of d/f of women choosing not to abort")
are central to their outcomes. With these assumptions, the equations
demonstrate that a decrease in the cost of abortion will raise both the abortion rate and the nonmarital birthrate. The authors explain:

> With abortion less costly the fertility rate is lower for sexually active
> women. With fewer women choosing to carry their babies to term, the
> mean disutility of single parenthood among women choosing to bear
> children declines, and there is a consequent decrease in the marriage
> rate(F). The out-of-wedlock birthrate therefore rises.
>
> *(Akerloff, Yellin, and Katz, at 302–303)*

For economists, as Milton Friedman explained in the mid-1930s, the test
of an equation's validity is not its internal coherence but its ability to explain
empirical data. Akerloff, Yellin, and Katz therefore test their model's pre-
dictions against the two other leading theories claiming to explain the increase in nonmarital births, and declare victory. William Julius Wilson, in
his examination of the urban underclass, had tied declining marriage rates
to increased male joblessness.[20] Akerloff, Yellin, and Katz cite three studies
that call his conclusions into question. Robert Mare and Christopher Winship, using cross-section data, estimate that at most 20 percent of the decline
in marriage rates of blacks between 1960 and 1980 can be explained by decreasing employment.[21] Christopher Jencks notes that the decline in the
fraction of married unemployed black men aged thirty to forty-four between
1960 and 1980 was only slightly higher (13 percent) than the decline in the
fraction of married employed black men (11 percent).[22] Robert Wood, in a
study published in 1995, found that only 3 to 4 percent of the decline in black
marriage rates can be explained by the shrinkage in the pool of eligible black
men.[23] Even Donna Franklin, referring to other studies still, concludes that
"a more rigorous analysis of the data has found that the unemployment of
black men explains only a small portion of the decline in marriage rates."[24]

Historians like Stephanie Coontz combine joblessness with other factors in an effort to create a composite picture of social change.[25] Economists treat joblessness as an isolated variable to be plugged into an equation and evaluated for its explanatory power. By that measure it has been found wanting.

The rival explanation, and the one that has attracted the greatest amount of political attention, is welfare. Charles Murray, author of *Losing Ground: American Social Policy, 1950-1980*, is perhaps the most quoted of the commentators who indict welfare programs.[26] The Great Society initiatives of the Johnson era, Murray argues, seduced the poor into dependence, eroded their commitment to self-reliance, family values, and the work ethic, and actually increased the poverty the programs were designed to alleviate. Aid to Families with Dependent Children (AFDC), in particular, discouraged marriage, encouraged divorce, and made single parenthood not only feasible but more attractive than the alternatives.[27] The problem with Murray's thesis is that, like Wilson's, it does not fit the data.

Welfare benefits and nonmarital birthrates do track each other from the 1960s through the early 1970s — the "welfare rights" era that eliminated the restrictions on unmarried mothers, expanded the public assistance roles, and produced the high point in the value of AFDC cash payments. Murray's difficulty is that nonmarital birthrates continued to rise as the value of welfare benefits declined steadily in the years since. Comprehensive efforts to test the correlation between welfare payments and behavior produce mixed results, with relatively small effects. Moreover, the studies that examine the post-1972 era and find some correlation tend to do so only for whites, not blacks. The only consistent correlation is the link between the generosity of welfare benefits and unmarried mothers' ability to live on their own.[28]

Akerloff, Yellin, and Katz claim a more persuasive explanation. They argue, first, that the shift in contraception and abortion practice was sufficiently large to constitute a significant "technological shock." The use of the pill by unmarried women at first intercourse, they report, jumped from 6 to 15 percent in just a few years, and the number of abortions to unmarried women, which was less than half the number of nonmarital births in the 1960s, grew tenfold or more so that by the 1970s unmarried women had 75 percent more abortions than out-of-wedlock births (at 306). These technological shocks then "induced unmarried women, who were willing to obtain an abortion if pregnant, to engage in premarital sexual relations while foregoing the promise of marriage in the event of a premarital conception. Moreover, their partners' empathy and willingness to marry declined once it was apparent that the woman herself was unwilling to obtain an abortion." The net result, the economists conclude, was to erode the bargaining position of women who wanted children, producing fewer marriages and greater retention of nonmarital babies. They explain:

> In the old days, if a woman wanted a child, she was typically able to exact a promise that the man would marry her. Thus, most premaritally conceived first births (about 60 percent for whites and 35 percent for blacks by our tabulations) resulted in marriage before the birth of the baby who was then, of course, kept by the woman. If the woman did not get married soon after the birth of the baby, the chances were less than 30 percent that the child would be kept. In the new world, however, after the legalization of abortion, there were two reasons why the baby would more likely be kept. First, unmarried women who wanted children would find it increasingly difficult to make (and also to enforce) a contract in which marriage was promised in the event of pregnancy. Since these women wanted children, they would naturally keep them. Furthermore, because women who would not want to keep a child born out of wedlock had easy access to contraception and the option to abort an unwanted pregnancy, a greater fraction of the children born out of wedlock would be wanted. It is thus no surprise that, despite the very large rise in sexual participation, the number of agency adoptions was halved from 86,000 to 43,000 in the five years following the introduction of abortion.[29]

Whereas in 1970 most children whose mothers did not get married were put up for adoption, by the late 1980s two-thirds of such children stayed with their mothers.

Akerloff, Yellin, and Katz do not so much reject Wilson and Murray as claim that their own theory offers a better explanation of the mechanism involved in increasing nonmarital births. These economists, like Gary Becker, are rational choice theorists. They are able to say without qualification that since "these women wanted children, they would naturally keep them" to describe circumstances in which 65 percent of mothers bearing nonmarital children reported that the children were either mistimed or neither wanted nor unwanted. Nonetheless, more than most economists, they pay attention not just to financial incentives (will having another baby result in higher AFDC payments) but to the psychological and cultural factors that underlie decision-making (will family, friends, and colleagues disapprove if a man fails to marry the mother of his child). This allows them to bridge much of the distance between other theories.

In addressing Wilson's jobs thesis, Akerloff, Yellin, and Katz argue that nonmarital births, rather than correlating with a decline in the number of marriageable men, correlate with a decline in the number of men willing to marry. This leaves open the question, of course, of whether, with declining stigma, some women are also deciding that they are better off without the men who impregnated them. But the economic theory does explain why marriage rates have dropped almost as much for the employed men who would presumably be more attractive mates as for the unemployed.

The economists' position on welfare is more complex. Liberals have simultaneously maintained that the "man in the house" rules of the 1960s and early 1970s contributed to family instability while denying the conservative charge that the increase in nonmarital births is a by-product of AFDC. Akerloff, Yellin, and Katz suggest that there may be some truth in all these conflicting positions. They note that the African-American shotgun marriage ratio began to fall earlier than the white rate and, unlike the pattern for whites, showed no significant change tied to the legalization of abortion. They attribute the differences to the influence of welfare benefits. Given the high percentage of black children who experience poverty (one third of black children will live in poverty more than 70 percent of the time compared to 3 percent of white children), African-Americans are inevitably more affected than whites by changes in welfare benefits. Akerloff, Yellin, and Katz posit that for "women whose earnings are sufficiently low that they are potentially eligible for welfare, an increase in welfare benefits has the same effect on out-of-wedlock births as a decline in the stigma to bearing a child out-of wedlock." Accordingly, they conclude, "the rise in welfare benefits in the 1960s may have had only a small impact on the white shotgun rate but resulted in a significant decrease in the black shotgun marriage rate" (at 310). By making the issue one of timing, of identification of which "technological shock" triggered the long-term shift away from the promise to marry as the price of sexual access, the economists are able to agree both with the conservatives that welfare played a role, and with the liberals that the critical role occurred in the 1960s and 1970s and that cutting benefits now will impoverish those already on welfare without having much impact on new mothers' marriage rates.

Figure 12.4

13

Economics *and* History
The Chapter Yet to Be Written

T HE very words "technological shock" indicate the ahistorical nature of Akerloff, Yellin, and Katz's analysis. "Shock" suggests a sudden, unexpected (if not necessarily, as *Webster's* suggests, scandalous) shift in behavior. "Technological" implies that the shift is a product of technical innovation — i.e., the pill — rather than a broader array of social or cultural forces. While the economists' analysis is more sophisticated than these words may suggest, their analogy to technological changes in wheat production reinforces the impression of a discrete, one-time shift in mores attributable to a single cause.

History provides a different perspective. However right Akerloff, Yellin, and Katz may be about the mechanisms involved in the decline of shotgun marriages, those events did not occur in isolation. The research that produced the pill was as much a response to greater demand as a cause of it; increased nonmarital sexuality and its consequences helped fuel political support for liberalized abortion policies. The critical factors in the economists' equations, represented by symbols such as "d/f" (women's disutility from single parenthood), are often themselves the product of a complex array of social forces. The single biggest factor in women's disutility, for example, may be the stigma associated with nonmarital births, which may in turn result from societal attitudes toward nonmarital sexuality, women's economic independence, the existence of a social safety net, and the incidence of single parenthood.

Moreover, the mechanism the economists charge with responsibility for the increase in nonmarital births may be implicated in a broader set of social phenomena. Consider, for example, Paula England and George Farkas's assessment of Gary Becker's claim that married women's greater employment is linked to the rising divorce rate. They observe that

> rather than marriages being less satisfactory when wives are employed, it may be that the financial independence women achieve from employment permits divorce in situations where marital dissatisfaction arises from nonemployment-related reasons. With more women employed, they are more able to support themselves outside of marriage, and men are less apt to have to face the shame of leaving a family destitute in order to divorce. In addition, nonpecuniary features of wives' employment experience provide information and contacts which make leaving a marriage a less frightening possibility. We suspect that these factors explain why increases in women's employment have increased divorce despite the lack of decreasing marital satisfaction.[1]

The process England and Farkas describe is remarkably similar to both Stephanie Coontz's observations about divorce *and* Akerloff, Yellin, and Katz's conclusions about nonmarital pregnancy. For England and Farkas, the "technological shock" is married women's workforce participation. Women's greater employment opportunities soften the consequences of divorce just as legalized abortion lowers the risks of nonmarital sexuality. Women become more willing to make decisions they would have avoided when the consequences were more dire, and men feel less obliged to put aside their own interests to protect the women. Over time, and sometimes a relatively short time, the effect may be a wholesale shift in social mores.

Considered cumulatively, these shifts transform institutions and society. Historians like Stone, Shorter, and Degler chart the transformation of the family as a process unfolding over centuries. Social scientists document the more immediate changes and offer tentative explanations. The greater difficulty, in attempting to track change from its midst, is making sense of the whole, and that difficulty is compounded when scholars move from the concrete — is the increasing nonmarital birthrate a product of more conceptions or fewer marriages? — to the less tangible. "What needs explaining," Lawrence Stone observed, "is not a change of structure, or of economics, or of social organization, but of sentiment."[2]

While there cannot yet be anything like the comprehensive answer historians offer, Mitt Regan, professor of law at Georgetown University, undertakes one of the first efforts to explore the question. Regan's topic is law.

He argues that the move from status to contract in family law, the movement that Sir Henry Maine celebrated more than a century ago, should more properly be seen as a twentieth-century innovation, and that time is ripe for a reconsideration of status. His reasons concern intimacy and identity, and they easily embrace what Lawrence Stone would have termed "sentiment."

Regan's starting point is a reexamination of the changes wrought by the Victorian era family in light of the more recent scholarship exploring the effect of modernity on identity. Regan uses the term "Victorian" to describe the emergence of the companionate family, characterized by the separate spheres of home and market, and locates these developments in the nineteenth century in the United States.[3] He notes that the Victorians "were the first to confront the widespread influence of modernism," of rapid change and the triumph of reason over tradition, and that this confrontation "provoked a fear that rising individualism would dissolve any sense of self that was rooted in communal responsibility."[4] For early moderns, in colonial America as well as Lawrence Stone's England, communal influence was pervasive. The household was the basic unit of production *and* reproduction in a hierarchical society in which church, community, and family overlapped. Without clear boundaries between public and private, the individual never escaped supervision. Phillippe Aries observes that

> The historians taught us long ago that the King was never left alone. But in fact, until the end of the seventeenth century, nobody was ever left alone. The density of social life made isolation virtually impossible, and people who managed to shut themselves up in a room for some time were regarded as exceptional characters: relations between peers, relations between people of the same class but dependent on one another, relations between master and servants — these everyday relations never left a man by himself.[5]

It is striking to visit an ancient village in the mountains of Italy and observe that, in the midst of empty hillsides, the homes in the town are crowded next to each other along narrow streets and passageways.

Regan identifies modernization with the emergence of large industrial organizations that dwarfed household enterprise, the growth of wage labor giving workers direct access to income, and a cycle of invention and obsolescence that created a pervasive sense of dynamism and instability, and gave rise to concern "about the fragmentation of the social order into an endless series of market struggles untempered by any moral restraints" (20).

The Victorian solution, Regan argues, was the withdrawal of the family from the larger society. The home became an emotional sanctuary in a cold and greedy world. Companionate marriage and a sharply developed sense of privacy — making the gulf between private and public life as wide as it could manage — were central to the remade family's success.[6] So, too, was the redefinition of family life in terms of prescribed roles that "required the exercise of restraint for a set of purposes that transcended the self." Regan argues that

> Entry into marriage involved automatic assumption of a specific role, a process that linked individual self-realization to adequate performance of the obligations associated with that role. For nineteenth-century culture, "[o]ne came to selfhood through obedience to laws and ideals," and few ideals were more important than those associated with family life. As a result, powerful cultural sanctions encouraged reliance on family roles as fundamental elements in the development of identity. For women, "[n]ineteenth century American society provided but one socially respectable, nondeviant role for women — that of loving wife and mother." For men, "[w]ork by the husband was a responsibility owed to the wife, and nothing more detrimental could be said about a man than that he did not support his wife and family."   *(28; citations omitted)*

Internalization of these role expectations linked cultivation of self-control to the achievement of social ends and insured that the private sphere was governed by something more than individual emotion. Regan concludes that "Victorian family law sought to reinforce this orientation by expressing those shared expectations about behavior through the vehicle of status. An individual's formal legal identity within the family reflected a relational identity that was intended to be a part of one's sense of self" (33). The result, in a world with fewer external constraints, was powerfully reinforced internal norms.

This Victorian construction of intimacy has not held; late twentieth-century family law, Regan declares, has rejected the Victorian emphasis on status. "If the Victorian era was marked by role identification, then the late twentieth century is marked by 'role distance' — a greater sense of an authentic self that stands apart from the roles that it may be asked to play" (34). Regan describes these developments as part of a movement from status to contract. Defining status as "a set of publicly imposed expectations largely independent of the preferences of the person who holds that status," he distinguishes Henry Maine's use of the same terms, noting that Maine addressed the shift from family to individual *within civil society; within the family*, status continued to order relationships for at least another century. Regan maintains that the individual has come to replace the family as the center of private life only as we have come to see ourselves within what Lawrence Friedman calls "the republic of choice."[7] Within this society, "[t]here has been a dramatic and pervasive weakening of the normative imperative to marry, to remain married, to have children, to restrict intimate relationships to marriage, and to maintain separate roles for males and females."[8] At each stage of modern life, the individual enjoys much greater freedom to structure relationships as she likes. She may choose, Regan maintains,

- to leave home at an earlier age, living on her own, with a roommate, or with whomever else she cares to associate;

- to become involved in an intimate relationship on a short-term, long-term, or any other basis;

- to marry and to structure the relationship as she wants, with or without children, with or without paid employment;

- to divorce on whatever grounds she deems appropriate;

- to have children, care for the children, entrust care of the children to the other parent or a nanny, juggle childcare with other activities, and do all of these things within or without marriage.

In making these decisions, intimate relationships become part of an individual's quest for authentic self-definition; the terms on which the relationships are conducted are negotiable rather than fixed, their endurance provisional rather than permanent, with even the decision to have children often resting on the children's contribution to the parent's growth and development (51; citations omitted).

Regan views these developments as a double-edged sword offering, on the one hand, the promise of more emotionally satisfying relationships, but, on the other, the loss of the family as a source of stable support. He insists, moreover, that each of the individual changes must be assessed, not standing on its own, but in the context of what he terms "our postmodern condition: the loss of the self as a coherent category of analysis" (68; citations omitted). In the 1996 movie *Multiplicity*, Michael Keaton plays a character who replicates himself, producing clones each slightly different from the others, in order to manage his complicated life and in order to manage a multiplicity of roles. Keaton's character is a metaphor for "postmodern life," for the "self-multiplication" that Kenneth Gergen (with no reference to the movie) defines as "the capacity to be significantly present in more than one place at a time."[9] Gergen is describing, not a fantasy of science fiction, but the product of the all too real technology of our time that shrinks space and time and multiplies the range of relationships in which we are involved. To illustrate Gergen's point, Regan gives us "Tom," corporate law firm partner, divorced father, and postmodern exemplar. Tom, in the course of a single day, may be a father, instructing his daughter in the virtues of self-restraint, a bachelor, bragging of his sexual conquests on the phone with friends, a dutiful son promising to visit his elderly mother in a city a thousand miles away, a demanding litigator preparing for a trial on the other side of the country in two weeks and willing to insist that junior colleagues work long into the night on little notice, an avid squash player looking forward to a tournament scheduled for the weekend, and a Sunday school instructor preaching faith and charity. As the number and intensity of these relationships increase, Gergen suggests that the notion of a stable self begins to dissolve. Identity becomes a fluid concept, and the idea of authenticity loses its meaning, for it assumes some underlying sense of self that is the basis for distinguishing superficial from more permanent versions of the self.[10] In a postmodern world, Tom's relationship with his daughter need be no more central to his identity than his performance at squash.

As history, Regan's account of the postmodern family is thin. The text is under two hundred pages, and more than half of the book addresses his call for a return to status as a way to encourage a relational sense of identity and responsibility in family matters. He relegates to a single sentence (with multiple footnotes) the "reasons for this evolution," acknowledging that "complex economic and social changes have contributed to it; as well as factors such as the increasing influence of Romanticism, the diminishing role of the family in the transmission of wealth, the emergence of a mass consumer society, and heightened gender consciousness" (33). He makes no effort to identify the mechanisms that produce particular changes the way Akerloff, Yellin, and Katz and many historians do. Yet, if he were to fill in the details, what he would describe is a process of transformation that is a lineal descendant of the changes Stone, Shorter, and Degler documented, and an emerging family that may be as distinct from the Victorian family Regan critiques as the Victorian family was from the early modern family that preceded it. The four areas of analysis the historians identified remain effective guideposts to the developments Regan describes.

FAMILIES   The critical development in the making of the Victorian family was the shift from households deeply embedded within networks of community and kin to nuclear families sharply differentiated from the larger society. The greater boundaries around the family came with the movement of men, paid labor, and market production out of the home, and women's assumption of responsibility for the family's remaining domestic activities.

Modern changes track the movement of women and the household's remaining activities into the market and the corresponding infiltration of the market back into the home. Conventionally married couples have increasingly come to depend on dual incomes, and single parents seldom have a choice at all. Working parents use McDonald's and Lean Cuisine to ease their domestic burdens, and lobby for on-site day care. The market response to increased demand is to supply much of what could previously be obtained only in the home, making single life easier in turn (and prompting Barbara Ehrenrich to comment that, before the advent of washing machines, frozen foods, wrinkle-free resistant fabrics, and 24-hour one-stop shopping, "the single life was far too strenuous for the average male").[11] Mitt Regan emphasizes that the converse is also true: much of what previously characterized the office has followed e-mail, voicemail, cell phones, faxes, and the Internet into the home. Technology spanning time and space successively reduces "down time" and any illusion of the home as a private space insulated from external influences (74).

The earlier integration of family and community placed the individual within a hierarchical web of relationships, everywhere supervised within a common frame of values. The new integration of home and market places the individual within a cacophony of shifting roles, pressures, and values.

MARRIAGE   The separate spheres, and the sexual division of labor that went with it, have given way to what Stephanie Coontz describes as co-provider families. Just as the modern family was more egalitarian and less stable than the premodern one, so too is the postmodern family more egalitarian and less stable still.

In the old order, the role of affection in the shift to companionate marriage involved the selection of a mate on the basis of love rather than familial obligation. Once married, a powerful set of societal forces — the role internalization Regan describes, the dependence Okin emphasizes, and the stigma that Akerloff, Yellin, and Katz attempt to quantify — kept couples together whether or not love endured. In the new era, affection has become the basis for not only selecting but keeping a mate. Regan cites Robert Bellah's findings that many modern couples "feel that their marriages are better than their parents' because of greater intimacy and sharing of feelings" (54). If this sense of intimacy fades, however, so does the most important reason for staying together. Companionship has replaced children — and necessity — as the modern families' reason for being.

CHILDREN   In raising the wall of private life between family and society, Phillippe Aries observes, the Victorian family reorganized itself around the child.[12] Quality replaced quantity as parents' primary concern, and child-rearing — particularly "mothers' efforts to inculcate in their children the values and traits of character deemed essential to achievement and respectability"[13] — became the middle-class family's most important responsibility. Charles Taylor describes the shift as one of sensibility: parents' love for their children moved from the banal to a matter of crucial importance.[14]

With the lowering of the walls between family and society, childrearing has changed from the family's central focus and mothers' primary occupation to one of a number of activities parents like Regan's Tom must balance. Regan observes that "marriage no longer automatically implies that a couple will have children. As fertility rates continue to decline over the long term, voluntary childlessness has become more prevalent as an acceptable way of life. Those who do have children now tend to have them later in life and to have fewer of them" (47). As children take up a smaller portion of their parents' lives, they also become less central to the family's organization and less critical to their parents' (and particularly their mother's) identity. Among the many results is a shift in parental roles and confusion in the allocation of responsibility. Recent movies are replete with mothers' guilt at juggling family and career and fathers' often painful discovery of the joys of parenthood. (In 1997's *Liar, Liar*, for example, it takes Jim Carrey's son's birthday wish that, for just one day, his father cannot lie for unscrupulous lawyer Carrey to learn just how much he loves his son, and how important it is for Dad, divorced or not, to show up for birthday parties.) Moreover, when parents do remain involved their roles have changed. Regan cites a study of the portrayal of families on television, which concludes that "[t]oday's TV parents are less likely to give their children rules or to pass on family beliefs and values. Rather, TV parents and kids tend to discover life's important values and beliefs in a process of mutual learning" (50). Shorter observes that, while the nineteenth-century nuclear family escorted children

adolescence to the threshold of marriage, today "the peer group is
ing up the task of adolescent socialization; and as the children move
through puberty, parental thoughts about good and bad, right and wrong,
and which way is up are becoming even more irrelevant to them."[15] Today's
children have become more like the children of bygone eras who encoun-
tered community mores, for better or ill, from relatively early ages. The shelter the nuclear family offered children has proved as transient as the conception of privacy that guarded it.

SEXUALITY   Edward Shorter identifies two great sexual revolutions. In
the first, which began in the late eighteenth century, affective sexuality was
linked to romance and marked by the celebration of married love — and a
dramatic rise in premarital conception and illegitimacy. In the second revolution, which began in the 1960s, Shorter links the increase in sexuality "to
hedonism."[16] The eighteenth-century revolution witnessed the incursion of
premarital intercourse into courtship; the later revolution into unmarried
life more generally with the final unlinking of coitus and "life-long"
monogamy.[17] This second revolution has witnessed not just increases in
sexuality and nonmarital births that dwarf the increases associated with the
first, but the disappearance of much of the disapproval — and most of the
social consequences — that once attended unsanctioned intercourse.

Regan (eschewing use of the term "hedonism") argues that today's pursuit of intimacy is "an individual quest for authentic self-definition rather
than, as with the Victorians, conduct that occurs within the context of a set
of relationships whose terms are prescribed by a common code of behavior"
(53). To capture the change, he invokes Richard Sennett's distinction between a nineteenth-century "seduction" and a twentieth-century "affair":

> A seduction was the arousal of such feelings by one person — not always
> a man — in another such that social codes were violated. This violation
> caused all the other social relations of the person to be temporarily called
> into question; one's spouse, one's children, one's own parents were in-
> volved both symbolically through guilt and practically if discovery of the
> violations occurred.

By contrast:

> It would seem illogical now for a person conducting an affair, whether
> inside or outside the bonds of marriage, to see it innately connected to

parental relations, so that whenever one makes love to another person one's status as someone else's child is altered. This, we would say, is a matter of individual cases, of personality factors; it is not a social issue.

(53; citations omitted)

This is not to say that all sexuality is sanctioned; only that the sensibilities surrounding it have changed. *Newsweek* put the subject of adultery on its cover and cited poll data demonstrating greater condemnation for the practice in the 1990s than twenty years earlier.[18] These results, however, may underscore, rather than undermine, Regan's larger point. Infidelity, writes Dr. Frank Pittman, isn't about "whom you lie with. It's about whom you lie to."[19] Extramarital sexuality is problematic in the postmodern world when it challenges the parties' understanding of their relationship to each other. The issue of obligation to a larger community appears to arise only in the military — and perhaps the presidency.[20]

Regan's account of the postmodern family is undoubtedly accurate; the issue is whether it is complete. Regan himself acknowledges that "the portrait I have sketched is a qualified one; . . . acceptance of the ethos I have described likely varies by region and class, and is most closely identified with so-called social elites: urban middle- and upper-middle-class professionals" (46). Existential angst and the literature on alienation and fragmentation of identity from which Regan draws is distinctly Western and quintessentially middle class. Regan ventures little speculation about the implications of his observations for other groups.

In the older histories, however, class is an important, if not always central, part of the story, and the results can be sobering. When Lawrence Stone first broaches the issue of class in sixteenth-century England, he describes the family and sexual mores of the period as a product of the middle and upper classes imposed on the lower classes through community supervision. With the move from the early modern to the modern family, the middle class exchanged community supervision for the internalized roles Regan describes. The poor were to an increasing degree on their own. Stone describes a dramatic rise in illegitimacy as a primary consequence, one he attributes to "a change of attitudes toward pre-marital sex on the part of some working-class women; a change in economic circumstances which left them more exposed to enticement and coercion to seduction; a change in social circumstances which deprived them of the moral stiffening provided by older relatives; and a change of economic and social circumstances which left the male seducers more free to refuse their traditional obligation to marry the girls whom they had impregnated."[21] Where Akerloff and Yellin see the contemporary move away from shotgun weddings as the product of a change in internalized mores, Stone sees the earlier shift as a consequence of the attenuated ties between family and community.

In the United States, historians are more inclined to discuss the significance of class in economic terms. Mary Ryan, in her finely etched portrait of nineteenth-century Utica, New York, describes the creation of Regan's Victorian family (and Stone and Shorter's "modern" one) as a self-conscious strategy to maintain class position in turbulent times. Between 1845 and 1856, the numbers of shopkeepers and craftsmen who had historically constituted the middle ranks of Utica society fell by half, and 40 percent of the city's residents were immigrants. The Protestant native-born responded, Ryan observes, by carrying through "an elaborate and largely successful strategy for reproducing the middle class." She explains that

> Prescient native-born couples began in the 1830s to limit their family size, thereby concentrating scarce financial and emotional resources on the care and education of fewer children. Second, . . . native-born Protestants initiated methods of socialization designed to inculcate values and traits of character deemed essential to middle-class achievement and respectability. Next, native-born parents tended to keep their children within the households of their birth for extended periods, often until their sons were well over twenty years of age. By this strategy, mothers and fathers prolonged their moral surveillance and material support of the second generation even as it advanced out of the home into the labor force. At the same time, the parental generation had created the educational institutions and financed the schooling that qualified their children for more skilled and lucrative occupations. As a result of these parental strategies, the native-born youth of the 1850s not only secured middle-class jobs but also circumvented the declining segments of the old middle class and won a foothold in white-collar occupations.[22]

Regan's Victorian family, in short, ably served the interests of the middle class.

While Ryan does not discuss the consequences for Utica's laboring masses, other writers emphasize the constraints that prevented the working poor from following suit. Elizabeth Pleck, for example, compares African-American and Italian-American families in the urban North at the turn of the century. Pleck emphasizes that both groups were desperately poor; few families in either group could securely rely on a single wage-earner's income, much less replicate the Utica middle class's complete separation of family from market. Cultural differences nonetheless dictated different responses. Pleck notes that in Italian-American families the wives were more likely to stay at home while the children worked; in African-American families the children were more likely to stay in school while the wives worked. School attendance figures for African-American boys in 1900 were double the Italian rate; black married women's labor force participation rates were several times the Italian rate.[23] Differences in childrearing contributed to disparities. Pleck observes that "Italians believed in close supervision of children, blacks in training for independence. Properly raised Italian children (*ben educati*) were never left alone. Mothers told their children to play with siblings and other relatives rather than with neighbors." African-American patterns, in contrast, were the result of slavery. Mothers as well as fathers had worked in the fields, sometimes leaving elderly black nurses to care for the children, but more often with older siblings supervising the young. Pleck concludes that

> The emphasis on children's education was embedded within a family's plans for its survival. Both groups may have shared the same parental concern for provision in old age, but expressed the concern through different strategies: for Italians, through the continued presence of at least one adult child as a wage earner in the household; for blacks, through the education and social mobility for the children. Both groups tried to plan for the future, but a black family may have placed greater emphasis on a child's schooling as the means of meeting long-term family needs. Thus, both Italians and blacks believed in self-sacrifice, but with a difference. Whereas Italian children often submerged their needs to those of their parents, especially their mothers, black mothers deprived themselves of necessities for the sake of their children.[24]

Neither group could afford to keep both mothers and children ensconced in the home until the children were safely married off sometime in their twenties. As a result, neither group met the standard for "good parenting" of the day, and while both strategies contributed to survival, neither provided a foundation for widespread movement into the middle class until the very different circumstances that emerged after World War II.

The class dynamic present in all these processes — the jump in the illegitimacy rates in England and France in the eighteenth century, and the rates of maternal and child labor in American cities in the late nineteenth — can be analyzed in terms of Akerloff, Yellin, and Katz's conception of "technological shock." With the withdrawal of family from community, the middle class compensated by investing far more family time (overwhelming the mother's) and resources (almost certainly thought of as the father's) in children. These investments produced human capital — education, conduct, and internalized moral codes — that paid off in a society that valued such traits without, particularly in the days before public education, systematically providing for their production. The very success of the middle-class strategy increased the disadvantages of the working poor, who could neither insulate their children from the more treacherous communities that came with urbanization nor secure the advantages of greater investment in education and childrearing.

14

And What About the Children?

I F children were the Victorian family's reason for being — and middle-class children its most prominent beneficiaries — then children have suffered most from its passing. Over the last several decades, every measure of childhood well-being from SAT scores to gum-chewing has registered a decline — and the declines correlate with the rise of single-parent families. The precise relationship between family form and children's well-being is nonetheless treacherous turf, analytically and politically. Correlations are not the same as causation (as the tobacco lobby continually reminds us), and identifying the causal mechanisms in family well-being is more compli cated — and inevitably less certain — than isolating the cause of lung cancer. The absence of the other parent alone is not enough to explain the result; children who have lost a parent to death do almost as well as children whose parents stay together, and considerably better than those whose parents divorce (who in turn do better than those whose parents never marry). Moreover, however strong the correlations, villifying single mothers on the basis of statistical data or nebulous pieties, as Dan Quayle discovered, or misleading anecdote (Ronald Reagan and Clarence Thomas come to mind) can and should produce a backlash of its own.

Navigating this minefield is thus for the stout of heart, and the leading voice in the effort to make sense of the data is Sara McLanahan's. McLanahan, a Princeton sociologist, is a divorced and remarried mother of three. Her work is sufficiently careful, detailed, and qualified to be cited by those on all sides of the controversy. She is nonetheless the scholar most identified with the proposition that "children who grow up with only one parent are less successful in adulthood than children who grow up with two parents."[1] To the dismay of some of her Princeton colleagues, McLanahan was willing to state unequivocally to a national television audience that

> What my research shows is that children who grow up apart from one of their parents are disadvantaged across a broad array of outcomes. In fact, almost any measure of child well-being that you look at, these children are disadvantaged. They are more likely to drop out of school, they have lower grade-point averages, they are more likely to become a teen mother, or to have a child outside marriage, and, if they do marry, they are more likely to divorce. So almost any outcome that you look at you see this gap between the performance of children who live with both parents for eighteen years and the other children. And this occurs regardless of the social class background of the child. It occurs regardless of the race of the child. It is there regardless of the sex of the child. This differential, which is an increase in risk between two and three times greater than the risk [of negative outcomes in intact families], . . . occurs across all these outcomes.[2]

McLanahan emphasizes that she did not enter the field to disparage single mothers. Indeed, what prompted her initial research was a desire to respond to reporter and writer Ken Auletta. Auletta had written a series on America's underclass in the *New Yorker*, in which he tied criminality, drug use, and a host of other problems associated with the poorest segments of society to family structure. McLanahan was sure that the data would prove him wrong. Instead, she was the one who changed her mind. The conclusion that her research most systematically documents is that, even when race, poverty, and income status are factored into the equation, children who grow up in a single-parent family are disproportionately at risk on nearly every measure of well-being.[3] There is nothing controversial about these findings — even single mothers' staunchest defenders argue that, given the disadvantages of single parenthood, it would be remarkable if children in two-parent families did not enjoy advantages. The controversial question is why.

The portion of McLanahan's research cited most often by those who defend single parents is the work that ties a large source of children's disadvantage — about half, McLanahan concludes — to income. The single most striking difference between families with two parents and those with one (particularly if the lone parent is a woman) is money. Approximately one in two mother-only families is below the poverty line compared with less than 13 percent of intact families.[4] The reasons are straightforward.

Women, on average, earn less than men; women with children earn less than those without; single parents face greater constraints in the jobs they can manage than do married parents; and parents who would be struggling financially even if they stayed together are disproportionately likely to grow apart, whether because of death, divorce, or the failure to marry in the first place.[5] Neither child support nor government assistance begins to make up for the gap in wages between two-parent and single-parent families. McLanahan finds that "[n]ot only are mother-only families more likely to be poor than other families, but also the dynamics of their poverty experience are different. . . . Among mother-only families, poverty lasts longer and is more severe."[6] Despite these disparities, many earlier studies made no attempt to take income differences into account. McLanahan demonstrates that, once statistical measures control for income, 50 percent of the disparities in school achievement and teen pregnancies between two-parent and single-parent families disappears.[7] She argues further that, at least for children whose parents break up during the children's early adolescence, "the income effect is not simply a reflection of the fact that poor families are less likely to remain intact. These findings provide strong evidence that it is not just low income per se but the *loss* of economic resources associated with family disruption that is a major cause of lower achievement of children whose parents divorce."[8] She would make reducing the economic insecurity of children growing up in single-parent families her first priority.

McLanahan, however, does not stop there. Observing that income differences cannot explain why children in stepfamilies do worse than children in two-parent families, she goes on to examine what she terms differences in "parenting." She begins by noting that

> We suspect that parental involvement and supervision are weaker in one-parent families than in two-parent families. In one sense, this advantage is simply a matter of numbers: one parent has less time and authority than two parents who can share responsibility and cooperate with each other. In another sense, however, it is due to the fact that single-parent families and stepfamilies are less stable in terms of personnel (grandmothers, mothers' boyfriends, and stepfathers are more likely to move in and out), which creates uncertainty about household rules and parental responsibility.[9]

McLanahan then attempts to parse out the contributions her measures of "single parenting" make to poor outcomes for children the same way she tested for the effect of income. Her conclusion is that differences in parental involvement and supervision account for over half of the differences in the high school dropout and early childbearing rates, and all of the difference in idleness among boys.[10] (In other words, single parents who display the same level of parental involvement and supervision as parents in intact families produce children who are still more likely to drop out of school or have children at an early age, but their sons are equally able to find and keep steady jobs.) These results are dramatic and suggest that differences in household composition account for as much of the disadvantages that single-parent families face as differences in income. McLanahan cautions, however, that other studies, while confirming the income effects, have found weaker correlations with parenting practices and therefore "we are less confident of the parenting results . . . than the income results" of the study.

McLanahan completes the analysis by comparing the level of community resources available to two-parent and single-parent families. She finds that children in single-parent families live in communities with fewer resources, move more often, and, as a result, have weaker community connections. She finds the strongest statistical correlations between residential mobility and teen birth and high school dropout rates. When mobility is combined with decreases in income, it explains almost all the differences between the high school dropout rates of single-parent and two-parent families and, even without considering income, much of the difference between two-parent and stepparent families.[12] McLanahan concludes that "[s]ince many parents are in a position to reduce the number of times they move, and since judges are often in a position to limit or minimize residential mobility, these findings may be especially useful to parents and policymakers in improving the lives of children."[13]

The implications of McLanahan's research are controversial, at least in part, because McLanahan focuses on the ways in which single-parent families are most likely to be different from two-parent families and places the responsibility for negative outcomes there. In this sense, her work echoes Gary Becker's. He expresses the advantages two parents offer in terms of specialization. Dads free to specialize in the workforce earn dramatically more than single moms; the income gap is therefore likely to be unbridgeable. A married Mom, with Dad's support, can provide her children substantially more involvement and supervision (not to mention field trip participation) than one who parents on her own. McLanahan prefers Susan Moller Okin's perspective. She believes that women will achieve equality only when men assume an equal share of responsibility for children. Partnership, on something akin to William Galston's terms, is nonetheless essential. McLanahan links the best outcomes for children with intact families, stepfamilies, and single-parent families in which both parents contribute to the children's financial and emotional support. Martha Fineman would place McLanahan with those eager to reforge the links between men and women through joint custody, child support, and limits on custodial parents' autonomy.

Beyond Fineman's feminism, McLanahan's work is subject to two types of challenges. The first is empirical. While few scholars challenge her work directly, more maintain that it is incomplete. McLanahan's primary culprits are the differences in financial and parenting resources associated with a reduction from two parents to one. Other researchers focus on factors less inevitably tied to family structure. Andrew Cherlin, working together with other scholars on British data, has conducted longer-range studies that find many of the difficulties linked to parental separation are present *prior to* the breakup, largely as a result of the parental conflict that precedes separation. His more recent research, however, also finds long-term emotional consequences, such as increased rates of aggression or depression, linked to divorce.[14]

Other researchers tie negative consequences to the custodial parent's adjustment (i.e., stressed or depressed adults parent less effectively) or to the interaction between marital quality and postseparation circumstances. (Indeed, Paul Amato and Alan Booth find that divorce may benefit children from high-conflict relationships).[15] These scholars suggest that factors associated with divorce, rather than divorce itself, correlate most closely with negative outcomes for children. Kristin Luker, in her account of the politics of teenage pregnancy, questions whether any study can effectively control for all the differences that separate single parents from parents in other families. She emphasizes that the women who become teen moms are more disadvantaged as a group than those who postpone childrearing, and even studies that attempt to account for quantifiable factors such as sociocconomic background have difficulty assessing "the cognitive-psychological factors and the unobserved differences that may subtly separate the kinds of people who become teen mothers from those who do not."[16] Given that, even within the same family, women who give birth earlier tend to be more troubled than those who postpone childrearing, it is difficult to conclude, Luker argues, that the prospects for their children would have improved had these more troubled mothers simply waited longer to become pregnant.[17] The energy spent on single parenthood, critics like Luker maintain, would be more productively spent alleviating the inequality, conflict, and poverty that produce it.

The more radical challenge, however, comes from those who believe that McLanahan does not go far enough in linking negative outcomes to family structure. David Blankenhorn introduces his book, *Fatherless America*, with the declaration that

> Fatherlessness is the most harmful demographic trend of this generation. It is the leading cause of declining child well-being in our society. It is also the engine driving our most urgent social problems, from crime to adolescent pregnancy to child sexual abuse to domestic violence against women. Yet, despite its scale and social consequences, fatherlessness is a problem that is frequently ignored or denied. Especially within our elite discourse, it's largely a problem with no name.[18]

David Popenoe seconds Blankenhorn's conclusions. He writes that "beyond being merely a second adult or third party, fathers — men — bring an array of positive inputs to a child, unique and irreplaceable qualities that women do not ordinarily bring. Despite their many similarities, males and females are different to the core. They think differently and act differently. Differences have universally been found in aggression and general activity level, cognitive skills, sensory sensitivity, and sexual and reproductive behavior. By every indication, the expression of these differences is important for child development."[19] McLanahan, unlike Blankenhorn and Popenoe, does not link the negative outcomes she identifies with single-parent families to the absence of the father per se, and the empirical record, which strongly supports McLanahan's cautious claims, is decidedly mixed on Blankenhorn's and Popenoe's bolder ones. That gender differences exist, and that men and women "parent" somewhat differently is not in dispute. That these differences make the presence of a mother and a father (and, Blankenhorn argues, preferably biological ones) indispensable to children's well-being is another matter.

While fatherhood may once have been a neglected field, the literature attempting to measure fathers' influences has grown exponentially over the last several decades. Studies confirm that men and women interact with their children in different ways (mothers use touch in order to comfort a child, fathers to excite), in different amounts (mothers do more), with different consequences (fathers emphasize discipline and control, mothers monitoring and supervision).[20] Early studies found that boys growing up without fathers had greater difficulty with sex-role and gender-role development, school performance, psychosocial adjustment, and perhaps the control of aggression. More recent studies find that enhanced paternal involvement correlates with increased cognitive competence (and higher grades), greater empathy, less sex-stereotyped beliefs, and a more internal locus of control (not to mention greater teacher appreciation of field trip participation). All the studies find that fathers can effectively parent even small children on their own, and most divorce studies find that mothers and fathers do about equally well, with mixed results on the importance of the same-sex parent to older children.[21] Taking the studies together, however, Michael Lamb writes, in the introduction to the third edition of his book on *The Role of the Father in Child Development*, that the critical question becomes not that differences exist, but *why* they exist. His answer: the context in which parenting occurs is more important than gender differences between parents in explaining fathers' influence. He observes, first, that

> fathers and mothers seem to influence their children in similar rather than dissimilar ways. Contrary to the expectations of many psychologists, including myself, who have studied paternal influences on children, the differences between mothers and fathers appear much less important than the similarities. Not only does the description of mothering resemble the description of fathering (particularly the version of involved fathering that has become prominent in the late 20th century) but the mechanisms and means by which fathers influence their children appear similar to those that mediate maternal influences on children.[22]

Lamb reports, second, that the parent's individual characteristics are less important than the quality of the parent's interaction with the child (warm nurturing men contribute more to the development of their sons' masculinity than more masculine and remote fathers), and, third, that the individual relationship between parent and child may be less important than the family context in which it occurs. He emphasizes that "positive paternal influences are more likely to occur not only when there is a supportive father-child relationship but when the father's relationship with his partner, and presumably other children, establishes a positive familial context. The absence of familial hostility is the most consistent correlate of child adjustment, whereas marital conflict is the most consistent and reliable correlate of child maladjustment."[23] Thus, fathers who spend additional time with their children have the most positive impact when their partners welcome

and encourage the involvement, and father absence is harmful, Lamb concludes, "not necessarily because a sex-role model is absent, but because
many aspects of the father's role — economic, social, emotional — go un-
filled or filled inappropriately."

Lamb's conclusions echo McLanahan's. Intact families do better than
single-parent families not because a biological father and mother are necessarily indispensable to children's well-being, but because intact families
bring a greater array of economic, social, and emotional resources to childrearing. Nancy Dowd, in her defense of single-parent families, maintains
that the "direct impact of fathers on their children . . . is 'essentially re-
dundant'" and that grandmothers and other female friends or kin can play
the same role. She nonetheless observes that the "strongest claim for a
unique role for fathers . . . is that when fathers strongly support the
mother in a full-time parenting role, their presence has significant, though
indirect, benefits for children. Two parents are better than one not because
they are opposite sexes, but because one, ideally, provides economic and
emotional support to the one who is parenting."[24] David Popenoe, despite
his insistence that "fathers — men — bring . . . unique and irreplaceable
qualities" to parenting and his opposition to single-parent families, concedes that much "of what fathers contribute to child development, of
course, is simply the result of being a second adult in the home. Other
things being equal, two adults are better than one in raising children. As the
distinguished developmental psychologist Urie Bronfenbrener has noted,
the quality of the interaction between principal caregiver and child depends
heavily 'on the availability and involvement of another adult, a *third party*
who assists, encourages, spells off, gives status to, and expresses admiration
and affection for the person caring for and engaging in joint activity with
the child.'"[25] Both sides of the debate cite McLanahan because her research
documents the irrefutable — all other things being equal, two parents are
better than one.

Where the two sides part is on the definition of what makes "other things
. . . equal." Parents who part are not identical to parents who stay together. Never-married mothers differ from married mothers in ways that go
beyond the fact that they do not marry. The benefits associated with parents who stay together voluntarily do not necessarily accrue to children
whose parents remain together because they see no other option. It is possible to demonstrate conclusively that children have suffered from family
instability without uncritically embracing proposals to restrict divorce or
nonmarital births.

These differences are not merely ones of statistical methodology. The increasing number of single-parent families is not a random phenomenon. Nonmarital births, although increasing in incidence across the spectrum, disproportionately affect those made more vulnerable by age, race, and socioeconomic status (figures 14.1, 14.2, and 14.3). Divorce, with rates high enough to affect everyone, still disproportionately affects the poor (figure 14.4).

McLanahan's statistics attempt to measure the impact of family structure by controlling for race, income, and other indicia of socioeconomic status. When those controls are relaxed, and when the impact of family status is *combined* with the impact of race and poverty, the result is accelerating inequality that makes disparities among children dramatically greater than those among their parents (figures 14.5 and 14.6).[26]

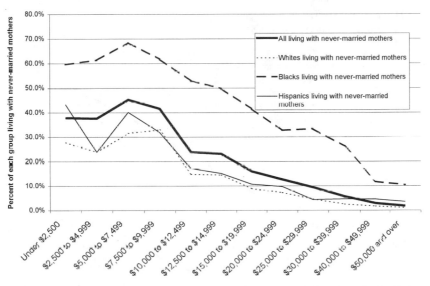

Figure 14.1 Percent of children under 18 living with never-married mothers, by family income and race, 1998. Author's depiction of data from U.S. Census Bureau, "Unpublished Tables — Martial Status and Living Arrangements: March 1998" (www.census.gov/prod/99pubs/p20-514u.pdf).

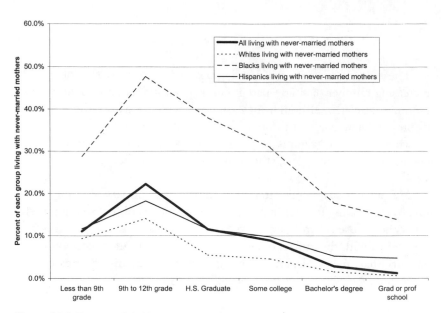

Figure 14.2 Percent of children under 18 living with never-married mothers, by education and race, 1998. Author's depiction of data from U.S. Census Bureau, "Unpublished Tables — Martial Status and Living Arrangements: March 1998" (www.census.gov/prod/99pubs/p20-514u.pdf).

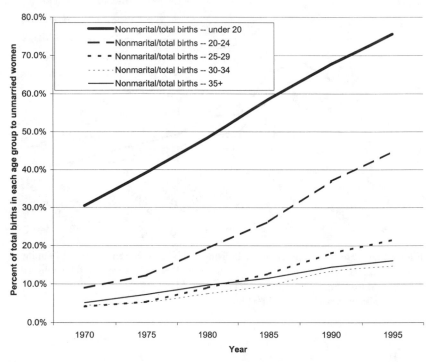

Figure 14.3 Nonmarital births as a percentage of total births by age. Author's depiction of data from U.S. National Center for Health Statistics, *Vital Statistics of the United States* (annual); *Monthly Vital Statistics Reports*; and *Statistical Abstract of the United States* (1980, 1998). See also Appendix, figures A.7–A.9.

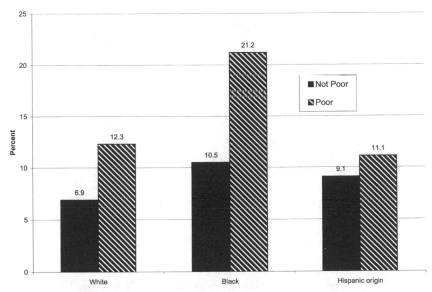

Figure 14.4 Percent of poor and non-poor two-parent families discontinuing* within two years, by race.

*"Discontinuation" is defined as marital separation. *Source:* U.S. Bureau of the Census, "Current Population Reports, Series P23–179," *Studies in Household and Family Formation* (Washington, D.C.: GPO, 1992). (The two-year periods are from December 1983 to December 1985 and from April 1985 to April 1987.)

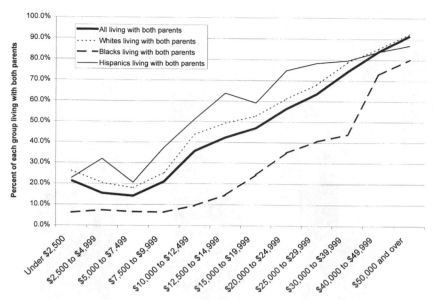

Figure 14.5 Percent of children under 18 living with both parents, by family income and race, 1998. Author's depiction of data from U.S. Census Bureau, "Unpublished Tables — Marital Status and Living Arrangements: March 1998" (www.census.gov/prod/99pubs/p20-514u.pdf).

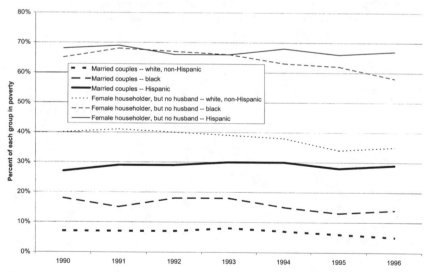

Figure 14.6 Percent of children under 18 living in poverty, by race and family structure, 1990–1996.* Author's depiction of data from Federal Interagency Forum on Child and Family Statistics. *America's Children: Key National Indicators of Well-Being, 1998* (Washington, D.C.: GPO, 1998), table ECON1.A, at 70.

*The descriptions of race and ethnicity (i.e., "white," "black," and "Hispanic") are those in the original report. The term "Hispanic" refers to people who may be of any race. The children are children under 18 related to the householder by blood, marriage, or adoption.

15

Conclusion

T HE first part of this book ended with the example of Murphy Brown, and the question of just how enduring our family mores really are. By recasting the question in a historical framework, part 2 has suggested that society's ability to influence family behavior is almost as much an issue as the content of family values. Dealing with changes in family form and function involves not only the sexual revolution of the 1960s but the changing relationship between family and society that has been steadily unfolding (if Lawrence Stone is correct) for more than half a millennium. This larger perspective suggests that, even with respect to issues about which there may be broad consensus — for example, that two parents are better than one — the ability to produce anything close to universal conduct is very much in doubt. Indeed, the philosopher Charles Taylor has written a pessimistic volume in which he questions whether it is possible to reconcile a coherent moral order with the nature of modern identity at all.[1]

Taylor's pessimism comes, in part, from the passing of the institutions that once made family norms close to universal, both in understanding and, to a surprising degree, in practice. The first — and much studied — transformation came with the separation of family and society, with the end of integrated communities in which family, production, and religion seamlessly overlapped and in which "nobody was ever left alone." Within these older communities, a tailor's standing might depend equally on his relationship with his father and his customers; the minister could be expected to restrain domestic violence *and* predatory pricing.[2] The concept of privacy, in both its legal and physical senses, was largely unknown, and at least one of the consequences was a lot less sex and a greater ability to regulate that which occurred. After all, Taylor notes, before the seventeenth century, hallways were unusual, and the only route from one part of a house to another might be through the master bedroom.

The change now upon us is the passing of Regan's Victorian family, and with it the substitution of family for community as the stable anchor of a changing society and the essential locus for the moral instruction and supervision of the young. The separate spheres, and the distinctive role of women within the domestic sphere, were critical to the result. Not only did Victorian mothers devote renewed attention to young children (Stone emphasizes that the better care that reduced infant mortality rates *before* the twentieth-century advances in combating infectious diseases), but women were central to a web of relationships that provided for the supervision of adolescents. Mary Ryan underscored the role of the Utica middle class in escorting sons as well as daughters into early adulthood and marriage in their mid-twenties. Teens would not escape close adult supervision until after World War II.

The separate spheres depended, however, on the permanence of marriage, which relied in turn on the internalization of the roles associated with it, and the restriction of alternatives. Gender-based marital roles, Regan observed, linked "individual self-realization" to the fulfillment of social obligations. Nineteenth-century American society provided but one socially respectable, nondeviant role for women — that of loving wife and mother. Work by the husband was a responsibility owed to the wife, and nothing more detrimental could be said about a man than that he did not support his wife and family.[3] Women's dependence, reinforced by their lack of opportunities outside marriage and the atrophy of the kinship and community ties of earlier eras, made single parenthood in any form perilous, and for both men and women too flagrant a violation of the social norms associated with family resulted in a wholesale loss of class standing. For despite its success, the Victorian family was never as universal as the family it replaced. Community surveillance had enforced the norms of an earlier era — for example, with English townsmen denying grazing rights to those they considered deviant or French charivari intervening in the home of a drunken neighbor thought to be too abusive to his wife. The Victorian family, which dealt with violence within the family by denying its existence, depended to a much greater degree on internalized norms, and a larger family investment in producing them.

As a result, the creation and maintenance of the Victorian family was very much a class-based affair, following Ackerloff, Yellin, and Katz's model of "technological shock." The middle classes, less insulated from social change than the upper classes and with more resources than the lower classes, led in the creation of the new norms. These norms — companionate marriage, greater investment in children, maternal devotion to the home — provided a buffer from a riskier society and set the standards by which the poor were to be judged in their requests for assistance. The poor were then doubly dis advantaged: they disproportionately suffered from the decay of the older era (more dangerous cities and weaker restraints on sexual predation in eighteenth-century England, for example) at the same time that they had difficulty securing the advantages of the new order (nonworking mothers, secondary education). Rising illegitimacy, among the more visible barometers of social change in most eras, was largely a lower-class affair. During times of rapid change, shifting family mores served to replicate class advantage. Societal disparities eased only with stabilization in the rate of change and more widespread prosperity.

In our era, the process of creating a new set of family norms, spurred by the changing role of women in the postindustrial economy and the reorganization of the family around it, is well under way, and it is no less class-based than the changes that preceded it. While American society may not be able to reach a consensus on "family values," the middle class has embraced a new strategy for success. Its tenets are that:

1. Women, like men, should invest in their own earning capacity and postpone childbearing (if not always marriage) until their educations are complete and their careers established. Men (with the possible exception of Donald Trump) should consider the financial as well as reproductive contributions of potential mates.

2. Unmarried women are free to join unmarried men in sexual activity. Consent (and perhaps condoms) have replaced betrothal as the key indicia of legitimate behavior, with women bearing ultimate responsibility for unplanned pregnancies, and men serving as guarantors should the child claim support from the father or the state.

3. The ideal relationship is an egalitarian one in which both partners contribute financial support and caretaking services commensurate with family needs (if not always gender-based equality).

4. Marriage is a contingent rather than a permanent institution.

These changes offer obvious advantages for those who make them work, including both greater financial security (two paychecks produce more income and better ability to deal with layoffs) and greater freedom within individual relationships. These new norms also contribute to the atrophy of the older forms of restraint that channeled family relationships. The equation of sex and reproduction has been shattered, and that between marriage and parenthood is under assault. As with earlier changes in family form, the shifts play out along class lines. Delayed childbearing correlates directly with socioeconomic status and, even controlling for parental income, women with the best chances in life are the ones most likely to postpone pregnancy. At the same time, the negative consequences of single parenthood, whatever its cause, are borne most heavily by the children whose families have the least income. Donna Franklin's thesis that these changes in family practices "ensure inequality" applies not just to African-Americans but to the society at large.

The challenge these changes pose is not the ultimate one of judgment (the shifts have clearly benefited some and hurt others), but rather how to rebuild support for families within a structure that requires managing greater individual freedom within an ever more far-reaching and complex web of relationships. Analyzed in terms of the categories that frame historians' perspectives on the changing family, the family of the 1990s has already taken its place beside the early modern family of sixteenth- and seventeenth-century England and the Victorian family that succeeded it. A comprehensive chart (figure 15.1) summarizes these changes and differences.

The renegotiation of the relationship between the adults is well under way. Women in the workplace, even if not universal, define the norm. The relationship between men and women is no longer governed by either the separate spheres or the double standard. Marriage has shifted from an institution premised on lifelong commitment to one that celebrates companionship — and permits either party to terminate the arrangement when it fails to fulfill its promises. The transformation that remains incomplete is the relationship to children.

Early modern and Victorian societies provided for children through marriage. The marital link, which defined "legitimacy," provided clear lines of connection and responsibility. And when marriage itself changed from an arranged affair to one based on choice, internalized gender roles served to link the voluntary institution to social obligations — chief among which were obligations toward children. Lawrence Friedman's "republic of choice" provides no such automatic connections. Sex need not indicate openness toward parenthood; parenthood creates no obligation to marry; marriage implies no particular organization for meeting the needs of children. Suc-

Family Type	Early Modern	Modern/ Victorian	Post-Modern/ The 1990s
Family/Community Primary relation- ships	Full integration Vertical/ Hierarchical[1]	Parallel Separate spheres	Partial integration Horizontal[2]
Marriage	Permanent institu- tion	Lifelong obligation	Terminable at will
Mate selection	Arranged by par- ents	Chosen by spouses	Chosen by spouses
Primary purpose	"Little Common- wealths"[3]	Childrearing	Companionship
Children	Instrumental: advance family's dynastic ambi- tions	Central: Quality> quantity	Optional?
Sexuality	Reproduction, pleasure optional	Reproduction and pleasure within marriage	Pleasure, reproduc- tion optional

[1]Vertical in the sense that family relationships within the family were hierarchical; the father ran the family in all its myriad roles and directed the relationships with other parts of the community.

[2]Horizontal in the sense that the family's interactions with the community may be ordered along a number of horizontal lines such as separate provision for day care or tennis lessons, Mom and Dad's employment relationships, adolescent friendships, etc.

[3]The phrase is from John Demos, and he used it to describe the role of the family as a public institution tightly integrated into a well-ordered society as a source of everything from economic production to dependent care. See Demos, *A Little Commonwealth: Family Life in Plymouth Colony* (New York: Oxford University Press, 1970).

Figure 15.1

cessful parents, like those of old, find ways to meet their children's needs; society has fewer tools to direct those less likely to succeed on their own.

At the conclusion of his book on the postmodern family, Mitt Regan argues that the antidote to this fragmentation of family life involves a return to status. He chooses the term "status" to distance himself from the contractual model identified with the "republic of choice" and the idea that each relationship is a discrete exchange independent of all that came before it. Regan seeks instead to "create an identity whose freedom of action is circumscribed by one's relationship to others."[4] He observes that

> the use of status reflects a relational notion of obligation. That is, certain relationships by their nature are seen as characterized by vulnerability and dependence, which makes inappropriate a regime of unqualified private ordering. In each case, the law reflects the view that the stronger party owes certain responsibilities to the weaker, responsibilities that flow from the fact of the relationship itself rather than solely from individual choice.[5]

Regan links status to the creation of a "structure of meaning within which the individual can make sense of her existence" (94). He seeks to invest the roles of husband, wife, mother, father with something more than the sum of the individual choices of their occupants, and to use the idea of family to bridge the gulf between isolated individuals and mass society.

While Regan speaks eloquently of communal obligations, his analysis of how this is to come about focuses almost entirely on the relationship between spouses. His proposals would eliminate the marital rape exception, uphold the conclusive presumption that the mother's husband is the father of her child, preserve some role for fault in the divorce process, and expand the role of alimony. He provides a compelling prescription for more fulfilling intimate partnerships. But although he begins his book with the acknowledgment that "being a father has been perhaps as important an impetus for this book as being a scholar" (5), the relationship to children receives less attention than the one between adults.

I believe that if Regan is right, if status holds the key to a renewed sense of obligation that connects family roles to community needs, it will come not just from reconsideration of the relationship between spouses but of that between parents and children. The definition of status that Regan develops is that of "a legal identity that is subject to a set of publicly imposed expectations largely independent of the preferences of the person who holds that status" (9). At a time when intimate relationships may vary widely, parenting involves a more predictable set of obligations. Marriage may no longer involve dependence; childhood inherently does. The emotional vulnerability of intimate partners may not rise to a level of societal concern; that of children is more likely to do so. The obligations of one partner to another (physical care, financial support, emotional reciprocity) may be hard to prescribe between able-bodied adults; the obligations of parents toward their children are more readily the subject of legal enforcement.

If family obligation is to be rebuilt on lines of status — indeed, if it is to be rebuilt at all in a way that links individual obligation to societal needs — then parenthood may be the only remaining candidate. Parenthood may play the part marriage once did of initiating young men and women into a socially sanctioned role whether or not they would voluntarily embrace all of the role requirements. Unlike the marriages of the 1990s, parenthood is a permanent relationship; it is also one of dependence and trust. It involves expectations that society is capable of imposing on those who resist, but it is also a role capable of being expressed in terms of universal ideals. We are in the midst (with help from church, state, and Hollywood) of remaking our images of parenthood. And while the emerging ideals start with the middle-class struggle to redefine the combination of family care and career, the hope for remaking family life depends on their widespread applicability. The law, with the central role Regan assigns it of defining and enforcing the content of status, will be instrumental in that process.

Part III

From Partners to Parents

The Legal Revolution

THE law school curriculum is sometimes divided into private law and public law courses. Private law — contracts, torts, property — addresses relationships between private parties. While the state occasionally imposes measures thought to advance the common good, private law seeks overwhelmingly to honor the commitments which the parties have undertaken to govern themselves. Public law — criminal law, business regulation, and, par excellence, constitutional law — addresses the relationship between the state and its citizens, and the imposition of responsibilities necessary to advance community welfare. Family law, which has long policed the boundary between public and private, lies somewhere in between. So long as the family was seen as a central unit of society, there was a significant public stake in its governance. The state policed marital formation and dissolution, mandated marital terms, and drew sharp distinctions between marital and nonmarital relationships. Marital status, with wedding rings on public display, governed rape, inheritance, and identity.

In the new era, courts and legislatures are busy disentangling (and reweaving into different strands) the public and private dimensions of family law. Sexual relationships are becoming more distinctly private, more a matter of personal preference and private bargaining, and at the same time more subject to the rules that govern other private relationships. A man can today be prosecuted for raping his wife. Parent-child relationships in contrast are becoming more public, both in the sense that they are attaining greater visibility in their own right as the public importance of marriage fades, and in the sense that the state has become more willing to enforce public expectations of parents. Couples can renegotiate their relationship to one another, but the state continues to define their relationship to their children.

This last section of the book examines the legal changes underlying this process in three stages. The first two chapters ask what is left of the older understandings of family that governed the last century and a half of family law. Chapter 16 considers the challenge same-sex relationships pose to the traditional connections between sex, marriage, and reproduction, while chapter 17 contrasts the treatment of older couples (the extraordinarily wealthy Burrs of 1843 and the Connecticut Wendts of 1998) with that accorded young couples with children. Both chapters explain why, for different reasons, the relationship between the adults provides a less firm footing than it once did for protecting the interests of minors.

The next three chapters address the terms on which the law is rebuilding parental obligation. Chapter 18 contrasts the status-based nature of child support with the more contractual nature of spousal obligation and explains how, for all but the wealthiest couples, child support has become the most important financial obligation to survive a breakup. Chapters 19 and 20 then explore contemporary custody conflicts. Custody has replaced fault as the most emotionally charged issue at divorce and has provided the forge for a revitalized definition of parenthood. The conflicts, while a measure of the respective merits of mothers and fathers, turn on the newly emerging norms of egalitarian parenting and parental obligation. Custody now holds the moral center of family law.

The final two chapters explore the changing relationship between family, state, and community. Changing economic organization and its impact on the relationship between men and women appears to have made greater family instability a permanent part of society, and the two-parent family a less reliable institution for advancing society's interest in children. Chapter 21 examines welfare reform as an element in the redefinition of responsible motherhood, and the terms of humanitarian assistance, while chapter 22 concludes that the dichotomy between family autonomy and state intervention is a false one. State support is pervasive — and has been at least since the initial provision of public education. Instead, the more central transformation is in the nature of adolescence. While the community still interacts with small children through their parents, adolescents have emerged from the cocoon of the separate spheres — and few adolescents emerge as butterflies.

16

The Meaning of Marriage

MARRIAGE once defined family relationships. Uncertainty over its continuing role is among the most emblematic markers of family change. In the legal world, where legislatures rarely tinker with so sacrosanct an institution, the greatest challenge has been not so much to define marriage as to define what it is not. *Baehr v. Lewin*,[1] the Hawaii Supreme Court case addressing same-sex marriage, is perhaps the most influential marriage case in a generation, and crafting the basis for Hawaii's refusal to recognize same-sex unions has proved a more difficult task than articulating the grounds for opposition.

Figure 16.1

Shortly after the Hawaii Supreme Court decided *Baehr*, the Markkula Center for Applied Ethics at Santa Clara University assembled a panel to discuss the developments. There, Professor Peter Kwan explained that, before the Hawaii decision, there were two types of legal challenges to a state's refusal to acknowledge same-sex marriage. The first, based on the Constitution's due process clause, recognized marriage as a fundamental right. The landmark case of *Loving v. Virginia*, which in 1967 had struck down antimiscegenation laws barring marriage between blacks and whites, had recognized the freedom to marry as "one of the vital personal rights essential to the orderly pursuit of happiness by free men."[2] This fundamental right for many, however, had not prevented subsequent cases from defining marriage as "a union of man and woman, uniquely involving the procreation and rearing of children."[3] If marriage, by definition, only applied to heterosexual unions, the refusal to recognize same-sex relationships could not be said to deny gays and lesbians a fundamental right. The second challenge, grounded in equal protection principles, alleged that the ban on same-sex marriage constituted discrimination on the basis of sexual orientation. The Supreme Court's 1986 decision in *Bowers v. Hardwick*, however, which held that there is no constitutionally protected right to engage in sodomy and that homosexuals are not a constitutionally protected suspect class, had made litigation on these grounds futile.[4]

Legal developments had been so unpromising that when a gay male couple[5] sought to challenge Hawaii's refusal to recognize same-sex marriages, they initially had trouble securing counsel. Gay rights organizations considered the case hopeless and worried that a challenge might create more bad law for their cause. The couple finally enlisted Dan Foley, an environmental attorney without experience in gay and lesbian litigation, to represent them, and Foley based his legal challenge on a modified due process argument that legal experts at the time did not think would be enough to overcome the hostile precedents. The Hawaii court in *Baehr*, however, executed an end run around the earlier cases. First, since it based its reasoning on Hawaii's state constitution, the highest court to hear the case would be the Hawaii Supreme Court, insulating the case from review by the more conservative Supreme Court of the United States. Second, even though Foley had raised only a due process challenge, the State of Hawaii's counsel, in an offhand remark, had insisted that "of course," this wasn't a sex discrimination case, and the court seized on the suggestion. The Hawaii Constitution, unlike the federal one, expressly banned sex discrimination, and the *Baehr* court held that the refusal to recognize same-sex marriage may therefore be unconstitutional.[6] If a man and a woman each seek to marry a woman, the court reasoned, only the man may do so, the woman may not, and thus the result turns on a sex-based classification. Such classifications, Kwan explained to the Markkula Center audience, are subject to the strictest scrutiny and violate the Hawaii Constitution unless the State can show that "(a) the statute's sex-based classification is justified by compelling state interests, and (b) the statute is narrowly drawn to avoid abridgements of the applicant couples' constitutional rights."[7] The adverse precedents in other states did not apply to *Baehr*'s *sex* discrimination claim, and the Hawaii Supreme Court remanded the case to the trial court to determine whether the state could demonstrate a compelling interest in banning same-sex marriages.

The second panelist was Lee FitzGerald. FitzGerald is a Santa Clara graduate. Each year, for the previous thirteen years, Santa Clara religious studies professor Fred Parrella had invited him to speak to his class on the "Theology of Marriage." FitzGerald echoed the equal protection concerns of the Hawaii court. He described his long-standing relationship with another man, their prosaic middle-class existence, and the contract they had drawn up to govern their relationship because they could not marry. They were responsible citizens. They paid their taxes. They ordered their lives and their relationship in accordance with society's norms in all respects but their choice of a mate. Why, Fitzgerald asked, echoing the claims of the plaintiffs in *Baehr v. Lewin*, were they denied the right to marry?

Parrella himself was the last to speak. His views were the least known to the audience, and the room quieted in anticipation as he began to speak. He was the oldest of the panelists, a professor of religious studies at a Catholic institution who planned to address same-sex marriage within the Christian tradition. What would he say? Parrella began with a theological perspective on marriage. Acknowledging that defining marriage is "an elusive enterprise" even for the married, he proposed that

> Marriage is an unconditional, lifelong commitment between two persons who promise to share all of life and love, home and hearth, body and soul; marriage necessarily involves the fullest of communciation, the deepest of understanding, and the strongest of personal loyalty and trust between two people.[8]

Parrella noted that, as a theological matter, marriage is not just a relationship between two people, but it is part of a search for meaning, a longing for intimacy and fulfillment in others as well as themselves. Within the Catholic tradition, marriage has moved (along lines Regan might approve) from a legal contract to a personal covenant before God; it is rooted, in the words of the Second Vatican counsel, in "the conjugal covenant of irrevocable personal consent." Moreover, while the Catholic Church once saw procreation as marriage's primary purpose, companionship has now joined reproduction as a central purpose of the enterprise, with the partners to "render mutual help and service to each other through an intimate union of their persons and actions."[9] With this understanding of marriage, Parrella queried, "What in the ideal order would prevent all of this from being said about two persons of the same sex in the same way these words can be spoken about a man and a woman?"

At the end of the presentation, a member of the audience asked with genuine mystification, "What is the objection to same-sex marriage?" Theologically, Parrella noted, there are three bases for objection. First, some fundamentalist groups rely on an appeal to authority: the Bible, read literally, forbids sodomy and some religions allow no further discussion. Second, many groups appeal to tradition: it is unnatural and therefore immoral, it has historically been prohibited. Third, Roman Catholic teaching provides that "in God's plan, sexual activity must always be open to . . . procreation as well as the creation of unity between two people." Homosexual intimacy, like intercourse with the use of artificial contraception, thus violates natural law.[10]

While the appeal to religious authority and tradition remains persuasive to many, the Santa Clara faculty audience found it an uncomfortable basis for public policy, and even many theologians have registered doubt about the continuing importance of procreation as a defining element of marriage. Catholic theologian and natural law scholar John Finnis is a notable exception. He argues that the dual purposes of marriage, the unitive goal of communion and companionship, on the one hand, and procreation, on the other, are not two separate objectives, but common elements of a single goal.[11] Although Finnis's natural law reasoning sometimes influences secular thought (and, indeed, as a philosopher Finnis has contributed to a natural law revival that goes beyond Catholic theological circles), it is hard to translate Finnis's objections to same-sex marriage into persuasive secular arguments. Finnis's reasoning reflects a way of thinking appropriate to an era in which most couples wanted children, their own sexual activity was the only practical way to obtain them, and fertility was a mysterious matter no secular authority could explain. It is harder to apply in an era of artificial conception and assisted reproduction, even without widespread acceptance of nonmarital sexuality. One suspects that if, in some brave new world, procreation could occur only in a test tube, the logical extension of this reasoning would be that sex was inappropriate altogether. Without appeal to theological fiat, it is difficult to insist on the continuing validity of the link between marriage and procreation.

Hawaii, in deciding what state interests to assert in the trial court, faced a similar challenge without the possibility of recourse to biblical authority and with considerable discomfort about a resort to natural law reasoning. The State's struggle to identify alternative grounds tells us much about the uncertain state of contemporary marriage. In its initial pleadings, Hawaii identified five state interests in opposing same-sex marriage:

(a) protecting the health and welfare of children and other[s] . . . ;

(b) fostering procreation within a marital setting . . . ;

(c) securing or assuring recognition of Hawaii marriages in other jurisdictions;

(d) protecting the State's public fisc from the reasonably foreseeable effects of State approval of same-sex marriage;

(e) protecting civil liberties.[12]

The State did not mention sex directly, and by trial the lawyers representing the State had abandoned all but the interest in fostering procreation in a marital setting. They lost handily.

The arguments the State presented to the trial court satisfied no one, and law professor Samuel Marcosson argues that this result was inevitable because the connection between the interests of children and the ban on same-sex marriage was "attenuated at best and non-existent at worst," and failed to present the real basis for objection: "the core belief that there is something intrinsically wrong with homosexuality, homosexual conduct, and homosexual relationships."[13] At an earlier stage in the case, Hawaii had identified public morality as an additional state interest in opposing same-sex marriage. Marcosson believes that the State abandoned the morality claim because to have presented it would have bolstered the charge that antigay animus was the motivating factor in the State's refusal to sanction same-sex marriage.

Marcosson is almost certainly right that a refusal to equate homosexuality and heterosexuality is central to any coherent ban on same-sex marriage. Eskridge, in his defense of same-sex unions, argues that homosocial relationships, including marriage-like partnerships, have been common throughout history. It is modern Western culture, he argues, that "is peculiarly hostile to same-sex unions," and he traces that hostility to the thirteenth century. "It was then," he writes, "that many secular governments enacted laws prohibiting 'crimes against nature' and that prior ecclesiastical laws came to be more stringently enforced."[14] Eskridge notes that Europe after 1200 became increasingly persecutory toward any kind of behavior that transgressed established gender lines, including independent behavior by women. But, of course, the era he is describing, historians' "early modern" era in Western Europe, is the era in which "no one was ever alone," nonmarital pregnancy was rare, relatively large portions of the population married late or not at all, and within marriage, the idea that sexual intercourse was legitimate only so long as it led to procreation was so deeply embedded that contraception was unthinkable. The opposition to same-sex marriage that Eskridge documents begins in at a time of deep-seated hostility toward sex of all kinds, with sex within marriage for the purpose of procreation the only exception.[15]

The more intriguing question then becomes why the hostility lasted beyond the eighteenth- and nineteenth-century's embrace of companionate marriage. The answer seems to be that the new era (Shorter's "modern" and Regan's "Victorian" one) tried to elevate conjugal love as an exception to the more general hostility toward sexuality rather than overthrowing the earlier constraints altogether. Maura Strassberg, in an effort to distinguish the objections to same-sex marriage from those to polygamy, has taken a fresh look at earlier theorists who strove to define the role of marriage in their day.[16] She starts with Franáois Lieber, whose *Manual of Political Ethics* influenced the U.S. Supreme Court's nineteenth-century pronouncements on marriage,[17] but the chronological account begins with Immanuel Kant. Kant's *Philosophy of Law* rests on the principle that no human being should be used as the means to satisfy another's desires. For sexual relations to satisfy the fundamental test of respect for persons, therefore, it is essential "that as one Person is acquired by another as a *res*, that same Person equally acquires the other reciprocally." This can only happen through marriage, which Kant characterized as a contract between two people for "lifelong possession of their sexual faculties."[18] Kant's version of the marital contract differed from earlier ones in that it proceeded from the consent of bride and groom, rather than from the negotiations of their parents, and it distinguished monogamous relationships from polygamous ones on the grounds that the latter did not involve an *equal* exchange. Nonetheless, sexual relations were permissible within the Kantian regime only within marriage, that is, only within a monogamous, lifetime union that elevated sexuality into something more than the satisfaction of physical desire.

Georg Hegel nonetheless found Kant's contractual notion of marriage "shameful." To the extent marriage is a contract, Hegel wrote, "it is a contract to transcend the standpoint of contract." For Hegel, marriage involves "a union on the level of the mind" in which the lovers achieve dissolution of individuality through unity with the beloved. This union involves not just an exchange between the spouses, but a public ceremony which through "the solemn declaration by the parties of their consent to enter the ethical bond of marriage, and its corresponding recognition and confirmation by their family and community" elevates marriage to a socioethical duty. While Hegel did not see procreation as the primary purpose of marriage in the sense in which it had been in earlier eras, he viewed children within a marital family as the objective embodiment of the unity of marriage, and monogamous, lifelong marriage in turn as essential to the proper rearing of children. Hegel carefully distinguished the institution of marriage, with its commitment to family and community, from "mutual caprice" and the "sensuous moment." Hegel like Kant used a revitalized definition of marriage to distinguish marital sexuality from sexuality's baser — and forbidden — forms, and he did so at a time when sexual attraction was becoming more central to notions of conjugal bliss.

François Lieber, Hegel's student at the University of Berlin in the early part of the nineteenth century, incorporated these ideals into a *Manual of Political Ethics*. In it, Lieber argued that only the family created by monogamous marriage allows human beings to reach their highest development. Strassberg explains that

> Monogamy accomplishes this by reinforcing romantic love, rather than sex, as the tie between the spouses. This in turn makes possible marriage as a permanent and exclusive union of different sexes. While Lieber recognized that sexual attraction arising out of the distinctively different nature of women might be the wellspring of family, he insisted that the family as a human, rather than animal, institution does not rest on mere sexual desire or the possibility of procreation. Monogamous relationships structured by reverence and romantic love encourage sexual continuance, which grounds family life on a long-standing, unselfish interest in another person. Conversely, when sexual relations are possible outside the monogamous family, sexuality itself becomes more emphasized. The selfishness which accompanies such a focus on sexuality invades the family and leads, in Lieber's view, to a weakening or destruction of parental interest in children's education and moral character, and to the reduction of women to sexual objects.[19]

Lieber linked these ideals not just to the idea of romantic love but to the specialized division of marital obligations. Strassberg continues: "By making women the distinctively different object of love and reverence, the modern institution of monogamous marriage creates a protected legal space within which women can devote themselves to the emotional support of husbands and children, thus making it possible for women to fulfill their highest potential as wives and mothers."[20] Like Hegel, Lieber then connected the family, as an institution built on lifelong exchange and a sexual division of labor, to its distinctive role in rearing children suitable to serve as citizens of a democracy.

Strassberg, in her embrace of same-sex marriage as consistent with Hegel and Lieber's ideal, attempts to separate the idea of unity and transcendence from procreation and a sexual division of labor. In the process, she articulates not just a justification for recognizing same-sex unions as marital, but a new marital ideal. She begins by noting that a major barrier to modern use of Hegelian theory is Hegel's "sexism," and the fact that his theory premises the "transcendent unity of monogamous love" on a radical distinction between men and women, in which women are viewed "arriving at a rather concrete and passive personhood through intuition and feeling, while men achieve a more universal personhood through conceptual thought." She even quotes Hegel as suggesting that "[t]he difference between men and women is like the difference between animals and plants. Men correspond to animals, while women correspond to plants." (at 1547; citations omitted). Strassberg nonetheless maintains that if "Hegel was wrong and social differentiation can be replicated in modern society by individuals taking on a number of different roles, then we can acknowledge Hegel's insight simply by insisting that the role of marital partner and parent be a valued and protected role in our society and that the unique ethics of the family be acknowledged" (1553). She argues further that not only are contemporary heterosexual unions compatible with this reformed ideal, but so too are same-sex relationships. She does so by emphasizing the two components she deems indispensable to the contemporary institution of marriage: (1) "romantic love and non-procreative sex" as important "expressions of personal individuality and as forces which break down barriers of independent individuality and establish a concrete unity of partners,"[21] and (2) civil recognition because it strengthens the legal and social connection between individuals, reconciles them to the apparent loss of personal liberty which social existence requires, and provides "a coherent point of social unification (through the commonality of the experience and the status of married persons) which counters the socially disintegrating effects of fully developed individuality" (1611–12). She embraces Regan's view of the role of marriage in the postmodern world and quotes him to the effect that "the legal status of being married fosters intimate commitment by limiting the vulnerability arising out of relationships that 'help shape personal identity.'"[22]

Regan, who argues that same-sex marriage is compatible with the "moral aspiration" of marriage as "responsibility based on the cultivation of a relational sense of identity," Strassberg, with her appeal to a Hegelian sense of transcendence, and Eskridge, who subtitles his book "from sexual liberty to civilized commitment," are ultimately in agreement. Same-sex marriage should be legally available because the marriage that would be recognized is not your father's (or perhaps more importantly) your mother's marriage. The new marital ideal would retain the ideal of transcendent unity, but not the notion of radically different and complementary partners. It would recognize the role of status relationships that regularize intimate unions and connect them to others while rejecting those based on gender and inequality. Finally, the new ideal would embrace the importance of commitment, fidelity, and sexual restraint without insistence on the missionary position or condemnation of those who choose not to marry. Eskridge argues that recognizing "same-sex marriages would contribute to the integration of gay lives and the larger culture, to a nonlegal form of civilizing gays. Marriage would contribute to this integration because same-sex marriage couples would be able to participate openly in this long-standing cultural institution. . . . Same-sex marriage would also civilize America. . . . This country would be edified — civilized, if you will — if it would end all vestiges of legal discrimination against its homosexual population. Essential to this project is the adoption of laws guaranteeing equal rights for lesbian and gay couples."[23] Essential to this project as well is the final separation of marriage, sex, and procreation as bearing any necessary legal relationship to each other.

These arguments, while they make the case for the continuing importance of marriage for adult partnerships, fail to address the full implications for the relationship between marriage and the state. When Hegel, distinguishing marriage from contract, emphasized the importance of a public ceremony, he did so to underscore the exchange of marital promises not just between the couple but between the couple and their respective families and communities. This exchange — and the community's very real stake in marriage as an institution — rested on the celebration of conjugal love to the exclusion of other forms of sexuality, the role of the marriage as not only the ideal but the only acceptable locus for childrearing, and the vulnerability of women because of the possibility of pregnancy and their role within the separate spheres. Civil marriage, to promote these state interests, involved a covenant with the community (and religious marriage a covenant with God) which the parties could not end or change on their own.

Given the significance of the state interest in marriage, public regulation of the institution was extensive. A central tenet of that regulation was insistence on the permanence of the relationship. During the early modern period, marriage had, in both religious and civil systems, been indissoluble. Fault arose (and really took hold during the Victorian era of companionate marriages) as a way to free an innocent spouse from the bonds of a union that had already ended through the actions of the other spouse. Fault-based divorce, to justify the dissolution of the bond with the community, had required the party seeking the divorce to show not only that the other spouse had breached his marital commitments, but that she was innocent of any wrongdoing. If both parties were equally responsible for the dissolution of their union, neither was entitled to a divorce even if neither party objected to the divorce. No-fault reforms passed in the 1960s and 1970s (and overdue for at least half a century) swept away this older body of the law without replacing it with a coherent alternative view of marriage.

The law in most states today allows either party to terminate the relationship at will. Some states — California the most notable among them — preclude any consideration of the reasons for the divorce, and impose only the most minimal of delays on divorcing couples. Other states have retained fault grounds for divorce on their books, but rarely use them to frustrate a party intent on ending a marriage or to provide a basis for a radically different distribution of marital assets from the one that would occur if the two parties were equally responsible for the divorce. The state has, for all practical purposes, withdrawn from the regulation of marriage. Mary Ann Glendon observes that "the traditionally central position of legal marriage in family has been extensively eroded everywhere," and Regan speculates that "high rates of divorce may indicate not so much a rejection of marriage as the fact that individuals' expectations of marriage are so high that they will not settle for anything less than the perceived ideal.[24] To the extent that marriage continues to foster transcendental unity, it is much like the transcendence associated with religion: the state permits it, encourages it, and (many argue) benefits from it, but maintains a clear distance. With marriage no longer serving to police sexuality, to link biological parents to their children, or to insure women lifelong protection within a defined relationship, modern law, in accordance with no-fault divorce principles, accords less legal protection to spousal relations than to contractual ones.

In Hawaii, the state ultimately asserted a single interest in opposing same-sex marriage: "fostering procreation in a marital setting." The evidence the state presented at trial focused overwhelmingly on the well-being of children who would be raised by gay and lesbian couples. Dr. Kyle Pruett testified that "biological parents have a predisposition which helps them in parenting children" and that "same-sex relationships do not provide the same type of learning model . . . because there is an overabundance of one gender and little information about the other gender."[25] Even the state's own witnesses, however, had no trouble concluding that gays and lesbians could be fit parents and that the influence of the parents' sexual orientation mattered little, if it mattered at all, compared to other factors affecting children's development. When it came time to rule, the trial court unequivocally declared: "The sexual orientation of parents is not in and of itself an indicator of the overall adjustment and development of children" and that the state therefore "failed to establish a causal link between allowing same-sex marriage and adverse effects on the development of children."[26] The question the court did not address was whether there continued to be a causal connection between the regulation of the relationship between parents in any form and the protection of children's interests.

Figure 16.2

17

Partnership Revisited

IN 1843, Sarah Burr sought a divorce a mensa et thoro, that is, a legal separation that was the only type of divorce then permissible in New York. Although the judicial record does not suggest that Mr. Burr was related to the infamous Aaron, Mrs. Burr's father's family, we are told, occupied the highest ranks in Connecticut society and the lower court had awarded her the extraordinary sum of $10,000 per year in alimony — more than the combined salaries of the chancellor, the secretary of state, the attorney general, and the comptroller. Mr. Burr appealed. The high court in New York consisted at that time of a chief justice and several members of the New York State Senate, all of whom issued individual opinions in the case. Senator Strong began with a recitation of the events leading to the separation:

> Perhaps no case has been presented to a court — certainly none is recorded — exhibiting greater inhumanity on the part of a husband towards his wife. Nurtured and reared in affluence, of a family of the highest respectability, mingling from her youth with a refined, educated and polished society, possessing talents of a superior order, accomplished, amiable, and beloved, in an evil hour she forsook the endearments of her home, and gave her hand to him who has since embittered every moment of her existence. . . . For thirty-five years, she was a meek and silent sufferer under the daily and death-dealing inflictions of one who had sworn at the altar of God to love, cherish and protect her. Almost within a month from the consecration of their nuptials, she exhibited the marks and ravages of a loathsome and noxious disease, the seeds of which he had already implanted in her system, there to germinate and grow till their deadly influence should prostrate her physical powers or

the grave should claim its weakened and premature victim. A common and sickly offspring for a few years of miserable existence bore about them the evidences alike of their own wretchedness and their father's shame and then went down to an early tomb. But it was not enough that the uncomplaining wife had been murderously visited with the plague-spots of her husband's leprosy. He must treat her with studied and malicious coldness, indifference and neglect, and at times with personal violence; address her in harsh, opprobrious, and abusive language; deprive her of necessary comforts and remedies in sickness, and in her ordinary health compel her servile and unworthy employments; coercing her at times to clean his self-defiled person — a work unfit to be required of the veriest menial, and proper only for himself. . . . During the whole period, and under the all provocations, Mrs. Burr conducted herself as a mild, respectful, affectionate, submissive and devoted wife. On no occasion did she resist the authority of her tyrannical lord, or seek to irritate his morose or excited temper. . . . She bore his profligacy, his intemperance, his neglect, his coldness, his cruelty, his brutality, until, prostrated by bodily disease and overwhelmed by mental anguish, she could bear with them no longer, and was forced to final separation. And then not until deprived of every other resource, and driven to the verge of starvation, did she venture to enter the courts of justice and spread her sorrows before the world.[1]

Perhaps unsurprisingly, the court voted seventeen to five to affirm the award. Nonetheless, alimony of this magnitude compelled discussion of the grounds for relief: was Mrs. Burr entitled only to a sum providing for her reasonable support or was she entitled to share in the wealth made possible by the Burr estate? In addressing the matter, there was never an issue of ownership of the Burr assets. The court characterized the half-million-dollar estate at issue in the case as "his," without much discussion of its origins or of Mrs. Burr's contributions to it. The only property that was "hers" was the $7,000 in separate property that she brought to the marriage, and which Mr. Burr got to keep as part of the legal separation. While one senator questioned the equity of the result, he quickly dismissed the thought, observing that

Marriage transfers title from the wife to the husband in absolute property, all the personal estate of which she is possessed at the time of the marriage, or which the husband reduced to possession during the coveture. . . . The law places the wife under the care, protection, and I may say, not the despotic, but the reasonable authority of the husband. If she had the right of claiming the restoration of property in cases of separation, she might be rendered too independent for domestic peace; more so than the law intended she should be.[2]

With Mr. Burr's ownership of the estate unchallenged, the issue in the appeal then became whether the alimony award, given its size, constituted a surreptitious liquidation of the estate. A dissenting senator emphasized that since Mrs. Burr was "a worthy, respectable and reasonable woman, there is no state or condition of the human mind, short of insanity, which can admit the belief that she either will or can desire to expend the sum of ten thousand dollars a year for her personal support or maintenance." The senator continued: "At her age it would be unsuitable, even ludicrous, to lavish the revenues of a principality in the adornment of her person, and she will not require to be fed like the profligate Egyptian courtezan with pearls dissolved in acid."[3]

In response, the majority agreed that an award of this size could not, in the court's words, be characterized as "pin money." Rather, Senator Strong justified the amount by a comparison with dower, that is, the law's provision for a wife to receive a one-third life interest in her husband's property at his death. Senator Strong asked rhetorically:

On what principle is the wife's dower allowed? Why should she not be restricted, where the property is large, to a comfortable maintenance and support? Why should she receive the income of one third of a vast and productive landed estate, towards the acquisition of which she may have contributed nothing?

He then replied:

The answer is obvious. Whatever increases his fortune is regarded by the law of civilized life as adding also to her prosperity. If he becomes rich, she is not to continue poor. . . . If a great abundance of wealth is thought so desirable by the husband that he has devoted a life of toil and perplexity to its accumulation, a just and fair proportion of it . . . [i]s supposed to be equally desirable and necessary for her, who has traveled with him for a long period in the same path of acquisition, whose mind has been bent and moulded constantly and for years towards the same

objects of pursuit which have engrossed his thoughts and invited his energies, and whose domestic economy, directed to the same purposes, has
been, if not the starting point, at least a leading auxiliary of his success.

(215–16)

The Burr case was decided at the dawn of the Victorian family. New York
did not yet permit final dissolution of marriage; it had not yet recognized a
married woman's separate property as her own; the husband's authority over
his household was still unquestioned. Yet the court recognized a conception
of partnership that would lay a basis for a more egalitarian approach to the
family in the years ahead. In the 1990s, this partnership ideal is under assault just as it is achieving its fullest realization.

In 1998, defining the nature of the marital partnership is as much an issue
as it had been in 1843. The intervening years — and the adoption of no-
fault divorce — have both strengthened the position of women and undermined the partnership understanding on which the Burr case rested. This
time Lorna Wendt, Connecticut housewife and divorcing corporate spouse,
raised the issue. Her executive husband, Gary, had asked for a divorce after
thirty-two years of marriage. She rejected the $10 million settlement he
proposed, insisting on half of the couple's total assets as a matter of principle. "You enter into this relationship as equal partners, 50–50," says Mrs.
Wendt. "To get out, it's still 50–50. All of the dinners I cooked, the clothes
I washed, the love and support I gave the children, are of equal value to the
paycheck."[4]

By 1998 the courts had moved a long way from the family law jurisprudence of the nineteenth century. Mrs. Wendt sought ownership of half the
estate, not a maintenance award that would leave management and control
in male hands. Connecticut law gave the court "equitable discretion," and
Mr. Wendt, conceding that divorce required division of the assets the couple had accumulated during the marriage, focused his disagreement on val-
uation and the treatment of future income. Nonetheless, the partnership
model Mrs. Wendt invoked was rooted in cases in which the couple's assets
paled in comparison with their needs. As in the Burr divorce, the Wendts'
wealth and the size of the award, because they underscored the distinctions
between need and entitlement, compensation and ownership, forced the
Connecticut court to address the very nature of their relationship.

In an opinion exceeding five hundred pages, the court began with a
recital of facts. There was none of the abuse that characterized the Burr case

and little discussion of the reasons for the divorce or assessment of the parties' moral character. Instead, the court describes the Wendts as a midwestern couple, who met as high school sweethearts, married upon Lorna's college graduation, and raised two children in accordance with a conventional and gendered division of responsibilities. Mrs. Wendt quit her job as a public school music teacher shortly before the birth of her first child; Mr. Wendt enjoyed a successful career as chairman, president, and chief executive officer of GE Capital Services, Inc., the largest division of General Electric Corporation, one of the largest companies in the world. The court summarized Mrs. Wendt's contributions as follows:

> She was an excellent representative of motherhood, very organized, a very good cook and a piano teacher for years. She did house cleaning, and "she even did windows." She paid the household bills, arranged for auto repairs and maintenance. She was a good role model for the children. Her duties included clothing, feeding, driving, music, school, conferences, church activities, clubs, lessons, kids' concerts and recitals, after school activities, car pools, doctors, being present in the house regularly, housecleaning, grocery shopping, kids' needs, kids' questions, games and school homework. She was extremely hospitable and social. . . . She related to men and women alike and was a cheerleader on a number of GE trips. She was extremely neat. The children were neat, their clothes had no stains and the house was immaculate. She ironed her husband's shirts, raised two children, entertained, sewed clothing, took the children to the doctor, attended Girl Scouts, went to school events, saw children's friends, used organizations skills and polished social skills. Guests were made to feel welcome in her house. She was a good cook. . . . She covered for her husband, i.e., gave reasons why her husband was not present at certain social events.[5]

The court also summarized Mr. Wendt's business skills, describing him as a "deal-maker" whose creation of leveraged buyouts was the seminal event in the industry. Colleagues characterized him as a "visionary" who exceeded the bounds of leadership, and accounted for an exceptional and consistent average annual growth rate of 20 percent per year over a ten-year period for his company. Moreover, he attended church, contributed to the community, changed his children's diapers, and went to their school recitals. The difficult issue for the court was how to balance the combination of contribution and need called for in the equitable distribution statute.

The trial court ultimately awarded Mrs. Wendt $20 million, less than the amount she initially claimed, but considerably more than the settlement Mr. Wendt had proposed.[6] Both parties have appealed, and the courts' discussion demonstrates the confusion that still attends marital dissolution. The Wendt court, in a fashion not unlike the Burr court, began by rejecting what Mrs. Wendt termed the "enough is enough" doctrine. Connecticut law professor Mary Moers Wenig had observed that, in informal surveys of marital distributions in the state, "the more there is, the smaller the percentage the non-propertied spouse receives."[7] Mrs. Wendt's attorney described the doctrine as an unstated policy that "with the award of x amount in alimony and property, any wife can support herself in the lifestyle to which she is accustomed, and, therefore, she 'needs' no further money." "Enough is enough" usually means, according to the court, that "the lion's share of the assets, usually in excess of eight figures, is awarded to the male corporate executive."[8] This position, like that of the dissenting senator in Burr, turns on the argument that assets accumulated during marriage belong to the wage earner, and the other spouse is entitled solely to enough for her support. Mrs. Wendt could easily enjoy the lifestyle to which she had become accustomed with considerably less than $20 million.

The trial court nonetheless coupled its rejection of "enough is enough" with rejection of the partnership theory Mrs. Wendt had advanced. In 1994 the Mississippi high court had described the marital partnership ideal:

> The wife contributed her share by rocking the cradle, keeping the house, and caring for the children. Although the husband was bringing in the income, still marriage is pretty much a 50/50 partnership as to property acquired during the marriage regardless of the role played by the parties. . . . We assume for divorce purposes that the contribution and efforts of the marital partners, whether economic, domestic or otherwise are of equal value.[9]

Many states, whether under a community property theory or Mississippi's common law partnership model, start with a presumption that marital assets should be divided equally. This partnership model equates domestic and financial contributions, but its primary motive is pragmatic. In most marriages, the couple's assets — typically, at best, a house, a car, and bank accounts that do not quite cover liabilities — are not substantial enough to justify the complicated and expensive inquiry that would be necessary to disentangle the couple's individual shares, and, even if the courts were eager to undertake the inquiry, there is no consensus on how to value their respective contributions. The two simplest "bright lines" rules therefore are deference to title (the name on the deed or the bank account) and equal division. In the modern era, equal division has won out. In the case Mrs. Wendt cited, Mississippi became the last common law jurisdiction to abandon reliance on common law title and the resulting award of the bulk of the property to the primary wage earner.[10]

Connecticut, however, the trial court ruled, had eschewed bright line rules altogether. State legislation required an individualized determination that balanced contribution and need. While the court need not detail its findings, it had to compare the parties' respective martial responsibilities. The result was a rambling five-hundred-page opinion (and legal fees that would dwarf the entire estate of a more typical divorce) that was most articulate in describing the grounds it rejected.

The Burr case is a model of clarity in comparison. In Senator Strong's opinion, with its emphasis on sharing and contribution, lifelong commitment was a defining feature of marriage. In marrying Mr. Burr, Mrs. Burr's primary loss was her opportunity to have arranged a better match. Absent marriage or inheritance, women were not expected to be self-supporting, much less amass a half-million-dollar estate on their own. Mrs. Burr expected to share in Mr. Burr's estate, not because her contributions necessarily equaled his but because their exchange was for life. It was his barbarity that drove her from the marriage, and his misconduct that guaranteed her an award equivalent to the dower right she would hold at his death.

In the Wendt case, the very idea of partnership is limited to the period in which the couple voluntarily remained together. Although Mr. Wendt initiated the divorce, the court did not inquire into the reasons for the dissolution, nor base any part of the financial award on the parties' relative culpability. When the court then rejected a presumption of equality in favor of proof of contribution, it had difficulty comparing incommensurable activities — and no basis on which to conclude that the contributions were equal. The court observed that Mrs. Wendt had "puffed up her contributions to GE," and noted that plaintiff's expert could not point to any testimony that "would lead her to believe that 'the defendant would not have been successful but for the plaintiff.'"[11] It rejected the $2 million tag Mrs. Wendt's experts placed on the services she provided over thirty-one years as the wrong standard of comparison, and dismissed as speculative the value of the career as a music teacher (and perhaps opera star) that she had given up to care for the children. While the court acknowledged Mrs. Wendt's unquantifiable (but still significant) contributions to her husband's career, and her uncontested right to continue to enjoy a standard of living commensurate with that of the marriage, it ruled that, taken together, these considerations did not justify an equal division of the couple's estate. The court then, without much further explanation except to valuation, awarded her almost half of the estate.

There are many ironies in this decision. The most immediate is that even as Mrs. Wendt lost the principle of equal division, she received an award that set precedent in Connecticut and sent concern through many a corporate boardroom. The most pervasive irony may be the fact that the developments that have strengthened women's positions in other ways — increased earning capacity, greater ability to exit from unhappy marriages, recognition of domestic contributions — undercut Mrs. Wendt's 50 percent claim here. The final irony is that the court, which relied heavily on Colorado law professor Ann Estin's scholarship, ignored what is perhaps her most salient contribution — recognition that existing law, which casts caretaking responsibilities as the most significant interest in need of protection at divorce, systematically fails to provide for them.

Estin drives home her point by comparing young parents with long-term homemakers. Suppose the Wendts had filed for divorce after ten years of marriage instead of thirty. They would have had two children, ages six and three. Mrs. Wendt would have last worked outside the home seven years before the divorce, and Mr. Wendt would have just accepted a new and still uncertain job at GE. Their assets, compared to the eight-figure estate they enjoyed twenty years later, would have been modest. Mrs. Wendt's claim to half — or more — of the house, the car, and the bank accounts that probably did not quite cover liabilities would be stronger than it was to the much larger estate the court divided in the 1990s.[12] But whereas in 1998 Mr. Wendt volunteered to pay Mrs. Wendt $250,000 a year in maintenance on top of the property settlement he offered, she is likely to have received short-term support in the mid-1970s, if she received alimony at all.

If the parties had divorced in 1975, the major assets of the marriage would have been the children, and Mr. Wendt's career. With marriage a partnership terminable at will, few jurisdictions would grant Mrs. Wendt a property interest in her husband's as-yet-unrealized earnings, much less a claim to almost 50 percent of his income potential, even though her sacrifices contributed to his ability to get the GE job as much, if not more, than they did to his later success.[13] Her strongest claim to a substantial settlement (including support) would therefore be either (a) the lost earning capacity she had suffered because of her caretaking responsibilities during the marriage and/or (b) the continuing impact of her caregiving responsibilities should she receive custody after the divorce. Neither would approach $20 million.

Estin notes with continuing irony that while the courts are quite willing to recognize the contributions of longtime homemakers like Lorna Wendt, they are much less willing to provide support for younger women who divorce in the midst of their caretaking responsibilities. Estin cites, for example, what she terms the "punchy and quotable" case of In re Marriage of Brantner to the effect that "[t]he new Family Law Act . . . may not be used as a handy vehicle for the summary disposal of old and used wives. A woman is not a breeding cow to be nurtured during her years of fecundity, then conveniently and economically converted to cheap steaks when past her prime."[14] She then contrasts the availability of support in cases of ongoing care and concludes that "maintenance awarded to facilitate the care of children is unusual. In the more than twenty states that have statutes incorporating caregiver maintenance provisions, the record of appellate court decisions indicates that only in a few jurisdictions do courts regularly apply a policy favoring caregiver support. In most states, the self-reliance norms now override the policies of caregiving."[15] In most states, had the Wendts divorced after ten years of marriage, Mrs. Wendt would have received half of the quite small marital estate, a few years of transitional support, and then been on her own while Mr. Wendt went on to earn "his" millions. Had Mrs. Burr, in contrast, had grounds to leave her husband at a comparable point in their marriage with sickly young children in tow, she is likely to have received a support award that lasted until death or remarriage.

There are, I suspect, two reasons for what Estin regards as incongruous results. The first is practical. Intimate partnerships involve, as Mitt Regan acknowledges, greater commitments than the law may be willing to recognize. When the parties live up to these commitments, the law honors the results; when the parties renege, the law may be unwilling to impose lifelong consequences. After all, long-term divorces are more likely to involve older men trading in their wives for a new model; Mr. Wendt remarried within months of the district court ruling to a woman he met during the year he requested the divorce.[16] Mrs. Wendt's award acknowledged contributions that had peaked during the children's minority and were largely complete by the time of the divorce. In short-term marriages, women are dramatically more likely to be the partner refusing to live with the spouse she married — and the courts appear to be more reluctant to allow them to leave with a substantial share of the marital assets. Courts honor the completed exchange, but not the executory one.

The second reason is doctrinal. With the adoption of no-fault divorce, the Uniform Marriage and Divorce Act and many state legislatures embraced the principle of the clean break. The legislation enacted a clear preference for use of the property division rather than spousal support to address need. Only in marriages with a large accumulation of assets could the courts provide compensation for the sacrifices involved in caretaking without imposing an ongoing relationship on the parties. To the extent that child care continues to restrict the caretaker's income, the UMDA preferred that it be included in the calculation of child support. The only obligation the drafters agreed should survive the divorce was the one to children.[17]

Figure 17.1

18

Child Support and the Parenthood Draft

B EFORE the Burr decision — and the subsequent rise of the Victorian family — children, like women, were seen as dependents whose well-being required male support and protection. The law recognized a paternal presumption in custody disputes, and almost no other provision for child support. Within the Victorian family and the partnership of the separate spheres, children were assigned to their mother's domestic realm and provided for legally, if at all, through the mother's dissolution award. In the 1990s, children's interests stand on their own. The courts recognize provision for children as both separate from the arrangements between the adults and independent of the justifications that govern adult relationships.

Consider the case of L. Pamela P. v. Frank S.[1] Frank S. (that is, Frank Serpico, the former New York City police officer who became famous for his accounts of police corruption) challenged a child support order on the grounds that L. Pamela P. had deliberately lied to him, telling him that she was using birth control when she knew quite well that she was not. Although L. Pamela P. denied any such conversation, the Family Court found in Frank S.'s favor and held, therefore, that instead of apportioning the child support obligation between the two parents in accordance with their means, the father's obligation would be "only in the amount by which the mother's means were insufficient to meet the child's needs."[2] In an opinion by Judge Wachtler (that is, Sol Wachtler, a once-eminent New York jurist who would later be forced to resign because of his bizarre harassment of his former paramour), the New York Court of Appeals disagreed with the Family Court. Wachtler explained that

Although at one time the objective of paternity proceedings was merely to prevent a child born out of wedlock from becoming a public charge, it is now well established that the appropriate emphasis must be upon the welfare of the child. . . . The primary purpose of establishing paternity is to ensure that adequate provision will be made for the child's needs, in accordance with the means of the parents. . . .

[I]n determining the parents' obligations to support their child, the statute mandates consideration of two factors — the needs of the child for support and education and the financial ability of the parents to contribute to that support. The statute does not require, nor, we believe, does it permit, consideration of the "fault" or wrongful conduct of one of the parents in causing the child's conception.[3]

At their core, partners' dissolution awards are contractual. They follow from the parties' agreements — express or implied — and principles of reciprocity. If Mrs. Wendt is entitled to half the marital estate, it is because the law implies an agreement to share marital fortunes and equates domestic and market contributions within marriage. If the Wendt award seems excessive, it is because of skepticism about the equality of the Wendts' particular exchange.[4] Child support, in contrast, follows neither from the parents' agreement with each other nor from the presumed equality of the exchange with their children. Child support rests to a much greater degree than spousal support on natural love and affection, and societal insistence that parents assume responsibility for the children they bring into the world. These sentiments, however, though almost universally shared, do not dictate particular dollar amounts; they do not, without considerable elaboration, support the conclusion that Frank S. should pay support determined by a percentage of his income rather than by the child's unmet needs.

Legally imposed child support starts, as Wachtler's opinion suggests, with protection of the public fisc, and the concern is an ancient one. The first Anglo-American child support legislation was the English Poor Law Act of 1576. Triggered by the combination of rising "bastardy" rates and poor relief, the act was designed to persuade young women to name the father of their children so that the scoundrel could be assessed the state's cost of raising them — unless of course he remedied the matter by marrying the mother.[5] Under these acts, the father's debt was to the state. Nonmarital children in sixteenth-century England were unlikely to remain with their mother if the father did not marry her, and she had no right to compel payment from the father if she managed them on her own. The father could contribute voluntarily, but he was legally compelled only to offset the imposition on the public fisc resulting from his immorality.[6] If the mother were to try to take him to task on her own, she — or in many eras her father — needed to pursue the tort of seduction.[7]

The first sustained effort to make unmarried fathers pay support for children in their mother's care came during the Progressive era. It is tempting to claim that these efforts mark the first true recognition of fathers' obligation to their children as well as the state, but like earlier (and later) interest in securing child support compliance, the Progressive reforms were motivated by rising divorce, nonmarital birthrates, and public welfare expenditures. By the early 1920s, every state but Alaska, Texas, and Virginia had authorized "bastardy" proceedings, often criminal in nature, that permitted mothers to initiate support actions against the fathers. Little evidence exists that the legal changes achieved the desired results: Mary Ann Mason reports that a Boston survey in 1914 indicated that only 13 percent of identifiable fathers were taken to court and only 7 percent ordered to pay anything at all — and three-fifths of nonmarital children continued to become wards of the state in the first year of their lives.[8]

Nonetheless, the turn-of-the-century reforms compelled a reexamination of child support in marriage dissolutions as well as in state welfare cases. Before the Progressive era, child support orders were virtually nonexistent. Divorce decrees provided for children, if at all, though the mother's alimony award. That order could be expected to take into account the family's food, clothing, and shelter needs without consideration of the children's expenditures separate from their mother's. If the mother received no alimony, the children were unlikely to receive support. Chancellor Kent, in what is probably the most quoted child support observation of the nineteenth century, explained in 1826 that the "obligation of parental duty is so well secured by the strength of natural affection that it seldom requires to be enforced by human laws."[9] Harry Krause provides a somewhat less benign explanation, one rooted in nineteenth-century notions of reciprocity and paternal authority:

> Choosing to rest most of his case on natural law and what we now call sociobiology, [Sir William] Blackstone[10] did not say that the support obligation he saw was founded on the reciprocal relationship of parent and child in the ongoing family, but I think it was. This reciprocity had an economic and a social component.

Economically, the support-obligated parent was entitled to the child's earnings until the child reached the age of majority. More importantly, economic reciprocity extended to the parent's old age. Support received by the young child morally and legally obligated the adult child to support the aged parent.

Socially, parent and child reciprocity involved an ongoing family life. Supporting parents had the emotional satisfaction of seeing their offspring grow up. They shaped their child's life. And their financial responsibilities were fairly minimal.[11]

Parents removed from their children's lives could hardly be expected to contribute much at all.

Progressive era courts faced the issue in a curious way. Many divorce decrees awarded the mother custody with no mention of support. When fathers then in fact contributed nothing at all, courts, invoking the new legislation, tried to hold fathers accountable, sometimes years after the decree. The fathers protested that the silent decree meant that they were off the hook. The states split on the question, with a majority rejecting the fathers' position and ruling that silence in a divorce decree did not eliminate the father's support duty.[12] California courts, however, disagreed, explaining that the minority position was not merely a procedural one: "When a parent is deprived of the custody of his child, and therefore of its services and earnings, he in no longer liable for its support and education."[13] The idea of reciprocity, as the linchpin of private obligation, died hard.[14] The notion that paternal obligation existed only in tandem with paternal authority lasted a while longer.

The modern interest in child support enforcement, like its predecessors, began with expanding AFDC rolls — and rising "bastardy" rates. Congress, frustrated by the Supreme Court's liberalization of AFDC eligibility requirements in the 1960s and 1970s, rediscovered the importance of fathers' financial contributions. By 1975, Congress had established an Office of Child Support Enforcement (now located within the Department of Health and Human Services). AFDC applicants were required to assign their rights to uncollected child support to the state, and to cooperate in establishing paternity and securing payments. To keep their AFDC funding,[15] the states established enforcement agencies operating in accordance with federal standards.[16]

Child support is nonethless likely to have remained of minor significance if it had not, a decade later, also become an issue for divorcing fathers, dads much more likely to have enough money to be worth pursuing. Where the Uniform Marriage and Divorce Act emphasized a complete break between divorcing spouses,[17] it recognized child support as the remaining obligation from the marriage. Provision for child support, unlike spousal support, was to take into account the children's impact on the custodial parent's earning capacity, and child support was presumed appropriate in all cases involving children. By 1989 the percentage of divorcing custodial parents with child support orders had increased from less than 50 to 72 percent.[18]

Despite these efforts, the real value of child support awards, controlled for inflation, dropped by 22 percent between 1979 and 1984. Over the next five years they would increase 10 percent (to $3,293 per year per child), but they were still lower in 1989 than they had been a decade earlier.[19] Garfinkel, Melli, and Robertson observe that "[l]ike Alice in Wonderland, the U.S. child support system has had to go faster just to stay in place."[20] Unmarried mothers increased from 19 percent to 30 percent of those eligible for awards over the course of the 1980s, and improved collection in some areas could not offset the increasing proportion of children in high-risk groups. While the number of unmarried mothers with child support awards increased from one in ten to nearly three in ten during the 1980s, the majority of nonmarital children received no child support at all, and for those who did the amounts remained dramatically less than they needed even though (almost all researchers have concluded) their fathers could afford to pay more.

Frank Serpico is one of the fathers in those statistics. Had the child been conceived decades earlier, Serpico would have experienced considerably more pressure (whatever the circumstances of conception) to marry the mother. If he did not, she might find it impractical to raise the child at all. Either way, the issue of child support would not arise. Indeed, even if the mother somehow managed to retain custody and sought child support under the laws on the books since the Progressive era, Serpico might still have managed to frustrate the paternity determination or evade collection of the small support amount the courts were likely to order.[21] The enforcement principle, if implemented at all, would have been limited to the standard the court rejected in 1983 — the child's relatively modest basic needs.

Through the 1980s and early 1990s, commissions and legislatures, prodded by increasingly stringent federal requirements, drafted mandatory state guidelines intended to increase child support awards.[22] No template of parental obligation existed to guide them. British author John Eekelaar argued that what a child needs is the ability to develop "its [the child's] capabilities so as to put it in the most favourable position they can reasonably achieve to realize its life-chances when it enters the adult world";[23] others argued that it was unrealistic and unfair to hold parents with otherwise limited involvement in their children's lives to such a standard.[24] The new guidelines ultimately proceeded from a more practical premise: the assumption that "need," however defined, was too nebulous to assess and that instead separated parents' contributions should match those of intact families. While each state adopted its own guidelines, all but four chose two standard methods designed to approximate the percentage of income intact couples spend on their children. The guideline drafters reasoned that (1) to do more would disproportionately place the burden of divorce on the non-custodial parent, and (2) to do less would disproportionately place that burden on the child.[25]

The cases that have most troubled the courts since have been the high- and low-end cases.[26] Indeed, in New York, the greatest deviations from the child support guidelines have been to award more where the noncustodial parent earns little, and less when he earns a great deal.[27] The high-end cases pose a challenge to the guidelines because, very much like the Burr and Wendt cases, they depart from any semblance of a relationship to the child's needs. While the courts have long recognized that wealthy children have a legitimate claim to the private schools, summer camps, and piano lessons that accompany their parents' lifestyle, no one, as Linda Elrod observes, "needs three ponies."[28] At some point, the courts fear, such awards move from the support category to a distribution of the estate. At least one court, however, faced with a case in which child support guidelines recommended an award substantially beyond the child's demonstrated needs, authorized creation of a "good fortune trust." The court reasoned that, while it might be a windfall to award the child an extra thousand dollars a month during his minority, the child was entitled to share in "the affluence of the parents," and wealthy parents typically provide postmajority assistance (college tuition comes to mind) for their children.[29] Other courts simply award less than the guidelines suggest.

In the low-end cases, two factors have been at play, both arising in ways that are deeply gendered. Where the child support guidelines provide for an award that does not, because of both parents' poverty, meet the child's basic needs — and the noncustodial parent (NCP) is male — the courts have been tempted to award more. The idea that every father has an obligation to earn enough to provide for his family is deeply ingrained. Where, however, the custodial parent can provide for the child's basic needs while the NCP can afford little — and the NCP is female — some commentators have questioned the propriety of any award.[30] The gender-neutral guidelines insist that every NCP contribute. The guideline drafters were eager to encourage all parents, whatever their circumstances, to acknowledge parental responsibility and play a role in their children's lives. Where the NCP is male, the small contribution may be his only contribution to a struggling family. Where the NCP is female, however, she is more likely to have agreed to the father's custody because of her own inability to care for the child. Noncustodial mothers are more likely than noncustodial fathers to remain in contact with their children with or without child support, and less likely to be able to contribute support that makes a difference in their children's lives.[31] For both men and women, an inflexible system may result in awards that they cannot afford to pay or hire an attorney to contest.

These new guidelines do not depart from previous practice in principle; parental obligation to children has been recognized as a matter of natural law since Blackstone. Nonetheless, the guidelines depart from centuries of practice in at least two respects: (1) the child support obligation, because it attempts to replicate the amounts intact families spend on their children, could, if fully enforced, have a greater impact on a noncustodial parent's standard of living than any sustained previous effort at enforcement; and (2) this imposition is independent of other family obligations. The historical emphasis in providing for children has been on marriage and the norms associated with it; the new guidelines allow parental obligation to trump other considerations. To date, the effects have been modest because enforcement remains sporadic, but child support collections have doubled since the Clinton administration took office in 1993, and they are likely to increase further still.

The results are most dramatic when partnership norms and parental norms are in conflict. L. Pamela P. v. Frank S., more than a decade and a half after it was decided, now looks utterly conventional; in the mid-1990s, fathers' rights groups on the Internet have been abuzz about the "babysitter" cases. The first, State ex rel. Hermesmann v. Seyer,[32] involved a teenage boy required to pay support for a child conceived in a relationship with his babysitter that began when the boy was twelve and the sitter sixteen. (He was thirteen and she seventeen by the time they conceived.) The sitter, initially charged as a juvenile with statutory rape, pleaded guilty to a reduced charge of contributing to a child's misconduct. She applied for AFDC benefits to help her care for her baby and, as a condition of receiving assistance, assigned her support rights to the state. The Kansas Department of Social and Rehabilitation Services (SRS) initiated a paternity action against Shane Seyer and sought reimbursement for the SRS support provided for Baby

Melanie. Shane argued in his defense that he was too young to have legally consented to the intercourse and he could therefore not be held responsible. The Kansas Supreme Court, like the New York high court before it, ruled that the mother's misconduct was irrelevant. Quoting a Wisconsin case, the court rejected "appellant's assertion that because he [the Wisconsin boy] was fifteen years old when he had intercourse with L.H., he was incapable of consent. . . . If voluntary intercourse results in parenthood, then for purposes of child support, the parenthood is voluntary."[33] The court concluded:

> This State's interest in requiring minor parents to support their children overrides the State's competing interest in protecting juveniles from improvident acts, even when such acts may include criminal activity on the part of the other parent. Considering the three persons directly involved, Shane, Colleen, and Melanie, the interests of Melanie are superior, as a matter of public policy, to those of either or both of her parents. This minor child, the only truly innocent party, is entitled to support from both her parents regardless of their ages.[34]

The court then went on to question the propriety of seeking a $7,000 judgment from a high school student and recorded with apparent mystification SRS's statement that it "had no intention of ever attempting to collect its judgment." On that note, the opinion ended, affirming the lower court order against Shane Seyer.[35]

The second case, *County of San Luis Obispo v. Nathaniel J.*,[36] arose in California in 1996. It is remarkable primarily for its facts. The court recited: "A 34-year-old woman seduces a 15-year-old boy and becomes pregnant. She gives birth to a daughter and thereafter applies for Aid to Families with Dependent Children. Is the child's father obligated to pay child support even though he is a victim of statutory rape? We conclude he is."[37]

These cases demonstrate the nature of the modern child support obligation. The parent's responsibilities to the child are in one sense absolute. They do not depend on marriage, or the other parent's behavior. The child cannot waive them, nor can anyone else on her behalf. At the same time, they are quite limited. The issue in all three cases was recognition of paternity, and financial support. In neither of the "babysitter cases" did the State even expect to collect. No one sought to compel the reluctant fathers to play a more active role in their children's lives (though, as Karen Czapanskiy reminds us, their right to do so would have been protected had they chosen to exercise it).[38] Instead, what these cases do is to establish the background for the ongoing negotiations between father and mother, parents and state.

In an earlier era, the "rules," as Akerloff, Yellin, and Katz demonstrated, were designed to persuade the woman to say "no," and failing that, to convince the man to marry her. Marriage was the only way for a father to vindicate his responsibility to the child and, more centrally, to the mother for what was often the understood terms of her consent. In the new era, women may engage in sex for the same reasons as men — with no promise to marry needed or implied. The state, however, still demands a guarantor. The obligation not to impose the consequences of the sexual act on the public fisc is, in these cases, subject only to the father's ability to pay, and the state's ability to make him.[39] The mother has no ability to alter the father's obligation except by staying off welfare. The child's right to share in his father's station in life is more of a default rule. One of the reasons child support collection rates in nonmarital cases are so low is that many of the mothers never seek support in the first place. Their reasons are varied. They include the father's poverty, his disappearance, fear of his reaction, and the desire to exclude him from a further role in the child's life. They may also include a

Figure 18.1 "Child support."

mother's sense that it is unfair to seek support from the father if he had no role in the decision to forgo contraception, or the one not to seek an abortion. The father's position in these cases, as Frank Serpico can attest, is the same as the woman's in an earlier era who relied on a man's unenforceable promise that he would marry her.

19

The Remaking of Fatherhood

HAMLET: I see a cherub that sees them. But, come; for England!
  Farewell, dear mother.
KING CLAUDIUS: Thy loving father, Hamlet.
HAMLET: My mother: father and mother is man and wife: man and
  wife is one flesh; and so, my mother. Come for England!

— William Shakespeare, *Hamlet* 4.3

I F parental obligation no longer depends to the same degree on marriage, what about parental prerogatives? Fatherhood — or at least the legal recognition of fatherhood — once depended almost entirely on marriage. A father who recognized his responsibility toward his children married their mother; if he did not, the law might not recognize his relationship with them at all. In England, the law went so far as to declare an illegitimate child "*filius nullius*" (literally, the child of no one), with no rights to inherit from father or mother. In the United States, nonmarital children were viewed as part of their mother's — but not their father's — families. The father might, as we explored in the last chapter, bear some responsibility to the extent that his nonmarital child imposed a burden on the state, but the child had no claim to his father's name, property, support, or companionship.[1] In 1972, Illinois conclusively presumed that every father whose children were born outside marriage was unfit, for that reason alone, to take custody of them.[2]

The legal redefinition of fatherhood began with Peter Stanley's challenge to that Illinois statute, and the process has continued apace ever since. The completed part is the dismantling of fatherhood by marriage; the unfinished business is the construction of a definition to take its place. The debate is a hotly contested one, and there are three positions: (1) that fatherhood, like motherhood, is biological and should be accorded legal recognition absent a father's behavior abandoning or forfeiting his rights; (2) that fatherhood, like motherhood, should depend on a demonstration of bonding, commitment, and nurturance essential to children's needs; and

(3) that fatherhood and motherhood are fundamentally different and complementary roles. The Supreme Court's struggles with the question, though central only to the demolition of the older understandings of fatherhood, frame the state court battlegrounds in which the debate is likely to be resolved.

Law professors, in introducing their students to the mysteries of legal analysis, delight in asking their classes to synthesize a line of cases. Law, at least in the Anglo-American tradition, is a product of common law method. Judges decide one case at a time, tying the outcome to the case's particular facts. Judges then address the next case on a similar topic within the framework created by the first. At the end of the process — three, four, five cases later — the professor asks whether the cases can be synthesized, that is, whether they provide a coherent framework with which to address the topic or whether they are hopelessly in conflict. The Supreme Court cases addressing fatherhood are a law professor's ideal. They are cases decided by the nation's highest court, a court that often eschews family law matters, and therefore are of major importance in themselves. And, to the professor's gratification and the class's torment, they zigzag in sufficiently interesting twists and turns (without ever quite tripping over themselves — and without quite resolving the issue) to pose the requisite intellectual challenge.

Peter Stanley, with the assistance of legal aid lawyers seeking to restore his welfare benefits, filed the initial challenge. Stanley, whether the law recognized it or not, had been an active father to his three children. He had supported them, lived with their mother "intermittently" for eighteen years, and, in regard to the two children whose custody was at issue in the case, for all of their lives. When Joan Stanley died, the State of Illinois declared the children wards of the state because they had no legally recognized parent or guardian and placed them with court-appointed caretakers.[3] Stanley challenged the Illinois statute as a violation of his rights to equal protection (the law treated unwed fathers differently from married fathers and unwed mothers) and due process (the law deprived unwed fathers of a fundamental liberty interest — the companionship, care, custody, and management of their children — without a hearing). The Supreme Court agreed, recognizing that the "interest of a man in the children he has sired and raised . . . undeniably warrants deference" and that illegitimate children "cannot be denied the rights of other children because familial bonds in such cases were often as warm, enduring, and important as those arising within a more formally organized family unit."[4]

Stanley, particularly as depicted by the majority,[5] represented the clearest possible case for the recognition of an unmarried father's parental role. Stanley had *established* his parenthood over an eighteen-year period, had supported his children, had done so with Joan Stanley's support and encouragement, and she had died, leaving the state as the only opposing interest. Nonetheless, Chief Justice Burger's dissenting opinion acknowledged Illinois's concern that in order to provide for children's welfare "it is necessary to impose upon at least one of the parties legal responsibility for the welfare of [the child]," and that the parties entrusted with legal rights and responsibilities in connection with the child signify "their willingness to work together . . . towards the common end of childrearing."[6] The majority opinion left open how the states might address these issues without marriage as the final arbiter of fatherhood.

The Supreme Court revisited the issue in a trio of cases that reached the High Court over the next decade (although it would not be until the 1990s that the issue became the popular subject of tabloids and made-for-TV movies). In the first case, *Quilloin v. Walcott*, the Court reembraced the distinctiveness of marriage. Leon Webster Quilloin fathered a son in 1964. The mother married another man in 1967, and, after nine years in which the new husband cared for the child, he sought to adopt eleven-year-old Darren, with the approval of mother and son. Georgia law provided that while either parent may veto the adoption of a marital child, the mother alone could arrange for the adoption of a nonmarital one.[7] Quilloin, like Stanley, argued that the statute violated his rights to equal protection (the law treated unwed fathers differently from married fathers and unwed mothers) and due process (the law deprived unwed fathers of a fundamental liberty interest in their children). This time, however, the Court sided with the state. Observing that an unmarried father might be subject to essentially the same child support obligation as a married father, the Supreme Court nonetheless emphasized that Quilloin had never had custody of the child and thus had "never shouldered any significant responsibility with respect to the daily supervision, education, protection, or care of the child." In contrast, the Court noted, "legal custody of children is, of course, a central aspect of the marital relationship, and even a father whose marriage has broken apart will have borne full responsibility for the rearing of his children during the period of the marriage."[8] Under any standard of review, the Court therefore concluded, the courts could take this difference in the extent of commitment to the welfare of the child into account, and Quilloin, while afforded notice and a hearing, could not veto Darren's adoption.

In the second case, *Caban v. Mohammed*, decided in 1979, the Court recast the issue in terms of the comparison between unmarried mothers and unmarried fathers, and the father fared better. This time, mother and father had lived together and shared custody of their two children until the oldest was four, and the father had maintained a relationship with the children after the separation. Mother and father each married others; both couples sought custody, and the mother supported her new husband's petition to adopt the children. New York law, like the Georgia statute in *Quilloin*, gave the unwed mother a veto over any adoption unless her parental rights were terminated, but allowed the father only notice and a right to be heard on the issue of whether the adoption furthered the children's best interests. The Supreme Court invalidated the statute, finding that the "gender-based distinction" was not "required by any universal difference between maternal and paternal relations" and that such distinctions "discriminated against unwed fathers when their identity is known and they have manifested a paternal interest in the child."[9]

In the third case, the Court attempted to reconcile the decisions. Justice Stevens, a dissenter in *Caban*, wrote the majority opinion in *Lehr v. Robertson* in 1983. His opening sentence framed the issue as "whether New York has sufficiently protected an unmarried father's inchoate relationship with a child whom he has never supported and rarely seen in the two years since her birth,"[10] and concluded that it did. New York maintained a "putative father registry" that permitted any man who wished to claim paternity to register with the state. Jonathan Lehr had not registered. Lorraine, the mother of his two-year-old daughter Jessica, had married Richard Robertson eight months after the girl's birth, and when Robertson petitioned to adopt Jessica, the court examined the putative father registry, found no father listed, and proceeded with the adoption without providing Lehr notice or a hearing despite the fact that Lehr had filed a paternity proceeding in the interim.[11]

In his opinion for the Court, Justice Stevens acknowledged both that the "intangible fibers that connect parent and child have infinite variety" and that the "institution of marriage has played a critical role both in defining the legal entitlements of family members and in developing the decentralized structure of democratic society."[12] For an unwed father, Stevens observed, what triggers constitutional recognition is not biology alone but an existing relationship substantial enough to merit constitutional protection. Stevens emphasized that

> The significance of the biological connection is that it offers the biological father an opportunity that no other male possesses to develop a re-

lationship with his offspring. If he grasps that opportunity and accepts some measure of responsibility for the child's future, he may enjoy the blessings of the parent-child relationship and make uniquely valuable contributions to the child's development. If he fails to do so, the Federal Constitution will not automatically compel a State to listen to his opinion of where the child's best interests lie.[13]

Stevens united the Supreme Court's conflicting decisions on fatherhood by taking the existence of a paternal relationship as a given. *If* a father's relationship with his children is a substantial one, that relationship merits constitutional protection. *If* a father has not established a paternal bond with his children, the inquiry ends there. Justice White's dissent, which would recognize the biological connection as "itself a relationship that creates a protected interest," raised the additional issue of the father's opportunity to establish the type of relationship Stevens demanded. While Stevens stated that Lehr "has never had any significant custodial, personal, or financial relationship with Jessica" and "did not seek to establish a legal tie until she was two years old," White noted that

According to Lehr, he and Jessica's mother met in 1971 and began living together in 1974. The couple cohabited for approximately two years, until Jessica's birth in 1976. Throughout the pregnancy and after the birth, Lorraine acknowledged to friends and relatives that Lehr was Jessica's father; Lorraine told Lehr that she had reported to the New York Department of Social Services that he was the father. Lehr visited Lorraine and Jessica in the hospital every day during Lorraine's confinement. According to Lehr, from the time Lorraine was discharged from the hospital until August 1978, she concealed her whereabouts from him. During this time Lehr never ceased his efforts to locate Lorraine and Jessica and achieved sporadic success until August 1977, after which time he was unable to locate them at all. On those occasions when he did determine Lorraine's location, he visited with her and her children to the extent she was willing to permit it. When Lehr, with the aid of a detective agency, located Lorraine and Jessica in August 1978, Lorraine was already married to Mr. Robertson. Lehr asserts that at this time he offered to provide financial assistance and to set up a trust fund for Jessica, but that Lorraine refused. Lorraine threatened Lehr with arrest unless he stayed away and refused to permit him to see Jessica. Thereafter Lehr retained counsel who wrote to Lorraine in early December 1978, requesting that she permit Lehr to visit Jessica and threatening legal action on Lehr's behalf. On December 21, 1978, perhaps as a response to Lehr's threatened legal action, appellees commenced the adoption action at issue here.[14]

Lehr's account depicts the adoption proceeding as part of a systematic effort to prevent him from developing a relationship with his child. For Justice White, the state's refusal to provide Lehr notice and a hearing before severing his parental ties made the state complicit in that effort.

The opinions in all these cases addressed the relatively narrow issue of the scope of constitutional protection to be afforded nonmarital fathers' relationships with their children — that is, the extent to which the Constitution invalidates state legislation, such as the adoption procedures at issue in *Lehr*, *Caban*, and *Quilloin*, which interferes with parental ties. What the Court did not directly address was the father's obligation to establish a parental relationship and the mother's duty to let him. On this issue the dissents (perhaps because they need not speak for the Court) are more revealing than the majority opinions. In *Lehr*, White started from the premise that the "usual understanding of 'family' implies biological relationships," and that "but for the actions of the child's mother," Lehr would have had the kind of significant relationship that the majority insists is entitled to constitutional protection. Stevens's dissenting opinion in *Caban* observed in contrast that

> This case concerns the validity of rules affecting the status of the thousands of children who are born out of wedlock every day. All of these children have an interest in acquiring the status of legitimacy; a great many of them have an interest in being adopted by parents who can give them opportunities that would otherwise be denied; for some the basic necessities of life are at stake.[15]

Stevens equated children's interests with "the status of legitimacy," and wished to facilitate adoptions that would provide that status, whether by the mother and her husband or by an unrelated couple. He believed that a rule giving mothers of newborns the exclusive right to consent to adoption would be justified because it "gives the mother, in whose sole charge the infant is often placed anyway, the maximum flexibility in deciding how to best care for the child. It also gives the loving father an incentive to marry the mother, and has no adverse impact on the disinterested father."[16] He assumed, as generations had before him, that a custodial mother was more likely to act in the child's interests than a noncustodial father, and that the state's interest (one Stevens was ready to call "compelling") lay with "the prompt, complete, and reliable integration of the child into a satisfactory new home at as young an age as is feasible."[17] Fathers in this view were expected to establish a relationship with the mother or depart the scene.[18] White, in his *Lehr* dissent, had recognized the father's biological tie as constitutionally significant independently of the father's role in establishing a family unit designed for caretaking.

To command a majority, Stevens's opinion for the Court in *Lehr*, unlike his dissent in *Caban*, retained the emphasis on paternal responsibility without the link to marriage — and without a maternal obligation to facilitate the father's involvement. The new battleground for paternal recognition then became newborn adoptions, with the states left to wrestle on their own with the question of just how much recognition to give nonmarital fathers. These myriad responses have been so divergent that the experts disagree on how to catalogue them. There are, however, at least four categories:

- At one extreme, Massachusetts and Tennessee have retained legislation that requires only the mother's consent to place nonmarital children for adoption. Even then, Massachusetts and Tennessee allow fathers notice and the opportunity to seek custody if they file a declaration seeking to assert parental responsibilities and if paternal custody is in the child's best interest.[19] The Massachusetts legislature amended the statute to give fathers somewhat greater rights, but Governor Weld vetoed the statute and the legislature failed to override his veto. Mississippi, the last state to deny unwed fathers notice of the adoption proceeding, had its adoption statute declared unconstitutional in 1998.[20]

- At the other extreme, many states preclude adoption absent the consent of mother and father, unless the nonconsenting parent has abandoned the child, cannot be found, or can otherwise be shown to be unfit. The *Baby Jessica* case, which became the subject of a made-for-TV movie, and the almost equally famous *Baby Richard* case, both of which ended with the dramatic removal of older children from the adoptive parents with whom they had lived all their lives, involved such statutes.[21] Indeed, in the *Baby Richard* case, the trial court initially ruled that biological father Otakar Kirchner had abandoned

Richard and was therefore unfit because he had had no contact with him during the thirty days following his birth. Yet Otakar, told that the baby had died, continued to inquire about the child, and offered financial assistance and filed an appearance in the adoption proceeding a month after learning of the child's existence (and within three months of his birth). The Supreme Court of Illinois reversed the trial court three years later, finding that Otakar's parental rights had not been properly terminated, and that, as a fit parent, he was entitled to custody without consideration of Richard's "best interest."[22]

In between these extremes are the states that require fathers to take action to acquire an adoption veto. Deborah Forman divides these states into two groups:

- Some states establish technical requirements that grant veto power to all fathers who are married to the mother, appear on the birth certificate, establish paternity, file with a putative father registry or the like. Nebraska requires unwed fathers to file a notice of intent to claim paternity within five days of the child's birth, and strictly enforces the time limits (barring, in one case, a notice of paternity *nine* days after birth).[23]

- Other states condition paternal vetoes on a demonstration of substantial commitment to the child. New York and California provide the leading decisions, both striking down statutes that required fathers to maintain a relationship with the mother as a precondition for recognition. New York law had required that, for the father to acquire the right to a veto, he had to establish that "he lived with either the mother or the child continuously for six months prior to the adoption; he admitted paternity; and he provided reasonable financial support to the mother for birth expenses."[24] Addressing the question that the U.S. Supreme Court had never reached, the New York Court of Appeals (the highest court in the state) ruled that fathers "have a constitutional right to the opportunity to develop a qualifying relationship with the infant," and that "the difficulty with the 'living together' requirement stems from its focus on the relationship between father and mother, rather than mother and child."[25] California went a step further. The state statute at issue provided a paternal veto if the father "*receives the child into his home* and openly holds out the child as his natural child."

The California high court concluded that the father's ability to "receive the child into his home" was "entirely within the mother's control" and declared the statute unconstitutional on that grounds. The court then concluded that "when the father had come forward to grasp his parental responsibilities, his parental rights are equal to those of the mother."[26]

The line of Supreme Court decisions that began in 1972 with *Stanley v. Illinois* was thought to herald a new era of fathers' rights. Florida Judge John E. Fennelly describes *Stanley* itself as a response to the Court's recognition of a new era of social mores and a product of the Court's "counter-culture" phase.[27] The cases since then are sufficiently varied to lend support to almost any theory of fatherhood in between the "marriage only" and "biology only" extremes suggested in the dissents. Law professors Janet Dolgin and Barbara Woodhouse have taken up the challenge of reconciling the decisions and exploring the intermediate approaches.[28] Dolgin, who also has training as an anthropologist, argued in 1993 that the key to the Supreme Court's fatherhood jurisprudence lies not with a radically new conception of fatherhood, but through a much more conservative effort to re-create the unitary family. After a detailed analysis of each case, she concluded that

> In sum, the unwed father cases . . . delineate three factors that make an unwed man a father. These are the man's biological relationship to the child, his social relation to the child, and his relation to the child's mother. *Stanley* through *Lehr* seem to suggest, and have certainly been read to say, that a man can effect a legal relation to his biological child by establishing a relationship with that child. However, the facts of those cases belie that as the accurate interpretation. . . . A biological father does protect his paternity by developing a social relationship with his child, but this step demands the creation of a family, a step itself depending upon an appropriate relationship between the man and his child's mother.[29]

Central to Dolgin's conclusion was her analysis of the last of the Supreme Court's fatherhood cases, *Michael H. v. Gerald D.* Justice Scalia introduces the case, noting that "[t]he facts of the case are, we must hope, extraordinary."[30] The case begins with Carole D., an international model with a Hollywood lifestyle, married to French oil executive Gerald D. Two years into the marriage, Carole has an "adulterous affair" with her neighbor, Michael

H. She bears a child, Victoria D., in May 1981, naming Gerald on the birth certificate but telling Michael that he may be the father. In October, Gerald moves to New York to pursue business interests, while Carole stays with Victoria in California. Blood tests establish a 98 percent probability that Michael is the father, and Carole spends three months with him in Jamaica in early 1982, with Michael treating Victoria as his child. By the end of March, however, Carole and Victoria return to California and move in with Scott K. (Scott whom? you may ask. He is not relevant to the legal outcome, but Scalia relishes including him in the recital of the facts.) Carole and Victoria visit Gerald in New York during the spring, and again during the summer, then vacation with him in Europe, returning in between to California and Scott. In November 1982 a spurned Michael files a filiation action to establish paternity. Carole, who has lived with Gerald in New York from March to July of 1983, reconciles with Michael in August, and they live together with Victoria for eight months. One month after signing a stipulation that Michael is Victoria's father, however, Carole leaves him for good. By June 1984, Carole has returned to New York and Gerald, where she is living at the time of the Supreme Court decision, along with Victoria and two other children born into the marriage. Michael, spurned permanently it would appear, seeks visitation rights, and the trial court rules against him on the basis of a California statute that conclusively presumes a child born to a married woman living with her husband to be the husband's child.

Here, the experts claim, is a biological father who has established a social relationship with his child, held himself out as her father, lived with her mother, and contributed to their support. Certainly a statute that refuses to recognize his almost certain paternity, and treats his request for visitation no better than it would a stranger's, cannot meet the constitutional standard set in the line of cases from *Stanley* to *Lehr*. The Supreme Court found *Michael H.* so troubling that it produced no majority opinion to explain the case's resolution. While the justices voted five to four to uphold the California statute, only one other justice joined Scalia's plurality opinion in its entirety, and two joined it in part. Justice Stevens concurred only in the judgment (which means that he disagreed with Scalia's reasoning), and four justices dissented in two separate opinions.[31] So fractured a decision carries less weight as precedent, and it is accordingly difficult to determine its significance outside the specific issue (the conclusive paternity presumption) presented in the case. (Even then, California amended the statute soon after the case to make it easier to secure blood tests within two years of the child's birth.)[32]

Dolgin argues that the key to Scalia's opinion (and thus the outcome of the constitutionality of the statute) lies with his declaration that the earlier line of cases "did not establish a liberty interest on the basis of 'biological fatherhood plus an established parental relationship — factors that exist in the present case as well.' Rather, as the plurality viewed them, the unwed father cases rested 'upon the historic respect — indeed, sanctity would not be too strong a term — traditionally accorded to the relationships that develop within the unitary family.'"[33] Those fathers who prevailed — Stanley and Caban, but not Quilloin, Lehr, or Michael H. — had established a unitary family of biological father, mother, and child before their cases reached the Supreme Court. The father's relationship with the child alone, however well established, did not control the results.

The more celebrated of the state cases, despite the stength of their paternal rights proclamations, appear to bolster Dolgin's arguments. *Baby Jessica*, *Baby Richard*, and *Raquel Marie* all involved fathers who had not only reconciled with but also married the mothers of their children before their cases reached precedent-setting resolutions. The fathers who did not rarely gained custody even if they won skirmishes along the way.[34] Unitary families, not single dads, were winning out. Indeed, by the mid-1990s, the leading advocates of the importance of fatherhood were calling for renewed attention to marriage as the only reliable way to link fathers to their children.[35]

Barbara Woodhouse presents a somewhat different view of the same events, exchanging Dolgin's concerns with what the Supreme Court decided for an emphasis on what it should declare. Woodhouse begins her article with Dr. Seuss's "Horton Hatches the Egg," the fable of Horton the Elephant who, when asked to relieve a mother bird "just for awhile," sits on her nest for fifty-one days. The faithless Mayzie Bird finally returns from her Florida vacation to claim "her" egg only as the egg is ready to hatch and the work is done. Horton watches ("with a sad heavy heart") as just then "the egg burst apart" and the baby comes out with "EARS, AND A TAIL AND A TRUNK JUST LIKE HIS!" The crowd looking on names the new animal an "elephant-bird" and shouts in unison, "it should be, it should be, it SHOULD be like that!" And so too, Woodhouse argues, should be fatherhood. She heads her argument "Horton and the Idea of Fathering as Mothering" and maintains that

> In reimagining fathering to make it more responsive to children's needs,
> I suggest that we change the legal and cultural meaning of "fathering"

until it looks more like the nurturing conduct we attribute to "mothering." Shifting the focus from procreation to gestation, from genetic ownership to parenthood earned through functional nurturing, asks that fathers "do" for their children from the very beginning. Rather than indulge a nostalgic yearning for "unpaid mother-love," society should demand the same qualities of service and commitment from "father-love."[36]

Woodhouse, in reviewing existing law, decries the scant recognition that fathers like Horton, who bear no genetic relationship to their children, receive. She is ambivalent about the New York and California decisions that distance the father's relationship to his child from that with the pregnant mother as though the two were independent. She ends the article by reiterating Dr. Seuss's refrain "it SHOULD be like that" as the critical question, and asking

> Is this the proper measure and timing for an unmarried father's taking of responsibility? How does his conduct towards the mother or siblings reflect on his commitment to the child? What distinguishes the self-dealing "fleeting impregnator" from the foolish but generous "thwarted father," deserving of constitutional concern?[37]

In short, has the would-be father demonstrated that he is capable of mothering?

Dolgin's and Woodhouse's analyses, while radically different from each other, together address the two faces of responsible fathering: either the ability to create, in one form or another, a "unitary family" that unites mom and dad in complementary roles *or* a father's ability to perform the essential attributes of mothering and fathering himself. Fatherhood advocate David Popenoe, for example, while dismissive of feminist efforts to describe fathering as mothering, nonetheless identifies two primary roles for the fathers of infants: support for the mother-child bond and development of a strong emotional attachment between father and child.[38] Where the critics disagree is on the desirability of fathering alone. Long ago, in his *Stanley* dissent, Chief Justice Burger dismissed the possibility altogether, stating flatly that

> the biological role of a mother in carrying and nursing an infant creates stronger bonds between her and the child than the bonds resulting from

the male's often casual encounter. This view is reinforced by the observable fact that most unwed mothers exhibit a concern for their offspring either permanently or at least until safely placed for adoption, while unwed fathers rarely burden either the mother or the child with their attentions or loyalties. Centuries of human experience buttress this view of the realities of human conditions and suggest that unwed mothers of illegitimate children are generally more dependable protectors of their children than are unwed fathers.[39]

In rejecting Burger's biological determinism (and the insistence on marriage that went with it), the courts have nonetheless retained Burger's conviction that biology alone matters less for men than for women in securing commitment to their offspring. Dolgin argues that the new test depends, practically if not always doctrinely, on the father's ability to secure a helpmate: the biological mother is preferable, but later cases suggest that Grandma (the moving force in some of the cases in any event) or a wife unrelated to the child may be sufficient.[40] Woodhouse argues that fatherhood should depend much more directly on a commitment to nurturing by the men themselves, but that such a commitment, though made to the child, inevitably involves a web of relationships necessary to the child's well-being.

State courts, convinced that the Constitution requires separating the father's relationship to his child from that with the mother, have displayed their greatest discomfiture in explaining how these relationships fit together in the emerging definition of parenthood. *Baby Emily*, if only because of the torturous twists and turns that attended the case's journey through the legal system, presents one of the more telling examples. The Florida trial court, considering, as in the *Baby Richard* case,[41] whether the biological father had abandoned his child, ruled initially that "[u]nder any definition of abandonment, the natural father has not, in fact, abandoned the natural mother or the child. He has exhibited every available means of attempting to contest the adoption, and his desire to have the custody of and to be with his natural daughter was unrefuted during the time of the hearing."[42] Thirteen months later, the trial court granted a rehearing because Baby Emily had not been represented by independent counsel — and then reversed its decision, finding that the father had provided the mother with no financial, emotional, or psychological support during the pregnancy, and that his prebirth conduct did not, therefore, demonstrate a settled purpose to assume all parental responsibilities after the birth. The first appellate panel to hear the case reversed the trial court in a two-to-one decision; the full appellate court granted a rehearing and voted six to five to reverse the case again, this time finding that the father had abandoned Emily. Finally, the Supreme Court of Florida ruled against the father, producing additional dissents in the process.

What is remarkable about the case is that it should have been easy. The Florida legislature had specifically amended the applicable statute to provide that, in determining whether a father has abandoned his child, "the court may consider the conduct of a father toward the child's mother during her pregnancy,"[43] and the trial court found that the biological father, a convicted rapist (though this was legally irrelevant to the outcome) who (more relevantly) had been physically and emotionally abusive toward the mother, "showed little to no interest in the birth mother or the unborn child," and provided the mother, who had lost her job because of an automobile accident and was malnourished during the pregnancy, "no financial or emotional support except during the time they were living together."[44] What apparently made this case so difficult for the myriad Florida courts who ruled on the case was that it required linking the father's abandonment of the child to his treatment of her mother. Justice Kogan, in his Florida Supreme Court dissent, explained:

> My objection is this: The fact that unwed biological fathers have a constitutionally protected "opportunity interest" in their offspring necessarily implies that they must at least be given the "opportunity" to exercise it. . . . This in turn means there must be a period of time after birth during which such a biological father has a right of access to the child. . . .
>
> Absent conduct detrimental to the fetus, hatred of the mother does not necessarily imply hatred of the child.[45]

The majority, in contrast, saw no constitutional issue because they saw the father's behavior toward mother and unborn child as inextricably intertwined.[46]

The courts' efforts to deal with a father's relationship with his unborn child do require separating the essential components of parenthood from the historical institution of marriage. Marriage, as both proponents and opponents of same-sex marriage acknowledge, policed sexual morality in order to reinforce the links between procreating and parenting, supported and encouraged a sexual division of labor that united women's nurturance with men's financial support, and tied the increasingly private institution of the family to a larger set of societal obligations. Scalia's opinion in *Michael H.* is striking, not because of his references to the "unitary family" (whatever "unitary" means on the basis of the complicated facts of that case), but because it is the only case in the lot that harkens back to this earlier understanding of marriage. The Scalia footnote in which Justices Kennedy and O'Connor refused to join squarely embraced the historical tradition regarding "the rights of an adulterous natural father" and found that he had none. None of the other modern cases turn so decisively on disapproval of the circumstances of the child's conception or on so clear a demarcation between the rights of a married father and an unmarried one.[47]

Instead, the state cases have struggled to rewrite the earlier ideas of provision for children into an emerging definition of parenthood. Legal recognition of fatherhood, as a status distinct from both biology and marriage, now serves some of the same purposes legitimacy once did in establishing lines of responsibility between fathers and their children. In the process, the courts are not so much creating a new model of parenthood (Arnold Schwarzenegger and Billy Crystal notwithstanding, men are unlikely to give birth — or hatch eggs — any time soon) as deciding which elements of the marital model continue to apply to obligations centered on children. Connecting fathers and nurturance has been a central element of the dispute. Ironically, it is those associated with fathers' rights, and the claim that fathering is distinct from mothering, who see the involvement of two parents as critical; they object, in these cases, only to the biological mother's role in determining the extent of the father's involvement. Feminists like Barbara Woodhouse who would recast fathering as mothering, precisely because they acknowledge fathers' ability to nurture on their own, create a basis for single fatherhood. They remind us in the process that motherhood has long been associated with the subordination of the mother's interests to the child's, and they would condition legal recognition of fatherhood on the demonstration of conduct that is often assumed, on the basis of biology alone, for women. Both groups, however, agree that, for fathers, the assumption of parental responsibility involves something more than participation in conception. Commitment to a newborn ought to involve, at a minimum, sufficient concern for the biological mother not to endanger the baby's well-being during pregnancy, and adequate parenting involves nurturance whether the father nurtures the baby himself or secures the services of someone else. Perhaps most importantly, the parental commitment (unlike modern marital ones) needs to be permanent, not, as some commentators have suggested, a trial run at fathering for a brief period after birth.[48] *Baby Emily* should have been an easy case under any standard.

Doonesbury by Gary Trudeau

Figure 19.1

20

Child Custody at Divorce

Ground Zero in the Gender Wars

U NWED fathers seeking custody of their newborns — despite their symbolic importance (and headline potential) — are rare. Divorced dads seeking greater contact with their children are not. And if the precise issues in adoption disputes are not always well-defined, the battle lines in the custody wars at divorce are so well drawn that they can be better described as opposing trenches. On one side are those who would identify children's well-being with continuing contact with both parents. They favor joint custody, liberal visitation, and limitations on custodial parent's autonomy that secure the involvement of the other parent. In the other camp are those who argue that genuinely shared custody approaching an equal division of responsibility for the child is rare, and that children's interests lie with the well-being of the parent who assumes the major responsibility for their care. This group favors primary caretaker provisions to govern custody, greater respect for the custodial parent's autonomy (including greater freedom to move), and greater concern for both the physical and psychological aspects of domestic violence. The joint custody camp has won the major battles but not yet the war. The courts and the helping professions overwhelmingly associate children's interests with continuing contact with both parents; the remaining conflicts concern the terms on which the contact is to take place. At issue in these disputes are not just the legal rules governing divorce but the norms for family relationships more generally.

Custody paradigms have always reflected the dominant ideology of the family. Mary Ann Mason titled her history of child custody "from father's property to children's rights," and, in colonial America, the early modern paradigm of hierarchical — and patriarchal — families gave fathers almost unlimited authority over their children.[1] During this period, a dying husband might name a distant uncle guardian of his children before entrusting legal responsibility to a woman, however devoted the mother to her children or the husband to his wife.[2] Nonetheless, neither divorce nor custody fights were common, and Mason reports almost no recorded custody disputes between fathers and mothers before the nineteenth century.

Divorce itself, as something more than an occasional tragedy, was a product of the Victorian family. The number of American divorces tripled between 1870 and 1890, and by the turn of the century 40 percent of the reported cases mentioned children.[3] In the family of the separate spheres, with its relatively greater gender equality and maternal governance of the home, childrearing was the mother's responsibility and, over the course of the nineteenth century, custody presumptions shifted from father to mother, at least for a child of "tender years." Nonetheless, the maternal presumption, justified in part by mother's greater moral standing, was mediated by the fault grounds necessary to obtain the divorce. A mother who unjustifiably left her husband or took up with another man (even if her affair followed her husband's adultery or desertion) could be deemed unfit. In an 1854 New York case, the court awarded custody of a four-year-old girl to her father because of the mother's adultery, even though the mother believed that the father had obtained a final divorce, and her affair occurred only after the marriage had dissolved because of his adultery during the period in which mother and father lived together. The court explained that "there may be no difference in the sin of the man and the woman, who violated the laws of chastity. . . . But we do know, that in the opinion of society, it is otherwise . . . for when she sins after this sort, she sins against society . . . her associations are with the vulgar, the vile and the depraved. If her children are with her, their characters must be, more or less, influenced and formed by the circumstances which surround them."[4] Mason observes that the shift in custody standards from a paternal presumption to a best-interest test favoring mothers occurred inconsistently over the course of over half a century, and that even with allowances for maternal fitness, it did not fully displace the paternal presumption until well into the twentieth century.[5]

The maternal presumption came under attack, in turn, with the shift toward more egalitarian families in the latter half of the last several decades. By 1973, New York courts were willing to declare that "[t]he simple fact of being a mother does not, by itself, indicate a capacity or willingness to render a quality of care different from that which the father can provide."[6] State courts would increasingly question the constitutionality of gender-based preferences, and between 1960 and 1990 nearly every state backed away from the "tender years presumption" as a decisive factor in custody awards. The period from 1960 to 1990 similarly marked the move away from fault and, for most states, the role of sexual conduct as a primary test of parental fitness. In combination, these changes dismantled the older system of custody standards without a ready replacement.

Joint custody began to fill the gap, at least in its 1970s incarnation, with parental experiments. Two divorcing parents, motivated perhaps by egalitarian sentiments and a shared desire to continue their children's involvement with both parents, would propose joint custody as a way to realize their ideals. In 1970, however, only one state statute explicitly provided for such a result, and the courts in a number of states were unwilling to authorize the arrangement, parental agreement notwithstanding.[7] Such cases, though relatively few in number, helped fuel support for legislative recognition of joint custody. California, which had led the country in no-fault reform, also led in the modern embrace of joint custody legislation. In 1979, California enacted legislation that declared: "[I]t is the public policy of this state to assure minor children of frequent and continuing contact with both parents after the parents have separated or dissolved their marriage" and that the first order of preference in awarding custody was to "both parents jointly . . . or to either parent."[8]

Joint custody initially enjoyed broad support. Within three years of the California legislation, every state legislature had considered the issue, and over thirty had enacted some form of recognition for joint custody.[9] The leading opposition came from law professor Joseph Goldstein, child analyst Anna Freud, and psychiatrist Albert Solnit, who had published *Beyond the Best Interests of the Child* in 1973. The authors, drawing on psychoanalytic theory, identified children's well-being with the stability of their relationship with a "psychological parent" with whom they had bonded. Goldstein, Freud, and Solnit observed that

> Children have difficulty relating positively to, profiting from, and maintaining contact with two psychological parents who are not in positive contact with each other. Loyalty conflicts are common and normal under such conditions and may have devastating consequences by destroying the child's positive relationships to both parents. A "visiting" or visited parent has little chance to serve as a true object for love, trust and identification since this role is based on his being available on an uninterrupted day-to-day basis. Once it is determined who will be the cus-

todial parent, it is that parent, not the court who must decide under what conditions he or she wishes to raise the child. Thus, the noncustodial parent should have no legally enforceable right to visit the child, and the custodial parent should have the right to decide whether it is desirable to have such visits.[10]

When I took a class in "Psychoanalysis and the Law" during the 1970s from Jay Katz, a psychiatrist and colleague of Joseph Goldstein's, he described advising divorcing fathers (as part of his psychiatric practice) to defer to the custodial mother and (typically) her new husband, and to hope to reestablish a relationship at the time the child started college.

By the 1980s, this advice had become untenable to divorcing fathers. With divorce rates increasing in the wake of no-fault reforms, more fathers wanted continuing contact with their children, and more women supported their calls for involvement. Katharine Bartlett and Carol Stack wrote the classic feminist defense of joint custody in 1986, arguing that

> From the point of view of ideology, rules favoring joint custody seem clearly preferable. Joint custody stakes out ground for an alternative norm of parenting. Unlike the "neutral" best interests test or a primary caretaker presumption, these rules promote the affirmative assumption that both parents should, and will, take important roles in the care and nurturing of their children. This assumption is essential to any realistic reshaping of gender roles within parenthood. Only when it is expected that men as well as women will take a serious role in childrearing will traditional patterns in the division of childrearing responsibilities begin to be eliminated in practice as well as in theory.[11]

While Bartlett and Stack shared feminist reservations about the way joint custody had been implemented in practice, particularly the courts' refusal to give sufficient weight to the importance of women's employment or their concerns about domestic violence, they identified a more equal division of child care responsibilities as central to women's hopes for greater equality. Women's increasing workforce participation, together with feminism's emphasis on equality, Jay Folberg observed, led in turn to fathers' greater participation in intact families, and greater expectation of continued involvement at divorce.[12]

These fathers were the moving force behind the joint custody legislation that swept the country. In California, James Cook, president of the Joint

Custody Association, helped draft the new legislation and secure its passage. He explained that the major purpose of the new law "was to deter divorcing parents who might otherwise be prone to pursue sole parent custody for purposes of vindictiveness, leverage, or extortion."[13] Borrowing a page from the feminist handbook that attributes greater influence to more prominent labels, fathers' rights groups named their complaint "parental alienation syndrome." They argued that many mothers, angry because of the conflicts that produced the divorce, poisoned their children's relationships with their fathers and obstructed the father's efforts to maintain a relationship with their children. Custody and visitation fights, explained James Cook, had replaced fault-based accusations as the new divorce battleground. These fathers embraced joint custody and the "friendly parent provisions" that provided for the award of custody to the parent most likely to insure the continued involvement of both, as a way to secure recognition of a right to continued contact with their children and to enhance their bargaining power in the custody and visitation wars.[14]

Joint custody in practice has been closer to Cook's vision of greater paternal security than to Bartlett and Stack's ideal of equal sharing. While public attention has focused on parents who propose joint custody on their own, and who devise alternating arrangements in which the child shuttles between two homes, joint custody in practice rarely involves fifty-fifty divisions of responsibility. California law, for instance, distinguishes between legal custody and physical custody. Joint legal custody addresses decision-making responsibility, and it is effectively available for the asking. During the 1980s, California courts awarded joint legal custody in 79 percent of all divorces (including a number of cases in which neither party requested it), despite the fact that the child resided solely with the mother in two-thirds of those cases.[15] In Wisconsin joint legal custody awards increased during the same period from 18 percent to 81 percent of the total, with the majority of children subject to these awards residing solely with their mothers.[16] While the effect of joint legal custody is primarily symbolic since one parent typically has physical custody and primary decision-making responsibility, it does grant both parents, however marginally involved in their child's upbringing, effective veto rights over medical and psychological care, and the ability to force a court decision over such charged disputes as whether to choose a religious or a public school.

Joint physical custody, in contrast, requires that the child reside with both parents, usually on an alternating basis. In Wisconsin joint physical custody awards increased from 2 percent in the early 1980s to 14.2 percent a decade later.[17] In the relatively affluent California counties where joint custody first took hold, joint physical custody awards accounted for 20 percent of the total by the mid-1980s.[18] Even then there is no requirement that "shared care" be shared equally, and the term can refer to anything from a strictly equal division of responsibility to little more than what used to be called visitation. In the overwhelming majority of cases in which the division is not equal, the child spends more time with the mother, with one California study finding that in *every* case of unequal division, the mother had the larger share.[19] In Wisconsin about half the joint physical custody cases (6.3 percent of all awards) involved equal custody shares, while the remainder (5 percent) resembled sole custody with visitation, with the mothers assuming primary custody in over 80 percent of the cases.[20] Joint custody has increased the time fathers spend with their children without approaching an equal division of child care responsibility.[21]

As joint custody became more common, reservations about these practices increased. Karen Czapanskiy summarized the major feminist objections in an article called "Volunteers and Draftees: The Struggle for Parental Equality." Czapanskiy maintained that "[f]athers are given support and reinforcement for being volunteer parents, people whose duties toward their children are limited, but whose autonomy about parenting is broadly protected. Mothers are defined as draftees, people whose duties toward their children are extensive, but whose autonomy about parenting receives little protection." From this perspective, she argued, "what is wrong with joint custody is that it adds rights rather than responsibilities. And what many parents and children need are responsibilities rather than rights."[22] Unlike other feminists, however, Czapanskiy did not favor substituting a primary caretaker preference, which would favor sole custody for the parent who had undertaken the primary child care responsibility during the marriage. Instead, she suggested "parenting plans" (already mandated in some states), which would require individually tailored agreements detailing custodial schedules, expressing parental understandings (e.g., watching *The Simpsons* is allowed, watching *South Park* is not), and planning for future undertakings such as basketball camp and college tuition. In Czapanskiy's model, these plans would advance a fifty-fifty division of parental responsibilities, with the provision of greater financial resources to offset greater assumption of care. While the results fall well short of Czapanskiy's call for full equality (and the courts have never seriously entertained her proposals that they enforce custodial responsibilities as strictly as financial ones), courts and counselors in many states have embraced parenting plans' greater flexibility, and joined California in taking residential time into account in the calculation of child support. Czapanskiy followed her *UCLA Law Review* article with a new piece observing, with some concern, that securing a greater share of residential custody had become the most effective strategy for those who wished to lower their child support payments, and that the reductions did not correspond to an offsetting decrease in the primary custodian's expenses.[23] A more recent study cites increased child support compliance by parents with joint custody (that is, parents with joint custody paid a higher percentage of the amount set) as a major indicator of its success. Feminist reservations notwithstanding, the continued involvement of both parents following divorce has become the new ideal.

Joint custody critics have enjoyed greater success in questioning custody terms in ways that do not involve a frontal assault on the ideal of shared parenting. The most serious concerns address the use of joint custody to resolve otherwise intractable parental disputes. Two issues dominate the discussion. The first is the extent to which the courts should police domestic abuse in custody proceedings. In 1991 law professor Naomi Cahn reviewed the role of domestic violence[24] in the legal provisions governing custody and discovered that, in most states, either the law was silent on the issue or it took the position of the *Baby Emily* dissent — that father and mother's relationship with each other was irrelevant to the relationship with their children. Cahn noted to her surprise that, while the invisibility of domestic violence has often been attributed to the separate spheres' sharp boundaries between home and market,

> the exclusion of parental violence as a factor in custody decisions is relatively new. Prior to approximately 1970 both fault-based divorce and custody decisions focused on the morality of parental conduct. Courts, as well as state legislatures, used "cruelty" as a basis for divorce and child custody awards, generally granting custody to the parent who had been the subject of the cruelty and denying custody to the parent at fault. As the focus in custody decisions has changed from parental rights to the best interest of the child, the relationship between the parents has become increasingly irrelevant.[25]

Cahn presented as an example a Maryland case in which the mother had been abused for seven years, but "nonetheless agreed to joint physical custody because she was '[t]errified that he would disappear with the children.' Although her husband was subsequently investigated for child abuse and neglect, the court upheld their joint custody agreement . . . , [observing according to the woman] that: 'A person may be violent and vindictive towards a spouse and yet be the best, most loving, caring, parent in the world. And may even in the presence of the other spouse exhibit something towards the kids that he/she normally wouldn't do because he/she is irritated with the other spouse.'"[26] Many courts, Cahn concluded, interpreted the best interest standard to make such abuse relevant to custody determinations only if it directly affected the children or occurred in their presence.[27]

Cahn addressed a moving target. Although as recently as 1989, fewer than sixteen states had statutes discussing the role of domestic violence in custody determinations, by 1997 over forty states and the District of Columbia had statutes on point.[28] The state statutes varied, with some incorporating a rebuttable presumption that it is not in the best interests of the child to be placed in sole or joint custody of a parent who has perpetrated domestic violence, and others recognizing domestic violence as a mitigating factor in other determinations such as parental abandonment or abduction that might be precipitated by the physical abuse.[29] Nonetheless, the new statutes marked greater recognition that parental conduct toward the other parent affected children's well-being, and that physical abuse, in particular, was unacceptable.[30]

These statutes, while providing a basis for dealing with the more egregious cases, do not deal with the other half of the issue: the problem parental conflicts of all kinds pose for custody decision-making.[31] In joint custody cases in particular, virtually all observers have expressed concern about the judicial temptation to "split the baby" by imposing joint custody on two otherwise fit parents who so distrust each other that each seeks custody on his or her own. Maccoby and Mnookin, in their study of California divorce, looked separately at the cases that were resolved later in the divorce process (cases they presumed to involve higher conflict disputes) and found that 40 percent of these high-conflict cases resulted in joint custody awards, typically with mother residence, compared to less than 25 percent of the cases resolved earlier. Maccoby and Mnookin called this result the "most disturbing finding" of their study.[32] In the Wisconsin study, Melli, Brown, and Cancian examined the length of time and the number of court appearances it took to obtain a divorce. They found that cases of unequal shared custody required the longest period and the most appearances to resolve, while equal shared custody cases took the least. They concluded that "[c]ases where the outcome is equal shared custody had generally low levels of dispute, while those with an unequal shared custody award were the most contentious. This suggests that parents with equal shared time are very different from those who negotiate or are given an unequal shared custody award."[33] The Wisconsin study replicated the California findings that high-conflict cases were *more*, not less, likely to result in joint physical custody awards, and that unlike the more amicably settled joint custody cases, the high-conflict type was more likely to result in primary mother residence.

High-conflict cases involve, on a more regular basis than other divorces, physical threats, psychological manipulation, fathers who lack confidence in mothers' parenting ability, mothers who dismiss the value of paternal contact, protracted legal disputes, and ongoing conflict over parenting practices. Social science research documents the negative effect such conflict has on children's well-being, and even the most stalwart joint custody advocates acknowledge that shared parenting requires a level of parental cooperation that not all parents can provide.[34] Partly because of these concerns, California amended its custody statute in 1989 to make it clear that state law established "neither a preference or a presumption for or against joint legal custody, joint physical custody or sole custody, but allows the court and the family the widest discretion to choose a parenting plan which is in the best interests of the child or children" (and then amended it again in 1994 to restore the joint custody presumption in cases in which both parents agreed).[35] Other states, including the minority with a presumption in favor of joint custody, similarly emphasize case-by-case decision-making. The challenge is how to manage parental conflict within a system that emphasizes the continuing role of both parents. Janet Johnston, in her review of high-conflict cases, concluded that custody arrangements should, at the very least, seek to minimize further antagonism. Like Czapanskiy, she prefers parenting plans with detailed custody provisions to open-ended awards that require ongoing parental coordination. And she emphasizes the importance of insulating children from exposure to violence, substance abuse, and psychological disturbance.[36] The "best interest" rubric, under which most joint custody awards are made, requires consideration of the impact of the parental relationship on children.

The other cases commanding disproportionate judicial energy are the "move-away" cases. Mom and Dad divorce, establish nearby residences, and amicably resolve custody. Then, one of them moves. If it is a noncustodial parent, no legal issue arises. It is up to the moving parent to continue (or not continue) visitation. If a custodial parent moves (and 75 percent will within four years of the divorce), the courts may intervene. While an order directing a parent not to move ("John Smith must reside for the next eighteen years in Honeyoe Falls") raises constitutional concerns, an order conditioning custody on residence within the area is less likely to do so.[37] ("Sole custody of John Smith, Jr., is conditioned on John Smith, Sr.'s residence in Honeyoe Falls.") Some states require the custodial parent to seek permission before taking the children out of the area; other states require the parent challenging the move to file a motion seeking a change of custody in order to raise the issue. No easy resolution exists for many of these disputes. If the move is far enough, permitting it may effectively end the noncustodial parent's involvement with the children; forbidding it may be a major imposition on the custodial parent's autonomy, including the ability to remarry, obtain better employment, or secure greater family support.

In 1996 the high courts in New York and California each decided major relocation cases within twenty-one days of each other. In both states, the moving mothers won in accordance with controversial new standards thought to favor custodial parents. Yet the differences in the way the courts approached the two cases illustrate the continuing tensions over the judicial role in managing family disputes. Before *Tropea v. Tropea*,[38] New York was one of the most restrictive jurisdictions. State law presumed that, if the move would deprive the noncustodial parent of "regular and meaningful access to the child," the move would ordinarily not be in the child's best interest, absent a demonstration of "exceptional circumstances." The custodial mother in *Tropea* wished to move from Syracuse to Schenectady (two-and-a-half hours away) in order to marry a Schenectady architect with whom she was expecting a child. The Judicial Hearing Officer denied her petition, concluding that her desire for a fresh start with a new family was insufficient to justify the disruption in the noncustodial parent's relationship with his children. "Exceptional circumstances" required something closer to a "concrete economic necessity" to gain approval under New York law.[39]

The Court of Appeals (the highest court in New York) reversed. The court noted that the older rule had proceeded from the premise that children can obtain an abundance of benefits from "the mature guiding hand and love of second parent" and that, consequently, geographic changes that significantly impair the quantity and quality of parent-child contacts are to be "disfavored." The court nonetheless held that

> Like Humpty Dumpty, a family once broken by divorce cannot be put back together in precisely the same way. The relationship between the parents and the children is necessarily different after a divorce and, accordingly, it may be unrealistic in some cases to try to preserve the

noncustodial parent's accustomed close involvement in the children's everyday life at the expense of the custodial parent's efforts to start a new life or to form a new family unit. . . . [I]t serves neither the interests of the children nor the ends of justice to view relocation cases through the prisms of presumptions and threshold tests that artificially skew the analysis in favor of one outcome or another.[40]

The court found the custodial parent's proposed move to be consistent with the children's best interest and therefore granted the petition to move she had been required to file under New York law.

In *Burgess v. Burgess*,[41] the California couple had agreed to joint legal custody and, as in *Tropea*, sole physical custody to the mother and liberal visitation for the father. Less than a year later, the mother accepted a job transfer and planned to move forty minutes away. She explained that the move was "career advancing" and would permit greater access for the children to medical care, extracurricular activities, and private schools and day care facilities. The father testified that he could not maintain his current visitation schedule if the children moved to Lancaster; he wanted to be their primary caretaker if the mother relocated.[42] The Court of Appeal, relying on the public policy of this state "to assure minor children frequent and continuing contact with both parents" concluded that mother could not retain sole physical custody absent a showing that the relocation was "necessary."[43]

The California Supreme Court reversed. It acknowledged that we live in "an increasingly mobile society," and concluded that the Court of Appeal had erred in requiring a determination of necessity.[44] The court emphasized that, in an initial determination of custody, the standard is solely one of the child's best interest; there is no basis for "imposing a specific additional burden of persuasion on either parent to justify a choice of residence as a condition of custody." "Moreover," the court held, "construing [the] Family Code . . . to impose an additional burden of proof on a parent seeking to relocate would abrogate the presumptive right of a custodial parent to change the residence of the minor child. . . . It has long been established that the 'general rule [is that] a parent having child custody is entitled to change residence unless the move is detrimental to the child,' and the showing necessary to establish detriment was a substantial one."[45]

Both New York and California thus rejected earlier precedents inhibiting moves. Both objected to placing too great a burden on custodial parents' autonomy or granting too much deference to the importance of the other parent's convenience or continuing contact. Nonetheless, the two decisions also differed considerably in their approach. The New York high court objected vehemently to the "bright line" rule opposing moves; it substituted a flexible fact-specific best interest test that required consideration of the reasons for the move. The California Supreme Court, in contrast, objected to too great an inquiry into the custodial parent's subjective motives.[46] It imposed a bright line rule instead, favoring moves by a parent with sole custody absent a strong showing of detriment. The centerpiece of both decisions, however, was a strong shift in emphasis. Prior decisions had assumed the continuing importance of both parents' continuing contact with the child; the new decisions required that the courts' evaluate the quality and quantity of the parents' respective contributions.

The existing state of custody law satisfies no one. Feminists declare that women are losing the custody wars (Martha Fineman's *The Neutered Mother* has the most creative rhetoric); fathers' rights groups insist that mothers are blocking fathers' access to their children (David Blankenhorn's "Every child deserves a father" is the most prominent slogan).[47] Richard Gardner sounds like Martha Fineman when he decries the "burgeoning of child-custody disputes unparalleled in history" and attributes the cause to "the replacement of the tender-years presumption with the best-interests-of-the child presumption and the increasing popularity of the joint-custodial concept."[48] Custody law is riddled by irony but also by an increasing coherence. A single source supplies both: the insistence that the law recognize the continuing ties of parents and children without a corresponding insistence that parents stay together.

In a 1998 symposium, Professor John Gregory, a veteran observer of the family law world, emphasized that

> Many observers, parents as well as mental health experts, lawyers, and judges, believe that children are injured substantially if denied interaction and relationship with both parents. Whatever conclusions should be drawn from the data, however, there is no doubt that judicial decisions, and increasingly, statutory formulations make assumptions which benefit non-custodial parents' visitation interests. It is assumed, and not infrequently stated explicitly, that it is in the best interest of a child to have continuing contact and a continuing relationship with the noncustodial parent. Indeed, the common judicial warnings against denial of all visitation or restriction of even supervised visitation indicate the social value assigned to non-custodial parent-child relationships.[49]

The result is that while domestic violence may be cause for caution in considering joint custody, even cases of clear parental misconduct rarely sever parental ties. Nonetheless, the courts are reconsidering the extent to which parents' behavior toward each other necessarily affects their relationship with their children.

Consider, for example, the infamous case of Woody Allen and Mia Farrow. When they began a relationship in the early 1980s, Mia had seven adopted children. She and Woody adopted an eighth, Dylan, they had a biological son, Satchel, and Woody adopted one of Mia's younger children, Moses. In 1991, not long after Woody's adoption of Dylan and Moses became final, he began an affair (and later married) Mia's college-age daughter Soon-Yi Previn. Mia accused Woody of molesting their daughter Dylan and sought to cut off his contact with their three children. The trial court found that Woody's behavior with Soon-Yi was inappropriate, that it had adversely affected the other children, that the evidence (though inconclusive) suggested that the abuse Mia alleged did occur, and that Woody was unable to understand the impact of his behavior on the children. Nonetheless, the court terminated only his visitation with Moses, and only because Moses, by then in his mid-teens, wanted nothing to do with Woody.[50] Although Mia Farrow "won" the case in the technical sense that the court upheld her side of the appeal, neither parent's position was fully vindicated. Instead, the court provided for continuing visitation in a supervised setting because of its conviction that Woody had a positive role to play in Dylan's and Satchel's lives.

In similar fashion, parental alienation, though often charged (it was, for example, Woody Allen's primary accusation against Mia Farrow), rarely results in a change of custody. Mary Ann Mason reports that, in a 1996 survey on child custody evaluation practices, 75 percent of psychologists indicated that they would favor an award of custody to Parent A if Parent B often attempted to alienate the child from the other parent.[51] Yet Richard Gardner, the author of *The Parental Alienation Syndrome*, recommends a custody shift in only a small percentage of alienation cases, and even then records his disappointment that the courts so rarely follow his advice.[52] What explains the discrepancy? The survey that Mason cites discusses parental alienation in the abstract: if alienation were the only issue under consideration, we would all prefer that it not occur. In the same survey, 77.7 percent of the psychologists would award custody to the parent who exhibits better parenting, 69.8 percent would favor the parent with whom the child has the closer emotional bond, and so on, through a list of thirty factors. The survey does not reveal who would receive custody when the "better" parent is the one who alienates, and Gardner maintains that "the primary psychodynamic factor operative for most PAS mothers is the desire to maintain the psychological bond with the child."[53]

The real-life case of *Renaud v. Renaud*[54] illustrates the dilemma. The father's affair with a coworker precipitated the divorce. The mother filed what the court termed an "excessive number of petitions" alleging abuse. The court found the mother had imagined abuse where there was none, the "baseless suspicions had adversely affected [the minor] in that he is no longer as loving towards [father] as he once was" and, should they continue, the accusations could seriously compromise the father-son relationship. The trial court nonetheless awarded the mother sole parental rights and responsibilities, limiting the father to visitation. The father appealed.

The Vermont Supreme Court affirmed the mother's custody award. The father had contended that "the court's express findings that the mother had undermined the child's relationship with father" made the custody award an abuse of discretion, but the Vermont court emphasized that custody was not a reward for good behavior. The court acknowledged that "a child's best interests are plainly furthered by nurturing the child's relationship with both parents, and a sustained course of conduct by one parent designed to interfere in the child's relationship with the other casts serious doubt upon the fitness of the offending party to be the custodial parent."[55] Nevertheless, the court found that the child had an extremely close emotional relationship with his mother, and that upsetting the relationship was likely to hurt him. The court accordingly upheld the mother's custody award, noting that "the court specifically ordered mother to encourage the child to develop a warm and loving relationship with father, forbade either parent from making disparaging remarks about the other in the minor's presence, and ordered extensive visitation with father totalling about fifty percent of the minor's time."[56] In the nasty Renaud divorce, custody commanded center stage, the child's psychological bond to his mother was the critical determinant, and judicial energy principally served to protect the father's continuing relationship with his son.[57]

Custody battles have become ground zero in the gender wars because they are among the few remaining family law disputes where courts judge adult behavior. Mia Farrow and Gail Renaud both felt wronged by their partners' infidelity. The fault system would have given voice to at least Gail's sense of betrayal (and Mia's, had she and Woody ever married), the tender years presumption would have given both mothers custody, and visitation was likely to happen informally, if it occurred at all. In the new system, the custody determination carries the full symbolic and practical weight of the adults' conflict. Maintaining parental ties is the new sine qua non of responsible parenthood — and a possible lever in the effort to exact revenge on the other spouse. The emphasis on parental cooperation then increases the importance of potentially disqualifying conduct: domestic violence, child abuse, and parental alienation carry greater significance as they become the limited exceptions to the principle of shared parenting. And, in this context, the courts still pass judgment. While neither the *Allen* nor the *Renaud* courts considered the father's infidelity to their partners,[58] they ruled that Woody's behavior with Soon Yi and Dylan had harmed his children, and that Gail Renaud's baseless allegations against her faithless ex-husband were bad parenting. Custody decisions — and the connections between parents and children — hold the new moral center of family law.

Figure 20.1 "Parenting plans."

21

Welfare Reform and the Permissibility of Motherhood

Marriage, particularly the marriage of the separate spheres, united male wage earners and female caretakers. Fatherhood apart from marriage founders (at least once paternity is established) on caretaking — to provide nurturing, single fathers must either re-create the unitary family by adding a mother or assume the responsibilities on their own. Single motherhood, on the other hand, has long foundered on money — without a full-time wage earner (and, until recently, without a full-time *male* wage earner), few families could be self-supporting.

The historical strategy for uniting financial independence and caretaking has been insistence on marriage, and the corresponding stigmatization of divorce and nonmarital procreation. Even if uncomplicated by social ostracism, however, single parenthood becomes viable only if the caretaker can secure a source of support outside marriage — from her family, the state, the father, or her own wages. If any single factor underlies family change, it is surely women's workforce participation and their relatively greater ability to support themselves and their families on their own. That single parenthood is more viable does not necessarily mean, however, either that it is desirable or universally possible. The question remains therefore whether a new ethic will take hold that embraces single parenthood as an acceptable choice — and what the terms of that embrace will be.

Much of our understanding about "permissible" motherhood is forged within the privacy of the nuclear family, and therefore off the public stage. Welfare, particularly in the form of the Aid to Families with Dependent Children program (AFDC), is the notable exception. The contrast between these public and private conceptions of motherhood had created tensions in the administration of the program since its inception during the Progressive era. In *Wake Up Little Suzie*,[1] Rickie Solinger captures these tensions in bold relief by contrasting the role of adoption and welfare in containing the consequences of teenage sexuality in the 1950s. For both blacks and whites, that decade's increasing rates of unmarried teen sex were a striking departure from earlier practices.[2] To portray the two communities' differing responses, she tells the stories of Sally Brown and Brenda Johnson, one white, the other black, but both sixteen, unmarried, and pregnant in 1957. Both girls are composites: the quotes, attitudes, experiences, and details of their stories are drawn from actual cases. Solinger presents Sally's story first.

The Friday after Thanksgiving, [Sally] . . . told her mother that she was pregnant. Mrs. Brown told Mr. Brown. Both parents were horrified — furious at Sally and particularly at her boyfriend, Tim, a local "hood" they thought they had forbidden Sally to date. In October, Sally told Tim about the first missed period and in November, the second. It was obvious to Sally that Tim's interest in her was dwindling rapidly. She felt heartsick and scared. . . .

The Monday following Thanksgiving . . . Mrs. Brown put her own plan into action. She contacted the high school and informed the principal that Sally would not be returning for the second half of her junior year because she'd been offered the wonderful opportunity to spend the Spring semester with relatives in San Diego. She then called up the Florence Crittenton Home and arranged for Sally to move in after Christmas vacation. . . .

At the maternity home, Sally took classes in good grooming, sewing, cooking and charm. In her meeting with the Home's social worker, Sally insisted over and over that she wanted to keep her baby. The social worker diagnosed Sally as borderline schizophrenic with homosexual and masochistic tendencies. She continued to see Sally on a weekly basis.

In mid-June, after the birth of a 7 pound 14 ounce boy, Sally told her social worker that she wanted to put the baby up for adoption because, "I don't think any unmarried girl has the right to keep her baby. I don't think it's fair to the child. I know I don't have the right."

On June 21, Sally's baby was claimed and later adopted by a Philadelphia lawyer and his infertile wife. Before Sally's 17th birthday in July, she was back home anticipating her senior year in high school. She had been severely warned by the social worker and her parents never, ever, to tell anyone of this episode and to resume her life as if it never happened.

Brenda's story is quite different.

Brenda's mother picked up on [her pregnancy] . . . in September when Brenda was beginning her third month. Mrs. Johnson had been concerned and upset about the situation, sorry that Brenda would have to leave school and disgusted that her daughter was thinking about marrying Robert, her 19-year-old boyfriend. On the day she discovered the pregnancy, she said to Brenda, "It's better to be an unwed mother than an unhappy bride. You'll never be able to point your finger at me and say, 'If it hadn't been for her.'"

At first, Robert stayed around the neighborhood. He continued to be friendly, and he and Brenda spent time together during the first half of Brenda's pregnancy. As she got bigger, though, she felt sure that Robert was spending time with other girls too. . . .

As Brenda got close to her due date, she worried how she would take care of a baby. There was no extra space in the apartment and no extra money in the family budget for a baby. Brenda asked her mother and older sister about giving the baby up, maybe to her mother's relatives in South Carolina, but her mother told her firmly, "You put your child away, you might as well kill him. He'll think no one wants him."

In early March, Brenda had a girl she named Jean in the maternity ward of the local public hospital. Brenda told the nurse, "I love the baby as much as if I was married." Having no money of her own, and having been offered little help from Robert who she heard had left for Florida to find work, Brenda went to the Welfare Office. There she received a long, sharp lecture about young girls having sex that taxpayers would have to bear the costs of. She was told she would have to find Robert if she wanted to get on welfare and that the welfare people would be watching her apartment building for him. The welfare worker asked Brenda if she knew what happened in some places to girls in her situation who got a second baby. The worker told her that in some states, a girl with a second illegitimate child would lose her welfare grant. She also said that some people liked the idea of putting a repeater in jail or making it impossible for her have any more bastards.[3]

In both cases, the girls violated societal norms by becoming pregnant and met with their families' disapproval. Neither married the father of their child, in part because neither man was terribly attractive when compared to the alternatives. There the similarities end.

Sally's family chooses adoption (Sally, like Brenda, is ambivalent) because of the powerful norms designed to discourage single parenthood. Sally's parents arrange for a private home that shares their interest in seeing the adoption completed. The home places their grandson with an infertile couple (a Philadelphia lawyer and his wife, no less) who will secure for the child the advantages of married middle-class life. Sally's education can proceed on course and, so long as she is quiet about the matter, her marital prospects should be unaffected. Sally and her son's middle-class standing have been preserved in the face of conduct that in an earlier era would have ostracized both.[4]

Brenda's family encourages her to keep the baby in large part because she cannot secure the advantages that accrue to Sally from adoption. Fewer couples were available to adopt African-American children, public agencies often discouraged those willing to do so, private agencies willing to take black clients were rare, and the prospects for a black child separated from his family could be bleak.[5] Precisely because the adoption process was perilous, single parenthood met with greater support within the African-American community, and Brenda's marital prospects were affected much less than Sally's might have been by the child's presence.[6]

While Brenda's circumstances are thus different from Sally's, the very force of the pressure necessary to persuade Sally to give up her child ensured the hostile reception Brenda would receive. The stigma that persuaded Sally to leave school during the pregnancy (with the isolation making her presence at the maternity home that much easier to secure) contributed to Brenda's expulsion in circumstances with fewer educational alternatives. The conventional (and in this case white and middle-class) wisdom that marriage or adoption were the appropriate responses to an unwed pregnancy ensured that the support available to Brenda would be limited and grudgingly given. Sally's parents' insistence on adoption protected her and her child from the harsher aspects of the norms against unwed pregnancies without a frontal assault that might have challenged the norms directly. Even social workers eager to assist African-Americans " 'felt uncomfortable' when confronted with unwed mothers who kept their children."[7] Maud Morlock, head of the U.S. Children's Bureau, "nurtured a hope that, someday, blacks would feel the stigma of illegitimacy as keenly as whites," and, Solinger reports, "imagined that this development would be an impressive signal of 'Negro progress.'" The remarkable part of Brenda's story, in the context of 1950s America, is that she received aid at all. Had her story not been set in Manhattan, the caseworker's response might well have been worse.

This dynamic contributes not just to racial disparities in the well-being of children but to persistent racialization of the issues underlying family behavior. Had, for example, Brenda been white — and white working-class teenagers were more likely than their middle-class counterparts to become pregnant and less likely to place their babies for adoption[8] — she still would have met with a chilly response from the social worker. Nonetheless, the support Brenda receives from the African-American community is strengthened by the hostility they know Brenda will receive from whites and the conviction that adoption is not a viable option for black babies. The social worker, aware in turn of the different norms among African-Americans, approves of neither Brenda nor the support she receives. Brenda may thus perceive the societal response to her pregnancy as racist even if the disapproval is identical to that accorded a white unwed mother, and the public identification of single parenthood with African-Americans — and with lower-class whites — would reinforce its unacceptability for girls like Sally.

Solinger's account of social attitudes in the 1950s describes in microcosm the conflicts that have always bedeviled public support for childrearing. The motivation for supplying aid is to vindicate, not undermine, mainstream values. Yet aid recipients may not be able to replicate ideal family behavior because of the circumstances that make them more likely to need assistance in the first place. The result is that aid programs are a better barometer of middle-class mores than of the needs of the clients they are supposed to serve. Welfare reform in the 1990s is the most recent of these clashes. Like its predecessors, the new legislation says more about evolving notions of motherhood than the conditions of the poor.

The nineteenth-century's middle-class conception of motherhood justified the initial provision of state aid. Progressive-era reformers were moved by the plight of urban women, often immigrants, unable to care for their children because of their husband's death or desertion and the assumption that no fit mother could provide for children on her own. Until the turn of the century, the major charitable response had been to make the children wards of the state. (Newt Gingrich's orphanages had once been real.) During the Progressive era, Linda Gordon observes, "the State acknowledged the inviolability of the relation of mother and child, its own stake in the preservation of the home, and the unique social value of the service rendered by mothers in maintaining their homes when fathers 'drop out.'"[9] By 1919 thirty-nine states and the territories of Alaska and Hawaii authorized direct funds for children to stay with their parents.[10]

The new institutionalized state assistance built contradictions into the program from the outset. The first was a practical one: the program sought to promote the objective of mothers caring for children in their homes without providing sufficient funds to do so. Mason observes that

> All single mothers were in the same bind, whether their single parenthood was the result of the death or desertion of their husbands, or the fact that they had never married. A "worthy" mother was one who devoted full time to her children, did not work outside the home, and led a conspicuously virtuous life with no male companionship. The reality of life for most single mothers was that, even if they were fortunate enough to warrant mothers' aid, they could not make ends meet. Their choices were limited: if they worked outside the home, they would not meet the conditions for aid, and ran the danger of being considered "neglectful," especially if they had to leave their children unattended for any period of time. This could be grounds for removal. If they sent their older children out to work so that they could remain in the home with younger children, that was also considered neglect. If they took in male boarders so that they could remain in the home, that was considered inappropriate, if not downright immoral. If they received help from males not their relatives, prostitution would be surmised.[11]

Complicating matters further was the fact that all these practices — child labor, maternal employment, male boarders — were common even among married couples for some of the immigrant groups who were major recipients of aid. Practices that were tolerated as part of the idiosyncratic values of foreign immigrants became matters of concern when state aid, administered by disapproving social workers, was awarded to those engaged in the activities. The cultural clash that Solinger identifies with race in the 1950s was an ethnic one at the turn of the century (with African-Americans and Mexicans largely excluded from participation).[12] "Americanization" became a major objective of the aid programs.

The state legislation authorizing assistance sidestepped direct conflict with mainstream mores by restricting eligibility. As late as 1931, most single mothers — and even more of those receiving assistance — were widows, and Mason observes that "less than half the states allowed pensions for women whose husbands were feebleminded or incapacitated, and most states refused to grant aid to divorced women whose husbands were still alive or to wives whose husbands had deserted."[13] During an era in which "poor man's divorce" consisted of desertion, state authorities were reluctant to substitute public aid for the support fathers were supposed to provide, at least in part because of fear that doing so would prompt the disappearance of even more men. Moreover, if married mothers separated from their husbands were suspect, unmarried and adulterous mothers were by definition unfit. Massachusetts law, in keeping with the sentiment of the era, declared that giving support to mothers of illegitimate children would "offend the moral feeling of respectable mothers and would do violence to a traditional sentiment that is inseparable from a respect for virtue."[14] The law was not without effect. In 1914 more than three-fifths of the illegitimate children born in Boston would become wards of welfare agencies in the first year of their lives.[15]

These early public assistance programs originated with the states; Congress federalized them with adoption of Aid to Dependent Children (ADC — later Aid to Families with Dependent Children, or AFDC) as part of the Depression era's Social Security System. By the 1930s, many European nations provided child allowances to all parents irrespective of income. These programs were often natalist in origin, spurred by concern about declining birthrates among "native stock." In the Unites States, increasing the population was never a primary objective, and universal assistance for children never took hold. Instead, support continued to be tied to women's market limitations. Unemployment compensation and old age social security were the most visible (and controversial) aspects of the New Deal legislation, and even women's advocates thought that such provisions, together with the extension of social security survivors' benefits to widows and orphans, offered the most promise for dependent women and their children. The ADC program, much more of an afterthought identified with pensionless widows, proposed to cover children under sixteen for whom there was "no adult person, other than one needed to care for the children, able to work and provide a reasonable subsistence compatible with decency and health."[16] The final bill limited coverage to children who had "been deprived of parental support or care by reasons of the death, continued absence from the home, or physical or mental incapacity of a parent" and permitted each state to impose "such other eligibility requirements — as to means, moral character, etc. — it sees fit."[17] In deference to the Southern states concerned about a potential loss of African-American and Latina workers, the legislation excluded domestic and agricultural workers from coverage. AFDC had been conceived of, and largely remained, a survivors' benefits insurance program.

As a national program committed to children's well-being, AFDC would undergo a wholesale transformation by the end of the 1960s. The role of widows as the primary beneficiaries would disappear. Whereas in 1937, widows constituted 43 percent of the ADC caseload, by 1961 the combination of lower death rates and more comprehensive public and private provision of survivors' benefits reduced their number to 7 percent.[18] At the same time, the conditioning of benefits on "moral" eligibility became increasingly anachronistic for a generation caught up in the sexual revolution. Particularly after Lyndon Johnson's declaration of war on poverty, state support became more of a claim of right and less one of charity.

The federal agency charged with administration of the program responded gradually to these changes, disallowing barriers to aid based on illegitimacy alone and eliminating most of the state restrictions that legislation in the 1930s had authorized. By the mid-1960s, the most common remaining restrictions on eligibility focused on the presence of a "man in the house" (detected through unannounced midnight home visits known colloquially as "Operation Bedcheck"), whose income would be deemed available to the recipient family.[19] The stated rationale for the rule was a financial one, but its practical effect was linked to the more traditional supervision of recipients' morality. In one of the more prominent welfare rights decisions of the 1960s, the Supreme Court invalidated these provisions, holding in 1968 that

> Congress has determined that immorality and illegitimacy should be dealt with through rehabilitative measures rather than measures that punish dependent children, and that protection of such children is the paramount goal of AFDC. . . . [I]t is simply inconceivable, as HEW has recognized, that [any state] . . . is free to discourage immorality and illegitimacy by the device of absolute disqualification of needy children.[20]

The Court held that the states could not simultaneously find the parents "unfit" and leave the children in these "unfit" homes without assistance. Mary Ann Mason hailed the changes as marking "the first time in American history poverty alone was not an accepted condition for removing children from their parents, no matter what their marital status or with whom they chose to live."[21] By 1997, of the 90 percent of AFDC families without a father, 37 percent of the recipients would be separated, divorced, or widowed while 53 percent would fall into the never-married category.[22]

These victories did not eliminate the contradictions underlying the AFDC program; indeed, they added new ones. The most direct concerned the program's shifting objectives. "Mothers' pensions," though justified by children's needs, were triggered by the father's death or disappearance. AFDC benefits, once the state liberalized eligibility requirements (and used survivors' benefits to protect widows and orphans), were overwhelmingly triggered by divorce and illegitimacy. Solinger's comparison of Sally and Brenda illustrates the resulting cognitive dissonance. AFDC made it easier for Brenda to exercise a choice that middle-class whites viewed to be unacceptable — the choice of keeping the child and raising it within a single-parent family.

The shift in the 1970s from adoption to abortion as the preferred response to unplanned pregnancy did little to dissipate the tensions. An entire generation came of age after the legalization of abortion grappling with its moral dimensions. The issue was not just whether abortion should be an option, but whether it could be a morally justified one. And the issue was not limited to the abstract or the political. Few sexually active women, in an era in which women were deferring marriage at historic rates, did not at some point confront the possibility that they might be pregnant, and consider the alternatives. Many who never did become pregnant came to the conclusion, morally as well as practically, that abortion was preferable to improvident childbirth. For those who chose abortion, the conviction that it had been an appropriate choice could be a deeply held one. Dr. Curtis Boyd, in describing his decision to continue performing abortions in the face of worsening harassment from organizations like Operation Rescue, reprinted the following letter of thanks.

Dear Dr. Boyd,

In 1973 you gave me an abortion. I was 26 years old, new in town, waiting tables. I am now 42 with two boys 4 & 9. Although both of their fathers left when I was pregnant, I was ready to love, nurture, and support them. I often think how different it would have been had my abortion been impossible. I don't know which would have been worse — being a confused, inadequate, impoverished mother; twisting my soul by giving the baby away; or experiencing an illegal abortion. I'm especially grateful to doctors like you. I'm sure you must take a lot of flack and see a lot of troubled women. But you make it possible for so many women to have healthy families. Thank you and Merry Christmas.[23]

"Healthy families" were associated with delayed childbearing in a decade in which U.S. fertility rates reached an all-time low. AFDC's more focused emphasis on the well-being of children also brought more focused concern about a program directly subsidizing children who — in accordance with both the prevailing conservative (chastity) and liberal (abortion) virtues of the day — should never have been born.[24]

The changing market position of women not only aggravated the dissonance, it eliminated the central justification for the program. All women were effectively being told that they were needed in the labor market. Feminism encouraged ambitious young women to seek their fortunes. All but the wealthiest families were coming to depend on two incomes, and the fragility of marriage made dependence perilous even for the middle class. Defending the domesticity of poor women, who historians remind us have almost never had the luxury of staying out of the labor market, became increasingly untenable. With family law scholars like Ann Estin documenting the wholesale lack of support for caretaking at divorce,[25] AFDC constituted what may have been the last remaining legal recognition of the Victorian family's insistence on mothers' domestic role.

These contradictions almost certainly would have led to reformation of the program long before the 1990s were it not for the larger conflict in which discussions of the program took place: the ideological divide between right and left on the appropriate role of the state. By the 1960s, AFDC advocates supported the program not because they shared its emphasis on the nineteenth-century ideals of middle-class motherhood, but because they saw government assistance in attaining a minimum level of well-being as a basic societal obligation that should be extended toward everyone. These advocates would have combined more generous social programs with relaxed eligibility restrictions: sex, pregnancy, marriage, children — all would be matters of individual choice. State support for employment, child care, and the immediate needs of children would be available irrespective of marriage. United Nations resolutions and international treaties began to champion such positive as well as negative rights,[26] and Daniel Patrick Moynihan proposed a negative income tax, guaranteeing a minimum income to all, as an official in a *Republican* administration. Within this framework, AFDC's major failing was that it did not go far enough.

By the time of Ronald Reagan's election in 1980, these views were in retreat. Free-market libertarians who wished to diminish the role of government joined with traditional moralists who opposed state subsidization of
behavior they found offensive. Their movement gathered force as nonmarital birthrates reached one-third of the national total, and Charles Murray
published op-ed pieces about the "coming white underclass."[27] The conservative coalition exploited the contradictions at the core of the AFDC program, the public hostility to government in general, and welfare recipients
in particular to propose limiting the program or abolishing it altogether.
Democrat Bill Clinton won election in 1992, promising to "end welfare as
we know it."

The welfare scholars most influential in charting the reforms were liberals, not conservatives. Harvard professors David Ellwood and Mary Jo
Bane joined the Clinton staff to help draft new welfare legislation. As aca-
demics, one of their principal insights had been that the welfare population
could be seen as two different groups with different characteristics: numer-
ically greater short-term recipients who, on average, remained on welfare
less than two years, and longer-term recipients, averaging total periods of
AFDC aid of more than five years, who received the bulk of the benefits.
Bane and Ellwood explained the paradox this way:

> Suppose that a [hospital] has 100 beds, 99 of which contain very long-
> term patients. The 100th bed is used by short-term patients, each of
> whom stays in the hospital for only one day. Over the course of one year,
> there will be 464 patients in these beds — 99 long-term patients and
> 365 short-term patients. Thus, the fraction of patients ever in the hos-
> pital over the course of the year who are short-term is very high — 79
> percent (= 365/464). On the other hand, at any point during the year, 99
> percent of all the beds will house long-term patients. Thus, because the
> longer-term patients are more likely to show up in a patient count at any
> point during the year, they dominate the hospital "caseload" at any
> point.[28]

These two groups differed in ways that went far beyond the length of their
time on welfare. The short-term group was, on average, older, better educated, with more labor market experience. It used AFDC as a kind of "income insurance," providing transitory protection against income losses arising from a divorce, job loss, or other income-threatening event. These
recipients use welfare benefits for a short period of time, get back on their

feet, and then leave the welfare system never to return."[29] The long-term recipients, the majority of whom were cycled on and off welfare, tended to be a less employable group. At the beginning of their first welfare receipt, "nearly two-thirds of longer-term recipients had neither a high school diploma nor a GED; half had no work experience; and two-thirds were under the age of twenty-five. Nearly three quarters had never been married."[30] And while welfare recipients on average had fewer children than the nonwelfare population, the longer-term group had more.

Welfare "reform," with the Republican Congress passing more draconian legislation than Clinton proposed, targeted long-term recipients. With the distinctions between the two groups in mind, Ellwood had suggested that no individual be entitled to welfare benefits for more than two years at a time, or five years cumulatively. He also recommended raising the minimum wage, expanding the earned income tax credit, creating a refundable child care credit, preserving subsidies for child care and medical insurance, and improving child support enforcement.[31] The Republican Congress adopted the time limits without much of the employment support. In the summer of 1996, Congress passed and, over the objection of many in his own administration, the president signed the Personal Responsibility and Work Opportunity Reconciliation Act of 1996. The act did indeed end "welfare as we knew it." It projected $54 billion in savings, primarily by slashing benefits to legal immigrants (benefits largely restored by subsequent legislation); it adopted a five-year cap on the receipt of federally funded assistance; and it established stringent new work requirements, imposed through state participation rates (e.g., 25 percent of a state's AFDC caseload had to obtain employment by the end of the first year). Its most radical changes, however, were structural. The act dramatically increased the authority of the states over cash assistance for needy families, with the federal contribution limited to a fixed block grant, and it abolished the entitlement to assistance so that even applicants who met the stringent new requirements were not guaranteed aid.[32] AFDC as a federal guarantee to needy families — and as a symbol of the sanctity of mothers' presence in the home — was at an end.

Welfare reform was fought on the battleground of permissible motherhood. The preamble to the "Personal Responsibility" Act stated that "prevention of out-of-wedlock pregnancy and reduction in out-of-wedlock birth are very important Government interests" and that the policy contained in the statute is intended to address the crisis of out-of-wedlock childbearing.[33]

Although Congress, fearing that its efforts would be declared unconstitutional, stopped short of conditioning public assistance on marital status, the legislative history clearly demonstrates that the purpose of the act was to promote marriage, marital parenting, and paternal support.[34]

Welfare reform's most vehement critics have similarly cast the issue in terms of the value of mothering. Santa Cruz University political science professor Gwendolyn Mink, in a chapter entitled, "Why Should Poor Single Mothers Have to Work Outside the Home? Work Requirement and the Negation of Mothers," argues that

> More intrusive and patriarchal than any national welfare policy we've ever known, the Personal Responsibility Act tells the poor single mother that if she doesn't participate in a father-mother family, she surrenders her right to care for her children. Although outside work can especially compromise a poor mother's ability to attend to her children's schedule and range of needs, the PRA makes it the paramount requirement for poor mothers who are persistently single. In impairing their capacity to meet their personal responsibilities as parents, the PRA thus repudiates them as mothers.[35]

Welfare reform in practice, however, comes closer to television's *Grace Under Fire* than it does to a return to the situation in Hawthorne's *Scarlet Letter*. Welfare recipients overwhelmingly leave the rolls for work, not marriage, and their new image is one of struggling single parenthood rather than a quest for new partners (or even romance). Columbia law professor Carol Sanger, in a thoughtful article on mothers separating from children, observes that "[c]urrent welfare reforms are premised on the belief that a working mother as role model is more important for poor children than whatever they may gain from a homebound but publically supported mother."[36] The media depictions of "reformed" recipients have been markedly more positive than the welfare images before the new act, with the *New York Times* running a front-page story (a year after the act's passage) declaring that "As Rules on Welfare Tighten, Its Recipients Gain in Stature."[37]

Welfare reform has the potential — particularly when the economy worsens, time limits expire, and less generous states take a meat-ax to what is left of the protections it offers — to make poor children's material circumstances substantially worse. There will inevitably be a residual group of mothers who, because of substance abuse, psychological trauma, or physical limitations, cannot succeed in the workplace, and the most recent studies indicate that domestic violence, invisible in the legislative debate, is a major obstacle to workplace success.[38] Despite these limitations, welfare reform is already remaking the image of motherhood in ways that suggest that new reforms (should the liberals regain sufficient support to make them happen) will be built into a model of working parenthood rather than domesticity. Mary Jo Bane, for example, tells the not atypical story of Donna, a Boston mother of five, with six-year-old twins, who left welfare for a job as a parent aid worker at a children's service agency. Her story is at least initially a success: she has more income, greater self-esteem, and the conviction that she is a better role model for her children. Her younger children, however, are having difficulty at school. Two have been diagnosed as hyperactive, and the youngest has a learning disability. Her job leaves her with less time to help them with homework and to coordinate their activities at and after school. An educational or medical crisis could easily force her to choose between her job and her children's well-being. Even if that happens, however, the focus will be different from the older program. The triggering event (at least in the public mind) will not be the birth of a fifth nonmarital child, but the absence of adequate afternoon care, flexible family leave, school advocates capable of negotiating the bureaucracy for students with learning disabilities, or expanded medical coverage — in short, issues in which the middle class and the poor are more likely to share an agenda for rebuilding the infrastructure supporting children.[39]

True reform will accordingly require rethinking the connections between children and society. The older model rested on the family combination of breadwinner and homemaker. ADC, ultimately renamed Aid to *Families* with Dependent Children, sought to compensate for the wage earner's absence in an era when a full-time homemaker was deemed critical to children's well-being. The new model instead treats the family's connection to the labor market as essential, and holds that societal support should complement rather than undercut that participation. There are two challenges to this change.

The first is to reverse the decades-long disinvestment in children. Even if welfare reform, a booming economy, and community initiatives reduce the number of improvident births, they are unlikely to stem the long-term increase in family instability, and that increased instability has widened the gap between societal wealth and the well-being of the next generation. Greater employment may improve the lives of welfare moms and their families, but they will still need assistance in securing adequate education, day care, medical insurance, and support for children with special needs. The elimination of aid based on family structure (and, perhaps more importantly, the growing multiplicity of family forms) increases the importance of direct support for children. Congress recognized this to some degree when it extended medical benefits for children, but perhaps the most disturbing aspect of welfare reform implementation has been the 54 percent drop in insurance coverage for former recipients.[40]

The second challenge will be to reconnect children and communities. In a provocative new book, Harvard sociologist Orlando Patterson takes on what he terms the myth that African-Americans compensate for greater family instability with a richer network of kinship ties. Instead, he concludes, on the basis of his own and other sociological research, that poor African-Americans are the most isolated group in society. He explains that marriage is not just a source of immediate support but of access to a wider network of societal ties, and that marriage outside of one's immediate ethnic, geographic, or social circle is a type of "cultural dowry" that multiplies connections and resources. Patterson emphasizes that

> Through sheer, baseless repetition, and through nonrepresentative case studies of a few Afro-American housing projects by urban anthropologists, it has become an accepted belief that large networks of support and natural neighborhood communities are out there waiting to be developed and built on. Would that this were so. But my own analysis of rep resentative samples of national network surveys confirms what other scholars have found: The typical Afro-American has a much smaller network of friends and kinsmen than other Americans do. And, what was most unexpected, the proportion of members of this attenuated network who are kinsmen is smaller than in other Americans' networks. There are no "hoods" out there.[41]

The result, Patterson concludes, is that poor African-American children have less access to the "network of ties that structures the flow of information that both socialize people as they grow up and provide social resources critical for competent functioning in society."[42]

Patterson's immediate topic is gender relationships within the African-American community, and he proposes greater emphasis on the educational success of African-American men, rewriting their sexual and behavior codes, encouraging marriages (particularly by black women) that cross racial and other social lines, dispersing racially concentrated ghettos, and increasing the support for childrearing, support that he views as critical to accomplishing his other objectives.[43] Nonetheless, the problem he identifies is a more general one. Welfare recipients have been triply isolated by their lack of access to marriage, employment, and, for inner-city blacks, the white suburbs where resources are in greater supply. Children within single-parent families share their mother's isolation if she stays home with them, and are too often left on their own or with slightly older siblings if she is employed. Middle-class communities are slowly — but much *too* slowly — increasing the available supervision for the children of "two wage-earner" families. For low-income parents, even if married but especially if single, the lack of community support constitutes a crisis. In this sense, poor, inner-city African-American children represent the "canary in the mine" whose difficulties reflect a more sensitive reaction to the changing circumstances that challenge society as a whole.

Figure 21.1

Renegotiating Childhood

Subj: Sign up for FREE XXX now!
Date: 98-06-05
From: DMcdo59630

Erotic Pics/Chat

Free Nude Pics! CLICK HERE

Hot Sexy Sweeties

Celebs! Teens! Hookers!

Hairy Men and
thier [*sic*] Brut Wangs! CLICK HERE

Click Here To Be Removed From Mailing List

THIS spring we suggested that our sixteen-year-old son introduce the Argentine exchange student staying with us to America OnLine. When we checked our e-mail that evening, we discovered the message printed above. Our son insisted that all he had done was to go into one of the chat rooms, that the message was unsolicted. We believed him. When we first subscribed to AOL when he was eleven, our house quickly became a magnet for every sixth-grade male in the neighborhood. At first, we were delighted to find that our efforts to interest our children in computers were so successful. Then we figured out how to view the graphic attachments to the e-mail messages stored on our hard drive. This time, the sixteen-year-olds demonstrated no rapt absorption in the computer suggesting eagerly awaited communications. The graphic e-mails had gone commercial (if no more polished in vocabulary or spelling), and their purveyors were only too willing to come to us, with or without a formal invitation. Between the two incidents, we had installed parental blocks on the computer. While they may shield our younger children from accidentally wandering into an inappropriate website, they did not obstruct the e-mail solicitations. We are persuaded that any determined teenager who cannot find his way around the blocks is unprepared for life in a high-tech world. After all, with only a mild demonstration of interest, there is now an industry designed to assist him.

Childhood has changed, and the paradigm that had defined it, guided it, and governed it for the last three centuries is about to give way. Childhood, as something that lasts much beyond toddlerhood, is the Victorian family's greatest invention. Earlier eras had, by the age of seven, treated children as miniature adults, and did not invest overly much concern in them either as individuals or as a distinct part of the population. As children became the Victorian family's reason for being, childhood gained "as a special, and increasingly prolonged, period of social moratorium, of subordination and lack of adult responsibilities."[1] The nuclear family provided a thick wall of protection that insulated children from the larger world until they were ready to be shepherded into responsible adulthood, and claimed in return a large measure of deference to parental authority.

Within this system, the legal regulation of childhood has been not so much about children as it is about the relationship between families and society. Law schools address children's legal standing in courses entitled "Children, Families, and the State," and these courses, which include as much constitutional law as family law, begin with a classic set of cases that articulate a libertarian approach to the family. In the process of articulating a relatively static conception of the relationship between parents and children, these cases miss much of the changing relationship between adolescents and society.

Meyer v. Nebraska and *Pierce v. Society of Sisters* typically start the semester. Barbara Woodhouse describes the two cases as "liberal icons," in which "the Supreme Court of the [conservative] *Lochner* era struck down state laws from Western and Midwestern states prohibiting the teaching of foreign languages in the elementary grades and requiring that all elementary students attend public school."[2] The cases not only remain good law, and their principles so thoroughly embraced, that Justice Brennan, in his *Michael H.* dissent, observed that "I think I am safe in saying that no one doubts the wisdom or validity of those decisions."[3] Woodhouse, whose objective is a revisionist one, explains that at least one reason the cases have been accepted so uncritically is their role in opposing the anti-German and anti-Catholic hysteria of their day. The statute at issue in *Meyer* prohibited the teaching of a foreign language (German in the case that presented the issue to the Supreme Court) to any child who had not completed the eighth grade. The Oregon statute at issue in *Pierce*, which had been sponsored by the American Legion, backed by the Populist and Progressive leadership in Oregon, and passed with the support of the Ku Klux Klan, required every child between eight and sixteen to attend public school. Woodhouse observes that "[t]he guiding sentiment behind the Oregon law . . . seems to have been an odd commingling of patriotic fervor, blind faith in the cure-all powers of common schooling, anti-Catholic and anti-foreign prejudice, and the conviction that private and parochial schools were breeding grounds of bolshevism."[4] Even in our modern era of restrictions on bilingual education, Brennan is still correct that barring private schools or foreign language instruction altogether would be constitutional anathema.

Woodhouse has no interest in resurrecting a prescribed curriculum. Instead, her concern lies with the image of the family on which the decisions rest. In what Woodhouse describes as "the dramatic focal point" of *Meyer v. Nebraska*, Justice McReynolds (whom Woodhouse describes as "the most bigoted, vitriolic, and intolerant individual ever to have sat on the Supreme Court") invoked the specter of Plato's Republic. He wrote:

> For the welfare of his Ideal Commonwealth, Plato suggested a law which should provide: "That the wives of our guardians are to be common, and their children are to be common, and no parent is to know his own child, nor any child his parent. . . . The proper officers will take the offspring of the good parents to the pen or fold, and there they will deposit them with certain nurses who dwell in a separate quarter; but the offspring of the inferior, or of the better when they chance to be deformed, will be put away in some mysterious, unknown, place as they should be." In order to submerge the individual and develop ideal citizens, Sparta assembled the males at seven into barracks and entrusted their subsequent education and training to official guardians. Although such measures have been deliberately approved by men of great genius, their ideas touching the relation between individual and State were wholly different from those upon which our institutions rest.[5]

Neglecting the religious liberty and intellectual freedom arguments developed in oral argument, McReynolds based his opinion on parents' right to control their children.

Pierce v. the Society of Sisters built on the *Meyer* foundation. The brief for the Society of Sisters, in opposing compulsory public education, argued that

> Children are, in the end, what men and women live for. Through them parents realize, as it were, a measure of immortality. . . . All that we missed, lost, failed of, our children may have, do, accomplish in fullest measure. . . . For them parents struggle and amass property and put forth their greatest efforts and strive for an honored name. . . . In this day and under our civilization, the child of man is his parent's child and not the state's. Gone would be the most potent reason for women to be chaste and men continent, if it were otherwise.[6]

Justice McReynolds agreed. In an opinion that Woodhouse describes as a "sequel and anticlimax" to *Meyer*, McReynolds reiterated "the liberty of parents and guardians to direct the upbringing and education of children under their control." "The child is not the mere creature of the State;" the majority opinion held, "those who nurture him and direct his destiny have the right, coupled with the high duty, to recognize and prepare him for additional obligations."[7] In her article, "Who Owns the Child? *Meyer* and *Pierce* and the Child as Property," Woodhouse concludes:

> Was the child private property of parents or a public resource? In the language of children's rights, the public child had needs that created rights that became, through legislation, positive claims on the community. In the language of laissez-faire, the parent controlled the destiny of the private child in keeping with its station in life. The Court in *Meyer* rejected Plato in favor of Spencer.[8]

Woodhouse does not find it surprising that the Supreme Court that decided *Meyer* and *Pierce* also invalidated federal legislation restricting child labor.[9]

Janet Dolgin picks up the story where Woodhouse leaves off. She begins her analysis in the 1970s with *Yoder v. Wisconsin,*[10] and concludes that the case, even as it reiterated *Pierce*'s parental rights perspective, modernized it in exactly the fashion Woodhouse's analysis suggests. *Yoder* (like Dolgin's article) starts with the issue *Pierce* left open: the constitutionality of compulsory school attendance laws. If parental autonomy were as absolute as the Supreme Court suggested in the 1920s, the state would have no power to compel attendance at any school. The Amish parents in *Yoder*, concerned that no high school could insulate their children from the "worldly influences" they feared, wished to keep their teenagers out of school altogether. They were charged with violation of the Wisconsin law that mandated school attendance for children under sixteen who had not graduated from high school. Chief Justice Burger's decision declaring the law unconstitutional relied expressly on *Pierce* in holding that

> The history and culture of Western civilization reflect a strong tradition of parental concern for the nurture and upbringing of their children. This primary role of the parents in the upbringing of their children is now established beyond debate as an enduring American tradition.[11]

Dolgin observes, however, that *Yoder* did not recognize a general parental right to object to compulsory education. While *Pierce* had invalidated mandatory *public* education for all who objected, *Yoder* created an "arguably unique" exception for the Amish. Indeed, the Court expressly rejected any absolute parental rights over their children, explaining that

> There is no doubt as to the power of a State, having a high responsibility for education of its citizens, to impose reasonable regulation for the control and duration of basic education. . . . [A] State's interest in universal education, however highly we rank it, is not totally free from a balancing process when it impinges on fundamental rights and interests, such as those specifically protected by the Free Exercise Clause of the First Amendment, and the traditional interest of parents with respect to the religious upbringing of their children so long as they, in the words of *Pierce*, "prepare them for other obligations." 268 U.S., at 535. It follows that in order for Wisconsin to compel school attendance beyond the eighth grade against a claim that such attendance interferes with the practice of a legitimate religious belief, it must appear either that the State does not deny the free exercise of religious belief by its requirement, or that there is a state interest of sufficient magnitude to override the interest claiming protections under the Free Exercise Clause.[12]

The Court, in applying this balancing test, then concluded that a year or two of additional formal education would do little to prepare Amish children "to participate effectively and intelligently in our open political system" or "to be self-reliant and self-sufficient participants in society" at the same time that compulsory attendance would conflict directly with Amish religious beliefs. Even as it declared that the "primary role of the parents in the upbringing of their children is now established beyond debate as an enduring American tradition," the *Yoder* decision rested directly on the parents' interest in directing their children's *religious future* rather than parental autonomy as an abstract right.

Dolgin, after establishing the limits of *Yoder*'s embrace of parental rights, nonetheless sets it together with *Meyer* and *Pierce* in opposition to a children's rights model championed by Justice Douglas in his *Yoder* dissent. Douglas opined that "[w]here the child is mature enough to express potentially conflicting desires, it would be an invasion of the child's rights to permit such an imposition without canvassing his views."[13] He described the Court's decision as imperiling "the future of the student, not the future of the parents."[14] He thereby recognized children as autonomous individuals with interests distinct both from their parents and from the state. Dolgin concludes that "[e]ven today, almost three decades after the Court decided *Yoder*, Justice Douglas's understanding of children and of the parent-child relationship in that case contrasts markedly with almost all Supreme Court jurisprudence involving conflicts between parents and the state."[15]

Where Dolgin finds some support for Douglas's views is not in the conflicts between parent and state, or between parent and child, but rather in those cases that involve direct conflict between child and state. Dolgin cites two cases from the 1960s as establishing the high-water mark of children's rights. In *In re Gault*, the Supreme Court granted juveniles many of the same procedural rights as adults in criminal proceedings.[16] In *Tinker v. Des Moines Independent School District*, the Supreme Court recognized the First Amendment right of high school students to wear black armbands to class.[17] These cases, however potentially revolutionary in their implications, spawned few progeny that survived the counterculture era in which they were decided. The equivalent in the 1990s was more likely to take the form of prosecuting the children, at ever younger ages, as adult offenders, and then granting them the full range of adult protections — and penalties.

While staying well clear of a children's rights model outside the criminal context, the Supreme Court, Dolgin notes, has nevertheless backed away from *Meyer* and *Pierce* in a discomfiting case-by-case reexamination of family relationships. She uses two cases, *Parham v. J.R.* and *Bellotti II*,[18] to frame what she calls the "transforming traditional model." She chooses *Parham* and *Bellotti II* because the "conflict between the two cases is obvious."[19] In doing so, she uses a method familiar to every law professor and casebook author: choose two cases with seemingly irreconcilable results and ask students to discern their commonality. The responses may offer a glimpse into the inner workings of American law — and, perhaps more reliably, the inner workings of student thinking.

Dolgin's choice of *Parham* and *Bellotti II* appears well suited to the exercise. *Parham* reiterated Supreme Court support for parental authority, echoing *Meyer*, *Pierce*, and *Yoder*. The case involved the involuntary commitment of children to state mental institutions at their parents' behest. The district court had ruled the statute unconstitutional for its failure to provide the children with the right to contest their commitment in an adversary proceeding. The Supreme Court overturned the lower court's ruling, upholding, instead, the constitutionality of the Georgia procedures. The Court explained that

> Our jurisprudence historically has reflected Western civilization concepts of the family as a unit with broad parental authority over minor children. . . . Surely, this includes a "high duty" to recognize symptoms of illness and to seek and follow medical advice. The law's concept of the family rests on a presumption that parents possess what a child lacks in maturity, experience, and capacity for judgment required from making life's difficult decisions. More important, historically it has recognized that natural bonds of affection lead parents to act in the best interests of their children. . . .
>
> Nonetheless, we have recognized that a state is not without constitutional control over parental discretion in dealing with children when their physical or mental health is jeopardized. [Yet simply] because the decision of a parent is not agreeable to a child or because it involves risks does automatically transfer the power to make that decision from the parents to some agency or officer of the state.[20]

The Court concluded that the State was more than able to protect itself from the risk that some parents might "dump" unruly children into state facilities through its own admission procedures, which required a medical determination that the child was a suitable candidate for treatment. So long as the state concurred that hospitalization was appropriate, the Court refused to grant children the right to contest their parents' preferences for their treatment.

Bellotti II, decided like *Yoder* and *Parham* in the late 1970s, became the first in this long string of cases to recognize children's interests that might be at odds with those of their parents. *Bellotti II* involved the constitutionality of state provisions that required minors to obtain their parents' consent before obtaining an abortion. The Supreme Court held such laws to be constitutional only if they provided for a judicial bypass procedure that left open the possibility of abortion without parental consent.[21] The Court observed that

> A pregnant minor is entitled in such a proceeding to show either: (1) that she is mature enough and well informed to make her abortion decision, in consultation with her physician, independently of her parents' wishes; or (2) that even if she is not able to make this decision independently, the desired abortion would be in her best interests.[22]

Dolgin observes that "the decision in *Bellotti II*, in contrast with that in *Parham*, focused on protecting the choices of the child involved against the contrary choices of their parents."[23] In her effort to reconcile the two decisions, Dolgin concludes that both recognize the limits of childhood autonomy and decision-making power, but that more pervasively they represent the limits of the Supreme Court's jurisprudence of childhood. Dolgin concludes that "in the late 1970's, the frame within which the Court securely countered attacks against challenges to traditional visions of family life a half century earlier began to totter. . . . [T]he remarkable force of traditional understandings of childhood and of the parent-child relationship began to wane, but not yet to falter absolutely."[24]

In a larger sense, however, the libertarian parent-child model had already begun to falter by the time *Meyer* and *Pierce* were decided in the 1920s. Barbara Woodhouse writes that "McReynolds's defense of the privatized family and flat rejection of public control of child-rearing as 'wholly different' from American institutions were all the more ardent and categorical, because they denied present reality. By 1923, the family citadel was crumbling under assaults from common schooling, child welfare, juvenile justice, child labor laws, and a host of government assumptions of paternal prerogatives designed to standardize child-rearing and make it responsive to community values."[25]

The true patriarchal model of parenthood, one that treated children as no more than their fathers' property, had given way well before the 1920s. There was a time when a father's power over his children was so absolute that it included the right to put them to death and, indeed, in some societies fathers might be seen as having an obligation to do so if their children's behavior sufficiently threatened public well-being or if the larger claims of God (Abraham and Issac come to mind) or community were sufficiently compelling. Father as Old Testament Patriach, however, had passed into history well before the nineteenth century. Even the early modern family, which Lawrence Stone describes as still embodying close to absolute parental authority and routinely harsh discipline ("Spare the rod, spoil the child" was the motto for *this* era in childrearing), recognized some limits to parental claims and at least the possibility of prosecution for pedicide.

Nonetheless, the revolution (many historians would claim the very invention of childhood) came with the Victorian family. At least in its initial stages, however, the Victorian conception of childhood had remained a private matter. Where the absolute patriarchs of old had monitored the morals and manners of their offspring as part of their obligation to the community, the Victorian family conducted its moral instruction for the children's benefit. Wealthier parents financed the initial expansion of secondary and higher education to secure their children's position in society, and bore the opportunity cost involved in keeping women and children out of the labor market as the price necessary to police the boundary between the increasingly dangerous public and the private spheres. Perhaps most centrally, the middle class led in the substitution of quality for quantity, investing much more love, attention, instruction, and supervision in each of their children — and making the nuclear family much more central to that result, not just during infancy but into early adulthood. Nineteenth-century capitalism, like its late twentieth-century equivalent, increased the economic distance between the top and bottom layers of society, and the middle class reaped the benefits of its greater investment in human capital by preparing its sons to occupy (and its daughters to marry within) the higher-paid managerial and professional ranks in the new industrial order.

Were this the end of the story, children would remain their parent's "property," if more akin to pampered thoroughbreds than ill-treated draft horses. By the end of the nineteenth century, however, three additional forces converged and ultimately altered the relationship between family and state. First, the success of industrialization had increased the demand for a larger quantity of skilled labor than parental investment alone was likely to supply, and many capitalists welcomed government subsidization of their training costs. Second, the populist reaction against increasing inequality generated support for public education as an essential component of an empowered citizenry and an egalitarian society. Third, progressive reformers, who had internalized the new childhood ideal, sought to ameliorate the circumstances of the less privileged (and particularly the immigrant poor) by extending the benefits of middle-class childhood to a broader segment of the population. These three movements came together in their recognition of a societal interest in children independent from the value parents themselves might assign to their young.

To be sure, these movements, neither singly or together, sanctioned wholesale intervention in the family. Enlightened industrialists, progressives, and even populists were not much more likely than Justice McReynolds to sanction Plato's ideal; they came together most forcefully in their support for subsidized (rather than compulsory) public education. By the 1920s, the battle lines were being drawn, not over teaching German in elementary school but over mandatory education (whether public *or* private) and restrictions on child labor. Working-class parents, and particularly the immigrant Catholic working poor of the urban north, correctly perceived that these measures reflected disapproval of their parenting practices and a corresponding infringement of their autonomy in the name of their children.

Seen in this light, the decisive battles occurred not before the Supreme Court, but in the forty-eight state legislatures that ultimately restricted child labor and provided for compulsory education to an increasing degree at public expense. These battles have been so conclusively settled that the more recent ones over home schooling and the Amish become the exceptions that prove the rule rather than a frontal challenge to the ideal. Woodhouse is right that the Supreme Court's celebration of parental autonomy in *Meyer* and *Pierce* was anachronistic at the time the cases were decided. By the 1920s, children were becoming an increasingly important *public* concern. The skirmishes along the way established dividing lines between federal and state authority, academic standards and the suppression of cultural expression, mandatory curricula versus mandatory schools. Were *Meyer* and *Pierce* to be rewritten today, their outcomes would be the same, but the reasoning would be that of *Yoder*: the states' unquestioned right to prescribe curricula becomes constitutionally troublesome when it conflicts with other established interests, not because it clashes with parental autonomy as an abstract ideal.

If *Meyer* and *Pierce* are sideshows, what of their resurrection in the more recent cases of *Parham* and *Bellotti II*? The key to understanding these cases is their allocation of responsibility between parents and state. *Parham* involved involuntary incarceration in a mental institution. Presumably, the child's behavior required attention, and treatment at the institution was the parents' preferred solution. The child's attorney argued that the free care available at a state institution created the risk that parents would choose to "dump" troublesome teens on state hospitals at public expense. The Court's response: the State could — and did — protect its own interests through an independent evaluation of the suitability of the proposed care. The case, though it invoked the ideal of parental authority, amounted to no more than the conclusion that a third determination, through a separate hearing ostensibly on the child's behalf, would serve no greater purpose (while imposing greater expense) than the combined result of the parents' and the hospital staff's separate conclusions.

Bellotti II, and the subsequent judicial bypass cases, create no greater insight into the constitutional status of parent-child relationships. Abortion is so emotionally and politically charged a subject that most commentators treat it as sui generis. Moreover, the birth of a child, in Anglo-American law, has long served as the marker replacing one parent-child relationship with another as the unit of legal analysis. Nonetheless, even a cursory examination of abortion decisions suggests that too unilateral an emphasis on parental autonomy is unsustainable as an approach to these cases. First, there is no clear principle of parental autonomy in operation. If parents would like their daughter to have an abortion, and she refuses to consent to the procedure, few medical professionals would proceed, and the parents would be powerless to compel a different result. "Parental autonomy" can only prevent an abortion, not compel one. Second, the consequences of a decision to proceed with a pregnancy cannot be contained within a discrete family unit. The result compels a pregnant teen to become the mother of a child she does not want. Once the baby is born, the reluctant mother acquires far greater independence in deciding how to care for the child than she enjoyed in deciding to give birth. While the judicial bypass procedure satisfies no one (and offends those who believe abortion is never sanctioned), it is hard to argue that it represents much of an intrusion into functioning parental relationships, much less a blow for children's independence.

The larger issue underlying these cases, and one much harder to address within the confines of Supreme Court decision-making, is the interaction between parents and society in providing for children. The *Parham* parents relied on state assistance to provide for their troubled son; the *Bellotti II* parents failed to insulate their daughter from a pregnancy neither appeared to want. Helen Fisher, in her sociobiological account of monogamy, adultery, and divorce, argues that many scholars confuse the advantages that accrue from the nuclear family in caring for infants with those necessary for provision for adolescents. She observes:

One might argue that with the origin of dependent teenagers, parents became obliged to remain together longer to provide for their dependent young. But as I pointed out in Chapter 5, divorces tend to cluster around the fourth year of marriage — about the duration of human infancy. Nowhere in the world do people characteristically remain together to raise their young through their teenage years, then systematically depart.

Since our ancestors did not adopt the reproductive strategy of extending their partnerships to rear adolescents, nature took a creative tack: human kinship evolved. What an ingenious twist: a web of related *and unrelated* individuals locked in a formal network of ties and obligations, an eternal unbreakable alliance dedicated to nurturing their mutual offspring, their mutual DNA.[26]

Fisher's analysis has sociobiology's flaws as well as its strengths: her statement is overly general and it is only loosely tied to the empirical literature from which it develops. Nonetheless, her insight is an important one — the Victorians' emphasis on the nuclear family in providing for adolescents is anomalous, a larger kinship group (Hillary Rodham Clinton's *It Takes a Village* comes to mind) the norm. The challenge for the 1990s has been to attempt to deal with the fragility of the nuclear family in providing for older children at a time when the very conception of extended kinship groups seems impossible to reconcile with a highly mobile and rapidly changing society. What Dolgin describes as the traditional understandings of the parent-child relationship have not just "begun to falter," they are increasingly irrelevant to the most significant challenges to our ability to provide for children. Parents, whether married or single, full-time professionals or stay-at-home caretakers, cannot hope to meet all of children's needs on their own.

In this context, the case that is perhaps most emblematic of the changing status of childhood is one unlikely to be included in family law texts — *Reno v. ACLU*. Among the forces that most threaten Victorian notions of childhood are the technological innovations that invade the home and increasingly make the image of childhood as a protected period of innocence a chimera. In response, Congress passed the Communications Decency Act (1997), legislation designed in principal part to shield minors from the type of blandishments with which this chapter began. The American Civil Liberties Union challenged the statute's constitutionality almost immediately after it was signed. In oral argument before the Supreme Court, the Deputy Solicitor General began his defense of the statute by observing that

> The Internet is a revolutionary advance in information technology. It also provides a revolutionary means for displaying patently offensive, sexually explicit material to children in the privacy of their homes.
> With as many as 8,000 sexually explicit sites on the World Wide Web alone at the time of the hearing, and the number estimated to double every 9 months, the Internet threatens to render irrelevant all prior efforts to protect children from indecent material.
> All of the laws regulating the display of indecent material in theaters and book stores, on radio, TV, cable, and telephone, all of these approach insignificance when the Internet threatens to give every child with access to a connected computer a free pass into the equivalent of every adult bookstore and video store in the country.[27]

The government's argument failed to sway the Court in large part *because* of the pervasiveness of Internet communications and the difficulty of segregating transmission intended for adults from those available to children.

The Communications Decency Act had banned the knowing transmission of "obscene or indecent" materials to any recipient under age eighteen as well as the knowing sending or display of "patently offensive" messages in a manner available to minors under the age of eighteen. The American Civil Liberties Union and nineteen other plaintiffs alleged that the terms "indecent" and "offensive" were vague and overly broad, and that the act would therefore chill constitutionally protected speech. In upholding their argument, the Supreme Court agreed that "[i]n evaluating the free speech rights of adults, we have made it perfectly clear that '[s]exual expression which is indecent, but not obscene is protected by the First Amendment.'" The government attempted to counter that prior cases had drawn a distinction between transmitting indecent materials to minors and transmitting them to adults. Indeed, in 1968 the Supreme Court had rejected the argument that First Amendment guarantees are independent of age, upholding the constitutionality of a New York statute that prohibited selling objectionable materials to minors. The Supreme Court in *ACLU v. Reno* acknowledged the precedent, observing that "we relied not only on the State's independent interest in the well-being of its youth, but also on our consistent recognition of the principle that 'the parents' claim to authority in their own household to direct the rearing of their children is basic in the structure of our society.'" The Court nonetheless held the case inapplicable to the Communications Decency Act, explaining that

> In arguing that the CDA does not so diminish adult communication, the Government relies on the incorrect factual premise that prohibiting a transmission whenever it is known that one of it recipients is a minor would not interfere with adult-to-adult communication. The findings of the District Court make clear that this premise in untenable. Given the size of the potential audience for most messages, in the absence of a viable age verification process, the sender must be charged with knowing that one or more minors will likely view it. . . .
>
> The District Court found that at the time of trial existing technology did not include any effective method for a sender to prevent minors from obtaining access to its communications on the Internet without also denying access to adults. The Court found no effective way to determine the age of a user who is accessing material through e-mail, mail exploders, newsgroups or chat rooms.[28]

Concluding that the scope of the CDA's coverage was "wholly unprecedented," the Court invalidated the legislation.

Reno v. ACLU is by no means the last word on Internet regulation.[29] Nonetheless, the case involved the Court's clear preference, driven by its First Amendment analysis, for narrowly tailored measures that would permit parental control over material coming into their homes over an approach that would make widely disseminated communications safe for minors. The next battleground in this issue is likely to be Internet usage at public libraries. The battle lines involved in the library debate capture almost precisely the larger positions on the role of children in society. At one end are conservative groups who oppose library access to obscene material generally. Closely allied with them are parental groups who believe that libraries should install filtering devices or take other measures to restrict minors' access to offensive materials. These parental groups, however, divide on an issue central to the debate about the relationship between community and children: some believe that the library has an obligation to censor children's access in accordance with community standards while others insist that libraries should defer to the parents' particular preferences. (Most in this group would therefore impose the most restrictive parental preferences on all children, but if an individual parent authorizes access for her children to adult material, they would permit it.)

At the other extreme are those who oppose all restrictions. They, too, divide into two camps: those who oppose library censorship because they believe that the selection of appropriate material will vary from child to child and age to age and must therefore remain a parental responsibility, and those who oppose all censorship irrespective of age.

I believe that much of this discussion misses the role of libraries in the modern age. I acquired new insight into that role one year when I decided to grade exams at home. I spent the first part of the day in wonderful and productive isolation until the time my nanny was due to bring the children back from school. Then, seeking to escape the distractions they would bring, I left for the local public library. I got there just before school let out, and watched as a steady stream of students from the parochial school down the street marched in, in uniform, and stayed until their parents picked them up. These students were generally between the fifth and eighth grades, an awkward age when they had become too old for after-school programs and too young to go home by themselves. They often came in groups, sat down at the library tables, and began homework or chatted quietly. If they became bored, they wandered outside or into the library stacks. The librarians intervened if they became too loud, but did not otherwise supervise their activities. Nonetheless, the solitary character of morning library usage gave way to a vibrant, if necessarily subdued, social center during those afternoon hours.

When I listen to debates over library Internet access, I picture my local library as a test of the debaters' contact with reality. Parental supervision was nonexistent, and at odds with the caretaker role the library had assumed. Librarian intervention was also limited, and almost entirely concerned with insuring that the students did not overly interfere with the library's other patrons. At the same time, the library computers never became the object of the type of rapt attention that my home computer has occasionally become. There are, I think, two reasons. The first is lack of privacy. The library computer screen is visible enough to deter anyone likely to be embarrassed by the association with graphic material. The second is the library policing of group behavior. Without the protection of a wall of privacy or the bravado of the group, adolescent behavior is much less an issue.

These dilemmas frame the challenges in negotiating childhood in the era now upon us. Hillary Clinton is right that, over the course of much of human history, it has taken a village to shepherd children from toddlerhood to adulthood. The Victorian era's creation of childhood as a distinct — and privatized — period of life firmly ensconced within a domestic — and feminine — preserve is no longer tenable. The positions in the library debate that strike me as the most preposterous are those that depend on parental supervision. In my local library the children were there *because* of the unavailability of their parents. In this debate, as in *Meyer, Pierce, Yoder, Parham,* and *Bellotti II,* the emphasis on the sanctity of parental authority becomes more insistent as it becomes less relevant. There are only two choices: making community spaces safer for children or better preparing children to negotiate a more perilous world on their own. Libraries do not necessarily have an obligation to install filtering devices,[30] but they do have one to ensure that it is not groups of middle school students who set the terms for library usage.

Figure 22.1 "Children and the Internet."

From Partners to Parents

The Unfinished Revolution

I N this book, I have argued that family law is in the midst of a transformation from partners to parents as the centerpiece of family obligation. To chart this transformation, I have divided the book into three parts — philosophical, empirical, and legal — in an effort to show that there is a remarkable degree of consensus about much of that process — and about identification of the divisions that remain. The first part of the transformation, the dismantling of marriage as the exclusive determinant of family connections, is complete and well documented in every discipline that has undertaken the task. The second part — the revitalization of the law of custody, child support, and community obligation addressing parental relationships — is under way, with substantial agreement about the broad framework in which these changes are occurring. The unfinished portion of the transformation is the renegotiation of the partnerships — between men and women, family and community — necessary to make parenthood successful. Because we are in the midst of the process, because the critical issues combine the normative with the descriptive, and because the renegotiation takes place along the fault lines of gender and class, the most contentious of the issues about the future of the family occur here.

To understand these divisions it is useful to return to the conclusions on which the first section of the book ended. In that first part, I presented the following grid that compared the four positions in the debate in terms of the importance of the two-parent family and specialization between home and market (figure 23.1):

| | Two-Parent Family | Two Parent Family |
	Favor	*Neutral*
Specialization		
Favor	*Becker:* Specialization linked to traditional family	*Fineman:* Specialization irrespective of family structure
Specialization		
Neutral or Oppose	*Galston:* Two-parent family irrespective of specialization	*Okin:* Egalitarian roles irrespective of family structure

Figure 23.1

I then noted the destabilizing effect of Murphy Brown. What I did not comment upon is the gender division.

The two men — Becker and Galston — differed on specialization, but favored the provision of child care within the two-parent family. The two women — Okin and Fineman — also differed on specialization, but disagreed with the men on the importance of keeping couples together. These differences are related to their varying philosophical perspectives, but they are also directly connected to the respective strength of men and women's bargaining positions in the emerging family order. This gender division corresponds to the largest practical disagreement underlying modern family law disputes: the issue of whether the law should promote the continued involvement of both parents in their children's upbringing or whether it should place greater priority on securing support for those providing the care. The issue underlies all of family law as it affects the terms on which marriage and divorce should occur, the principles that should govern support and custody, and the relationships that the state should recognize and support. Recasting the philosophical divisions in the book in terms of solutions, the philosophical chart (figure 23.2) can be redrawn in the following terms:

	Two-Parent Family *Favor*	Two-Parent Family *Neutral*
Specialization *Favor*	*Becker:* Discourage inefficient divorce; oppose subsidies	*Fineman:* Provide support for caretaking independently of marriage
Specialization *Neutral or Oppose*	*Galston:* Discourage divorce in families with children; add waiting periods	*Okin:* Equalize contributions to caretaking within and without marriage

Figure 23.2

To understand why these divisions are gendered ones, it is useful to return to Gary Becker's initial analysis.

Becker defended the "traditional family" (conflating family arrangements from hunter-gathers to the Victorians) in terms of the advantages of specialization and the need for long-term contracts (marriage) to encourage the exchange. Susan Moller Okin objected to the enterprise because of the inherent vulnerability that came with limited market involvement. What both acknowledged, but neither made central to their argument, was the extent of the gender premium that came, not from the arrangement in a particular marriage, but simply from being male. Most historians, however much they reject Fredrich Engels' generalizations, date the rise of the patriarchal family (with its insistence on lifelong monogamy and the double standard) to the emergence of agricultural economies — and the concentration of real property ownership in male hands. Most historians, however much they reject industrialization as the sole explanation for the family of the separate spheres, acknowledge the link between these changes in family form and a labor reorganization that afforded only middle-class men access to the higher-paying professional and managerial jobs of the new industrial order, and working-class men exclusive access to the better-paying manufacturing positions. Even Donna Franklin, in her account of the African-American's family quite different history, emphasizes that its most patriarchal period came during the sharecropping era, with its almost exclusive male access to share-cropping contracts. The size of the male premium and its importance to the survival and social standing of the next generation, together with the dependence of those "choosing" the domestic sphere, made marriage as a long-term proposition necessary — and possible on something close to a universal basis.[1] Indeed, Susan Westerbrook Prager reports that, during the nineteenth-century debate on the adoption of community property in California, opponents argued that

> This proposition, I believe, is calculated to produce dissension and strife in families. The only despotism on earth that I would advocate is the despotism of the husband. There must be a head and there must be a master in every household; and I believe this plan by which you propose to make the wife independent of the husband, is contrary to the laws and provisions of nature — contrary to all of the wisdom which we have derived from experience.[2]

Becker and Okin agree that these long-term marriages were largely marriages on what today would be viewed as "male" terms, and what secured female consent was the lack of alternatives. Prager concluded that "[t]o these men marriage was held together by little more than male dominance complemented by the complete subjection of the wife. The institution was based on power and dependency; to tamper with these foundations, let alone accord the spouses equal status in property matters, would destroy the institution."[3]

Prager's California delegate (Mr. Botts), in the context of a community property debate, incorporated the arguments made back East against the married women's property acts and what ultimately became women's relatively greater independence within the family of the separate spheres. History proved him at least partly right. In the nineteenth century, women's greater economic independence, however minimal in today's terms, corresponded with a greater degree of family instability. It also, however, remade the terms of the marital bargain in both normative and practical terms so thoroughly that even today's conservatives do not advocate depriving women of their property ownership (though a 1998 Southern Baptist convention did admonish women to obey their husbands as the key to marital success). Couples adjusted — and preserved a large measure of domestic tranquility — by internalizing these new roles as central parts of marriage.

To the extent that today's relationships are undergoing a similar transformation, it is because of a modern economic reorganization, at least comparable to that of the last century, that has increased the demand for women's market labor and increased women's relative ability to make it on their own. The gender gap, to be sure, remains, but it retains its greatest significance above the "glass ceiling"; there remain relatively few women who enjoy the entrepreneurial success of a Gary Wendt. Below the upper-management ranks, there has been a steady expansion of higher-paying supervisory positions in traditionally female occupations, some retrenchment in male middle-management circles, and a dramatic loss of earning power among less skilled males. Marriage is no longer a woman's only (or even necessarily a secure) avenue to family life or middle-class status; divorce, while still costly financially, need not imperil the means of self-support. The terms on which women are willing to marry and stay married have shifted accordingly.

A recent article in the *Journal of Marriage and the Family* (which newspaper headlines described as "New Study Confirms What Men Have Always Known; The Key to a Happy Marriage Is Doing What Your Wife Says") underscores the point. Of course, the actual research was somewhat more complicated than the newspaper headlines suggested. The authors designed an examination of 130 newlywed couples to determine which kinds of marital interactions were most likely to predict divorce. Five years later, they compared the intact marriages with those ending in divorce and found that

> The marriages that wound up happy and stable had a softened start-up by the wife, that the husband accepted influence from her, that he de-escalated low intensity negative affect, that she was more likely to use humor effectively to soothe him, and the that he was more likely to use positive affect and de-escalation to effectively soothe himself.

Conversely, the pattern predicting divorce was

> negative start-up by the wife, refusal of the husband to accept influence from his wife, wife's reciprocation of low intensity negativity in kind, and the absence of de-escalation of low negatively from the husband.[4]

The authors concluded that negative exchanges between spouses were characteristic of all marriages and that therapists could afford to ignore them. The problem, they suggested, was "the escalation of negativity and only by the husband, which we believe is an index of the husband's refusal to accept influence from his wife." They went on to argue that

> If we assume that this sequence is, in fact, an index of the refusal of some husbands to share power with their wives by rejecting the demands she makes, then the issue in therapy becomes not one of getting the couple to apply the brake in the face of negative affect reciprocity, but in getting husbands to share power with their wives. Usually the wife brings marital issues to the table for discussion, and she usually brings a detailed analysis of the conditions in which the problem occurs, its history, and suggestions for a solution. Some men, those whose marriages wind up stable and happy, accept influence from their wives, and some do not. Most sociological analyses of marriage emphasize the loss of power that men have experienced over the last 40 years with the loss of the breadwinner role and with women's emergence in the workplace.[5]

What these sociologists demonstrate is that it takes a different strategy — and different internalized roles — to make contemporary relationships work. It should not be surprising that women initiate 70 percent of all divorces.

The debate over family relationships takes place within this changing dynamic. Barbara Dafoe Whitehead (otherwise known for her article "Dan Quayle Was Right") argues that a changing culture of ideas has shaped divorce practice. She writes:

> Beginning in the late 1950's, Americans began to change their ideas about the individual's obligations to family and society. Broadly described, this change was away from an ethic of obligation to others and toward an obligation to self. . . .
>
> This ethical shift had a profound impact on ideas about the nature and purpose of the family. . . . More than in the past, satisfaction in this [the family] sphere came to be based on subjective judgments about the content and quality of individual happiness rather than on such objective measures as level of income, material nurture and support, or boosting children onto a higher rung on the socio-economic ladder. . . . The family began to lose its separate place and distinctive identity as the realm of duty, service and sacrifice. Once the domain of the obligated self, the family was increasingly viewed as yet another domain for the expression of the unfettered self.[6]

Considered in gender terms, however, the references to "duty, service and sacrifice" translate into the roles of the separate spheres. "Work by the husband," Mitt Regan reminds us, "was a responsibility owed to the wife, and nothing more detrimental could be said about a man than that he did not support his wife and family." Conversely, women were expected to be loving wives and mothers — and to subordinate their own interests to those of their husbands and children. If their husbands fulfilled their duty of support, if they fulfilled "such objective measures as level of income," women had a duty not to complain. Whitehead acknowledges that, between 1890 and 1920, in the now famous Indiana community known as Middleton, "two-thirds of divorces were granted on the grounds of non-support."[7] Husbands' rejection of their wives' influence would not have been grounds, legally or practically, for divorce in 1920 unless the husbands lost their jobs in the process.

Whitehead, like Galston, ends her book with a call to dismantle the divorce culture. She writes:

> Our civic and religious traditions offer a vision of the obligated self, voluntarily bound to a set of roles, duties, and responsibilities, and of a nation where sacrifice for the next generation guides adult ambitions and purposes and where wholeness of self is found in service and commitment to others.[8]

What Whitehead does not explore is what these ideals mean in the context of modern relationships. Does it mean that a wife has a duty to remain with a husband who rejects her influence? That a husband must defer to his wife's choices about the children's schooling, neighborhoods, and geographic mobility? That both parents should remain employed if necessary to pay for private school tuition? That at least one parent should expect to sacrifice his career prospects for the children, and the other should then (and only then?) be obligated to remain with her partner for life? When Whitehead calls for "service and commitment to others," what terms does she have in mind?

Becker, Okin, Fineman, and Galston frame the alternatives. Becker and Fineman represent the extremes, not just because they embrace diametrically opposed positions with respect to the role of the state, but because of the implications of their positions for men and women's respective bargaining power. Becker's emphasis on privatization would favor both eliminating AFDC and other child subsidies and enforcing the private agreements that were rendered illusory with no-fault divorce. The result would make it relatively more difficult to raise children outside of marriage, encourage women to devote a larger share of their energies to the domestic sphere, and make it harder for both spouses to divorce. Gary Wendt might find that he had to pay more than half of the estate to leave his wife of thirty-two years; the younger women who initiate the majority of divorces would find it harder to leave the men who reject their influence — and harder to change the balance of intact relationships. While Becker does not address the balance of power within these unions, William Kristol does. He maintains that women, unlikely to come to these conclusions entirely on their own, must be taught "to grasp the following points: the necessity of marriage, the importance of good morals, and the necessity of inequality within marriage." Men, being stronger, "are likely to enjoy their liberation at the expense of women," and women should accordingly recognize that the price they pay for marriage and morality is "submission to the husband within the family."[9] The Southern Baptists, who might also advise women to submit "graciously," would agree.

Fineman, in contrast, proposes a system likely to maximize women's power in family relationships. She emphasizes recognition of the mother-child dyad as the defining element of family, with those who nurture (male or female) receiving custody and subsidization independently of family structure. Her proposals would alleviate the major element in women's dependence — and lack of bargaining power — and condition male participation in childrearing on either assumption of the primary caretaker role or their partner's consent. Linda Hirshman and Jane Larson's *Hard Bargains* (1998) maintains that the necessary complement to Fineman's vision of equality within the family is genuine protection of women's autonomy in sexual relationships as well.[10] Nancy Levit, however, cautions that men have historically been excluded from the nurturing role, and that until the welcome mat is laid out for them, it is unrealistic to expect full participation.[11] Fineman's critics allege that keeping the door closed will be the necessary effect of her proposals.

Okin and Galston prefer both an intermediate position with respect to the role of the state and greater sharing rather than a division of responsibilities within the family. They differ on how to accomplish that result, and their differences, like those between Becker and Fineman, occur on the fault lines of gender. Okin tends to advocate reforms that increase equality within intact families and enhance women's bargaining power at divorce. She would therefore encourage men and women to share childrearing responsibilities in ways that do not subordinate one partner's career to the other, and to assume an equal division of postdivorce responsibilities in ways that make it easier for women to leave unhappy relationships. She would oppose a return to fault or other restrictions on divorce that would disproportionately burden women's possibilities for exit, but she avoids extended discussion of feminist concerns that joint custody and other efforts to secure men's continuing involvement do so at the price of women's autonomy. To realize the type of equality Okin advocates requires that men and women share responsibility for children; Okin is neutral on the issue of whether this takes place in two-parent families because of her insistence that the exchange occur on something closer to women's terms.

Galston shares Okin's preference for more egalitarian families; he differs from Okin in the relative priority he accords to keeping parents together. The issue he evades is the degree of coercion he is willing to use to accomplish the task, and on whom it should be applied. Galston's proposal for a braking mechanism on divorce, most experts conclude, is unlikely in itself to have much influence partly because most couples reach the point of no return before they approach the legal system, and partly because it does not address divorcing couples' motivation. Two strategies might succeed in keeping couples together: Becker's traditional one of restricting the alternatives, by making it more difficult for men to enjoy new relationships and women to survive on their own, or Fineman's more radical one of insisting that the price men have to pay to secure relationships with their partners and children is behavior women find acceptable. Galston, though embracing welfare reform proposals that make it harder for poor women to raise children on their own, is less clear on the intended effect of his middle-class reforms. Yet leaning hard on someone is necessary to their success.

What none of the authors address directly is the question of "sentiment," of the internalized roles necessary to make these models work. The early modern family dealt with children by giving fathers decision-making power over everything, the separate spheres by recognizing mothers' authority within the home. Both did so by encouraging the secondary parent's deference to the primary one (at least within their respective spheres). Becker would revive these terms. Fineman would abandon the requirement that both parents remain involved. Okin and Galston require a model of parental partnership.

The model that offers the greatest possibility of success, the one that provides some common ground between feminists and fatherhood advocates, is a supportive partnership model. Children do better when both parents are involved; they do better still when the second parent's involvement supports the first's. The question then becomes how to encourage mutually respective and supportive relationships in a system powerless to impose them directly. The courts and the public may be farther ahead of the theorists in exploring what the new model of partnership means. The renegotiation that is occurring between parents fits within the framework of parental obligation the courts are in the process of building:

CREATION   Marriage once meant preparation for parenthood. Today, married couples may wait a decade before having children and find, once the child is born, that parenthood changes their lives — and their relationship to each other — far more dramatically than marriage. Societal pressure in the early days of parenthood still provides greater support for a specialized division of labor than an egalitarian one. Employers are more understanding of maternal leave than paternal leave, and early infancy is a period in which the divergence in gender roles is likely to be greatest. Yet the renegotiation of supportive partnerships most critically needs to take place here. We need idealized images — and something close to Regan's conception of status roles — that encourage fathers to join mothers in newborn care, both on their own and as supportive partners. Embedded in my memories of my firstborn's early days of life is the deep conviction that I would have never learned to nurse without my husband's assistance. Negotiating the rest of our childrearing responsibilities was much harder, but the early days in the hospital set the tone for much of what was to come.

The stakes for this transition may be higher than we realize. Although most theorists have argued that specialized marriages are likely to be more stable, Margaret Brinig and Frank Buckley found that married women's workforce participation *lowers* the likelihood of divorce.[12] Brinig's more recent work with Steven Nock finds, in a complementary way, that relationships in which either spouse assumes the disproportionate share of women's traditional responsibilities are more likely to break up, and that these effects are amplified when the other spouse agrees that the result is unfair.[13] It is hard to imagine stable relationships without at least a working agreement on an appropriate division of responsibility.

UNMARRIED COUPLES   The challenges are greater for unmarried couples. The emerging model of motherhood emphasizes the need for women to invest in their financial and emotional self-sufficiency, or to consider adoption or abortion as alternatives. It also encourages men to think of themselves as guarantors ready to contribute to abortion, child support, or caregiving if the mother fails to work matters out on her own. The more difficult issue is the extent to which partnership is an indispensable element of responsible parenthood. The issue is a volatile one. Dan Quayle differed most markedly with Murphy Brown's creators over his insistence on the father's distinctive role, and perhaps the most emotionally charged issue beneath the surface of the gay and lesbian marriage debate is recognition of same-sex partnerships as a state-sanctioned locus for childrearing. At the same time, many women prefer to follow the example of the African-American community and enlist support from a wider circle of friends and relatives who may — or may not — include the biological father while other women, often those with fewer options still, have agreed to the father's custody when they could not raise the child on their own. Between 1995 and 1998 the number of single fathers increased by 25 percent.[14]

The solution to this dilemma, while inherently a complex one, also involves a partnership model, if only to identify the parents who fail to qualify. Welfare reform, however contested, is part of a debate on the terms of single motherhood. If women are to win recognition of a right to parent alone, it must be on terms that provide for the child's needs. Legal recognition of paternity is moving toward what Judge Fennelly termed a "step up or step out" approach, that is, fathers need to establish a relationship with their children at birth or to make room for someone who will. The secret to the puzzle of the Supreme Court's zigzags is the Court's preference for parental partnerships, with new husbands given preference over fathers who failed to establish an ongoing relationship with the child at birth. Fatherhood, as the New York and California high courts finally recognized, may not involve an ongoing relationship with the mother, but it involves at least enough cooperation with a parental partner to secure the child's well-being.

MAINTENANCE   Once parental bonds are established, it is not so much that the criteria for maintaining them changes as that the presumption against severance increases substantially. For mothers and fathers who have assumed a parenting role, the child's interests will ordinarily lie with the continuation of those bonds. Direct harm to the child presents the clearest exception; inability to cooperate with the other parent presents a basis for hesitation. The clearest way to encourage supportive partnerships, however, is at their inception. We need greater support for relationships based on cooperation and mutual respect.

A critical need in making this happen is greater ability to manage conflict within relationships. Kate Bartlett and Angela Harris argue that the structure of family relationships plays a major role in domestic abuse. They observe:

> The role of dominance in the incidence of domestic violence is undisputed. In a national survey of 2,143 families in the late 1970's, less than 3 percent of wives in couples that followed an egalitarian pattern of decisionmaking had been violently attacked in the preceding year. The corresponding figures for wives in wife-dominant couples was 7 percent, and for wives in husband-dominant couples over 20 percent. . . . Similarly, family violence rates are highest in states where women have the lowest economic and educational status. . . . Husband-beating was also most frequent in husband-dominant households (15 percent) as compared to wife-dominant households (6 to 10 percent) and egalitarian ones (under 5 percent). . . . Child abuse is also more frequent in husband-dominated households.[15]

In some ways, these problems may be ones of transition. Male-dominated households were once the norm. With the move to more egalitarian relationships, men and women's expectations may be more likely to diverge, with conflict resulting from the disagreements. Internalizing egalitarian norms and delegitimizing the resort to violence may help provide a better foundation for maintaining relationships. The model I constructed at the end of part 1 suggests that the major choice that lies ahead will be between more relatively egalitarian partnerships or even more single-parent families.

PARENTING APART   Cooperation is hardest to achieve in the midst of war. Perhaps the greatest challenge for divorcing parents is to establish parenting models in which the couple refrain from taking out their hostility toward each other on their children. Joan Kelly notes that, in warring families, the negative consequences of divorce appear before the breakup; she emphasizes counseling that establishes a basis for future cooperation as the most pressing need at divorce. Joint custody standards should incorporate recognition that abuse and excessive conflict can be disqualifying factors.

Baby Emily, after all the twists and turns of its tortured passage through the Florida courts, is emblematic of the emerging model of parenthood. The mother, unable to secure financial independence or the father's emotional support, turned to adoption. The father insisted on custody without a demonstration of either financial commitment or emotional stability. The

Florida courts finally ruled that the father's respect and concern for the child's mother was a matter of major importance for the child as well. If the father had met that test, the mother could not exclude him from a say in deciding the child's future, but then she would have been much more likely to do so in the absence of a judicial decree.

Parenthood, of course, is a status of ancient origin that requires no legal recognition to be a major part of our lives. The social construction of parenthood has nonetheless been governed for centuries by marriage and the partnerships that connect adults to children. With the shift in those adult relationships from societally imposed status relationships to matters resting to a far greater degree on private choice, parenthood now stands in its own right as the public status on which the law is rebuilding family obligation. The process is not just a matter of legislation and case law. For many of my generation who thought we knew what to expect from relationships, parenthood — with its demands, external expectations, gender divisions, and emotional intensity — took us by surprise.

The legal shift from partnership to parenthood as the legal basis of family obligation is now largely complete. The clearest shifts are those in divorce adjudications, with child-centered issues the focus of most proceedings. The changes look something like this (figure 23.3):

	Old System	New System
Central relationship	Husband-wife	Parent-child
Determining feature	Marriage	Conception +
Duration	Death or Divorce	Age of Majority
Most important financial division	Property or alimony	Child support (for all but the wealthy Wendts)
Key determinant	Fault	Custody
Power to settle	Parties alone (modern law)	Parents + court

Figure 23.3

Under this system:

- Parents have no obligations to each other other than those voluntarily assumed, and even those may be terminated at any time.

- Parent-child ties begin at birth and are the same for marital and non-marital children. They can be transferred (adoption) or terminated by the state, but not abandoned.

- Children's rights stand independently of the mother and father's relationship to each other. Thus, child support is independent of visitation, a parent cannot contractually forgo a child's right to support, and parental fault (e.g., adultery) is irrelevant.

The changes in partnership will take longer to realize, and their success depends on the understandings that occur outside of court. Like the changes that produced the Victorian family, the transformation now under way is proceeding from a mix of economic restructuring and cultural renegotiations. If the changes appear, much like their nineteenth-century counterparts, to require more from men, it is because the underlying shift in bargaining power is one that has reduced the size of the male premium. Even in Gary Becker's model, men have to pay a higher price to stay in marital relationships than they did when women enjoyed fewer alternatives.

This transformation, if to a large degree inevitable, is often needlessly destructive, and custody disputes — precisely because they are so central to the process — are major contributors to the carnage. A winner-take-all custody system may give a parent with only somewhat less involvement either no incentive to stay involved at all or a major incentive to fight to the bitter end. Conversely, a mindless emphasis on joint custody is often threatening to mothers, particularly if they are locked into hostile relationships or feel at a disadvantage in litigation with better-financed mates. Richard Gardner, though more often cited by father's rights groups, attributes much of what he terms "parental alienation syndrome" to women's insecurity in a system that fails to acknowledge their relationship with children. A clearer understanding of the terms of engagement, one that starts with a presumption of both parents' continuing involvement but also recognizes clear grounds for disqualification, would benefit everyone.

The other partnership in the midst of renegotiation is the one between family and state, and it is proceeding along two parallel tracks. The first concerns the state's terms of recognition for struggling families. Welfare reform, with its redefinition of permissible motherhood, has occupied center stage, but the state has also assumed a greater role in establishing paternity and securing child support as well as preventing abuse and neglect. These changes undoubtedly have an ideological component, but they also proceed from the need to replace marriage and divorce as the central determinants of family legitimacy. And they are not without effect. In the first half of the 1990s, child support collections doubled, and teen pregnancies, with greater emphasis on abstinence and contraception and an economy encouraging greater investment in the future, dropped by 14 percent across the board and 21 percent for African-Americans.[16]

The second track concerns the relationship between adolescents and community. Greater instability appears to be a permanent part of family life, and even intact families have greater difficulties insulating their teenagers from the perils of society than they did a half century ago. This renegotiation is complex and multifaceted, but it is to a large degree independent of the issue of which families of small children the state chooses to support. Instead, it involves rebuilding the community infrastructure that looks out for children, socializes them into adult roles, and bridges the gaps that families fail to fill. For the state and for local communities as well as for the legal system, the transformation is one that requires a shift in focus from adult interests to children's standing on their own.

Shortly after the birth of my first child, a friend, who was herself six months pregnant, asked me if I felt more "mature." With the stress of childbirth and sleepless nights still fresh in my mind, I answered an emphatic "no." Three years later, during a walk in the park with what by then had become two children, I understood what she meant. A large dog approached us and began to bark. I have always been terrified of dogs, but this time I quickly gathered the one-year-old into my arms, held my three-year-old close to me, and confronted the intruder. The amazing thing to me was that I felt almost no fear. I no longer had the luxury; I was a parent.

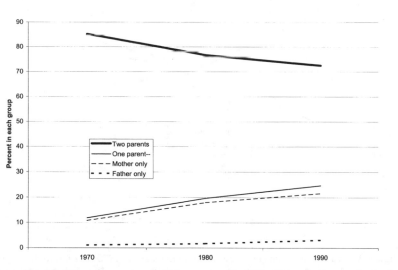

Figure A.1 Living arrangements of children under 18, 1970–1990 — all races. Author's depiction of data from U.S. Bureau of the Census, Current Population Reports, P23–180, *Marriage, Divorce, and Remarriage in the 1990's*, table M (Washington, D.C.: GPO, 1992).

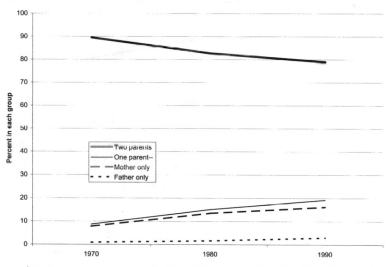

Figure A.2 Living arrangements of white children under 18, 1970–1990. Author's depiction of data from U.S. Bureau of the Census, Current Population Reports, P23–180, *Marriage, Divorce, and Remarriage in the 1990's*, table M. (Washington, D.C.: GPO, 1992).

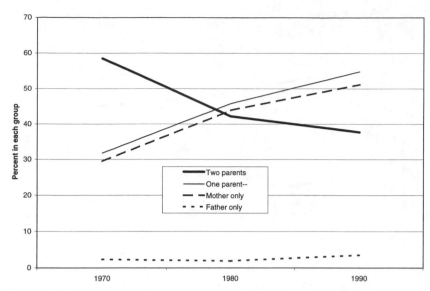

Figure A.3 Living arrangements of black children under 18, 1970–1990. Author's depiction of data from U.S. Bureau of the Census, Current Population Reports, P23–180, *Marriage, Divorce, and Remarriage in the 1990's*, table M. (Washington, D.C.: GPO, 1992).

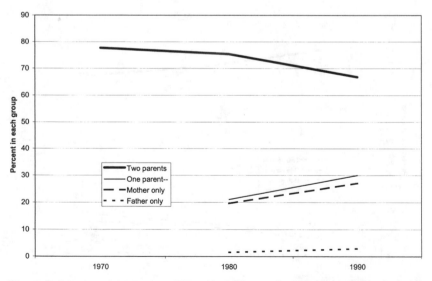

Figure A.4 Living arrangements of Hispanic children under 18, 1970–1990. Author's depiction of data from U.S. Bureau of the Census, Current Population Reports, P23–180, *Marriage, Divorce, and Remarriage in the 1990's*, table M. (Washington, D.C.: GPO, 1992).

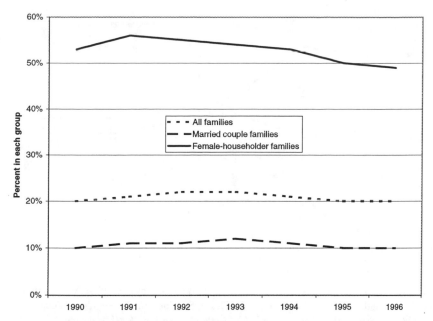

Figure A.5 Percent of children under 18 in poverty by family status, 1990–1996. Author's depiction of data from Federal Interagency Forum on Child and Family Statistics, report, America's Children 1998, table ECON1.A (www.childstats.gov/ac1998/econ1a.htm), visited June 30, 1999.

Figure A.6 Divorce rate, 1960–1996. Author's depiction of data from U.S. National Center for Health Statistics, *Vital Statistics of the United States*, annual; *Monthly Vital Statistics Report*; Bureau of the Census, unpublished data.

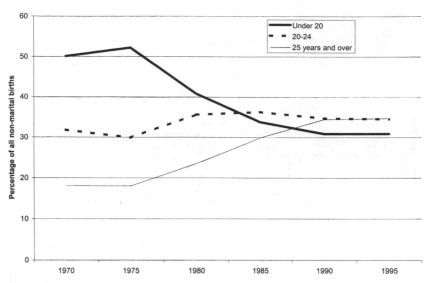

Figure A.7 Distribution of live births to unmarried mothers by age, 1970–1995. Author's depiction of data from National Center for Health Statistics, *Health — United States, 1998, with Socioeconomic Status and Health Chartbook*, table 8, p. 178 (Hyattsville, MD: NCHS, 1998) (www.cdc.gov/nchswww/data/hus98.pdf), visited July 19, 1999.

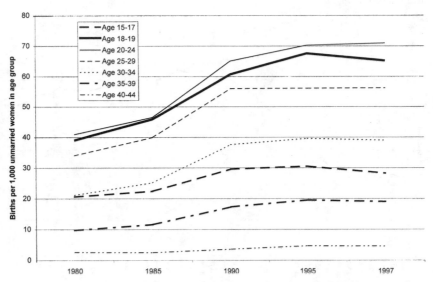

Figure A.8 Nonmarital birthrates, by age of mother, 1980–1997. Author's depiction of data from Federal Interagency Forum on Child and Family Statistics, report, America's Children 1999, table POP6.A (www.childstats.gov/ac1999/pop6a.htm), visited July 29, 1999.

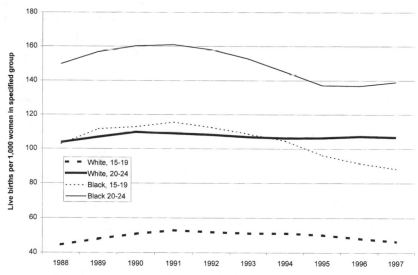

Figure A.9 Birthrates by age and race of mother, 1988–1997. Author's depiction of data from *National Vital Statistics Reports* 47.18 (April 1999): table 4.

Introduction: From Partners to Parents — The Second Revolution in Family Law

1. *In the Matter of Raquel Marie X.*, 76 N.Y.2d 387, 559 N.E.2d 418, 559 N.Y.S.2d 855 (1990). The father must also openly acknowledge his paternity during such period and pay reasonable pregnancy and birth expenses in accordance with his means (Domestic Relations Law at 111 [1] [e]).

2. Ibid., 76 N.Y.2d at 395.

3. Ibid., 76 N.Y.2d at 405, 406.

4. *In the Matter of Raquel Marie X.*, 173 A.D.2d 709, 570 N.Y.S.2d 604, 605 (1991). The court required that an unwed father express "a willingness to himself to assume full custody of the child — not merely to block his adoption by others."

5. See "Symposium: Morality, Public Policy, and the Future of the Family," *Santa Clara Law Review* 36 (1996): 267.

6. Lenore Weitzman deserves credit for first attaching the word "revolution" to divorce. See Weitzman, *The Divorce Revolution: The Unexpected Social and Economic Consequences for Women and Children in America.*

7. *Stanley v. Illinois*, 405 U.S. 645 (1972).

8. Barbara Welter, "The Cult of True Womanhood: 1820–1860," *American Quarterly* 18 (1966): 151, 152. Welter writes: "The attributes of True Womanhood, by which a woman judged herself and was judged by her husband, her neighbors and society, could be divided into four cardinal virtues — piety, purity, submissiveness and domesticity. Put them all together and they spelled mother, daughter, sister, wife — woman. Without them, no matter whether there was fame, achievement or wealth, all was ashes. With them she was promised happiness and power."

1. Economics and the Family: Reformulating the Old Order

1. Gary S. Becker, *A Treatise on the Family* (1981), ix.

2. David D. Friedman, *Price Theory: An Intermediate Text.*

3. Robin West, "Authority, Autonomy, and Choice: The Role of Consent in the

Moral and Political Visions of Franz Kafka and Richard Posner," *Harvard Law Review* 99 (1985): 384.

4. Richard A. Posner, "The Ethical Significance of Free Choice: A Reply to Professor West," *Harvard Law Review* 99 (1986): 1431–48.

5. Milton Friedman, *Essays in Positive Economics*.

6. Becker, quoted in Richard Thomson, "Profile: Economist of the Mind," *The Independent*, October 18, 1992, 11.

7. Becker, *Treatise on the Family* (1981), 14. Subsequent page numbers are cited in the text and, unless otherwise noted, are from the first (1981) edition.

8. Becker, *A Treatise on the Family, Enlarged Edition* (1991), 33.

9. Becker emphasizes "that 'deviance' is used only in a statistical, not a pejorative, sense" (*Treatise on the Family*, 24).

10. Lloyd Cohen, "Divorce and Quasi Rents: Or, I Gave Him the Best Years of My Life," *Journal of Legal Studies* 16 (1987): 267.

11. Cohen emphasizes that another way of thinking about the asymmetry is that men reap the greatest advantages during the peak childrearing years that tend to come early in the relationship; women enjoy the greatest benefits as the children grow older and their husband's earning capacity reaches its peak. Cohen, "Divorce and Quasi Rents," 287.

12. Allen M. Parkman, *No-Fault Divorce: What Went Wrong?*

13. Becker invokes the Coase theorem to express skepticism about the impact of any legal change. An economic imperialist like Becker, Ronald Coase is a seminal figure in the introduction of economic analysis to law. See Ronald H. Coase, "The Problem of Social Cost," *Journal of Law and Economics* 3 (1960): 1–44. In the early sixties, Coase wrote that, absent transaction costs, legal changes might redistribute wealth but were unlikely to affect outcomes. Coase gave the example of a railroad that ran through wheat fields, giving off sparks that occasionally caused fires. Without transaction costs, Coase argued, either the farmers would pay the railroad to take effective precautions or the railroad would pay the farmers for the damage to their crops. Either way, the parties would bargain until they reached the optimal outcome, i.e., one that maximized the joint welfare for the farms and the railroad. Becker argues that married couples should similarly be expected to negotiate. In a fault-based system that effectively requires the consent of the other spouse for a divorce, the party who most wants the divorce would have to pay a higher price than in a no-fault system, *but*, Becker concludes, there would be no reason to believe that the overall divorce rate would change.

Coase also argued, however, that with transaction costs, the railroad could effectively be made to pay the farmers for their losses, but the farmers were unlikely to be able to organize in a way that would permit them to pay the railroad enough to stop its harmful activity. Coase's larger point was that it would often be the effect of transaction costs, rather than efficiency considerations, that should determine the choice of which laws to enact. Becker discounts the transaction costs that might prevent married couples from bargaining efficiently, but even a cursory examination of the factors that might prevent a couple from providing effective guarantees of fault-free behavior counsels hesitation. It is interesting to consider, for example, what security a wife might demand as a precondition to giving up a well-paying job to care for the children. Becker, *Treatise on the Family* (1991), 331. See, more generally, Robert C. Ellickson, *Order Without Law: How Neighbors Settle Disputes* (Cambridge: Harvard University Press, 1991).

14. Ira Ellman, "The Theory of Alimony," *California Law Review* 77 (1989): 1. See also June Carbone, "Economics, Feminism, and the Reinvention of Alimony: A Reply to Ira Ellman," *Vanderbilt Law Review* 43 (1990): 1463.

15. See, e.g., Susan Faludi, *Backlash: The Undeclared War Against American Women*: national surveys indicate that "less than a third of divorced men say they were the spouse who wanted the divorce, while women report they were the ones actively seeking divorce 55 to 66% of the time" (26); Sanford L. Braver, Marnie Whitley, and Christine Ng, "Who Divorced Whom: Methodological and Legal Issues," *Journal of Divorce and Remarriage* 20 (1993): in a sample of 378 families, interviewer found that in two out of three cases the parties identified the wife as the first party to want out of the marriage (1); National Center for Health Statistics, *Monthly Vital Statistics Report* 38 (May 21, 1991): in 1988, divorces involving families with children (64.9 percent) were filed by women (2); *Healthpoint: Mills-Peninsula Hospital* (January-February 1992), reporting on a study by Joan Kelly, which found that women under age forty-five were significantly more likely to initiate divorce than their husbands while the rates for men and women above age forty-five were even.

2. Feminism and Political Theory: The Traditional Family and Its Discontents

1. Quoted from the back cover of Okin's *Justice, Gender, and the Family*. The *Oxford Dictionary of Philosophy* provides the following definition of distributive justice: "Justice, distributive. The problem is to lay down principles specifying the just distribution of benefits and burdens: the outcome in which everyone receives their due. A common basis is that persons should be treated equally unless reasons for inequality exist, after that the problems include the kind of reasons that justify departing from equality, the role of the state in rectifying inequality, and the link between a distributive system and the maximization of well-being." Simon Blackburn, ed., *The Oxford Dictionary of Philosophy*.

2. Susan Moller Okin, *Justice, Gender and the Family*, 7–8. Subsequent page numbers are cited in the text.

3. Okin, 93. See also John Rawls, *Political Liberalism* (New York: Columbia University Press, 1993), which moves away from his emphasis on "original position."

4. Cited in Okin, *Justice, Gender, and the Family*, 94.

5. Albert O. Hirschman, *Exit, Voice, and Loyalty: Response to Decline in Firms, Organizations, and States*.

6. Okin, *Justice, Gender, and the Family*, 157–59. Okin bases her conclusions on power within the family on two studies: Robert O. Blood, Jr. and Donald M. Wolfe, *Husbands and Wives: The Dynamics of Married Living* (New York: Free Press, 1960), and Philip Blumstein and Pepper Schwartz, *American Couples* (New York: Morrow, 1983).

Okin notes that the Blood and Wolfe study, "though informative, is now outdated and unreliable in the way it interprets its own findings." She protests that "the authors' biases are apparent throughout, from their labeling of the less powerful husband 'Caspar Milquetoast' to their pronouncement that families ranging from husband dominance to 'extreme egalitarianism' are 'appropriate,' but that wife-dominance is a 'deviant' and 'not normal' reversal of marital roles" (156–57). Of course, Blood and Wolfe may have been using the term "deviant" in the same sense that Becker did, as a statistical rather than a normative statement.

7. Okin, *Justice, Gender, and the Family*, 160–67.

8. Mahony, *Kidding Ourselves*, 227.

9. Nigel Hamilton, *JFK: Reckless Youth*, 41.

10. James B. Stewart, *Blood Sport: The President and His Adversaries*, 69–70.

11. The story, however, may be apocryphal. "The story about the school nurse is not true, but it is a good one," Hillary Clinton is reported to have said. "Family File: Hillary's a Busy Lady, but She's Not That Busy," *Los Angeles Times*, June 15, 1994.

3. Feminism and Economics: Becker Meets Okin

1. Becker, *Treatise on the Family* (1991), 37.

2. Okin, *Justice, Gender, and the Family*, 172.

3. Becker, *Treatise on the Family* (1981), 350.

4. Ibid.

5. David D. Friedman, *Price Theory*, 596–97. Peg Brinig and I have also argued that women's labor market participation has resulted in more, rather than less, specialization. See, e.g., June Carbone and Margaret F. Brinig, "Rethinking Marriage: Feminist Ideology, Economic Change and Divorce Reform," *Tulane Law Review* 65 (1991): 953.

6. Okin, citing Bergman, in *Justice, Gender, and the Family*, 153; see also Barbara R. Bergman, *The Economic Emergence of Women*, 263. Men assumed somewhat greater responsibility in the 1990s, but even fatherhood advocates acknowledge that women still perform twice as much child care as men — and twenty years ago they were performing three times as much. For a summary of the data, see Nancy Levit, *The Gender Line: Men, Women, and the Law*, 44.

7. Susan Faludi summarizes the data in *Backlash: The Undeclared War Against American Women*, 15, 17, 36–39.

8. Okin, *Justice, Gender, and the Family*, 157.

9. Becker, *Treatise on the Family* (1981), 331. I would like to thank Bill Sundstrom for reminding me of this point.

10. Shoshana Grossbard-Shechtman, *On the Economics of Marriage: A Theory of Marriage, Labor, and Divorce*. Grossbard-Shechtman, who uses even more equations and opaque language than Becker, develops her theory over the course of two chapters that defy succinct summarization. Nonetheless, she describes the model's principal insights as "the hypotheses that labor force participation of married women varies with the sex ratio of those eligible for marriage, that income changes influence wives' labor sup-

ply more than husbands', that group differences in patterns of division of spousal labor influence the elasticity of female labor supply, and that a positive correlation between achievement in markets for labor and spousal labor can provide an additional explanation for the backward-bending supply of labor. The theory also offers interesting insights regarding consumption, fertility, and marriage" (51). The starting point for Grossbard-Shechtman's observations is that the conventional labor market and the marriage market are interrelated, and that, for example, increased income will affect both the supply and demand of household labor, marriage, and divorce.

11. See statistics in Grossbard-Shechtman, *On the Economics of Marriage*; also, see statistics in ch. 1, n. 15, of the present volume.

12. Weitzman, *The Divorce Revolution*, 346.

13. See, generally, Michael S. Kimmel, ed., *Changing Men*.

14. The literature on race and gender roles is complex. Popular accounts report a gulf between black men and black women. See, e.g., Ellis Cose, "Black Men and Black Women," *Newsweek*, June 5, 1995, 66; Michelle Wallace, *Black Macho and the Myth of the Superwoman*; Ellis Cose, *A Man's World*, 64. Cose cites surveys as finding that 42 percent of black men, compared to 32 percent of white men, held a primarily "recreational" view of sex while fewer than 9 percent of black women, compared to more than 21 percent of white women, saw pleasure as the primary purpose of sex.

More rigorous studies confirm the existence of gender differences among blacks that follow different patterns from those among whites. See, for example, Noel A. Cazenave and George H. Leon, "Men's Work and Family Roles and Characteristics," in Kimmel, ed., *Changing Men*. Cazenave and Leon summarize the literature as finding that "social class and SES [socioeconomic status] operate differently for black and white respondents. For white respondents, being middle class and of a high SES are associated with less sex typing and more liberal gender roles. For black respondents these factors are correlated with greater sex typing and conservatism on gender-role items than they are for either white middle-class respondents or black working class respondents" (245).

15. It is interesting, in this respect, to consider the case of Japan. A recent newspaper account summarizes the trends:

> Between the skyhigh cost of living and an oppressive, male-dominated society, Japanese women seem to have seized upon their own form of revenge: They have stopped having babies.
>
> Figures released over the weekend by the Health and Welfare Ministry showed that a mere 1.18 million babies were born in Japan last year, the lowest figure since the government began calculating the statistics in 1899. The ministry calculated that the average Japanese woman now produces an average of 1.43 babies in her lifetime, compared with 2.05 babies per American woman.
>
> Any figure below 2.08, demographers say, means an inevitable decline in a country's population. . . .
>
> [Critical to the falling birth rates, explained Haruo Sagaza, who teaches population studies at Waseda University's department of human science] are the

male-centered values of Japanese society, which assumes that it is the responsibility of the woman alone to raise children. As long as Japanese women work,
they have freedom and their own money; once they become pregnant, their career choices diminish and they are forced to stay at home.

After knowing freedom, today's women prefer not to step into a marriage
that will make them give up a lot of what they have, Sagaza said, calling the
trend the "single-ization" of women.

(Michael Zielenziger, "Japanese Women Having Fewer Babies,"
San Jose Mercury News, July 9, 1996, 8A)

16. Victor R. Fuchs, *Women's Quest for Economic Equality*, 8.

4. Law, Public Policy, and the Feminism of Difference

1. See Fineman "Implementing Equality: Ideology, Contradiction, and Social
Change," *Wisconsin Law Review* 1983 (1983), at 789. Fineman incorporated and expanded her account of Wisconsin divorce reform in *The Illusion of Equality*. Fineman
moved from Columbia to Cornell while this book was in production.

2. See June Carbone, "Equality and Difference: Reclaiming Motherhood as a Central Focus of Family Law," *Journal of Law and Social Inquiry* 17 (1992): 471.

3. Fineman, "Implementing Equality," 849–50. The bill was narrowly defeated in
the state senate after having been passed by the assembly.

4. Fineman, *The Illusion of Equality*, 63.

5. Ibid., 3.

6. When I first began to write about family law in the mid-1980s, two years after
the publication of Fineman's Wisconsin article, I was firmly counseled not to criticize
no-fault. When I later wrote a review of her book, *The Illusion of Equality*, Fineman sent
me a note indicating that she felt ostracized and later ignored when criticism of no-fault
reforms became acceptable.

7. I am using the term "feminist method" here in two senses. First, women's use of
equality to advance their interests is centuries, not decades, old and has been a long-
standing part of women's claims to greater participation in society. See Susan Groag Bell
and Karen M. Offen, *Women, the Family, and Freedom: The Debate in Documents*, 97, 99.
Second, Okin's work employs feminist method in a modern sense as well, however, in
that it does what Kate Bartlett describes as "asking the woman question." Katharine T.
Bartlett, "Feminist Legal Methods," *Harvard Law Review* 103 (1990): 829. That is,
Okin systematically examines the family by asking what the impact of the family's institutional arrangements is on women, and whether that impact can be reconciled with
conventional accounts of justice. In this sense, the "feminist" part of Okin's method is
the act of making visible the previously assumed features of the family that disadvantage
women — and violate conventional notions of equality as justice.

8. Fineman, *Illusion of Equality*, 190.

9. Ibid., 29. Or as Carol Sanger puts it, "Distracting women from motherhood

seemed to be the key to a better life." Carol Sanger, "M Is for the Many Things," *Review of Law and Women's Studies* 1 (1992): 1301, 1306.

10. Catherine Crier, "Keys to the White House — A Glimpse at the Race," *CNN Transcripts*, September 6, 1992, Transcript no. 50–7.

11. Fineman, *Illusion of Equality*, 174.

12. Fineman writes: "The very process of assuming caretaking responsibilities creates dependency in the caretaker — she needs some social structure to provide the means to care for others. In a traditional family, the caretaker herself, as wife and mother, is dependent on the wage-earning husband to provide for her so she can fulfill her tasks" (*The Neutered Mother, the Sexual Family, and Other Twentieth-Century Tragedies*, 163).

13. When Gary Becker uses the term "deviant," he is invoking a statistical term of art that means outside the norm with no necessary normative (in the sense of moral) implications. Fineman uses the term, on the other hand, to illustrate the stigmatization of motherhood outside of male control, and it carries with it clear normative (in all senses of the word) implications.

14. Fineman, *The Neutered Mother*, 165 (capitals in original).

15. Ibid., 233.

5. Liberal Feminism vs. the Feminism of Difference: Or, The Huxtables vs. Grace Under Fire

1. Through the 1980s and early 1990s, analysts divided feminism into two camps: the liberal camp seeking equality through "sameness" or identical roles for men and women, and the "difference" camp, which seeks recognition of the ways in which men and women differ, and equal respect for those traits and activities identified with the feminine.

This intramural feminist dispute crystallized in the mid-eighties over the issue of pregnancy leave. Congress had outlawed sex discrimination in the Civil Rights Act of 1964, but the Supreme Court concluded that discrimination on the basis of pregnancy was not sex discrimination because only women become pregnant and pregnancy, given women's special place in "the scheme of human existence," was in a separate category from other physical disabilities. Wendy W. Williams, "The Equality Crisis: Some Reflections on Culture, Courts, and Feminism," in Bartlett and Kennedy, eds., *Feminist Legal Theory: Readings in Law and Gender*, 24.

Pregnancy leave became a feminist rallying point, and Congress amended the statute to provide that "[W]omen affected by pregnancy, childbirth, or related conditions shall be treated the same for all employment-related purposes, including receipt of benefits under fringe benefit programs, as other persons not so affected by similar conditions in their ability or inability to work" (ibid., 25).

Some states, most notably California and Montana, went further. They passed legislation requiring employers to grant pregnancy leave and to guarantee the employee's job until her return. Male employees challenged the state laws as discriminating against them (they would enjoy no such protection from discharge in the event of a comparable physical disability; prostate surgery was the most popular example), and feminists filed supporting briefs on both sides of the issue. Liberal feminists backed the challenge, arguing that equality demanded only that women be afforded the same treatment that men enjoyed in comparable circumstances, and that special protections would make women more expensive to hire. They worried that the local diner, which provided leaves for no one, would balk at hiring employees entitled to time off. Difference feminists defended the state legislation, arguing that pregnancy leave was more central to women's workforce participation than other forms of temporary leave, and that recognition of such differences was not only appropriate but necessary, to equality. See, e.g., Christine Littleton, "Reconstructing Sexual Equality," 35–56, in Bartlett and Kennedy, eds., *Feminist Legal Theory* (Boulder: Westview, 1991).

2. *United States v. Virginia*, 116 S. Ct. 2264, 135 L. Ed. 2d 735 (1996).

3. On the issue of pregnancy leave, for example, the Supreme Court unequivocally upheld the statutes that provided for pregnancy leave without comparable leave for men. See *California Federal Savings and Loan Association v. Guerra*, 479 U.S. 272, 107 S. Ct. 683 (1987).

Fineman notes that "[e]ven some of the most hard-line sameness-of-treatment feminists have altered their positions in recent years, conceding that equality needs to be supplemented by an appreciation of difference in at least some narrowly defined class of situations. For example, Herma Hill Kay, one of the prominent early legal feminists, recently partially recanted her commitment to sameness-of-treatment by fashioning an 'episodic' approach to equality" (Fineman, *The Neutered Mother*, 40).

4. Conversation with Professor John DeWitt Gregory of the Hofstra University School of Law, Quebec City, Canada, June 13, 1996.

5. From 1966 to 1981, law school enrollment more than doubled, with the number of women increasing from 4 percent to 35 percent of the total. The increasing numbers of women masked a decline in the number of male students and kept the ranks of law school graduates growing into the mid-1980s. See *A Review of Legal Education in the United States: Law Schools and Bar Admission Requirements* (Chicago: American Bar Association, 1981) 54.

6. Weitzman, *The Divorce Revolution*. Weitzman documented the inadequate provisions for women and children at divorce. Her conclusion: "Just one year after legal divorce, men experience a 42 percent improvement in their postdivorce standard of living, while women experience a 73 percent decline." While Weitzman's figures proved to be an overstatement, her account sparked a decade of research addressing the gender-based inequalities that follow divorce.

For criticism of Weitzman's work, see G. Duncan and S. Hoffman, "What Are the Economic Consequences of Divorce?" *Demography* 25 (1988): 641 (reporting a 30 percent drop for women). For more general reviews, see Jana B. Singer, "Divorce Reform and Gender Justice," *North Carolina Law Review* (1989): 1103; Marsha Garrison, "Marriage: The Status of Contract" *University of Pennsylvania Law Review* 131 (1983): 1039; Herma Hill Kay, "Equality and Difference: A Perspective on No-Fault Divorce and Its Aftermath," *University of Cinncinati Law Review* 56 (1987): 1.

7. Which is not to say that Becker is a feminist.

8. Okin acknowledges that, in theory, affording greater protection for those rended vulnerable by their domestic responsibilities would also be more just than the current system. She claims, however, that the genderless family is still more just, in part, because of the impact on children. Okin, *Justice, Gender, and the Family*, 183–86.

9. Okin seems to recognize as much. She titles her last section "Protecting the Vulnerable," and a key part of her proposal advocates rewriting the terms of divorce to reflect "the gendered or nongendered character of the marriage." She explains: "The legal system of society that allows couples to divide the labor of families in a traditional or quasi-traditional manner *must* take responsibility for the vulnerable position in which marital breakdown places the partner who has completely or partially lost the capacity to be economically self-supporting. When such a marriage ends, it seems wholly reasonable to expect a person whose career has been largely unencumbered by domestic responsibilities to support financially the partner who undertook these responsibilities. This support, in the form of combined alimony and child support, should be far more substantial than the token levels often ordered by the courts now" (Okin, *Justice, Gender, and the Family*, 183). Moreover, Rhona Mahony, in her careful blueprint for achieving Okin's version of equality, emphasizes the need to revalue homemaking to make it more attractive for men as well as women (Mahony, *Kidding Ourselves*, 215–38).

10. Okin, *Justice, Gender, and the Family*, 179.

11. It is also probably not accidental that, in *The Cosby Show*, much of the work of parenting — driving the children to theater rehearsals? — takes place offstage, and the parents' presumably demanding jobs are never allowed to intrude on family life.

12. Fineman, *The Neutered Mother*, 104.

13. Okin, *Justice, Gender, and the Family*, 186.

14. Fineman, *The Neutered Mother*, 230–31.

15. See Okin, *Justice, Gender, and the Family*, 210n20 and 178.

6. Fineman and Becker: Feminism vs. Economics

1. Fineman, *The Neutered Mother*, 154.

2. "Moral hazard" is an economic term of art that refers to the tendency to spend other people's money more freely than one's own. Thus, economists assume that executives on an expense account spend more freely than they would on a vacation at their own expense and, in the context of Fineman's call for "subsidy (without strings)," it would refer to the incentives created for women to have more children than they would choose to have if they had to raise them without subsidies.

3. Becker, *Treatise on the Family* (1981), 356–57.

4. See, e.g., T. Paul Schwartz, "Marital Status and Fertility in the United States: Welfare and Labor Market Effects," *Journal of Human Resources* (negative correlation between Medicaid benefits and fertility; mixed results for AFDC); Margaret F. Brinig and Frank Buckley, "The Price of Virtue" (unpublished manuscript: combined Medicaid/AFDC benefits some correlation); and the more extended discussion of this issue in chapter 12 of the present volume, which suggests both that the expanded AFDC ben-

efits between 1965 and 1972 *did* have an impact on the increase in nonmarital birth-rates, and that changes after that period have had minimal impact.

5. Fineman notes, for example, that the image of runaway teen pregnancy is largely a myth. Teen fertility peaked in 1958, and increases in the late 1980s correlate more closely with the rising poverty levels of the era than with welfare. Fineman, *The Neutered Mother*, 115 (subsequent page numbers are cited in the text).

6. Thomas "chided her for taking public assistance, saying she was a prime example of everything that was wrong with welfare programs. 'She gets mad when the mailman is late with her welfare check,' Thomas said then. 'That's how dependent she is. What's worse is that now her kids feel entitled to the check too. They have no motivation for doing better or getting out of that situation.'" Kay Williams Graves, "Clarence Thomas' Sister Takes a Steady Step Up a Rocky Path," *Chicago Tribune*, August 4, 1991, 1.

7. And even that was possible only because of the availability of publicly funded day care (ibid.).

8. Martin conceived her first child in high school without being either married or on welfare and her fourth while she was caring for her aunt. She's also had an abortion. Kay Williams Graves, "Clarence Thomas' Sister Takes a Steady Step Up a Rocky Path," *Chicago Tribune*, August 4, 1991, 1.

7. Morality, Family, and the State

1. This is not to say, of course, that modern society in any way lacks discussion of sex or sexual mores. Richard Posner, a federal appellate judge, a former University of Chicago law professor, and law and economics' most prolific proponent, has even developed an economic theory of sexuality. He explains that his book, *Sex and Reason*, differs from Gary Becker's work because Becker writes about the family; sex is a different subject. Richard A. Posner, *Sex and Reason*, 8–9.

2. While even the Catholic Church no longer insists that procreation is the primary purpose of marriage, the most commonly recognized additional end is sexual companionship (Theodore Machin, *The Marital Sacrament*). Cohabitation without conjugal intercourse is, in most jurisdictions, not legally a marriage, and sex without marriage may still be illegal as well as sinful. See Immanuel Kant, *The Philosophy of Law*, 113 (justifying these conclusions as a product of "pure reason").

3. Michael Grossberg, *Governing the Hearth: Law and the Family in Nineteenth-Century America*, 64.

4. See Felicity Heal and Rosemary O'Day, eds., *Church and Society in England: Henry VIII to James I*, and Eric Williams Ives, *Anne Boelyn*.

5. Nathaniel Hawthorne, *The Scarlet Letter* (1850) (rpt., Boston: Houghton Mifflin, 1960).

6. Grossberg, *Governing the Hearth*, 64 (citing David Hoffman, *Legal Outlines*, 147 [1836]).

7. Moreover, many of the laws against fornication, sodomy, and adultery remain on the books and are, on occasion, enforced. See, in particular, *Bowers v. Hardwick*, 478 U.S.

186 (1986), and the recent actions by an Idaho prosecutor to bring enforcement actions against unmarried pregnant teens. Quentin Hardy, "Idaho County Tests a New Way to Curb Teen Sex: Prosecute — Pregnant Girls and Boyfriends Get Hauled into Court; Welfare is the Real Issue," *Wall Street Journal*, July 8, 1996, A1.

8. See Carl E. Schneider, "Moral Discourse and the Transformation of American Family Law," *Michigan Law Review* 83 (1985): 1803; Schneider, "Rethinking Alimony: Marital Decisions and Moral Discourse," *Brigham Young University Law Review* (1991): 197; and Schneider, "Marriage, Morals, and the Law: No-Fault Divorce and Moral Discourse," *Utah Law Review* (1994): 503.

9. Schneider, "Marriage, Morals, and the Law," 506. Schneider focuses primarily on no-fault divorce, arguing that it exemplfies a broader trend. He emphasizes, however, that "the trend away from moral discourse is only a trend, and not a full accomplished fact," and that not all states followed California's lead and eliminated consideration of fault altogether.

10. Ibid., 508–509. The hypothetical also specified that "Mrs. Appleby's religion forbids divorce, she still loves her husband and doesn't want to be separated from him, and she feels that her situation and status in the world depend on being married. She therefore detests the idea of divorce."

11. Schneider, "Marriage, Morals, and the Law," 516.

12. Schneider reports that he got similar responses from law school classes at the University of Connecticut and Brigham Young University, with somewhat more of an argument that Mr. Appleby was not morally entitled to a divorce at Connecticut than at Michigan, and an additional bit more than that at BYU (ibid., 516).

13. Schneider, "Marriage, Morals, and the Law," 520.

14. Michael Meyer reminds me that this reluctance does not extend to all areas of family life, and most particularly does not extend to domestic violence. Indeed, Schneider has been criticized for too narrow a construction of the idea of morality. See, generally, Meyer, "Morality, Public Policy, and the Future of the Family," *Santa Clara Law Review* 36 (1996): 267.

15. William A. Galston. *Liberal Purposes: Goods, Virtues, and Diversity in the Liberal State*, 3.

16. Galston, *Liberal Purposes*, 7, 82.

17. Jeremy Waldron writes that he is not aware of the use of this image [of neutrality] by any liberal writer before 1974, and concludes that the image of neutrality is relatively new to the liberal tradition. Waldron, *Liberal Rights: Collected Papers, 1981–1991*, 144.

18. Alasdair C. MacIntyre, *After Virtue: A Study in Moral Theory*. See also Galston's descriptions of the role of neutrality in modern defenses of liberalism (*Liberal Purposes*, 80–81).

19. Mary Ann Glendon, "Book Review: A Review of *Liberal Purposes: Goods, Virtues, and Diversity in the Liberal State* by William A. Galston," *George Washington Law Review* 61 (1993): 1955, 1957.

20. Galston, *Liberal Purposes*, 304.

21. Ibid., 304.

22. Galston, *Liberal Purposes*, 116. Indeed, Galston argues that religious tolerance within the liberal tradition is tolerance for beliefs rather than observances, and that this approach involves an "implicit" tilt toward religions characterized more by internal beliefs than external observance (e.g., various forms of Protestantism) and against religions in which piety is expressed through obedience to a system of law (e.g., Orthodox Judaism and Islam).

23. Galston, *Liberal Purposes*, 89.

24. Ibid., 284. In addition to his discussion of the family, Galston also emphasizes the role of religion and education in the process of inculcating liberal values (see 241–89).

25. Galston, "A Liberal Democratic Case for the Two-Parent Family," *The Responsive Community* 1 (1990–91): 14, 23–25. He also embraces Glendon's call to "put children first," particularly with respect to the division of assets at divorce.

26. Galston, *Liberal Purposes*, 286.

27. Family scholars have in fact engaged in a heated debate about just what obligations one spouse owes the other. This debate, however, has more in common with discussions of partnership dissolutions than with discussions of virtue. Courts almost never order quarrelsome partners to stay together (in the legal lexicon, courts frown on specific performance of a personal services contract). Rather, the question would be whether one party's breach of their agreement justified compensation of the other partners.

In similar terms, lawyers are skeptical that any legal change will keep divorcing couples together. Rather, they argue about the type of compensation Mr. Appleby might owe Mrs. Appleby. In partnership terms, he has breached their agreement to remain married and would owe compensation if he is determined to be the one at fault. Many states, however, preclude consideration of fault (including determination of which party is responsible for the divorce). In those states, he might still be responsible for spousal support tied to need and, in normative terms, can be said to have benefited from Mrs. Appleby's contributions to the marriage, including her responsibility for their daughter's uprbringing.

28. Immanuel Kant, *Philosophy of Law*. Kant's overriding principle was the idea that human beings should always be treated with respect and never merely as a means to an end. He further reasoned that, in sexual relationships, one necessarily treated the other as an object unless there was a mutual exchange for life in which each acquired a reciprocal right to the other.

8. What **Is** *the Purpose of Family Policy? Galston vs. Fineman — with the Others Watching from the Sidelines*

1. Galston, "A Liberal Democratic Case for the Two-Parent Family," 21.

2. Becker, *Treatise on the Family* (1981), 30–31.

3. See Nicole Sault, *Many Mirrors: Body Image and Social Relations*.

4. Galston, *Liberal Purposes*, 280.

5. Kantian ethics holds that human beings are independent moral agents subject to natural law, and that they should be treated as an end in themselves, not as means to end (Peter Angeles, ed., *The HarperCollins Dictionary of Philosophy*).

6. Galston does condemn, however, the "alarming relaxation of social, moral and cultural stigmas against out-of-wedlock births," citing a poll that revealed that 56 percent of all Americans believe that if a young person has a baby out of wedlock, no moral reproof should be made. He futher observed that "[a]mong Americans older than 55, only 29 percent felt this way. But among younger people aged 15 to 24, 70 percent said no reproof or judgment was appropriate," and urged that this attitude be reversed. Richard Louv, "Clinton Could Make 'Family' Popular Again," *San Diego Union-Tribune*, December 15, 1993, A2. The attitudes toward nonmarital births, however, correlate with attitudes toward nonmarital sexuality. Stephanie Coontz notes that in 1984, 60 percent of people aged 23–38 approved of casual sex, compared to only 28 percent of those older than 38 (*The Way We Never Were: American Families and the Nostalgia Trap*, 201).

7. Bruce Fretts, "THE EW POLL; Better Parent? Murphy Beats Dan!" *BPI Entertainment News Wire*, June 2, 1992 (from a telephone survey of 600 Americans taken for *Entertainment Weekly* on May 22–25 by the Gallup Organization; sampling error is plus or minus 4 percent).

8. "Quayle and the Boomerang Thing" (editorial), *Boston Globe* (city ed.), May 21, 1992, 20.

9. Ibid.

10. Although Richard Louv does quote him as observing that "[t]here is no disagreement between Clinton and Quayle on this issue, and 83 percent of the American public agrees that two stable parents are better than one. The issue is settled. The question now is, why are we so far from this ideal and how can we go forward to it?" Richard Louv, "Clinton Could Make 'Family' Popular Again," *San Diego Union-Tribune*, A-2.

11. Galston, *Liberal Purposes*, 231.

12. *Chambers v. Omaha Girls Club, Inc.* (8th Cir.) 834 F.2d 697 (1987).

13. See Regina Austin, "Sapphire Bound," *Wisconsin Law Review* 1989 (1989): 539.

9. Conclusion

1. Andrea H. Beller and John W. Graham, *Small Change: The Economics of Child Support*, 3.

2. For further discussion of this point, see Elizabeth S. Scott and Robert E. Scott, "Parents as Fiduciaries," *Virginia Law Review* 81 (1995): 2401–2476.

3. Fineman, *The Neutered Mother*, 230–33.

10. History and the Making of the Modern Family
(with Apologies to Edward Shorter)

1. Laura Kalman, *The Strange Career of Legal Liberalism*, 184. Kalman is quoting C. Vann Woodward quoting J. H. Plumb.

2. Friedrich Engels, *The Origin of the Family, Private Property, and the State* (1891), "Preface to the Fourth Edition" (1964), 7–8.

3. In modern writings, the term *patriarchal* is often used interchangeably with *sexist*. The word is used here, however, in its older descriptive sense to refer to a particular type of family form in which the father, as "patriarch," heads the household, exercises authority over family members and family holdings, and is eventually succeeded by his son, often in accordance with a system of primogeniture. Elman R. Service, *A Century of Controversy: Ethnological Issues from 1860 to 1960*, 15.

4. Translated as "mother-right" or "matriarchate" (1861). Bachofen used Aeschylus's *Oresteia* to illustrate the Greeks' changing views of family, and to challenge the prevailing Aristotelian notion that societies begin with a naturally occurring patriarchal family of father, mother, and children governed in accordance with principles of primogeniture. Service, *A Century of Controversy*, at 15.

Engels describes Bachofen's interpretation:

> For the sake of her paramour, Aegisthus, Clytemnestra slays her husband, Agamemnon, on his return from the Trojan War; but Orestes, the son of Agamemnon and herself, avenges his father's murder by slaying his mother. For this act, he is pursued by the Furies, the demonic guardians of mother-right, according to which matricide is the gravest and most inexpiable crime. . . . Orestes contends that Clytemnestra has committed a double crime; she has slain *her* husband and thus she has also slain *his* father. Why should the Furies pursue him, and not her, seeing that she is by far the more guilty? The answer is striking: "She was *not kin by blood* to the man she slew."

When Athena casts the deciding vote in favor of Orestes to break the tie among Athenian jurors, she insures the triumph of father-right over mother-right, and secures recognition of kinship through the male line. Engels, *The Origin of the Family*, at 11–12.

5. Lewis Morgan, *Ancient Society; Or, Researches in the Lines of Human Progress from Savagery through Barbarism to Civilization* (1877).

6. Engels, *The Origin of the Family*, 32–40. To prove his case, Engels adds as an appendix a report from *Russkiye Vyedomosti*, Moscow, October 14, 1892 (Old Style), which he noted is of interest "because it again demonstrates the similarity, even the identity in their main characteristics, of the social institutions of primitive peoples at approximately the same stage of development. Most of what the report states about these Mongoloids on the island of Sakhalin also holds for the Dravidian tribes of India, the South Sea Islanders at the time of their discovery, and the American Indians." He then quotes the report:

> The Gilyaks (described as "a little-studied tribe on the island of Sakhalin, who are at the cultural level of savagery") are acquainted neither with agriculture nor with pottery; they procure their food chiefly by hunting and fishing; they warm water in wooden vessels by throwing in heated stones, etc. Of particular interest are their institutions relating to family and the gens. The Gilyak addresses as fa-

ther, not only his own natural father, but also all the brothers of his father; all the wives of these brothers, as well as all the sisters of his mother, he addresses as his mothers; the children of all these 'fathers' and 'mothers' he addresses as his brothers and sisters. This system of address also exists, as is well known, among the Iroquois and other Indian tribes of North America, as also among some tribes of India. But whereas in these cases it has long since ceased to correspond to actual conditions, among the Gilyaks it serves to designate *a state still valid today*. To this day *every Gilyak has the rights of a husband in regard to the wives of his brothers and to the sisters of his wife*; at any rate, the exercise of these rights is not regarded as impermissible.   *(Engels, ibid., 164–65, italics in original)*

7. Engels, *The Origin of the Family*, 57–58.

8. Ibid., 65–66. Engels wrote: "In the great majority of cases today, at least in the possessing classes, the husband is obliged to earn a living and support his family, and that in itself gives him a position of supremacy, without any need for special legal titles and privileges. Within the family he is the bourgeois and the wife represents the proletariat."

9. See, in particular, Catharine A. MacKinnon, *Toward a Feminist Theory of the State*, 19–36.

10. The dividing line between history and anthropology, defined neatly today by such markers as departmental membership and choice of scholarly journals, was less well established in the nineteenth century. Thus, Henry Adams could cite Lewis Morgan's work as the "foundation of all future American historical scholarship" while modern scholars are more likely to refer to ethnology or anthropology than history in characterizing Morgan's scholarly standing (Service, *A Century of Controversy*, at 16). Service defines ethnology as a subdivision of anthropology, concerned with the comparative and genetic study of human culture (ibid., at xi).

11. See, e.g., Thomas R. Trautman, *Lewis Henry Morgan and the Invention of Kinship*, 237–65. Morgan's primary point, however, that Native Americans originated in Asia, is no longer in doubt.

12. Henry Maine, *Ancient Law*, 163–65.

13. Stephanie Coontz, *The Social Origins of Private Life: A History of American Families, 1600–1900*, 21–22.

14. Peter Laslett summarizes the developments:

The movement which led to the recovery and tabulation of all the known forms of the domestic group began as a reaction against historical, or rather historicist, anthropology and sociology. Up to that time the grand evolutionary theories of such men as Bachofen, Maine, Morgan and McLennan had held the field, theories which stated that there was a necessary succession of familial form to familial form as phases in the development of the whole human race. These earlier thinkers, deeply impressed with the Darwinian theory of the descent of man from the animals, and assuming a time scale which we know now to have been woefully abbreviated, had to face the problem of explaining how civilised, monogamous man evolved from Simian predecessors. They felt they had to account for the emergence from the "primeval horde" of the familiar group they themselves experienced and admired. They showed a strong disposition to moralise as well, and this seems to have been less successfully overcome by those who have come after than the evolutionary bias. The family was regarded as fundamental to society not only as its final structural unit, but as the receptacle of its values. . . .

[T]he whole body of evolutionary, historicist thinking about the family succumbed in the middle years of the present century before the attacks of the anthropological field worker, the empirical, comparative social scientist.

Much of value has, of course, been taken into the social sciences from these earlier thinkers, but there can be no doubt of their systems being consciously cast aside. Indeed there are those who would say that when nineteenth-century evolutionism was rejected, the only comprehensive theory of familial development ever proposed disappeared without anything being put in its place.

(Peter Laslett and Richard Wall, Household and Family in Past Time, *4–5)*

15. Bernard Bailyn's 1981 presidential address to the American Historical Association deplored "the absence of effective organizing principles" in contemporary historical work. "[L]arge areas of history, including some of the most intensively cultivated, have become shapeless, and scholarship is heavily concentrated on unconnected technical problems. Narratives that once gave meaning to the details have been undermined and discredited with the advance of technical scholarship, and no new narrative structures have been constructed to replace the old." Bailyn asked historians "to bring order into large areas of history and thus to reintroduce history in a sophisticated form to a wider reading public, through synthetic works, narrative in structure, on major themes, works that explain some significant part of the story of how the present world came to be the way it is." Kalman, *The Strange Career of Legal Liberalism,* at 142.

16. Laslett referred, for example, to standard text that described "three chief historical stages in the evolution of the family":

The large patriarchal family . . . in which the patriarch exercises more or less absolute control over his wife, his unmarried daughters and his sons and their wives and children . . . .

The small patriarchal family . . . composed of husband, wife and children, with generally the presence of one or two grandparents, one or more unmarried brothers or sisters of the parents, or other relatives.

The modern democratic family. The industrial revolution paved the way for the breakdown of the small patriarchal family and the emergence of the democratic family. In the United States, pioneer conditions, the rise of the public school, and the extension of democratic principles accelerated its development. (Laslett and Wall, Household and Family in Past Time, at 6. Citations omitted.)

17. Coontz, *The Social Origins of Private Life*, at 18, citing Laslett and Wall, *Household and Family in Past Time*, at 126.

18. Laslett and Wall, *Household and Family in Past Time*, at ix, 144. Laslett distinguished between "family," or biologically related individuals, and "households," those living together whether related or not, noting that larger households contained relatively few kin, with servants accounting for the major variations in size of households.

19. Peter Laslett, "Characteristics of the Western Family Considered Over Time," *Journal of Family History* 2 (1979): 98. Laslett had noted, even as his 1972 work was going to press, that the beginnings of research into household composition in Eastern Europe would be an important intellectual event (Laslett and Wall, *Household and Family in Past Time*, at xi).

20. Steven Mintz and Susan Kellogg, *Domestic Revolutions: A Social History of American Family Life*, 247. Laslett himself postulated four characteristics as the distinguishing feature of the family in the Western tradition: (1) the nuclear family form or simple family household; (2) the relatively late age of the mother during childbearing; (3) the relatively small age gap between spouses, "with a relatively high proportion of wives older than their husbands, and marriage tending toward the companionate"; and (4) the presence of servants as fully recognized members of the household. Peter Laslett, *Family Life and Illicit Love in Earlier Generations: Essays in Historical Sociology*, 13.

21. Stone's magnum opus, *The Family, Sex, and Marriage in England, 1500–1800* (1977) was eight hundred pages and together with his other work on the English family easily exceeds a thousand pages.

22. Stone, *The Family, Sex, and Marriage in England, 1500–1800*, abridged ed. (1979), 22. Stone identified the four key features of the modern family as (1) intensified affective bonding of the nuclear core at the expense of neighbors and kin; (2) a strong sense of individual autonomy and the right to personal freedom in the pursuit of happiness; (3) a weakening of the association of sexual pleasure with sin and guilt; and (4) a growing desire for physical privacy. Subsequent page numbers, cited in the text, are from the 1979 abridged edition unless otherwise indicated.

23. Stone, *The Family*, at 39–41. Stone is measuring the number who have not married by the age of fifty. Subsequent page numbers are cited in the text.

24. Stone, *The Family*, at 41–43. Stone reports that, by the eighteenth century, younger sons were marrying at average ages in their early to mid-thirties. He also concludes that small property owners and laborers in England and America married at median ages of twenty-seven or twenty-eight for men and twenty-five to twenty-seven for women from the sixteenth through the eighteenth centuries (ibid., at 42–44). Subsequent page numbers are cited in the text.

25. Stone, however, takes pains to point out that "Engels' theory that work brought equality between the sexes, and that the subordination of wives was a product of their transformation into a kept leisured class within the home, is not supported by the historical evidence" (Stone, *The Family*, at 411 and also at 140 and 417). Subsequent page numbers are cited in the text.

26. Stone, *The Family*, at 415. Stone rejects the modernization theories of Talcott Parsons and R. Nisbet along with Engels' Marxian analysis. As part of his argument, Stone notes that the changes in the family began as early as the mid-seventeenth century with the upper-middle and landed classes (even as many of those families remained dependent on hereditary estates and primogeniture) and spread downward to the laboring classes over the course of the next two centuries. Subsequent page numbers are cited in the text.

27. Stone, *The Family*, at 413. Cf. Shorter, *The Making of the Modern Family*, 5–6.

28. Stone, *The Family*, at 412. Cf. Carl N. Deglar, *At Odds: Women and the Family in America from the Revolution to the Present*, 8–9; also, Shorter, *The Making of the Modern Family*, at 5.

29. See, in particular, Carol Sanger, "Separating From Children," *Columbia Law Review* 96 (1996): 375.

30. Cf. Deglar, *At Odds*, at 9 ("The attention, energy, and resources of parents in the emerging modern family were increasingly centered upon the rearing of their offspring. . . . Parenthood thus became a major personal responsibility, perhaps even a burden"); also Shorter, *The Making of the Modern Family*, at 5 ("Whereas in traditional society the mother had been prepared to place many considerations — most of them related to the desperate struggle for existence — above the infant's welfare, in modern society the infant came to be the most important; maternal love would see to it that his well-being was second to nothing").

31. See also Shorter, *The Making of the Modern Family*, at 99: "before 1750 the lives of most young people were resolutely unerotic, and that traditional society succeeded quite effectively in suppressing (sublimating, if you prefer) the sex drives of the unmarried."

32. Engels, *The Origin of the Family*, at 72.

33. While Engels assumes that any marriage not motivated by economic considerations is one for love, Stone reasons that (1) many of these marriages are in fact motivated by accidental conception, and (2) while not much is known about the quality of these marriages, the available evidence suggests that they were less characterized by strong emotional bonds or a sense of equality between husband and wife than the marriages of the middle class (Stone, *The Family*, at 414). Finally, while Engels identifies promiscuity and prostitution with economic exploitation (and while Stone does too to some extent), Stone also points to evidence that suggests "that there was a small segment of the population, at the lowest social level, which failed to conform to the prevalent norms from generation to generation: a bastardy-prone minority group" (ibid., at 402).

11. Race, Class, and Controversy

1. See, e.g., Nathan Glazer's foreword to E. Franklin Frazier, *The Negro Family in the United States*, rev. and abridged ed., vii; and James Rhodes, *History of the United States from the Compromise of 1850*, 318, 332, 335.

2. See, e.g., Rhodes, *History of the United States*, 318, 332, 335. See also Herbert G.

Gutman, "Persistent Myths About the Afro-American Family," in Gordon, ed., *The American Family in Socio-Historical Perspective*, 467–89.

3. W. E. B. Du Bois (1909; rpt., Chicago: University of Chicago Press, 1978), 127–30.

4. For a discussion of the modern implications of Du Bois's work, see Donna Franklin, *Ensuring Inequality*, 5–6.

5. E. Franklin Frazier, *The Free Negro Family* (New York: Arno Press, 1968), 56n164.

6. Frazier, *The Free Negro Family*, at 72.

7. "Neither economic necessity nor tradition had instilled in her the spirit of subordination to masculine authority. Emancipation only tended to confirm in many cases the spirit of self-sufficiency which slavery had taught." Frazier, *The Negro Family*, at 102.

8. Daniel Patrick Moynihan, *The Negro Family: The Case for National Action* (Washington, D.C.: Office of Policy Planning and Research, U.S. Department of Labor, 1965). Moynihan, who went on to a Harvard chair and the U.S. Senate, was an assistant secretary of labor in charge of the office of Policy Planning and Research during the Kennedy and Johnson administrations. Civil rights was the salient issue of the day, and government officials had come to the conclusion that the "next and more profound stage" of the civil rights struggle would move beyond equal rights under the law to the provision of resources that would allow for full participation in American society. President Johnson had declared "war on poverty" and administration officials were to devise programs to address the underlying sources of inequality. Moynihan, determined to incorporate the results of social science research in the planning, was convinced that family structure was a major factor in the equation, and he prepared a report to bolster his views. The "Moynihan Report" ultimately became the basis for a major presidential address at Howard University and a White House planning conference. See Lee Rainwater and William L. Yancey, *The Moynihan Report and the Politics of Controversy*, 3, 17–37.

9. "Having demonstrated that the socioeconomic system, past and present, produces an unstable family system for Negroes, he [Moynihan] went on to discuss 'the tangle of pathology' (a phrase borrowed from Kenneth Clark's description of Harlem ghetto life). This tangle of pathology involves the matriarchy of the Negro family (by which he meant the tendency for women to fare better interpersonally and economically than men and thereby to dominate family life), the failure of youth (by which he referred to the fact that Negro children do not learn as much in school as white children and that they leave school earlier), higher rates of delinquency and crime among Negroes, the fact that Negroes disproportionately fail the Armed Forces qualification test (and that this suggests their poor competitive position in the job market as well), and the alienation of Negro men which results in their withdrawal from stable family-oriented society, in higher rates of drug addiction, in despair of achieving a stable life." Rainwater and Yancey, *The Moynihan Report*, at 5–6.

10. Moynihan himself, in his 1967 recapitulation of the dispute, observed with some bitterness: "The moment came when, as it were, the nation had the resources, and the leadership, and the will to make a total, as against a partial, commitment to the cause of

Negro equality. It did not do so . . . . The time when white men, whatever their motives, could tell Negroes what was or was not good for them is now definitely and decidedly over. An era of bad manners is almost certainly begun." Eliot Fremont-Smith, "Books of the Times: The Family Affair," *New York Times*, April 28, 1967 (quoting the February 1967 issue of *Commentary*). Moynihan, the liberal Democrat, would coin the term "benign neglect" in a later stint with the Nixon administration.

11. Franklin, *Ensuring Inequality*, at xvii. Donna Franklin observes that, although the Moynihan report would have been controversial standing on its own, the publicity surrounding it became linked with the Watt riots which occurred shortly thereafter, with the *Wall Street Journal* running a headline that read "Family Life Breakdown in Negro Slums Sows Seeds of Race Violence — Husbandless Homes Spawn Young Hoodlums, Impede Reforms, Sociologists Say." Franklin, ibid., 165–66; see also Rainwater and Yancey, *The Moynihan Report*, at 140–41.

12. Robert Staples and Leanor Boulin Johnson, *Black Families at the Crossroads: Challenges and Prospects*, 41.

13. Staples and Johnson, *Black Families at the Crossroads*, at 37.

14. Franklin, *Ensuring Inequality*, at 8.

15. Staples and Johnson, *Black Families at the Crossroads*, at 38.

16. William J. Wilson, *The Truly Disadvantaged*, at 173–74. Orlando Patterson is even more caustic: "[At the end of the 1960s,] the tide turned with the rise of Afro-American chauvinism and, in its service, a feel-good social science that condemned any and all explorations of the group's behavioral problems as racist or, when coming from Afro-Americans, reactionary. For nearly two decades, serious examination of this social wound was largely censored, with only a few literary figures and the occasional scholar daring to take it on. Fortunately, by the late eighties the tide had begun to turn again, thanks in good part to the works of Afro-American women writers and scholars." Patterson, *Rituals of Blood: Consequences of Slavery in Two American Centuries*, xi.

17. Herbert G. Gutman, "Long Together," *New York Times*, September 22, 1976. See also Kenneth Stamp, *The Peculiar Institution: Slavery in the Ante-Bellum South*: "The slaves had lost their native culture without being able to find a workable substitute and therefore lives in a kind of cultural chaos" (340).

18. Herbert G. Gutman, "Long Together," *New York Times*, September 22, 1976, and "In the South and in Harlem, Tenacity," *New York Times*, September 24, 1976. Gutman is summarizing findings from his *The Black Family in Slavery and Freedom*.

19. Gutman's observations take place within a larger debate on just how bad slavery was. The Moynihan report, in tracing family structure to slavery, began with Nathan Glazer's question: "Why was American slavery the most awful the world has ever known?" Moynihan's answer: "The only thing that can be said with certainty is that this is true. It was." Moynihan, *The Negro Family*, 15.

More recent scholarship, however, suggests that North-American slavery was not as bad as Glazer suggested. Robert W. Fogel and Stanley L. Engerman used econometrics to suggest that slave owners found slaves too valuable to be too badly abused. In particular, Fogel and Engerman concluded that "it was in planters' self-interest to encourage the stability of slave families and most of them did so"; slave families were rarely separated; it was not true that most slave families were matriarchal in form; and that only 9.9 percent of the rural black population in 1860 was mulatto, suggesting that sexual exploitation of slave women was relatively limited. Robert W. Fogel and Stanley L. Engerman, *Time on a Cross: The Economics of American Negro Slavery*, 5, 84, 85, 141.

Both Fogel and Engerman's methodology and conclusions have been controversial. For a list of critical reviews, see Franklin, *Ensuring Inequality*, at 22–23n26, who notes, however, that Fogel won the 1993 Nobel Prize in economics for his efforts.

20. Du Bois, *The Negro American Family*, at 9.

21. Melville J. Herskovits, *The Myth of the Negro Past*, 169. See also Carter G. Woodson, *The African Background Outlines*.

22. Niara Sudarkasa, "Interpreting the African Heritage in Afro-American Family Organization," in Harriett Pipes McAdoo, ed., *Black Families*, 37–53.

23. Sudarkasa observes that these core groups could be either patrilinear or matrilinear, but that most American blacks came from patrilinear groups (*Black Families*, at 41–43, 47).

24. Ibid., at 42. Sudarkasa also notes that the lack of conjugal boundaries extended to living arrangements as well. Husbands and wives had separate quarters within the compound, and in some matrilinear families, spouses resided in the separate compounds of their birth.

25. Sudarkasa, *Black Families*, at 44.

26. Another was payment of a "bride price" in patrilinear families that had to be returned in the event of divorce (ibid., at 47).

27. Ibid., at 44. The English family, with its emphasis on landed hereditary estates passed through the male line to a single member of the next generation (the eldest son), placed an extraordinary premium on legitimacy. In a consanguineal family, a wife's conception of a child with another man had the same impact on inheritance rights as the birth of a child to any other woman in the family. Accordingly, while spousal fidelity might be an issue, the consequences were considerably less than in a system of primogeniture.

28. Nathan Glazer, "On the Gutman Thesis," *New York Times*, September 29, 1976.

29. Wilson, *The Truly Disadvantaged*, at 87 (in 1993, 57 percent of all black children were living with a single parent); and Franklin, *Ensuring Inequality*, at 195–96 (between the early 1970s and the late 1980s the percentage of black families that had two parents fell from 63.4 to 40.6 percent; the percentage of newborn children whose mothers were unmarried increased from 35.1 to 62.6 percent).

30. Sudarkasa, *Black Families*, at 45, 46. Herskovits had attempted to link these developments to Africa.

31. Franklin, *Ensuring Inequality*, at 15, 17.

32. Ibid., at 15, citing Orville V. Burton, *In My Father's House Are Many Mansions: Family and Community in Edgefield, South Carolina* (Chapel Hill: University of North Carolina Press, 1985), 184.

33. Franklin, *Ensuring Inequality*, at 15 and 18. Orlando Patterson's new book,

which appeared as this book was going to press, draws on some of the same research to draw a less sanguine picture of slave families. He argues that the revisionist literature that shows that slaves primarily lived in two-parent families confuses family form with family dynamics. Even if men and women formed a stable reproductive unit, gender and sexual roles were markedly different from those of African or European two-parent families. Patterson emphasizes, in particular, the decimation of the roles of husband and father, the attenuation of paternal kinship relations, mother-child ties superseding those between husband and wife, an increase in domestic violence, and greater antagonism between men and women. Patterson, *Rituals of Blood*, 25–44.

34. There is some dispute, however, as to how early slave women started having children. Gutman argued that, given the importance of reproduction, slave women began to have children soon after puberty. Some of the more recent econometric evidence suggests that while slave women's mean age at first birth was a year or two younger than whites in the same period, they nonetheless averaged a three-year period of sexual abstinence after the onset of puberty. Franklin, *Ensuring Inequality*, at 16–17.

35. Ibid., at 13, citing Leon Litwack, *North of Slavery: The Negro in the Free States, 1790–1860* (Chicago: University of Chicago Press, 1961), 243. Franklin emphasizes that slaves had a clear proscription against a husband's philandering as well.

36. Eugene Genovese, *Roll, Jordan, Roll: The World the Slaves Made*, 465.

37. Sudarkasa, relying heavily on Gutman's data, observes that single women were likely to set up residences of their own during slavery only in two situations: (1) if her husband died or was sent off the plantation; or (2) if she "did not marry after having one or two children out of wedlock but continued to have children (no doubt often for the 'master'), she might have her own cabin built for her." She emphasizes that the "pattern of neolocal residence of an unmarried woman with children would have been virtually unheard of in Africa," and it was relatively rare among American blacks before the twentieth century. Sudarkasa, *Black Families*, at 46.

38. Franklin, while emphasizing the importance of two-parent families during slavery, devotes less attention to the quality of the relationships. Frazier had emphasized the creation of a matriarchy during slavery that, even in the context of a stable two-parent union, made "the Negro woman as wife or mother . . . mistress of her cabin" (*The Negro Family*, at 102).

39. Franklin, *Ensuring Inequality*, at 21.

40. The other factors Johnson cited were social and the continuing identification of female status with "breeding power." Charles S. Johnson, *Shadow of the Plantation*, 49.

41. Ibid. Johnson speculated that at least one reason why marriage in the event of a teenage pregnancy was not encouraged was that the family would lose their daughter's labor. He noted elsewhere, however, that "when children result from the deliberate philandering of young men," these men "are universally condemned" (ibid., at 67).

42. Franklin, *Ensuring Inequality*, at 37.

43. Johnson, *Shadow of the Plantation*, at 83. Franklin adds, citing other studies, that "the patriarchal family structure was more likely to exist in middle-class black families [and this] suggests that there was more resistance among wives in the lower-class house-

holds to the subordinate role they were granted after slavery. The wives in lower-income households probably had more egalitarian working relationships with their husbands in that they were working side by side, and were therefore more likely to challenge their patriarchal authority." Franklin, *Ensuring Inequality*, at 33.

44. Samuel Preston, Suet Lim, and S. Phillip Morgan, "African-American Marriage in 1910: Beneath the Surface of Census Data," *Demography* 29 (February 1992): 13. Franklin cites these demographers to question the census data on which Gutman relied to show the prevalence of two-parent families. According to Franklin, the 1910 data show that "African-American women were more likely than white women not to coreside with a spouse, if ever married," and she observes that while "black women may have married at higher or equal rates to those of white women, when these marriages were disrupted, black women were less likely to dissolve them legally — a point on which scholars agree. . . . This begins to explain how high rates of female headship, reported marriages, and nonmarital birthrates could exist simultaneously among African-Americans" (Franklin, *Ensuring Inequality*, at 37). If women who separated without divorce entered into a new relationship and bore additional children, the children would have been categorized as "illegitimate" whether or not the new relationship was consecrated as a marriage. Neither the black community nor the white community made much of the lack of a formal divorce, and Johnson concluded that the courts were lenient about the matter, "so long as the practice affects no one but Negroes" (Johnson, *Shadow of the Plantation*, at 49).

Franklin also observes, however, that, even taking into account the high rate of informal separations in the African-American community, widowhood was common, with Du Bois reporting in his turn-of-the-century study of African-Americans in Philadelphia that the mortality rate among Philadelphia's black males was "fierce," and that half of the African-American women with children in the 1880s were widows. W. E. B. Du Bois, *The Philadelphia Negro: A Social Study* (1889).

Carl Deglar, examining many of the same turn-of-the-century statistics, emphasizes the link between poverty and female-headed households, showing that, once studies control for income, much of the difference between black families and other families disappears. Deglar, *At Odds: Women and the Family in America from the Revolution to the Present*, 129–31.

45. Franklin, *Ensuring Inequality*, at 72.

46. Ibid., at 39, citing Kelly Miller, *Race Adjustments: Essays on the Negro in America* (New York: Neale, 1910), 173. Other accounts describe men leaving first in search of work and later sending for their families (see Staples and Johnson, *Black Families at the Crossroads*, at 52).

47. David Katzman, *Seven Days a Week*, 46–47.

48. Franklin, *Ensuring Inequality*, at 76.

49. Coontz, *The Social Origins of Private Life*, at 316. Beginning with the Depression, however, the importance of domestic service declined, as demand fell, and black women increasingly viewed the positions as demeaning. See Thomas J. Sugrue, *The Origins of the Urban Crisis: Race and Inequality in Postwar Detroit*, 24–25. Princeton: Princeton University Press, 1996.

50. Franklin, *Ensuring Inequality*, at 60.

51. St. Clair Drake and Horace Cayton, *The Black Metropolis*. Gutman, who documents the destruction of African-American traditions in the South as well as the narrowing of occupational opportunities in both relative and absolute terms in the North, argued that "the absence of a complex occupational hierarchy may have so weakened the Afro-American community as to prevent it from successfully organizing to compete with native white and immigrant groups. . . . [These developments] wiped out leadership and distorted the black community structure *above* the level of its family organization." Gutman, "Persistent Myths About the Afro-American Family," at 486.

52. Franklin, *Ensuring Inequality*, at 27. During the 1950s, the high point of both black and white fertility in this century, fertility rates were 33 percent higher for African-Americans than for whites (ibid., at 142).

53. Coontz, *The Social Origins of Private Life*, at 316. While black fertility rates remained much higher than white rates, the high fertility of African-Americans in the rural South, where the majority of African-Americans lived, skewed the overall totals.

54. Stanley L. Engerman, "Black Fertility and Family Structure in the U.S., 1880–1940," *Journal of Family History* 1–2 (1977): 134.

55. Franklin, *Ensuring Inequality*, at 80–81.

56. Ibid., at 86. In linking higher rates of nonmarital births to newcomers to the city, Franklin relies heavily on Frazier's research. More recent studies find, however, that at least in Boston and Philadelphia, the highest proportion of one-parent households was found among long-term residents, and that there were higher rates of single-parent families in southern cities than in northern ones. Stephanie Coontz, after reviewing this data, concludes that "female-headed families were associated with the urban poverty, unemployment, and underemployment rather than with the heritage of slavery or the direct effects of migration" (Coontz, *The Social Origins of Private Life*, 313).

57. Franklin, *Ensuring Inequality*, at 89.

58. Ibid., at 139. Franklin notes that in 1960, 41 percent of the black men in Detroit in an entirely black-populated census tract were jobless. In census tracts in Chicago, Los Angeles, and Baltimore, where 90 percent or more of the inhabitants were black, the rates ranged from 24 to 36 percent.

59. Franklin, *Ensuring Inequality*, at 107–10. Franklin points out, however, that a major factor in the initial increase was blacks' newfound willingness to resort to legal process rather than desertion, and official records may therefore overstate the extent of the increase.

60. Staples and Johnson, *Black Families at the Crossroads*, at 163.

61. Franklin, *Ensuring Inequality*, at 139. The figures are dramatic. In 1890 over 60 percent of African-Americans in the twenty to twenty-four-year-old age range were married, compared to less than 45 percent of white women in the same age group. In 1960 white married rates reached their height at 70 percent, while black rates were less than 60 percent. By 1979 about half of white women in their early twenties were married compared to less than 40 percent of African-Americans.

62. Patterson, *Rituals of Blood*, at 59.

63. David Fanshel, "A Study in Negro Adoption," *Child Welfare* (February 1959): 33. Franklin also reports that in 1960, 25 percent of maternity homes excluded African-Americans altogether, and Chicago courts threatened black mothers with child abandonment charges if they tried to put their babies up for adoption (*Ensuring Inequality*, at 138).

64. Franklin, *Ensuring Inequality*, at 164. Franklin's data is from Robert D. Grove and Alice M. Hertzel, *Vital Statistics Rates in the United States*, table 28; U.S. National Center for Health Statistics, *Vital Statistics of the United States* (1981), vol. 1, *Natality*, tables 1 through 32; *Monthly Vital Statistics Reports*: vol. 33, no. 6, supplement (September 28, 1984), table 17; vol. 34, no. 6, supplement (September 20, 1985), table 17; vol. 35, no. 4, supplement (July 18, 1986), table 18. See table 11.2 in main text.

65. Franklin, *Ensuring Inequality*, at 202–203. This compares with 39 percent of mother-only Latino families and 22 percent of white families.

66. Ibid., at 143. Franklin notes that for the entire population those most likely to be childless were "black women, born in the Northeast, married at older ages, college-educated, living in urban areas, and married to professional or white-collar workers rather than farmers or laborers. In short, childlessness was highest among the most economically stable and well-educated blacks" (at 199). Fertility rates for whites also vary with class, and much of the racial difference in fertility rates disappears when class is taken into account. See William P. O'Hare, Kelvin M. Pollard, Taynia L. Mann, and Mary M. Kent, "African-Americans in the 1990's," in Mark Robert Rank and Edward L. Kain, eds., *Diversity and Change in Families: Patterns, Prospects, and Policies*, 90–91 (observing that fertility rates were higher for low-income whites than low-income blacks).

67. Franklin, *Ensuring Inequality*, at 188–89. Franklin observes that between 1960 and 1980 the number of poor blacks living in urban areas had increased by 74 percent, with the majority shifting from rural to urban areas during that time period.

68. Staples and Johnson, *Black Families at the Crossroads*, at 170–71. The authors note that the racial gap in income has narrowed considerably for high school graduates and those with some college, but that the percentage of poor black children is higher than the percentage of poor black adults.

69. Ibid., at 103; Franklin, *Ensuring Inequality*, at 219.

70. Staples and Johnson, *Black Families at the Crossroads*, at 102–106. The authors observe that in a given year one of three black males employed in the labor force will suffer from unemployment. Franklin cites figures showing that while, "in 1970, only 9 percent of the young black males between the ages of twenty and twenty-four were neither employed nor in school, . . . by 1990 that figure had risen to 28 percent" (*Ensuring Inequality*, at 200).

71. Franklin, *Ensuring Inequality*, at 201, 203–204.

72. Ibid., at 198–205. Franklin notes that the birthrates for unmarried teenagers increased, but then stabilized and declined during the 1990s.

73. Charles E. Silberman, *Crisis in Black and White*, 94–95, quoted in Gutman, "Persistent Myths About the Afro-American Family," at 487.

74. Franklin, *Ensuring Inequality*, at 226–38. Perhaps because she is writing in the

more conservative 1990s, Franklin's proposals are in many ways more limited than those Moynihan envisioned. He believed that only guaranteed black male employment would make a significant difference to family structure, and envisioned a major commitment of government funds. See Rainwater and Yancey, *The Moynihan Report*, note 6.

75. William J. Wilson, *When Work Disappears: The World of the New Urban Poor*, xvii.

76. Staples and Johnson, *Black Families at the Crossroads*, at 45.

77. Franklin, *Ensuring Inequality*, at 217.

78. Gerald Early, "Poverty and Race in America: A Look at the Historical Changes in Black Family Life," *Chicago Tribune*, June 1, 1997, 5.

79. Franklin, *Ensuring Inequality*, at 145.

12. What Did Happen? Economics Revisited

1. Steven Mintz and Susan Kellogg note that at the time of the Moynihan report 25 percent of African-American women were divorced, separated, or living apart from their husbands compared to 7.9 percent of whites; black nonmarital birthrates had risen from 16.8 percent in 1940 to 23.6 percent in 1963 while white rates rose from 2 to 3 percent in the same period; and that female-headed households had climbed from 8 to 21 percent for African-Americans during the 1950s while the white rate remained steady at 9 percent. Mintz and Kellogg, *Domestic Revolutions*, 210.

2. Shorter, *The Making of the Modern Family*, 5–6.

3. David Popenoe, *Disturbing the Nest: Family Change and Decline in Modern Societies*, 1.

4. William O'Neill, *Divorce in the Progressive Era*, 6–7.

5. Table 12.1 from Andrew J. Cherlin, "Marriage Dissolution and Remarriage," in Mark Robert Rank and Edward L. Kain, eds., *Diversity and Change in Families: Patterns, Prospects, and Policies* (Englewood Cliffs, N.J.: Prentice-Hall, 1995), 306. Reprinted with permission.

6. Table 12.2 from Andrew J. Cherlin, "Marriage Dissolution and Remarriage," in Rank and Kain, eds., *Diversity and Change in Families: Patterns, Prospects, and Policies*, 307. Reprinted with permission.

7. Coontz, *The Way We Never Were*, at 23.

8. Ibid., at 25, 26. See also Mintz and Kellogg, *Domestic Revolutions*, at 178–79.

9. Coontz, *The Way We Never Were*, at 202–203.

10. Ibid., 39. Family patterns for blacks represented more of a continuation of earlier patterns. Moreover, increased teen sexuality led directly to more single-parent families, given blacks' more restricted access to adoption, or viable marriage. (See discussion in chapter 11 of the present volume.)

11. Coontz, *The Way We Never Were*, at 39–40.

12. Ibid., at 167.

13. Ibid., at 164.

14. Coontz, *The Way We Never Were*, at 166. The labor force participation rates of married women with a child below school age increased from 19 percent in 1959 to 29 percent in 1969 to 43 percent in 1979; by 1980, 50 percent of married women were em-

ployed (Roderick Phillips, *Untying the Knot: A Short History of Divorce*, 244). Phillips argues that women's greater labor market participation made it easier for men as well as women to divorce.

15. Phillips (*Untying the Knot*, at 246) notes that the major shift in attitudes favoring liberalized divorce appears to have occurred between 1968 and 1974, the period of the greatest increases in both divorce rates and liberalized divorce laws. He observes that "[i]t is impossible to ascertain whether changes in attitudes fostered more divorces or whether more divorces changed attitudes." For a somewhat different view of the role of changing attitudes, see Barbara Dafoe Whitehead, *The Divorce Culture*. For a more extended discussion of the causal issues, see Allen Parkman, *No-Fault Divorce: What Went Wrong?* 72.

16. Kristin Luker, *Dubious Conceptions: The Politics of Teenage Pregnancy*, 95.

17. George A. Akerloff, Janet L. Yellin, and Michael L. Katz, "An Analysis of Out-of-Wedlock Childbearing in the United States," *Quarterly Journal of Economics* 111 (1996): 279. Subsequent page numbers are cited in the text.

18. Figure 12.1 from Akerloff, Yellin, and Katz, "An Analysis of Out-of-Wedlock Childbearing in the United States," at 298. Reprinted with permission.

19. Equation 12.1 from Akerloff, Yellin, and Katz, "An Analysis of Out-of-Wedlock Childbearing in the United States," at 301. Reprinted with permission.

20. William J. Wilson, *The Truly Disadvantaged*.

21. Robert D. Mare and Christopher Winship, "Socioeconomic Change and the Decline of Marriage for Whites and Blacks," in Jencks and Petersen, eds. *The Urban Underclass*, 175–202.

22. Christopher Jencks, *Rethinking Social Policy*.

23. Robert G. Wood, "Marriage Rates and Marriageable Men: A Test of the Wilson Hypothesis," *Journal of Human Resources* 30 (1995): 163–93.

24. Franklin, *Ensuring Inequality*, at 217.

25. See, e.g., Coontz, *The Way We Never Were*, at 262: "The rise in divorce and unwed motherhood is a complex phenomenon, part of which is certainly a women's initiative and much of which occurs at all income levels. But we should not underestimate the connection of changes in marriage and out-of-wedlock childbearing to setbacks in male economic achievement. Regardless of race or educational attainment, young men aged twenty to twenty-four with earnings above the poverty level are three to four times more likely to marry than men of the same age with below-poverty earnings. Almost half the decline in marriage rates for young male high school dropouts, and virtually the entire decline for young black high school dropouts, is tied directly to their earning losses."

26. Charles Murray, *Losing Ground: American Social Policy, 1950–1980*, 10th anniversary ed. (New York: Basic Books, 1994).

27. Ibid., at 156–66. See also Coontz, *The Way We Never Were*, at 80, characterizing Murray's position.

28. For a review of the literature, see Brian L. Wilcox, Jennifer K. Robbennolt, Janet E. O'Keeffe, and Marisa E. Pinchon, "Teen Nonmarital Childbearing and Welfare: The

Gap Between Research and Politcal Discourse," *Journal of Social Issues* 52 (1996): 71–90.

29. Akerloff, Yellin, and Katz, "An Analysis of Out-of-Wedlock Childbearing in the United States," at 307–308. The economists acknowledge that the issue of how many women "want" children is an ambiguous one and point to data to the effect that 65 percent of mothers bearing nonmarital children in 1970 reported that the children were either mistimed or neither wanted nor unwanted. Their more formal description of the group is "woman who want children, and women who, because of indecision or religious conviction, have failed to adopt the new innovations [the innovations are birth control and abortion]" (ibid., at 280).

13. *Economics* and *History: The Chapter Yet to Be Written*

1. Paula England and George Farkas, *Households, Employment, and Gender: A Social, Economic, and Demographic View* (New York: Aldine, 1986), 65.

2. Stone, *The Family, Sex, and Marriage in England, 1500–1800*, abridged ed. (1979), at 414.

3. Lawrence Stone, ibid., and Phillippe Aries, *Centuries of Childhood*, describing England and France respectively, locate the analogous European developments in the eighteenth century, and most scholars would agree that these developments began earlier in Europe than in the United States. For the sake of consistency, I use Regan's term "Victorian" to describe these developments wherever they occurred.

4. Milton C. Regan, Jr., *Family Law and the Pursuit of Intimacy*, 4 (subsequent page numbers are also cited in the text). The process Regan labels "Victorian" is the same one that Stone terms "modern." Other American scholars agree with Regan's ascription of these events to the nineteenth century. See, e.g., Mary P. Ryan, *Cradle of the Middle Class: The Family in Oneida County, New York, 1790–1865* (Cambridge: Cambridge University Press, 1981).

5. Aries, *Centuries of Childhood*, 398.

6. Ibid. On these developments, see also Charles Taylor, *Sources of the Self: The Making of the Modern Identity*, 291–94, and Joan Williams, "Deconstructing Gender," *Michigan Law Review* 87 (1989): 789.

7. Lawrence Friedman, *The Republic of Choice*.

8. Regan, *Family Law*, at 46 (citations omitted).

9. Kenneth Gergen, *The Saturated Self: Dilemmas of Identity in Contemporary Life* (New York: Basic Books, 1991), 55.

10. Regan, *Family Law*, at 73.

11. Barbara Ehrenrich, "On the Family," *Z Magazine* (November 1995): 10.

12. Aries, *Centuries of Childhood*, at 413. Aries, like Stone, locates these changes in Europe in the eighteenth century.

13. Ryan, *Cradle of the Middle Class*, at 184.

14. Taylor, *Sources of the Self*, at 292.

15. Edward Shorter, *The Making of the Modern Family*, 270–71. Regan echoes

Shorter's conclusions, observing that "[o]nce they become adolescents, children often become part of a relatively autonomous 'youth culture' that to some degree displaces the family as an agent of socialization. Surveying the trend toward extrafamilial sources of support, one observer goes so far as to speculate that there is 'very likely to be an increasing proportion of the population who rely on friends for short-term help, and on kin for not much more than shared celebration of family holidays'" (*Family Law*, at 55)

16. Shorter, *The Making of the Modern Family*, at 16.

17. Ibid., at 161.

18. *Newsweek* reports that "[i]n 1974, the National Opinion Research Center at the University of Chicago surveyed attitudes toward extramarital sex. The view that adultery was 'always wrong' won majorities in every age group, but the margin was smallest among 18-to 29-year-olds; just 59 percent agreed with the proposition.

"But since then attitudes have undergone a remarkable shift. Twenty years later this same cohort, now in their 40s, condemned adultery by a much more resounding 74 percent. And people now in their 20s, who may have seen in their own families what happens when couples take adultery too lightly, show up in this survey as statistically the most sexually conservative group in America, tied with people in their 60s in their overwhelming rejection of marital infidelity." *Newsweek*, September 30, 1996, 56.

19. Pittman, quoted in ibid.

20. Indeed, *Newsweek* notes that the large majorities who disapprove of adultery in all circumstances do not find it to be a disaqualification for high office (at 58).

21. Stone, *The Family*, abridged ed. (1979), at 403. Shorter echoes Stone's conclusions, observing that "[w]hen illegitimacy became rampant in eighteenth-century France, virtually the only women to get pregnant were domestic servants, laundresses, seamstresses, spinners, and other such proletarian creatures. Out-of-wedlock pregnancy simply did not happen to nice girls from good families; or if it did, almost none of them carried to term a live-born infant subsequently registered as illegitimate" (*The Making of the Modern Family*, at 117).

22. Ryan, *Cradle of the Middle Class*, at 184–85.

23. Pleck notes, for example, that in 1896, at the lowest income levels (that is, families with husbands earning less than $200 per year), almost all the black wives worked compared to a fifth of Italian wives. Elizabeth Pleck, "A Mother's Wages: Income Earning Among Married Italian and Black Women, 1896–1911," 491–515 (quote at 497).

24. Ibid., at 506.

14. And What About the Children?

1. Irwin Garfinkel, Jennifer L. Hochschild, Sara S. McLanahan, eds., *Social Policies for Children*, 7. See also Sara S. McLanahan and Gary Sandefur, *Growing Up with a Single Parent: What Helps, What Hurts*.

2. *Frontline* (Public Broadcasting System): *The Vanishing Father* (1995; documentary), DeWitt Sage, producer (Alexandria, Va.: PBS Video, 1995).

3. McLanahan and Sandefur, *Growing Up with a Single Parent*, at 39–63.

4. Irwin Garfinkel and Sara S. McLanahan, *Single Mothers and Their Children: A New American Dilemma*, 14. See also McLanahan and Sandefur, *Growing Up with a Single Parent*, at 83, who use a different measure and 1992 data to find that whereas only 5.3 percent of two-parent families were below the poverty line, 26.5 percent of single-parent families were. For African-Americans, 48.8 percent of single-parent families were below the poverty line compared to 19.3 percent of two-parent families.

5. McLanahan and Sandefur, *Growing Up with a Single Parent*, at 87–88.

6. Garfinkel and McLanahan, *Single Mothers*, at 15.

7. McLanahan and Sandefur, *Growing Up with a Single Parent*, at 91.

8. Ibid., at 94.

9. Ibid., at 95–96.

10. Ibid., at 109–10. The study also controls for parental aspirations, but notes that differences in aspirations (e.g., expectations that a child will graduate from college) between two-parent and single-parent families are not statistically significant.

11. McLanahan and Sandefur, *Growing Up with a Single Parent*, at 111. The researchers also note that when they compare predivorce and postdivorce parental behavior to determine whether the lack of parental involvement was a product of the breakup, they find that "the decline in parental involvement and supervision can account for *all* of the increased risk of early childbearing among young women whose parents divorce during high school," but that the "difference in the risk of idleness among young men whose parents divorce and whose parents stay together . . . does not change when we adjust for differences in parenting before or after divorce" (ibid., at 114–15). In other words, for girls the *decline* in parental involvement and supervision following divorce correlates with increased risk of early childbearing; for boys, that *change* (as opposed to less parental involvement both before and after divorce) does not correlate with increased risk of idleness.

12. McLanahan and Sandefur, *Growing Up with a Single Parent*, at 130–33.

13. Ibid., at 133.

14. Frank Furstenberg, Jr., and Andrew Cherlin reported in 1991 that "conflict between parents is a fundamental factor that harms children's development and produces behaviorial problems. In many families, this conflict — and the harm it engenders — may precede the separation by many years" (Furstenberg and Cherlin, *The Family and Public Policy: What Happens to Children When Parents Part*, 64). Cherlin's most recent research, however, finds that, even controlling for children's predivorce behavior, the children whose parents stay together do better than those who split. Cherlin focuses on a different measure of children's well-being than McLanahan. His study focuses on emotional problems measured by behavior such as disobedience, aggression, depression, or anxiety. Andrew J. Cherlin, P. Lindsay Chase-Lansdale, and Christine McRae, "Effects of Parental Divorce on Mental Health Through the Life Course," *American Sociological Review* 63 (1998): 239–49. For a summary of the literature, see Paul R. Amato, "Life-Span Adjustment of Children to Their Parents Divorce," in *Children and Divorce: The Future of Children* 4 (Spring 1994): 143–64.

15. Amato reports that "[f]ollowing divorce, custodial parents often exhibit symptoms of depression and anxiety. Lowered emotional well-being, in turn, is likely to impair single parents' child-rearing behaviors. Hetherington and colleagues found that, during the first year following separation, custodial parents were less affectionate toward their children, made fewer maturity demands, supervised them less well, were more punitive, and were less consistent in dispensing discipline." Amato concludes that "[r]esearch provides clear support for this perspective. Almost all studies show that children are better adjusted when the custodial parent is in good mental heath and displays good parenting skills." Amato, "Life-Span Adjustment of Children," at 150 (citations omitted). The difference between these conclusions and McLanahan's is one of emphasis. McLanahan describes the lesser degree of parental involvement and supervision in single-parent families as though it were a product of fewer adults in the household. Amato describes it as a function of the custodial parent's psychological adjustment to the separation.

Amato and Booth's more recent study links the consequences of marital dissolution to predivorce marital quality. They report that "[f]or offspring residing with parents in poor-quality marriages, divorce does not appear to have negative long-term consequences for well-being. In contrast, offspring whose parents' marriages are not highly conflicted appear to suffer when the marriage ends. It is precisely under these conditions that children are most likely to view marital disruption as an unexpected and unwelcome event." Paul R. Amato and Alan Booth, *A Generation at Risk*, 204.

16. Kristin Luker, *Dubious Conceptions: The Politics of Teenage Pregnancy*, 130.

17. Luker emphasizes that disadvantaged women are more dependent than their better-off peers on assistance from relatives in managing childrearing, and that delay increases the likelihood that their mothers will not be there to help them or that the increased fertility problems will prevent them from having children altogether. See also Larry Wu, "Effects of Family Structure an Income on Risks of Premarital Birth," *American Sociological Review* 61 (1996): 386–406.

18. David Blankenhorn, *Fatherless America*, 1.

19. David Popenoe, *Life Without Father*, 139–40.

20. Ibid., 145. See also E. Mavis Hetherington and Margaret M. Stanley-Hagan, "The Effects of Divorce on Fathers and Their Children," in Michael E. Lamb, ed., *The Role of the Father in Child Development*, 205.

21. See Hetherington and Stanley-Hagen, "The Effects of Divorce," at 206, for a summary of the studies. They observe that while a number of the earlier studies suggest that children fare better with a parent of the same sex, two more recent studies, including a large-scale national survey, show no significant differences. In comparing mother-custody and father-custody households, this study further showed that, while children were better off on some measures with fathers, once the study controlled for income, children tended to be slightly better off with mothers. Amato, "Life-Span Adjustment of Children," at 154.

22. Lamb, ed., *The Role of the Father*, at 13.

23. Ibid.

24. Nancy Dowd, *In Defense of Single-Parent Families*, 31 (citations omitted). Dowd notes that, aside from the more general measures of children's well-being, there is an additional argument that two parents are necessary for "healthy sex-role identification." Dowd responds, however, that recent research has undercut some of these theories, while other scholars question the desirability of sex-stereotyped behavior and development (ibid., at 36–37). See also Nancy Chodorow, *The Reproduction of Mothering: Psychoanalysis and the Sociology of Gender*.

25. Popenoe, *Life Without Father*, at 139.

26. A 1998 survey of children's well-being reports that children under eighteen constitute 40 percent of the poor even though they are only a quarter of the overall population. Fifty-nine percent of children under six in female-headed households are poor compared with 12 percent of children under six in married two-parent families. Ten percent of white children lived below the poverty line compared with 40 percent of black and Latino children. Federal Interagency Forum on Child and Family Statistics, *America's Children: Key National Indicators of Well-Being* (Washington, D.C.: GPO, 1998), iii.

15. Conclusion

1. Charles Taylor, *Sources of the Self: The Making of the Modern Identity*.

2. Ibid., at 290–91.

3. Milton C. Regan, Jr., *Family Law and the Pursuit of Intimacy*, 28 (citations omitted).

4. Ibid., at 185. Regan associates the term "contract" with the "private" realm representing "the exercise of free will, which required protection from public influence" (ibid., at 90). He contrasts it with a "status" approach that regulates commercial exchanges in an effort to protect the more vulnerable.

Margaret Brinig, in her review of Regan's book ("Status, Contract, and Covenant," *Cornell Law Review* 79 [1994]: 1573), criticizes use of the term "status" because of its association with the gendered division of labor of the separate spheres, and suggests the term "covenant" instead to capture Regan's sense of relational exchanges.

Both the regimes which Regan and Brinig describe remain contractual, however, to the extent that they reflect (*a*) a voluntary enterprise undertaken by two people, and (*b*), an enterprise whose exchange is judged by principles of reciprocity. Both might depart from a "pure" contractual model by limiting the extent to which a weaker party can waive a right to alimony, but it is unclear to what degree either would insist on terms designed not to advance the interests of the spouses but rather the larger interests of society.

5. Regan, *Family Law*, at 92. Subsequent page numbers are cited in the text.

16. The Meaning of Marriage

1. *Baehr v. Lewin*, 74 Haw. 530, 852 P. 2d 44 (Haw. 1993). The "Lewin" in the case was John Lewin, the director of health for the state (and the official in charge of issuing marriage licenses). When Lawrence Miike replaced Lewin as director of health, the case

was recaptioned *Baehr v. Miike*, and thus opinions issued later in the case bear a different name.

2. *Loving v. Virginia*, 388 U.S. 1, 12 (1967).

3. For an account of the litigation leading up to *Baehr*, and the legal basis for recognition of same-sex marriage, see William N. Eskridge, Jr., *The Case for Same-Sex Marriage: From Sexual Liberty to Civilized Commitment*, 131. See also Maura Strassberg, "Distinctions of Form or Substance: Monogamy, Polygamy, and Same-Sex Marriage," *North Carolina Law Review* 75 (1997): 1501–1624 (quote at 1571; noting and rejecting the argument that marriage is a privilege that must be granted equally, if at all).

4. *Bowers v. Hardwick*, 478 U.S. 186 (1986). See Eskridge, *The Case for Same-Sex Marriage*, at 123, for a summary of the legal developments.

5. Pat Lagon and Joseph Melilo initiated the efforts to challenge Hawaii's ban on same-sex marriage. They were later joined by Tammy Rodriguez and Antoinette Pregil, and Ninia Baehr and Genora Dancel. The case is captioned *Baehr v. Lewin* because Baehr's name appears first on the complaint. For an account of Baehr and Dancel's involvement in the case, see Eskridge, *The Case for Same-Sex Marriage*, at 1–5.

6. The Fourteenth Amendment to the U.S. Constitution, one of the three constitutional amendments passed shortly after the Civil War to guarantee the rights of former slaves, provides that no state may "deny to any person within its jurisdiction the equal protection of the laws." The Hawaii Constitution, Art. I.5, in contrast, provides that "[n]o person shall . . . be denied the equal protection of the laws, nor denied the enjoyment of the person's civil rights nor discriminated against in the exercise thereof because of race, religion, sex, or ancestry."

7. *Baehr*, 852 P. 2d at 67. See Samuel A. Marcosson, "The Lesson of the Same-Sex Marriage Trial: The Importance of Pushing Opponents of Lesbian and Gay Rights to Their 'Second Line of Defense,'" *Journal of Family Law* 35 (1996–97): 721–53.

8. Fred J. Parrella, "Same-Sex Marriage," November 6, 1998 (unpublished manuscript on file with author).

9. Parrella, "Same-Sex Marriage," at 5.

10. Ibid., at 2. These justifications are in themselves controversial. The most quoted biblical passages are from Leviticus: "Thou shalt not lie with mankind as with womankind; it is *abomination*" (Leviticus 18:22); "If a man lies with a male as with a woman, both of them have committed an abomination" (Leviticus 20:13). Leviticus also recommends death for adulterers, those who lie with beasts, men who commit incest, and men who lie with men (Leviticus 20:10–16). William Eskridge notes that "[g]ay-friendly readers have interpreted this and other passages to be nothing more than references to 'unclean' practices, . . . but a more accurate reconstruction emphasizes the Old Testament's anxiety about male sexual intercourse" (*The Case for Same-Sex Marriage*, at 242*n*33). See also Daniel A. Helminiak, *What the Bible Really Says About Homosexuality*; Arlene Swidler, *Homosexuality and World Religions*; Derrick Sherwin Bailey, *Homosexuality and the Western Christian Tradition*; and John Boswell, *Christianity, Social Tolerance,*

and Homosexuality: Gay People in Western Europe from the Beginning of the Christian Era to the Fourteenth Century.

11. See John M. Finnis, "Law, Morality, and 'Sexual Orientation,' " *Notre Dame Law Review* 69 (1994): 1049. Same-sex marriage proponents respond that Finnis's argument suggests that infertile couples are not really married. Finnis disagrees, maintaining that "[p]arenthood and children and family are the intrinsic fulfillment of a communion which . . . can exist and fulfill the spouses even if procreation happens to be impossible to them." Finnis's position reflects a theological perspective at odds with much of the contemporary secular approach to sexuality and procreation. First, he starts from an Augustinian religious tradition that treats sexuality, not as a matter of personal fulfillment, but as a suspicious activity to be ordered to the acceptable end of procreation through the institution of marriage. Second, because the only appropriate place for sexuality is within an institution designed for procreation, openness to children is a defining element, in a natural law sense, of the spirit and letter of that institution. Twentieth-century religious teaching maintains that sex is not merely instrumental. It is okay to enjoy it, and even to plan it for a time of the month when the woman is likely to be infertile. Nonetheless, to enter into marriage opposed to procreation and determined to prevent it would mock the purpose of the institution. Finally, the individual's duty is to partake in the letter and spirit of religious teaching about marriage; conception, the subject of miracles in the Bible, is entrusted to God. The marriage of octogenarians, or a woman who has undergone a hysterectomy, is consistent with this tradition; voluntary sterilization is not. Accordingly, same-sex couples, who cannot maintain that their union is part of a divine plan for procreation, cannot marry while those who may be infertile can.

12. First Amended Pretrial Statement, *Baehr v. Miike*, No. CIV.A.91–1394, 1966 WL 694235, at *3 (Haw. Cir. Ct. Dec. 3, 1996).

13. Marcosson, "The Lesson of the Same-Sex Marriage Trial," at 722 and 723.

14. Eskridge, *The Case for Same-Sex Marriage*, at 35.

15. This is not to say that it is the only reason for the opposition that arose. See, e.g., Guido Ruggerio, *The Boundaries of Eros: Sex Crime and Sexuality in Renaissance Venice.* Nonetheless, to understand the depth of the opposition to same-sex marriage in religious circles, it is critical to understand the depth of the concern about sexuality. Fred Parrella writes that "[a] spirituality of the family has thus always remained something of an anomaly: either authentic spiritual growth was impossible for someone living in the world within the confines of a procreative relationship or, where marriage and the family was understood positively, spirituality existed *in spite of, beside*, or *above* one's state *in* life, not in and *through* one's role as husband, wife, father, mother. Thus, the statement of Vatican II 'that all the faithful of Christ of whatever rank or status are called to the fullness of Christian life and to perfection of charity' can only be understood as remarkable from an historical perspective." Parrella, "Towards a Spirituality of the Family," *Communio* 9 (1992): 127–41.

16. Strassberg, "Distinctions of Form or Substance," 1501–1624.

17. The major Supreme Court case to address marriage was *Reynolds v. the United States*, 98 U.S. 145 (1878), which upheld the constitutionality of the law barring polygamy. François Lieber, *Manual of Political Ethics, Designed Chiefly for the Use of Colleges and Students at Law* (2d ed., 1911).

18. Immanuel Kant, *The Philosophy of Law* (1887). See also Jeremy Waldron, *Liberal Rights: Collected Papers, 1981–1991*, 370–71.

19. Strassberg, "Distinctions of Form or Substance," at 1519, citing Lieber, at vol. 1:104–105*n*1, 122–25, 139, and at vol. 2:65, 110–11, 122–24.

20. Strassberg, "Distinctions of Form or Substance," at 1520, citing Lieber, at vol. 1:137–39. Lieber viewed women as different in nature from men and considered the maternal role essential to the development of our moral capacity of sympathy through simple care-giving, personal sacrifice, and affection, forming in turn the foundation for the development of friendship, charity, public spirit, and, ultimately, patriotism and social cohesion (Strassberg, at 1521; subsequent page numbers are cited in text).

21. Strassberg, "Distinctions of Form or Substance," at 1601. She combines this with the value of the unity of partners in allowing "such partners to experience their individuality as most real only in the context of a relationship in which they sacrifice their individuality, thus preparing individuals for identification with larger communities and the state."

22. Ibid., at 1612*n*607. Strassberg, like Eskridge, has crafted her argument to address the objections to same-sex marriage coming not just from religious groups but from the gay and lesbian community. Eskridge, in inimitable fashion, characterizes this as "the marriage-is-rotten argument." He notes that for gay men both the attraction and the opposition to marriage stem from its emphasis on monogamy. The early years of gay liberation celebrated the promiscuous lifestyle; in the 1990s, proponents of same-sex marriage welcome the commitment and stability it would encourage. Lesbian women have had greater success than gay men in maintaining long-term relationships without public recognition, and they are more vocal in their criticism of marriage. "Marriage is a great institution . . . if you like living in institutions," Paula Ettelbrick, one of Eskridge's key debating partners, argues. "Steeped in a patriarchal system that looks to ownership, property, and dominance of men over women as its basis, the institution of marriage has long been the focus of radical feminist revulsion" (Ettelbrick, quoted in Eskridge, *The Case for Same-Sex Marriage*, at 75). Strassberg responds by observing that marriage is likely to be inherently patriarchal "only if viewed as essentially arising out of a relationship between a man and a woman. Insistence on the fundamental significance of biological sex thus serves as a state-perpetuated foundation of the continuation of patriarchal ideas about gender roles and capacities. Under this view, extension of marriage to same-sex partners will serve to erase the importance of biological sex as a determiner of individual roles and, thereby, erode patriarchy" (Strassberg, "Distinctions of Form or Substance," at 1613).

23. Eskridge, *The Case for Same-Sex Marriage*, at 10.

24. Regan, *Family Law and the Pursuit of Intimacy*, at 66.

25. Pruett, quoted in Marcosson, "The Lesson of the Same-Sex Marriage Trial," at 727.

26. Quoted in ibid., at 731.

17. Partnership Revisited

1. *Burr v. Burr*, 7 Hill 207, 223–24 (N.Y. 1843).

2. *Burr*, 7 Hill at 227 (Senator Bockee).

3. Ibid., at 233 (Senator Bockee).

4. Marilyn Gardner, "When Marriage Ends, Should Partners Split Their Assets 50–50?" *Christian Science Monitor*, July 1, 1998, B8.

5. *Wendt v. Wendt*, 1998 Conn. Super. LEXIS 1023 (March 31, 1998).

6. The decision did not calculate the total value of either the judgment or the estate, and I have taken the estimates from the press statements of the lawyers. Mrs. Wendt's attorneys had claimed that the estate was worth as much as $200 million; Mr. Wendt valued it at 1 million on the date of separation, but acknowledged that it had doubled in value by the time of the trial court's decision. The court's valuation appears to be closer to Mr. Wendt's, and the amount awarded about half of the estate. See "GE Exec's Ex-Wife Gets Settlement," Associated Press, December 4, 1997.

7. Mary Moers Wenig, "The Marital Property Law of Connecticut, Past, Present and Future, *Wisconsin Law Review* 1990 (1990): 807, 873.

8. *Wendt*, at 31.

9. *Hemsley v. Hemsley*, 639 So. 2d 909, 914–15 (Miss. 1994). Mississippi had been, before this decision, the last state in the union to distribute property at divorce in accordance with common law title (that is, the party in whose name title was held got to keep the property). *Hemsley* was a 5–3 decision to replace the title system with a form of equitable distribution.

10. In this context, the term "partnership," though often associated with equal division, has no fixed meaning. Business partnerships, invoked as a comparison, are a specialized form of contract in which two or more colleagues form a separate business entity. The law governing their enterprise stems from their express agreement and the default terms that apply when the parties fail to specify otherwise.

To treat marriage as a partnership suggests only that the couple be recognized as creating a new entity — the marriage — that has an existence independent from the sum of their individual interests. This image, however, even as it seems to invoke Hegelian notions of transcendence, leaves open the question of what terms are to govern the relationship. When Mrs. Wendt conceives of marriage as a partnership, she means an arrangement between two people in which they agree to commingle their lives during the relationship and divide their assets upon dissolution 50–50. If marriage is to be governed in accordance with a bright line rule for division, her proposal probably makes the most sense, but it does so because of the nature of marriage rather than because business partnerships are invariably conducted that way. See Marjorie E. Kornhauser, "Theory v. Reality: The Partnership Model of Marriage in Family and Tax Law," *Temple Law Review* 69 (1996): 1413.

11. *Wendt*, at 29.

12. Richard A. Posner argues, perhaps with *Wendt* in mind, that a 50–50 division is hardest to justify for the superrich. He observes that "[w]hile [superrich husband] H's success in business might well be due in significant part to W's contributions, even if she never worked in the market, it is unlikely that the *fabulous* dimension of his success was." Posner, *Economic Analysis of Law* (5th ed.), 163. Posner's argument also applies to what Jane Rutherford calls the case of the "loser," who contributes neither to the family's domestic or market responsibilities but who might nonetheless claim 50 percent of the estate under an equal division rule. Rutherford, "Duty in Divorce: Shared Income as a Path to Equality." *Fordham Law Review* 58 (1998): 539–92 (quote at 589).

13. A few jurisdictions recognize a property interest in professional degrees, especially where one spouse supported the other through school, and the divorce occurs not long after graduation. In this case, the Wendts' respective parents paid for their education, and both parties worked during the period in which Mr. Wendt obtained his M.B.A. While it is possible that a court would find that her financial contributions to the degree were larger than his, it is also possible that a court would find that they were offset by his contributions to the family after graduation. The *Wendt* opinion includes a summary of the relevant case law, noting that Connecticut does not recognize a property interest in either degrees or income capacity.

14. 67 Cal. App. 3d 416, 419, 136 Cal. Rptr. 635, 637 (1977). See Ann Laquer Estin, "Maintenance, Alimony, and Rehabilitation of Family Care," *North Carolina Law Review* 71 (1993): 721–803. Estin notes that this decision is one of the earliest and best known in a long line of appellate decisions reversing short-term or transitional awards to longtime homemakers, and elaborating stringent standards to govern the lower courts' discretion in cases involving older wives. Ibid., at 739.

15. Estin, "Maintenance, Alimony, and Rehabilitation," at 739. Families with young children, unlike older couples, are unlikely to have a substantial accumulation of assets. Nonetheless, there is a debate in the literature over whether the property divisions in the cases with young children, which tend overwhelmingly to be equal divisions, reflect recognition of equal contribution or compensation for the custodial parent's greater need. Many would argue that the only way to provide for caretakers in these marriages is to award custodial parents either the bulk of the estate or 50 percent of the assets *and* substantial support. Both outcomes are rare. Compare Suzanne Reynolds, "The Relationship of Property Division and Alimony: The Division of Property to Address Need," *Fordham Law Review* 56 (1988): 827–916 (equal division recognizes contribution and ignores need) with Joan Krauskopf, "Theories of Property Division/Spousal Support: Searching for Solutions to the Mystery," *Family Law Quarterly* 23 (1989): 253–78 (equal division assumes unequal contribution and compensates for need).

16. Jim Yardley, "Executive, Once Spotlighted in a Divorce, to Wed Again," *New York Times*, August 16, 1998, 36.

17. For a more extended discussion of the UMDA, see Estin, "Maintenance, Alimony, and Rehabilitation," at 729 and 739. See also Margaret F. Brinig and June Carbone, "The Reliance Interest in Marriage and Divorce," *Tulane Law Review* 62 (1988):

855–905, in which Brinig and I laid out the difference between two possible justifications for the economic adjustments made at divorce. We argued that, at divorce, both parties could not realize their expectation interest in marriage (that is, the benefits that would accrue if the marriage continued) and that the law chose between them on the basis of fault. In this model, contribution is unnecessary; Mrs. Burr is entitled to the financial support that she would have received had the marriage continued because of Mr. Burr's breach of his obligations to her. In accordance with this theory, Mr. Wendt, whether divorced at thirty-five or fifty-five, would have been expected to continue to support his wife in accordance with the marriage's standard of living so long as he was the one who precipitated the breakup and she did not remarry.

The second model assumes that the marriage ends without the fault of either party. It then uses a restitution model to address the ways in which the marriage may have conferred a benefit on one party at the expense of the other. The two classic examples of this type of exchange are the degree cases and the homemaker cases. In both examples, one party incurs a loss (lost career opportunities, tuition expenses) in order to realize a benefit (children, a degree) from which both parties would benefit had the marriage continued. The divorce arbitrarily leaves one party with a disproportionate share of the loss while the other party retains the expected benefit. In these cases, the right to compensation is independent of fault. If the *Wendt* court had applied this analysis, it would have concluded that Mrs. Wendt had been amply compensated for her contributions to Mr. Wendt's degree by the higher standard of living they enjoyed during the marriage, but that she was entitled to at least the standard of living that she would have enjoyed had she invested in her own career instead of his.

The *Wendt* case as the court decided it, however, turned on a prior issue: allocation of an ownership interest in the estate. Here the issue is not forward-looking (where would the parties be if the marriage had continued) but backward-looking — what was the understanding of the parties with respect to their commingled lives. There were two possibilities: treat the marriage as an agreement to share their lives so long as the marriage lasts, and divide the accumulated assets equally, or apportion the accumulated assets on the basis of contribution, perhaps then adding an offset for need, or for inequities that arose from the timing of the divorce. The *Wendt* court claimed to be doing the latter, but then granted an award that came closer to the former.

18. Child Support and the Parenthood Draft

1. *L. Pamela P. v. Frank S.*, 59 N.Y.2d 1, 449 N.E.2d 713, 462 N.Y.S.2d 819 (1983).
2. Ibid., at 715.
3. Ibid., 59 N.Y.2d, at 5. Sol Wachtler, who at forty-two had become the youngest ever Chief Judge of the New York Court of Appeals, harassed Joy Silverman, a former lover who had left him, in an effort to persuade her to return and seek solace and assistance from him. During a period in which he was also trustee of the estate Silverman's stepfather had left her, Wachtler

invented and impersonated one David Purdy, a seedy private eye from Texas. Expertly disguising his own voice and handwriting, he made salacious threats to

Ms. Silverman and the wife of her new lover, David Samson (whom he also impersonated). To balance the vile Purdy character, he brought on the imaginary Theresa O'Connor and assumed her role as a church-goer who had hired Purdy but was leery of him.

Directing this phantom cast of characters, Wachtler as Purdy made phone calls and sent letters from New Jersey containing coarse threats to kidnap Ms. Silverman's 14-year-old daughter unless his demands for money were met. After a barrage of these warnings, in September of 1992 Ms. Silverman conferred with FBI Director William Sessions in Washington, D.C., who referred the case to . . . the Newark U.S. Attorney.

Judge Wachtler was arrested in November 1992. He argued that he was mentally impaired as a result of overdoses of Halcion and other mind-altering prescription drugs, but ultimately pleaded guilty to reduced charges and spent thirteen months in jail. Denis McInerney, "The Lawyer's Bookshelf: King of the Mountain; The Rise, Fall, and Redemption of Chief Judge Sol Wachtler," *New York Law Journal*, September 11, 1998, 2.

4. Mrs. Burr received a smaller portion of the couple's combined estate than did Mrs. Wendt, in large part because women in earlier eras were seen as contributing less to the accumulation of assets. See discussion of this in chapter 17 and in Brinig and Carbone, "The Reliance Interest in Marriage and Divorce," *Tulane Law Review* 62 (1988): 855.

5. Mary Ann Mason, *From Father's Property to Children's Rights: The History of Child Custody in the United States*, 25.

6. Ibid., at 98. Mason notes that English common law provided the father of a nonmarital child with neither a right to custody nor an obligation of support. American states varied considerably in the degree to which they followed English precedent.

7. For discussion of the history of the cause of action for breach of the promise to marry (which was abolished in the nineteenth century), see Margaret F. Brinig, "Rings and Promises," *Journal of Law Economics and Organization* 6 (1990): 203 (arguing that the rise of diamond-studded engagement rings came about as a form of liquidated damages after the promise to marry became legally unenforceable), and Jane Larson, "Women Understand So Little, They Call My Good Nature 'Deceit': A Feminist Rethinking of Seduction," *Columbia Law Review* 93 (1993): 374.

8. Mason, *From Father's Property to Children's Rights*, at 99.

9. Kent, quoted in ibid., 94.

10. Blackstone provided the classic justification for child support: "The duty of parents to provide for the *maintenance* of their children is a principle of natural law. . . . By begetting them, therefore, they have entered into a voluntary obligation, to endeavor, as far as in them lies, that the life which they have bestowed shall be supported and preserved. And thus the children will have a perfect *right* of receiving maintenance from their parents" (italics in original). William Blackstone, *Commentaries on the Laws of England* (1765–1769), vol. 1, cited in Harry Krause, "Child Support Reassessed: Limits of Private Responsibility and the Public Interest," *University of Illinois Law Review* 1989 (1989): 371.

11. Krause, "Child Support Reassessed," 367, 383.

12. See *State v. Langford*, 176 P. 197, 90 Or. 251 (1918) for a discussion of the different state positions. *Langford* involved a case in which the court had granted the divorce and awarded the mother custody without referring to child support in the decree. Ten years later, the father had paid no support and the issue before the court was whether to construe a divorce decree that awarded the mother custody without mentioning support as absolving the father of any further obligation. The Oregon court observed that a majority of jurisdictions interpreted such decrees as leaving the father's "natural" obligation unimpaired, while a minority concluded that no support was owed.

13. *Pacific Gold Dredging Co. v. Industrial Accident Commission*, 194 P. 1, 184 Cal. 462 (1920), cited in Mason, *From Father's Property to Children's Rights*, 212*n*95.

14. And may still not have died entirely. See Margaret F. Brinig, *The Contract and the Covenant: Beyond Law and Economics* (arguing that parental expenditures on young children still correlate with the likelihood that parents will live with their children when they become adults).

15. As a Justice Department attorney, I handled a case in the early 1980s that involved a challenge to the Georgia bastardy statutes. At that time, the only way to establish paternity in the state was to have the unmarried mother swear out a criminal arrest warrant against the father "for fornication and bastardy." Since the AFDC rules required recipients to cooperate with state efforts to secure child support, and since the criminal proceeding was the only way to do so in Georgia, the mothers, who had no great interest in swearing out arrest warrants against their boyfriends, challenged the Georgia proceeding as inconsistent with federal AFDC guidelines. The Georgia state legislature, to the frustration of the Georgia Attorney General's office, had refused to authorize a civil paternity action, and the parties to the litigation were convinced that the key to legislative action was a credible threat to cut off AFDC benefits to the state. The trial court judge deferred to the Department of Health and Human Service's (HHS) construction of its own statute, but the two HHS offices with responsibility in the matter had diametrically opposed views as to what the statute required. The HHS official with authority to act for the agency held his position on an "acting" basis and refused to take a position in the dispute. The parties settled the case without a ruling from the court, and Georgia has since adopted a streamlined civil paternity procedure.

16. See Krause, "Child Support Reassessed," 367, 372–73, and Paula G. Roberts, "Child Support Orders: Problems with Enforcement," *The Future of Children* 4 (1994): 101–20.

17. See, generally, Herma Hill Kay, "Equality and Difference," 1–90.

18. See Sanford N. Katz, "Historical Perspective and Current Trends in the Legal Process of Divorce," *The Future of Children* 4 (1994): 44–62 (52); and Jay D. Teachman and Kathleen M. Paasch, "Financial Impact of Divorce on Children and Their Families," *The Future of Children* 4 (1994): 63–83 (75).

19. Irwin Garfinkel, Marygold S. Melli, and John G. Robertson, "Child Support

Orders: A Perspective on Reform," *The Future of Children* 4 (1994): 84–100 (at 87). Compounding these results were low rates of compliance. In 1981 the most quoted initial study found no payment in 25 percent of cases in which child support orders had been issued, and partial payment in another 25 percent. A decade later, Census data showed that only 75 percent of the men and 63 percent of the women (8 percent of child support orders) with outstanding orders had paid *something* in 1991 — but a quarter still paid nothing at all. David Chambers concluded that "multiplying the number of custodial mothers due payments by the proportion who actually received payments, one can conclude that fewer than 40 of all custodial mothers actually received money from an absent father during the year." Only 24 percent of those potentially eligible both had an award and received the full amount. David L. Chambers, "Fathers, the Welfare System, and the Virtues and Perils of Child Support Enforcement," *Virginia Law Review* 81 (1995): 2575–2605 (at notes 6 and 54). See also Linda D. Elrod, "Child Support Reassessed: Federalization of Enforcement Nears Completion," *University of Illinois Law Review* 14 (1997): 695–709 (at 698*n*14).

20. Garfinkel, Melli, and Robertson, "Child Support Orders," at 87.

21. Harry Krause observed that, during earlier times, "[a]bsent parents were not pursued. Even for a legally established child support obligation, the absent father could all but choose not to pay. The obligation was rarely enforced effectively — especially not across state lines. Paternity — where in doubt — was rarely ascertained." Krause, "Child Support Reassessed," 370.

22. Linda Elrod terms these developments the "federalization of child support enforcement." Each state is now required to adopt mandatory child support guidelines limiting judicial discretion, and to streamline the procedures for establishing paternity. Congress has extended automatic payroll withholding to all new awards (including those which have never been in default), limited loan eligibility for those in arrears, facilitated interstate collection, and made evasion of child support a federal crime. Elrod, "Child Support Reassessed," at 698–709.

23. John Eekelaar, *Regulating Divorce*, at 102.

24. Leslie J. Harris, D. Dennis Waldrop, and Lori Rathbun Waldrop, for example, observe that (*a*) parental obligation has historically been rooted in the exchange between parental obligation and filial duty, and (*b*) "one reason absent fathers do not pay child support is that their loss of contact with and control over their children attenuates their sense of responsibility to the children." Empirical research supports their observations. Judith A. Seltzer's and S. M. Bianchi's work found that fathers who share decision-making about children with mothers are more likely to visit and pay support. Sanford L. Braver et al. explain these results in terms of a "social exchange" model in which noncustodial fathers engage in a type of cost-benefit analysis that balances, as part of a complex emotional calculus, the benefits the father receives from continued involvement with the child, the ease of visitation, the reactions of new partners, the father's personal commitment to the parenting role, and the reactions of his ex-spouse. These descriptions are empirical rather than normative, however. See Harris, Waldrop, and Waldrop,

"Making and Breaking Connections Between Parents' Duty to Support and Right to Control Their Children," *Oregon Law Review* 69 (1990): 689*n*39 (citing David Chambers, *Making Fathers Pay* [1979]); Seltzer, "Relationships Between Fathers and Children Who Live Apart: The Father's Role After Separation," *Journal of Marriage and the Family* 53 (1991): 79–101; Seltzer and Bianchi, "Children's Contact with Absent Parents," *Journal of Marriage and the Family* 50 (1988): 663–77; and Braver et al., "A Social Exchange Model of Nonresidential Parent Involvement," in C. Depner and J. Bray, eds., *Nonresidential Parenting: New Vistas in Family Living*, 87–108.

25. Hon. Judith Mitchell Billings, "From Guesswork to Guidelines — The Adoption of Uniform Child Support Guidelines in Utah," *Utah Law Review* 1989 (1989): 883–88 (859). The guideline drafters acknowledge, however, that because it is more expensive to maintain two homes than one, duplicating the percentage of income spent in intact families will not produce the same level of benefits for the child, and numerous observers have commented that even the higher standards in the new guidelines do not account for the full cost of childrearing. For a summary of the criticisms, see Margaret Campbell Haynes, ed., *Child Support Guidelines: The Next Generation* (Washington, D.C.: U.S. Department of Health and Human Services, April 1994).

26. For a comprehensive overview of these cases, see Laura W. Morgan, "Child Support and the Anomalous Cases of the High-Income and Low-Income Parent: The Need to Reconsider What Constitutes 'Support' in the American and Canadian Child Support Guideline Models," *Canadian Journal of Family Law* 13 (1996): 161.

27. Marilyn L. Ray, *New York State Child Support Standards Act: Evaluation Report, 1993*, xv.

28. See *Re Patterson*, 22 Fam. L. Rep. (BNA) 1416 (Kan. Ct. App. June 21, 1996) (attributing the "Three Pony Rule" to Professor Linda Elrod, one of the drafters of the Kansas Child Support Guidelines).

29. *Boyt v. Romanow*, 664 So.2d 995 (Fla. Dist. Ct. App. 1995).

30. See J. Thomas Oldham, "The Appropriate Child Support Award When the Noncustodial Parent Earns Less Than the Custodial Parent," *Houston Law Review* 31 (1994): 585.

31. See Oldham, "The Appropriate Child Support Award," 585.

32. *State ex rel. Hermesmann v. Seyer*, 252 Kan. 646, 847 P.2d 1273 (1993).

33. Ibid. (citations omitted). The court (after complaining about the inadequacy of the record) observed further that "[a]lthough the question of whether the intercourse with Colleen was 'voluntary,' as the term is usually understood, is not specifically before us, it was brought out in oral argument before this court that the sexual relationship between Shane and his babysitter, Colleen, started when he was only 12 years old and lasted over a period of several months. At no time did Shane register any complaint to his parents about the sexual liaison with Colleen." Ibid., 252 Kan. at 651.

34. *State ex rel. Hermesmann v. Seyer*, 252 Kan. at 655.

35. "Finally, we call attention to the fact that no issue was raised as to the propriety of the judgment against a youngster who was still a full-time student when these pro-

ceedings were commenced. When questioned in oral argument about the policy of SRS in seeking a judgment in excess of $7,000, counsel replied with the surprising statement that SRS had no intention of ever attempting to collect its judgment. Under such circumstances, the reason for seeking that portion of the judgment still eludes us" (ibid., 252 Kan. at 656). SRS, although it had joined Shane's parents in the suit, did not claim that they were liable for the judgment.

36. *County of San Luis Obispo v. Nathaniel J.*, 50 Cal. App. 4th 842, 57 Cal. Rptr.2d 843 (1996).

37. Ibid. The court further observed that "[t]he law should not except Nathaniel J. from this responsibility because he is not an innocent victim of Jones's criminal acts. After discussing the matter, he and Jones decided to have sexual relations. They had sexual intercourse approximately five times over a two-week period." The court also noted further that the state was only seeking to establish paternity, and to reserve the right to have a child support order entered at a time when Nathaniel had reached the age of majority and had the money to pay.

38. Karen Czapanskiy, "Volunteers and Draftees: The Struggle for Parental Equality," *UCLA Law Review* 38 (1991): 1415–81.

39. In John Eekelaar's words, "Indissoluble marriage has been replaced by the indissoluble responsibility of parenthood" (*Regulating Divorce*, 90).

19. The Remaking of Fatherhood

1. See Grossberg, *Governing the Hearth: Law and the Family in Nineteenth-Century America*; Mason, *From Father's Property to Children's Rights: The History of Child Custody in the United States*; and Mary L. Shanley, "Unwed Fathers' Rights, Adoption and Sex Equality: Gender Neutrality and the Perpetuation of Patriarchy," *Columbia Law Review* 95 (1995): 60–103 (at 67–69).

2. Illinois law defined the term "parent" to include "the father and mother of a legitimate child, or the survivor of them, or the natural mother of an illegitimate child, and . . . any adoptive parent." *Stanley v. Illinois*, 405 U.S. 645, 650 (1972).

3. After his wife's death, Stanley had asked a Mr. and Mrs. Ness to care for the children, and they were named the court-appointed guardians in the dependency proceeding. *Stanley*, 405 U.S. at 663n2 (Burger, C. J., dissenting).

4. *Stanley*, 405 U.S. at 651–52.

5. Chief Justice Burger's dissent presents a somewhat different view of the father, noting that he himself had placed the children with the Ness family, the state-appointed guardians, because he was unable to care for them after the mother's death; that he made no effort to be recognized as the father of the children until he discovered that he might lose welfare benefits if the state recognized someone else as the children's guardian; and that the oldest of the three children had been removed from the Stanleys' care in a neglect proceeding that had assumed father and mother were married — and still unfit parents. *Stanley*, 405 U.S. at 667 and note 5 (Burger, C. J., dissenting).

6. *Stanley*, 405 U.S. at 661n1 (Burger, C. J., dissenting).

7. *Quilloin v. Walcott*, 434 U.S. 245, 249 (1977). The father could, however, acquire a veto by "legitimating" the child through a procedure in which the father acknowledged paternity and the child acquired the right to inherit in the same manner as a marital child (Ga. Code Sec. 74–103).

8. *Quilloin*, 434 U.S. at 256.

9. *Caban v. Mohammed*, 441 U.S. 380 (1979).

10. *Lehr v. Robertson*, 463 U.S. 248, 249 (1983). In this case as well, the dissent presents a very different picture of the facts. The majority "assumes" that Lehr is the father, noting that the mother "has never conceded that appellant [Lehr] is Jessica's biological father" (ibid., at 250n3).

11. In addition to those persons named in the putative father registry, New York law also required notice to be given to those who have been adjudicated to be the father, those who have been identified as the father on the child's birth certificate, those who live openly with the child and the child's mother and who hold themselves out to be the father, those who have been identified as the father by the mother in a sworn written statement, and those who were married to the child's mother before the child was six months old. Lehr did not fit into any of these categories. A month after the adoption petition was filed, however, he sought to establish paternity and a right to visitation in a separate proceeding in another county. The court handling the adoption petition, however, stayed the paternity proceeding and signed the adoption order a short time later without giving Lehr formal notice or an opportunity to be heard. *Lehr*, 463 U.S. at 251–53.

12. *Lehr*, 463 U.S. at 256–57.

13. *Lehr*, 463 U.S. at 261–62.

14. *Lehr*, 463 U.S. at 268–69 (White, J., dissenting). Justice White's version of the facts could differ so markedly from Justice Stevens's because of the procedures involved. The lower court had processed the adoption without giving the putative father notice or an opportunity to be heard. The lower courts therefore made no findings of fact. The "facts" that White presents are those the father alleged. The mother may well have disputed or supplemented them.

15. *Caban*, 441 U.S. at 403.

16. *Caban*, 441 U.S. at 407.

17. *Caban*, 441 U.S. at 407–408. See also Chief Justice Burger's dissent in *Stanley*, which had echoed similar themes, concluding that the state could justifiably grant "full recognition only to those father-child relationships that arise in the context of family units bound together by legal obligations arising from marriage or from adoption proceedings." *Stanley*, 405 U.S. at 663 (Burger, C. J., dissenting). See also Janet L. Dolgin, "Just a Gene: Judicial Assumptions About Parenthood," *UCLA Law Review* 40 (1993): 637.

18. For a summary of this view, see Deborah L. Forman, "Unwed Fathers and Adoption: A Theoretical Analysis in Context," *Texas Law Review* 72 (1994): 967–1045. Forman notes, however, that the tendency of a pregnancy to trigger marriage or breakup is less for minorities than whites, and for teens than for older couples (ibid., at 993n170).

19. Forman, "Unwed Fathers and Adoption," 967–1045 (at 1001n221).

20. *Smith v. Malont*, Miss. Sup. Ct., No. 92–CA–01177 (*Family Law Reporter* 24 [September 24, 1998]: at 1589).

21. For an account of both cases, see Scott A. Resnik, "Seeking the Wisdom of Solomon," *Seton Hall Legislative Journal* 20 (1996): 363–430. For a list of statutes with similar provisions, see ibid., at 391n.

22. Susan Swingle, "Comment: Rights of Unwed Fathers and the Best Interests of the Child: Can These Competing Interests Be Harmonized? Illinois' Putative Father Registry Provides an Answer," *Loyola University Chicago Law Journal* 26 (1995): 703–53. Otaker ("Otto") and Daniella had been living together when she became pregnant. During the pregnancy, Otto visited his native Czechoslovakia and, while he was away, his aunt told Daniella that he had resumed a relationship with an old girlfriend. Daniella broke off the relationship, moved out of their apartment, and decided to place the baby for adoption. She instructed an uncle to tell Otto that the baby had died, refused to identify him as the father because of fear he would not consent to the adoption, and rejected his efforts at communication. Richard was born on March 16, 1991, and four days later Daniella consented to the adoption. On May 12, Daniella moved back into their apartment. Otto went to see a lawyer on May 18. The lawyer filed an appearance in the adoption proceeding on June 6. Otto and Daniella married in September. The Supreme Court of Illinois did not decide the case that would recognize Otto's parental rights until 1994. On April 30, 1995, the adoptive parents transferred four-year-old Richard to his birth parents. See Resnik, "Seeking the Wisdom of Solomon," 371–76. Resnik notes that, as with many of the other cases, the judicial opinions contain widely varying versions of the facts. See, in particular, the difference between the majority and the dissenting opinions at the intermediate appellate level. *In re the Petition of Doe*, 627 N.E.2d 648 (Ill. App. Ct. 1993).

23. Forman notes that such statutes have withstood constitutional challenge ("Unwed Fathers and Adoption," at 1001–10003).

24. Resnik, "Seeking the Wisdom of Solomon," at 393, citing *In the Matter of Raquel Marie X*, 76 N.Y.2d 855, 559 N.E.2d 418 (N.Y.S. 1990), cert. denied, 111 S. Ct. 517 (1990).

25. *In the Matter of Raquel Marie X*, 559 N.E.2d at 861, 863. The New York Court of Appeals further observed that "the State's objection [in ensuring swift, permanent placement] cannot be constitutionally accomplished at the sacrifice of the father's protected interest by imposing a test so incidentally related to the *father-child* relationship as this one, directed as it is principally to the *mother-child* relationship."

26. *Adoption of Kelsey S.*, 823 P.2d 1216 (Cal. 1992). Neither case resulted in an award of custody to the father, however. Rather, both resulted in remands to the lower court for a resolution of the custody issue in accordance with the new standards. In *Raquel Marie*, the lower courts found that the father's lack of concern and involvement with the mother also failed to demonstrate the requisite concern for the child she was carrying. In *Kelsey S.*, the California Supreme Court emphasized that the issue of custody was distinct from the issue of an adoption veto.

27. The Honorable John E. Fennelly, "Step Up or Step Out: Unwed Fathers' Parental Rights Post-Doe and E.A.W," *St. Thomas Law Review* 8 (1996): 259–311, (at 295).

28. See Barbara Bennett Woodhouse, "Hatching the Egg: A Child-Centered Perspective on Parent's Rights," *Cardozo Law Review* 14 (1993): 1747–1806; and Dolgin, "Just a Gene," 637–94. See also Katharine T. Bartlett, "Re-expressing Parenthood," *Yale Law Journal* 98 (1988): 293 (arguing that encouraging parental responsibility ought to be central to any approach to parenthood); Elizabeth Buchanan, "The Constitutional Rights of Unwed Fathers Before and After *Lehr v. Robertson*," *Ohio State Law Journal* 45 (1984): 313; and Shanley, "Unwed Fathers' Rights."

29. Dolgin, "Just a Gene," at 671.

30. *Michael H. v. Gerald D.*, 491 U.S. 110, rehearing denied, 492 U.S. 937 (1989).

31. Stevens interpreted the California statute differently from the other eight justices and based his decision on that interpretation. The two justices who joined Scalia's opinion in part dissented from a footnote that relied on "historical traditions specifically relating to the rights of an adulterous natural father" in defining the scope of the Constitution's liberty interest. The case also produced two dissenting opinions, one by Justice White and another by Justice Brennan (in which Justices Marshall and Black joined), that took very different approaches to the case. *Michael H. v. Gerald D.*, 491 U.S. 110 (1989).

32. Cal. Fam. Code Sec. 7541(b) (West 1994).

33. Dolgin, "Just a Gene," at 666. Scalia noted further that the "unitary family" "is typified, of course, by the marital family, but also includes the household of unmarried parents and their children." Ibid., at 667 (citations omitted).

34. The one exception of the celebrated lot, *Kelsey S.*, also involved a married man (just one not married to the mother of the contested child), and the recorded history of the case ends with a remand, not a final decision, for the father. There is no recorded decision of the remand, but Carol Gorenberg reports that, according to a legislative summary, the trial court found that the father did not fully commit to the child because he failed to emotionally and financially support the mother during the pregnancy. Carol A. Gorenberg, "Fathers' Rights vs. Children's Best Interests: Establishing a Predictable Standard for California Adoption Disputes," *Family Law Quarterly* 31 (1997): 169 (at 196*n*161).

For cases nonetheless awarding custody to the father, see *Jermstad v. McNelis*, 210 Cal. App. 3d 528, 258 Cal. Rptr. 519 (1989) (holding that the "natural" father, who sought custody within days of the birth, had equal rights with the mother in withdrawing her earlier consent to the adoption); and *Abernathy v. Baby Boy*, 437 S.E.2d 25 (1993) (allowing the father whose marriage proposal had been rejected by the mother to block adoption and assume custody).

35. See Blankenhorn, *Fatherless America*, at 201 (celebrating the "Good Family Man," and noting that it "would never occur to him — or to his wife or children — to make distinctions between 'biological' and 'social' fathering. For him, these two identities are tightly fused"). See also Popenoe, *Life Without Father*, 197–98.

36. Woodhouse, "Hatching the Egg," at 1757.

37. Ibid., at 1806.

38. Popenoe, *Life Without Father*, at 213.

39. *Stanley*, 405 U.S. at 665–66 (Burger, C. J., dissenting).

40. See, e.g., *Kelsey S.*, which involved a married father who had an adulterous affair and opposed the biological mother's efforts to place the baby for adoption so that he and his wife could take custody. *Jermstad v. McNelis*, the 1989 California case that allowed a father to withdraw his consent to adoption shortly after the child's birth, involved a father seeking custody together with his new wife. In *Ireland v. Smith*, 451 Mich. 457, 547 N.W.2d 686 (1996), the Michigan Supreme Court upheld an award of custody to a father whose own mother planned to care for the child, over the birth mother, who had placed the child in day care during her college classes.

41. Fennelly, "Step Up or Step Out," at 304–305. The underlying statutes are not, however, the same, with Florida requiring more of an assertion of paternal interest than Illinois to trigger the father's right to a veto in the first place.

42. Resnik, "Seeking the Wisdom of Solomon," at 376*n*67.

43. *In Re: The Adoption of Baby E.A.W. G.W.B.*, 658 So.2d 961 (Fla. 1995).

44. *Baby E.A.W.*, 658 So.2d 961, 967.

45. Justice Kogan went on to explain that while he would make an exception for those fathers who had abandoned their children, he would not tie abandonment to treatment of the mother, observing that "I am entirely unwilling to say that purely prenatal conduct ever can demonstrate abandonment with respect to the child absent clear and convincing proof that the biological father either (a) unequivocally, by word or deed, indicated a complete and unconditional prenatal abandonment of the child upon which others have reasonably relied, . . . or (b) recklessly or intentionally engaged in conduct that posed a significant risk of detriment to the fetus above and beyond what may be attributable to simple lack of socioeconomic resources." (*Baby E.A.W.*, 658 So.2d at 977).

46. On the issue of abandonment, the court holds: "Our review of the record shows substantial competent evidence to support the trial judge's finding of clear and convincing evidence that G.W.B. abandoned Baby E.A.W. The evidence in the record reveals that G.W.B. showed little to no interest in the birth mother or the unborn child. Once the birth mother moved out of the home, he provided no financial or emotional support. As the trial court noted, the evidence suggests that G.W.B. might have continued his passive stance toward the birth mother and the child had Danciu [the birth mother] not contacted him about adoption. Even then, the record shows that G.W.B. still did not make any move to provide financial or emotional support to the birth mother or the unborn child. We therefore approve the district court's decision affirming the trial court's finding of abandonment." (*Baby E.A.W.*, 658 So.2d at 967).

47. The most significant remaining exception is the limitation of the parental rights of fathers who impregnate the mother through rape.

48. See Kogan's dissent in the *Baby Emily* case, and Daniel C. Zinman, "Father Knows Best: The Unwed Father's Right to Raise His Infant Surrendered for Adoption,"

Fordham Law Review 60 (1992): 971, proposing that the father receive custody *pendante lite* (during the litigation) in contested adoptions.

20. Child Custody at Divorce: Ground Zero in the Gender Wars

1. Mason, *From Father's Property to Children's Rights*, 6–13. Massachusetts even enacted a statute in 1646 that provided that "[i]f a man have a stubborn or rebellious son, of sufficient years and understanding, viz. sixteen years of age, which will not obey the voice of his Father or the voice of his Mother, and that when they have chastened him will not harken unto them: then shall his Father and Mother being his natural parents, lay hold on him, and bring him to the Magistrates assembled in Court and testify unto them, that their son is stubborn and rebellious and will not obey their voice and chastisement, but lives in sundry notorious crimes, such a son shall be put to death" (ibid., at 11). There is no evidence, however, that executions under the statute ever occurred. Nonetheless, Mason notes that, consistent with the early modern family's looser boundaries between home and community, filial obligation was a community as well as a familial responsibility, and the community routinely punished rebellious children.

2. Mason, *From Father's Property to Children's Rights*, at 19–20. In England the father might grant the uncle both custody of the child and supervision of the estate. In colonial America, the guardianship was more likely to be limited to the estate. If the mother could not afford to care for the children, however, they might be apprenticed to a family who could, with the new family named as legal guardians. While children typically remained with their mothers, male guardians were often appointed so that "neither the child nor the widow may be injured in their rights and inherited property" (ibid., at 20; citations omitted).

3. Mason, *From Father's Property to Children's Rights*, at 54–55.

4. Ibid., at 63 (citations omitted). See also Jane C. Murphy, "Legal Images of Motherhood: Conflicting Decisions from Welfare 'Reform,' Family, and Criminal Law," *Cornell Law Review* 83 (1998): 688.

5. Mason reports, for example, that as late as the turn of the century, many cases routinely recited as governing law the common law maxim that "the natural right is with the father, unless the father is somehow unfit" (*From Father's Property to Children's Rights*, at 50).

6. Ibid., at 123 (citations omitted).

7. For an overview of joint custody history and legislation, see Jay Folberg, ed., *Joint Custody and Shared Parenting*, 160, 190. North Carolina enacted the first joint custody statute in 1957 (that is, the first statute explicitly authorizing custody to more than one person). Ibid., at 5. Many courts, however, found that they had broad discretion in deciding what type of custody to award, and did not need explicit statutory authorization (see ibid., at 160). Nonetheless, a Maryland court had declared in 1934 that joint custody was an arrangement "to be avoided, whenever possible, as an evil fruitful in the destruction of discipline, in the creation of distrust, and in the production of mental distress in the child" (Mason, *From Father's Property to Children's Rights*, at 130).

8. The legislation became effective on January 1, 1980. Cal. Civ. Code Sec. 4600(a)(1) (West 1981).

9. Folberg, ed., *Joint Custody and Shared Parenting*, at 159, 209, and appendix A. By 1995 the *Family Law Quarterly* listed forty-two states with provisions dealing with joint custody. See Linda D. Elrod and Robert G. Spector, "A Review of the Year in Family Law: Children's Issues Take Spotlight," *Family Law Quarterly* 29 (1996): 741, 771, app. table 2.

10. Joseph Goldstein, Anna Freud, and Albert Solnit, *Beyond the Best Interests of the Child*, 38. Joseph Goldstein wrote a decade later that their conclusion that noncustodial parents should have "no legally enforceable right to visit" their children was the most misunderstood aspect of the book. He explained that they did not oppose continuing contact between noncustodial parents and their children. Rather, they saw the effect of visitation orders as a "shift in the power to deprive the child of his 'right' from the custodial parent to the noncustodial parent. Visitation orders make the noncustodial parent — rather than the parent who is responsible for the child's day-to-day care — the final authority for deciding if and when to visit." Joseph Goldstein, "In Whose Best Interest?" in Folberg, ed., *Joint Custody and Shared Parenting*, at 52 and 55.

11. Katharine T. Bartlett and Carol B. Stack, "Joint Custody, Feminism, and the Dependency Dilemma," *Berkeley Women's Law Journal* 2 (1986): 9–41 (quotes at 28, 32–33).

12. Folberg, ed., *Joint Custody and Shared Parenting*, at 5.

13. James A. Cook, "California's Joint Custody Statute," in Folberg, ed., *Joint Custody and Shared Parenting*, at 169.

14. Cook, "California's Joint Custody Statute," at 169. See also Joanne Schulmann and Valerie Pitt, "Second Thoughts on Joint Child Custody: Analysis of Legislation and Its Implications for Women and Children," in Folberg, ed., *Joint Custody and Shared Parenting*, at 215, quoting James Cook to the effect that "[i]t's a new twist on the old game called keepaway. . . . We've tried to put a new handicap on the game by requiring the court to favor the most cooperative parent." For a full articulation of parental alienation as a syndrome, see Richard Gardner, *The Parental Alienation Syndrome: A Guide for Mental Health and Legal Professionals*.

15. Eleanor E. Maccoby and Robert H. Mnookin, *Dividing the Child: Social and Legal Dilemmas of Custody*, 107–108.

16. Marygold S. Melli, Patricia R. Brown, Maria Cancian, "Child Custody in a Changing World: A Study of Postdivorce Arrangements in Wisconsin," *University of Illinois Law Review* 1997 (1997): 773–800 (at 778).

17. Ibid., at 779. In Wisconsin the joint physical custody label is reserved for awards of at least 30 percent residential custody to one party, and not more than 70 percent to the other.

18. Mason, *From Father's Property to Children's Rights*, at 131. Joan B. Kelly, "The Determination of Child Custody," *The Future of Children: Children and Divorce* 4 (1994): 121–42 (at 125), cites three separate California studies, examining different data that put the figure somewhere between 17 and 34 percent.

19. Kelly, "The Determination of Child Custody," at 123 and n. 34.

20. Melli, Brown, and Cancian, "Child Custody in a Changing World," at 780.

21. Melli, Brown, and Cancian found that not only had the nature of custody awards changed, but the actual amount of time fathers spent with their children also increased, albeit less dramatically (ibid., at 784).

22. Karen Czapanskiy, "Volunteers and Draftees: The Struggle for Parental Equality," 1415–81 (quotes at 1416, 1468). For more pointed feminist criticism, see Martha Fineman, *The Neutered Mother*, especially the discussion in part 1, chapters 4 and 5.

23. Karen Czapanskiy, "Child Support, Visitation, Shared Custody, and Split Custody," in Haynes, ed., *Child Support Guidelines: The Next Generation*, 43–50.

24. Cahn defined "domestic violence" as "the use of physical or psychological force by one adult against another adult with whom there currently exists, or has existed, an intimate relationship," noting however that "this term is most frequently used as a euphemism for wife beating." Naomi R. Cahn, "Civil Images of Battered Women: The Impact of Domestic Violence on Child Custody Decisions," *Vanderbilt Law Review* 44 (1991): 1041–97 (quotes from 1042*n*5; citations omitted).

25. Cahn, "Civil Images of Battered Women," at 1043.

26. Ibid., at 1073, citing House Committee on the Judiciary, *Hearings on H.R. 172 Before the Subcommittee on Administrative Law and Government Relations*, 99th Cong., 2d sess., 1990 (testimony of Marcia Shields).

27. See, e.g., Cahn's reference to *Collinsworth v. O'Connell*, 508 So.2d 744 (Fla. Dist. Ct. App. 1987). The father in the case had exhibited violent and irrational behavior, which included throwing his wife to the ground, beating her when she was four months pregnant, and threatening to kill her, her father, and himself. According to Cahn, the court nonetheless "accepted a psychologist's conclusion that the man's 'past violence was related to the deterioration of his relationship with [his wife],' and was presumably unrelated to his fitness as a parent. The court apparently dismissed the battering that occurred while the woman was pregnant" as irrelevant to the custody proceeding. Cahn, "Civil Images of Battered Women," at 1073.

28. Lynne R. Kurtzf, "Comment: Protecting New York's Children: An Argument for the Creation of a Rebuttable Presumption Against Awarding a Spouse Abuser Custody of a Child," *Albany Law Review* 60 (1997): 1345. See also D. Kelly Weisberg and Susan Frelich Appleton, *Modern Family Law: Cases and Materials*, 842, reporting thirty-five states by 1995.

29. Weisberg and Appleton, *Modern Family Law*, at 842.

30. See Cahn, "Civil Images of Battered Women," for a summary of the effects of domestic violence on children, including their greater likelihood of becoming batterers themselves.

31. Many researchers find the level of conflict to be on a continuum. Janet Johnston, for example, notes a study of court-ordered mediation, which found that "in a startling 65 percent of families, domestic violence was alleged by one or both parents within the mediation session." A comparison sample of sixty randomly selected families found the rates of physical aggression to be thirty-six times lower. Janet R. Johnston, "High Con-

flict Divorce," in *The Future of Children: Children and Divorce* 4 (1994): at 168. Johnston notes, further, that the definition of "high conflict" can refer to at least three different dimensions: (1) domain — that is, the content of the dispute (e.g., distinctions between financial versus custody disputes); (2) tactics, such as the presence of physical aggression, verbal manipulation, etc., or the method of resolution; or (3) attitude, or intensity of the conflict.

32. Maccoby and Mnookin, *Dividing the Child*, at 58.

33. Melli, Brown, and Cancian, "Child Custody in a Changing World," at 788. The study also found that "[u]nequal shared custody cases also may be the result of more conflict between parents. Of the unequal shared custody cases, 34 percent had parents who were in dispute about custody, while only 6.4 percent of those with the outcome of equal shared custody were in dispute. Although only 51.5 percent of the divorcing parents were both represented by legal counsel in the divorce, 70.1 percent of the cases with an unequal shared custody outcome involved legal representation for both parents. Unequal shared custody cases also required the longest time to reach resolution (320 days as compared to 252 days) and, along with split custody cases, showed the greatest number of appearances before a judge" (ibid., at 799).

34. See Folberg, ed., *Joint Custody and Shared Parenting*, and Johnston, "High Conflict Divorce," for a summary of the literature.

35. Mason, *From Father's Property to Children's Rights*, 215n44; see also Weisberg and Appleton, *Modern Family Law*, at 848.

36. Johnston, "High Conflict Divorce," at 179.

37. See Weisberg and Appleton, *Modern Family Law*, at 909. For a more detailed comparison of these cases, see Pamela Markert, "Comment: Custody Relocation: More Questions Than Answers Result from High Court Opinions in California and New York," *Santa Clara Law Review* 38 (1998): 521–54.

38. *Tropea v. Tropea*, 87 N.Y.2d 727, 665 N.E.2d 145 (NY 1996).

39. In the companion case, *Browner v. Kenward*, 642 N.Y.S.2d 575 (N.Y. 1996), the custodial mother wished to relocate 130 miles away because her parents, with whom she lived, had relocated and she had lost her job. She testified that she had difficulty finding another job in the area that would permit her to find adequate housing, and that her son had a close relationship with his grandparents and cousins who would be in the new location. The lower court ruled in the mother's favor, influenced among other things by psychological testimony that the child would benefit by being away from his parents' bickering.

40. *Tropea*, 665 N.E.2d at 151.

41. *Burgess v. Burgess*, 13 Cal. 4th 25, 913 P.2d 473, 51 Cal. Rptr.2d 444 (1996).

42. *Burgess v. Burgess*, 13 Cal. 4th at 29–30.

43. *Burgess v. Burgess*, 13 Cal. 4th at 34.

44. The court observed that

As this case demonstrates, ours is an increasingly mobile society. Amici curiae point out that approximately one American in five changes residences each

year. . . . Economic necessity and remarriage account for the bulk of reloca-
tions. . . . Because of the ordinary needs for both parents after a marital dissolution to secure or retain employment, pursue educational or career opportunities or reside in the same location as a new spouse or other family or friends,
it is unrealistic to assume that divorced parents will permanently remain in the
same location after dissolution or to exert pressure on them to do so. It would
also undermine the interest in minimizing costly litigation over custody and require the trial courts to "micromanage" family decisionmaking by second-guess-
ing reasons for everyday decisions about career and family.

More fundamentally, the "necessity" of relocating frequently has little, if any,
substantive bearing on the suitability of a parent to retain the role of a custodial
parent. A parent who has been the primary caretaker for minor children is ordinarily no less capable of maintaining the responsibilities and obligations of parenting simply by virtue of a reasonable decision to change his or her geographical location.   (Burgess v. Burgess, *13 Cal. 4th at 35–36 (footnotes deleted)*

45. *Burgess v. Burgess*, 13 Cal. 4th at 34–35. In a footnote the court observed, however, that the case addressed only circumstances in which the moving parent had sole
physical custody. In a case of joint physical custody, the courts would have to consider
the custody issue on a de novo basis (starting from scratch) to the extent that the move
made continuation of the existing custody arrangement impossible. Ibid., at 40*n*12.

46. The court observed that "[o]nce the trial court determined that the mother did
not relocate in order to frustrate the father's contact with the minor children, but did so
for sound 'good faith' reasons, it was not required to inquire further into the wisdom of
her inherently subjective decisionmaking" (*Burgess v. Burgess*, 13 Ca. 4th at 34*n*5).

47. Fineman, *The Neutered Mother*, and David Blankenhorn, "The State of the Family and the Family Policy Debate," *Santa Clara Law Review* 36 (1996): 431.

48. Gardner, *The Parental Alienation Syndrome*, 2d ed. (1998), at xix; see also note 52,
below.

49. John Gregory, "Interdependency Theory: Old Sausage in a New Casing: A Response to Professor Czapanskiy," *Santa Clara Law Review* 39 (1999): 1037–51 (citing
the National Interdisciplinary Colloquium on Child Custody, *Legal and Mental Health
Perspectives on Child Custody Law: A Deskbook for Judges* [Washington, D.C.: NICCC,
1998]).

50. *Allen v. Farrow*, 197 A.D.2d 327 (N.Y. Sup. Ct. Appellate Division, 1994). The
court ordered supervised visitation with Satchel and Dylan, in part to insulate them
from the impact of the affair with their sister. Woody's participation in Dylan's therapy
did not have the desired effects, and the visitation was later ended.

51. Mary Ann Mason, *The Custody Wars*, at 164 (citing Marc J. Ackerman and
Melissa C. Ackerman, "Child Custody Evaluation Practices: A 1996 Survey of Psychologists," *Family Law Quarterly* 30 [1996]: 565).

52. Gardner generally favors custody awards to the primary caretaker and recommends a contrary custody choice only in what he terms the 10 percent or less of parental alienation cases that form the "severe" end of the spectrum. Nonetheless, Gardner's book changes in tone from the first edition, published in 1992, which emphasizes his frustration at the rare use of custody transfers to remedy the problem, to the second edition, published in 1998, which acknowledges a misuse of parental alienation syndrome to justify custody transfer in inappropriate cases. Gardner, *The Parental Alienation Syndrome*, 2d ed. (1998), at xxviii.

53. Ibid., at 167.

54. *Renaud v. Renaud*, 721 A.2d 463; 1998 Vt. LEXIS 257 (Vt. Supreme Court 1998).

55. *Renaud v. Renaud*, 721 A.2d at 466.

56. *Renaud v. Renaud*, 721 A.2d at 465.

57. The courts address parental rights more directly when children are not present. The newest cases to press the issue are tort cases, and while (as Frank Serpico can attest) the courts are reluctant to recognize wrongful parenthood, they are more willing to punish wrongful interference with the parental relationship. *Kessel v. Leavitt*, 1998 W. Va. LEXIS 135 (1998), has attracted the most attention.

John Kessel and Anne Conaty had a long-standing romantic relationship. They parted, but Anne shortly after learned that she was pregnant. They reconciled and became engaged. Anne testified, however, that she "became afraid of John and feared for her safety after the deterioration of their relationship." She left town, and John tried to reach her, professing an interest in both reuniting with her and blocking the adoption of the child. To frustrate John's involvement, Anne sought the services of a California attorney and placed the child for adoption in Canada. By the time John learned of Anne and the child's whereabouts, the Canadian adoption had become final. John sued Anne, her attorney, her parents, and her brother for fraud and tortious interference with his parental rights. The jury returned a verdict of $2 million in compensatory damages and $5.85 million in punitive damages, which the West Virginia Supreme Court of Appeals upheld.

The *Kessel* case is fraught with ironies. Had Anne been determined to frustrate John's paternity, she could have had an abortion. Had she chosen to keep the child, she was almost certain to retain custody. If she chose to move to California before the child's birth, few courts would consider intervening, and John would then bear the burden of establishing and maintaining a long-distance relationship with his child. Moreover, if John, like the majority of nonmarital fathers, lost interest, no court would require his presence in the child's life even if he were located nearby. One suspects that Anne's — and her lawyer's — chief offense was to deprive West Virginia of jurisdiction over the child's fate.

58. In *Renaud*, the father had alleged that the trial court placed undue weight on marital fault in the property division, but the Vermont Supreme Court rejected the allegation, noting that the trial court held that the father's fault in the marital breakup was

fully offset by the mother's dissipation of marital assets in bringing excessive motions, "and thus neither factor would be considered in the property division." The discussion of fault occupied one sentence in the opinion. *Renaud v. Renaud*, 721 A.2d at 468–69.

21. Welfare Reform and the Permissibility of Motherhood

1. Rickie Solinger, *Wake Up Little Suzie: Single Pregnancy Before Roe v. Wade*.

2. Stephanie Coontz, *The Way We Never Were: American Families and the Nostalgia Trap*. Coontz reports that in 1957, 97 out of every 1,000 girls between the ages of fifteen and nineteen gave birth, compared with only 52 of every 1,000 girls in 1983. The most notable difference: in 1960 only 15 percent of all teen births were to unmarried mothers; by 1986 the majority of teen births would be outside of marriage. In response, the number of white brides who were pregnant at the altar doubled during the 1950s, and adoptions increased by 80 percent. Ibid., at 202–203, 39–40.

Steven Mintz and Susan Kellogg note that black nonmarital birthrates rose from 16.8 percent in 1940 to 23.6 percent in 1963 while white rates rose from 2 to 3 percent in the same period; and that female-headed households had climbed from 8 to 21 percent for African-Americans during the 1950s while the white rate remained steady at 9 percent. Mintz and Kellogg, *Domestic Revolutions: A Social History of American Family Life*, 210.

3. Solinger, *Wake Up Little Suzie*, at 1–3.

4. Solinger emphasizes that, before World War II, adoption was rare. She quotes Justine Wise Polier, a justice in the New York City Children's Court, to the effect that before the war "the unmarried mother was viewed as a bad woman who must be punished. Her child was regarded as a child of sin, therefore unfit to be adopted into a decent home. Adoption was a rare and unusual thing, risked only with a brand new, beautiful and perfect baby known to have an excellent family history" (*Wake Up Little Suzie*, at 159).

5. Solinger cites a number of studies that showed that dramatically fewer African-American couples than white couples were found to have met the stringent agency criteria for adoption, and that while "a white unwed mother could assume a rapid placement, the black one knew that her child would be forced, in part because of agency practices, to spend months in foster homes or institutions before placement, if that was ever achieved" (ibid., at 199).

6. Nonetheless, Donna Franklin observed that the key change in the 1950s was the increasing number of African-American women who never married. Franklin, *Ensuring Inequality*, 165–66.

7. Solinger, *Wake Up Little Suzie*, at 202.

8. Ibid., at 224.

9. Linda Gordon, *PITIED But Not Entitled: Single Mothers and the History of Welfare, 1890–1935*, 38–39 (citations omitted). President Theodore Roosevelt posed the issue this way in 1909: "Should children of parents of worthy character, but suffering from temporary misfortune, and the children of widows of worthy character and rea-

sonable efficiency, be kept with their parents — aid being given to parents to enable them to maintain suitable homes for the rearing of the children? Should the breaking of a home be permitted for reasons of poverty, or only for reasons of inefficiency or immorality?" (Mason, *From Father's Property to Children's Rights*, at 91).

10. Mason, *From Father's Property to Children's Rights*, 92. Mason cites, as an example of such legislation, an Illinois statute providing that "[i]f the parent or parents of such dependent or neglected child are poor and unable to properly care for such child, but are otherwise proper guardians and it is for the welfare of the child to remain at home, the court may enter an order finding such facts and fixing the amount of money necessary to enable the parent or parents to properly care for such a child" (ibid., at 92).

11. Ibid., at 93.

12. Urban immigrants constituted a large percentage of those receiving aid. In Chicago in 1917, for example, two-thirds of those receiving assistance were foreign born. African-Americans and Latinos were often underrepresented or excluded altogether from such programs, especially in the South and Southwest. See Gordon, *PITIED But Not Entitled*, at 48.

13. Mason, *From Father's Property to Children's Rights*, at 92. Seventy-seven percent of the single parents at the turn of the century *were* widows, however (Gordon, *PITIED But Not Entitled*, at 19).

14. Mason, *From Father's Property to Children's Rights*, at 93. Hawaii, Nebraska, and Michigan were exceptions.

15. Ibid., at 99.

16. Gordon, *PITIED But Not Entitled*, at 277.

17. Ibid., at 277; and Lucy A. Williams, "The Ideology of Division: Behavior Modification Welfare Reform Proposals," *Yale Law Journal* 102 (1992): 719–746 (at 723n33).

18. Gwendolyn Mink, "Welfare Reform in Historical Perspective," *Connecticut Law Review* 26 (1994): 879–99 (at 880).

19. In addition, Louisiana deemed "unsuitable" homes in which the mother bore subsequent illegitimate children after the acceptance of assistance. See Williams, "Ideology of Division," 723n33.

20. *King v. Smith*, 329 U.S. 309, 2137–38 (1968). The Supreme Court based its decision on AFDC amendments and agency rulings that took place during the 1960s, not on the original legislative history. In doing so, the Court emphasized that the states could not, at the same time, declare a home unsuitable for children, and therefore ineligible for support, while taking no action to remove children from the home (ibid., at 2138–41). See also *Lewis v. Martin*, 397 U.S. 552 (1970).

21. Mason, *From Father's Property to Children's Rights*, 149. The "man in the house" rules, though designed to deter "immorality," were also thoroughly criticized for encouraging poor couples to split up. Under the AFDC system of the 1960s, mother and child might be financially better off on their own than with an impecunious father.

22. Jane Murphy, "Legal Images of Motherhood," *Cornell Law Review* 83 (1998): 101–87 (at 150).

23. Curtis Boyd, "The Morality of Abortion: The Making of a Feminist Physician," *St. Louis University Public Law Review* 13 (1993): 303, 305.

24. For a discussion of the rhetoric of welfare reform, see Linda C. McClain, " 'Irresponsible' Reproduction," *Hastings Law Journal* 47 (1996): 339. Critics in the 1990s often argue that the sentiment that "those" children should never have been born is racist in origin. Gwendolyn Mink, for example, quotes President Clinton to the effect that

> The poverty population of America [in the early days of welfare] was fundamentally different than it is now. . . . When welfare was created the typical welfare recipient was a miner's widow with no education, small children, husband dies in the mine, no expectation that there was a job for the widow to do or that she could ever do it, very few out-of-wedlock pregnancies and births. The whole dynamics was different then.

Mink goes on to ask: "What can he have meant? That if the welfare population were still 89 percent white and 61 percent widowed, as it was in 1939, welfare would not need to be reformed?" Gwendolyn Mink, *Welfare's End*, 22.

There is no question that racial stereotypes are pervasive in the welfare reform discussion. Studies on attitudes toward welfare recipients have found, for example, that the word "welfare" is a code word for "poor blacks," even though African-Americans are a minority (39 percent in the early 1990s) of the welfare population. Greg J. Duncan and Gretchen Caspary, "Welfare Dynamics and the 1996 Welfare Reform," *Notre Dame Journal of Law, Ethics, and Public Policy* 11 (1997): at 607 (citations omitted). Nonetheless, it is a mistake to conflate racial stereotyping (and even the corresponding hostility often associated with welfare discussions) with a conclusion that the American middle class would support white births to unwed mothers unable to support their children, particularly at times when the middle class of both races was emphasizing contraception, adoption, or abortion for their daughters and granddaughters.

25. See Ann Laquer Estin, "Maintenance, Alimony, and the Rehabilitation of Family Care," *North Carolina Law Review* 71 (1993): 721 (spousal support is premised on young mothers' full participation in the workforce). See also Murphy, "Legal Images of Motherhood," at 144 (child support guidelines similarly assume that mothers will work full time, with limited exceptions for those caring for the young children of the father paying support).

26. Barbara Stark, "Economic Rights in the United States and International Human Rights Law: Toward an 'Entirely New Strategy,' " *Hastings Law Journal* 44 (1992): 79; and Stark, "International Human Rights Law, Feminist Jurisprudence, and Nietzsche's 'Eternal Return': Turning The Wheel," *Harvard Women's Law Journal* 19 (1996): 169.

27. Charles Murray, "The Coming White Underclass," *Wall Street Journal*, October 29, 1993, A14.

28. Mary Jo Bane and David Ellwood, "The Dynamics of Dependence and the Routes to Self-Sufficiency" (1983; final unpublished report to the Department of Health and Human Services).

29. Duncan and Caspary, "Welfare Dynamics and the 1996 Welfare Reform," 605–632 (quote at 615).

30. Ibid., at 623.

31. David T. Ellwood, *Poor Support: Poverty and the American Family*, 88.

32. Mary Jo Bane and Richard Weissbourd, "Welfare Reform and Children," *Stanford Law and Policy Review* 9 (1998): 131–37. Bane introduces herself in this article as resigning "her position after President Clinton signed the welfare reform law in 1996."

33. Amy L. Wax, "The Two-Parent Family in the Liberal State: The Case for Selective Subsidies," *Michigan Journal of Race and Law* 1 (1996): 491–550.

34. Mink, *Welfare's End*, at 43.

35. Ibid., at 103.

36. Sanger, "Separating from Children," *Columbia Law Review* 96 (1996): 375, 499.

37. Jason Deparle, "As Rules on Welfare Tighten, Its Recipients Gain in Stature," *New York Times*, September 11, 1997, A1.

38. Joan Meier, "Domestic Violence, Character, and Social Change in the Welfare Reform Debate," *Law and Policy* 19.2 (April 1997): 205. Meier reports that "recent studies have found with surprising consistency that 15 percent to 30 percent of welfare recipients are current — and a staggering 50 percent to 60 percent are past (as adults) — victims of domestic violence" (ibid., at 206). See also Lisa D. Brush, who similarly finds high rates of domestic violence among the welfare population. She confirms that, once studies control for socioeconomic status, race does not have an impact on the incidence of domestic violence, but that domestic violence is more likely to interfere with white women's job participation. She also finds that while black welfare recipients have higher levels of education and experience than whites, they have a harder time finding and holding jobs, and are thus more vulnerable to welfare cutbacks.

39. Bane and Weissbourd, "Welfare Reform and Children," at 134–35. Donna's story did not specifically mention her marital status or the father of her children.

40. Congress recognized that one of the factors keeping welfare recipients on the rolls is the difficulty of finding jobs that offer medical benefits comparable to those available on welfare. In response, it separated Medicaid eligibility from eligibility for cash payments, and provided for transitional Medicaid benefits to protect those securing jobs without insurance benefits. Recent studies nonetheless report that

- Fifty-four percent of all people who lost Medicaid as a result of welfare reform became uninsured in 1997.

- More than half of those children who lost Medicaid coverage between 1995 and 1997 as a direct result of welfare reform were dropped unnecessarily from Medicaid.

- For recipients with incomes below the federal poverty line, 62 percent of adults and 57 percent of children became uninsured when they dropped Medicaid coverage. For those with slightly higher incomes, up to 200 percent of the federal poverty level, 45 percent of adults and 42 percent of children became uninsured when they dropped Medicaid coverage.

• Fifty-eight percent of minority children became uninsured when they lost Medicaid, as compared to 41 percent of white children.

Statistics and percentages are from the National Journal Group, Inc., "Welfare Reform Exacerbates Uninsurance Levels," *Health Line*, May 14, 1999.

41. Patterson, *Rituals of Blood: Consequences of Slavery in Two American Centuries*, xi–xii. Patterson identifies two myths: "One is that Afro-Americans have developed alternate forms of lasting and viable gender relations and alternate modes of child rearing. . . . [The other is] is the myth of the "hood," the belief that viable informal friendship patterns and communities exist, compensating for the breakdown or absence of more formal institutions" (ibid., at xi).

42. Patterson, *Rituals of Blood*, at 151.

43. Ibid., at 163–66.

22. Renegotiating Childhood

1. Lawrence Stone, *The Family, Sex, and Marriage in England, 1500–1800* (1979), 424.

2. Barbara Bennett Woodhouse, "Who Owns the Child?: *Meyer* and *Pierce* and the Child as Property," *William and Mary Law Review* 33 (1992): 995–1122 (quote at 996). See *Meyer v. Nebraska*, 262 U.S. 390 (1923) and *Pierce v. Society of Sisters*, 268 U.S. 510 (1925).

3. *Michael H. v. Gerald D.*, 491 U.S. 110, 142 (1989).

4. Woodhouse, "Who Owns the Child?" at 1017–18.

5. *Meyer v. Nebraska*, 262 U.S. at 401–402. See also Woodhouse, "Who Owns the Child?" at 1089 and at 1081 for the McReynolds quote. McReynolds also opined that "experience shows that this [instruction in a foreign language at an early age] is not injurious to the health, morals, or understanding of the ordinary child" (*Meyer*, 262 U.S. at 403).

6. Woodhouse, "Who Owns the Child?" at 1102.

7. *Pierce v. Society of Sisters*, 268 U.S. at 534–35.

8. Woodhouse, "Who Owns the Child?" at 1117. Woodhouse (at n. 660) notes that Herbert Spencer "places the private family at the core of society and finds absurd the notion that man might love his neighbor's child as his own" (Herbert Spencer *Principles of Sociology*, vol. 3, sec. 843).

9. The Supreme Court invalidated federal legislation that would have prohibited the transportation in interstate commerce of goods produced by children under fourteen, or children over fourteen who worked more than eight hours in a day or more than six days in a week, as a violation of the commerce clause. The result left the matter to the states. See *Hammer v. Dagenhart*, 247 U.S. 251 (1918) and *Bailey v. Drexel Furniture Co.*, 259

U.S. 20 (1922). Woodhouse notes that "[m]any middle class parents embraced the new notions of childhood, but conservative or traditional parents, particularly immigrant parents who depended on children's wages for survival, felt that compulsory education and labor laws infringed upon their rights in their children" ("Who Owns the Child?" at 1063).

10. *Yoder v. Wisconsin*, 406 U.S. 205 (1972). See Janet L. Dolgin, "The Fate of Childhood: Legal Models of Children and the Parent-Child Relationship," *Albany Law Review* 61 (1997): 345–431.

11. *Yoder*, 406 U.S. at 232.

12. *Yoder*, 406 U.S. at 222–25.

13. *Yoder*, 406 U.S. at 241–46.

14. *Yoder*, 406 U.S. at 245.

15. Dolgin, "The Fate of Childhood," at 387–88.

16. *In re Gault*, 387 U.S. 1 (1967).

17. *Tinker v. Des Moines Independent School District*, 393 U.S. 503 (1969).

18. *Parham v. J.R.*, 442 U.S. 584 (1979); *Bellotti II*, 443 U.S. 622 (1979).

19. Dolgin, "The Fate of Childhood," at 388.

20. *Parham*, 442 U.S. at 584, 600–603.

21. *Bellotti II* is one of a long line of Supreme Court cases to address the issue. In *Hodgson v. Minnesota*, 497 U.S. 417 (1990), which involved a challenge to a two-parent notification provision, Justice Steven's plurality opinion noted that "[d]uring the period between August 1, 1981, and March 1, 1986, 3,573 judicial bypass petitions were filed in Minnesota courts. All but 15 were granted. The judges who adjudicated 90% of these petitions testified: none of them identified any positive effects of the law. The court experience produced fear, tension, anxiety, and shame among minors, causing some who were mature, and some whose best interests would have been served by an abortion, to 'forgo the bypass option and either notify their parents or carry to term.' Among parents who supported their daughters in the bypass proceedings, the court experience evoked similar reactions."

See also Carol Sanger, "Compelling Teen Narratives: Teenage Abortion Hearings and Their Misuse," Faculty Workshop at Cornell Law School, May 2, 1997 (cited in Dolgin, "The Fate of Childhood," at 398n345).

22. *Bellotti v. Baird*, 443 U.S. 622, 643–44 (1979) (*Bellotti II*).

23. Dolgin, "The Fate of Childhood," at 396.

24. Ibid., at 400.

25. Woodhouse, "Who Owns the Child?" at 1090 (citations omitted).

26. Helen E. Fisher, *Anatomy of Love: The Natural History of Monogamy, Adultery, and Divorce*, 234.

27. *Reno v. ACLU: The Battle over the CDA*, Oral Argument of Seth P. Waxman on behalf of the Appellants, CNN Interactive, March 19, 1997, *http://207.25.71.25/US/9703/cda.scotus /transcript.html*. The amicus briefs filed in the case amplified Waxman's concerns. See, e.g., Brief for Amicus Curie Enough is Enough, et al. at 7–8, *Reno v.*

ACLU, 117 S. Ct. 2329 (1997): "About one-fifth of those who use the World Wide Web regularly seek out one or more of the over six hundred commercial pornography sites on the Web. Internet watchdogs report that approximately thirty-nine new pornographic sites appear daily. Pornographic entertainment on the Internet constitutes the third-largest realm of cyberspace sales, netting an estimated annual revenue of $100 million. In fact, it is common for popular adult Internet sites to receive more than two million visits during a one-month period. Sexually enticing invitations lure curious Net users to these sites, with some Internet sites using nothing more than a legal disclaimer to ensure that these 'adult-only' sites are actually visited by 'adults only.' These trends resonate with the American public, as one poll found that eighty-five percent of Americans are concerned about Internet decency."

28. *Reno*, 117 S. Ct. at 2329, 2347.

29. See, in particular, *ACLU v. Reno*, 31 F. Supp.2d 473 (E.D. Pa. 1999) (striking down as unconsitutional Congress's subsequent effort to craft more narrowly tailored legislation restricting transmission of pornography to minors).

30. See *Mainstream Loudoun v. Board of Trustees of the London County Library*, 24 F. Supp.2d 552 (E.D. Va. 1998) (declaring unconstitutional library policy limiting access to the Internet and adopting filtering software on library computers).

Conclusion: From Partners to Parents — The Unfinished Revolution

1. The relationship between the lower classes and the patriarchal family is a more complex one. In early modern England, the sexual behavior of the non-landowning classes appears to have been kept in check by limited mobility and widespread community supervision. Greater urbanization, with or without industrialization, produced greater family instability in both its early (sixteenth-century) and later (eighteenth-century) guises. Nonetheless, by the end of the nineteenth century, unionization, the emphasis on a "family wage," and other labor market changes produced a working-class male premium tied to manufacturing and other laboring jobs. (See the discussions in chapters 10 and 14.)

Franklin's account of the African-American family, though it acknowledges the role of different cultural values, also emphasizes that the small African-American middle class in many ways replicated *American* middle-class values, while the point of departure for the working class came with the move north and the creation of communities that often provided more stable job prospects for women than for men. (See the discussion in chapter 11, this volume.)

2. Remarks of a Mr. Botts, quoted in Susan Westerbrook Prager, "The Persistence of Separate Property Concepts in California's Community Property System, 1849–1975," *UCLA Law Review* 24 (1976): 1–82 (quote from 19–20). Prager reports that Mr. Botts went on to insist that, "I tell you Mr. Chairman, that if you introduce this clause, you must take care to carry along with it a speedy and easy and effectual way of procuring divorces, for they will come as sure as you live, as a necessary consequence" (ibid., at 18–19 and n. 96).

3. Prager, "The Persistence of Separate Property Concepts," at 19–20.

4. John M. Gottman et al., "Predicting Marital Happiness and Stability from New-lywed Interactions," *Journal of Marriage and the Family* 60 (1998): 5–22 (quotes at 17).

5. Gottman et al., "Predicting Marital Happiness," at 18. The authors also reported that "[t]he preliminary results suggest that the husband's rejection of influence from his wife is unrelated to the husband's age, income, occupation, or educational level. However, we found that the husbands who are more likely to reject influence from their wives are high on the MMPI [Minnesota Multiphasic Personality Inventory] hostility sub-scale (which assesses suspicious hostility), are smokers, are more likely to regularly use cocaine, were rated by observers as dominating their wives in the discussion in our oral history interview, make the major decisions in the family, have suffered financial or emotional hardships in the marriage, are physically shorter, report being healthier, and are more physically active in one-on-one competitive sports than men who accept influence from their wives" (ibid., at 19).

6. Whitehead, *The Divorce Culture*, 4–5.

7. Ibid., at 21.

8. Ibid., at 195.

9. William Kristol, "Women's Liberation: The Relevance of Tocqueville," in Ken Masugi, ed., *Interpreting Tocqueville's "Democracy in America,"* 492–93.

10. Linda R. Hirshman and Jane E. Larson, *Hard Bargains: The Politics of Sex.*

11. Levit, *The Gender Line*, 118–19.

12. Margaret F. Brinig and Frank H. Buckley, "No-Fault Laws and At-Fault People," *International Review of Law and Economics* 18 (1998): 325.

13. Margaret F. Brinig and Steven L. Nock, "Weak Men and Disorderly Women: Divorce and the Division of Labor" (unpublished manuscript). Brinig and Nock conclude that "women's work endangers marriages, regardless of which spouse does it." They also find that if either spouse does more of men's work, the marriage is more stable.

14. D'Vera Cohn, "More Men Becoming Single Dads," *San Jose Mercury News*, December 11, 1998, 17A. A majority of those with children under six (and 35 percent of the total) were never married. See also Patricia Paskowicz, *Absentee Mothers* (Totowa, N.J.: Allanheld, Osmun, 1982).

15. Katherine T. Bartlett and Angela P. Harris, *Gender and Law: Theory, Doctrine, Commentary*, 575, citing Lee H. Bowker, Michelle Arbitell, and J. Richard McFerron, "On the Relationship Between Wife Beating and Child Abuse," in *Perspectives on Wife Abuse*, at 164–65 "(child abuse twice as likely in husband-dominated household as in wife dominated household, and abuse tends to be more severe as well)."[15]

16. Sabin Russell, "Teenage Pregnancy Rate Falls: Study Attributes 20-Year Low to Abstinence, Contraceptives," *San Francisco Chronicle*, October 15, 1998, A1.

Ackerman, Marc J. and Melissa C. Ackerman. "Child Custody Evaluation Practices: A 1996 Survey of Psychologists." *Family Law Quarterly* 30 (1996): 565.

Akerloff, George A., Janet L. Yellin, and Michael L. Katz. "An Analysis of Out-of-Wedlock Childbearing in the United States." *Quarterly Journal of Economics* 111 (1996): 277–303.

Amato, Paul R. and Alan Booth. *A Generation at Risk*. Cambridge: Harvard University Press, 1997.

Angeles, Peter, ed. *The HarperCollins Dictionary of Philosophy*. New York: Harper-Collins, 1992.

Aries, Philippe, *Centuries of Childhood*. Translated by R. Baldick. New York: Knopf, 1962.

Austin, Regina. "Sapphire Bound." *Wisconsin Law Review* 1989 (1989): 539.

Bailey, Derrick Sherwin. *Homosexuality and the Western Christian Tradition*. Hamden, Conn.: Archon Books, 1955.

Bane, Mary Jo and Richard Weissbourd. "Welfare Reform and Children." *Stanford Law and Policy Review* 9 (1998): 131–37.

Bartlett, Katharine T. "Feminist Legal Methods." *Harvard Law Review* 103 (1990): 829.

———. "Re-expressing Parenthood." *Yale Law Journal* 98 (1988): 293.

Bartlett, Katharine T. and Angela P. Harris. *Gender and Law: Theory, Doctrine, Commentary*. 2d ed. New York: Aspen Law and Business, 1998.

Bartlett, Katharine T. and Carol B. Stack. "Joint Custody, Feminism, and the Dependency Dilemma." *Berkeley Women's Law Journal* 2 (1986): 9–41.

Becker, Gary S. *A Treatise on the Family*. Cambridge: Harvard University Press, 1981.

———. *A Treatise on the Family, Enlarged Edition*. Cambridge: Harvard University Press, 1991.

Bell, Susan Groag and Karen M. Offen. *Women, the Family, and Freedom: The Debate in Documents*. Stanford, Calif.: Stanford University Press, 1983.

Beller, Andrea H. and John W. Graham, *Small Change: The Economics of Child Support*. New Haven: Yale University Press, 1993.

Bergman, Barbara R. *The Economic Emergence of Women*. New York: Basic Books, 1986.

Blackburn, Simon, ed. *The Oxford Dictionary of Philosophy*. Oxford and New York: Oxford University Press, 1994.

Blankenhorn, David. *Fatherless America*. New York: Basic Books, 1995.

———. "The State of the Family and the Family Policy Debate." *Santa Clara Law Review* 36 (1996): 431.

Boswell, John. *Christianity, Social Tolerance, and Homosexuality: Gay People in Western Europe from the Beginning of the Christian Era to the Fourteenth Century*. Chicago: University of Chicago Press, 1980.

Boyd, Curtis. "The Morality of Abortion: The Making of a Feminist Physician." *St. Louis University Public Law Review* 13 (1993): 303, 305.

Braver, Sanford L., Marnie Whitley, and Christine Ng. "Who Divorced Whom: Methodological and Legal Issues." *Journal of Divorce and Remarriage* 20 (1993): 1–19.

Braver, Sanford L., S. A. Wolchik, I. N. Sandler, and V. L. Sheets. "A Social Exchange Model of Nonresidential Parent Involvement." In C. Depner and J. Bray, eds., *Nonresidential Parenting: New Vistas in Family Living*, 87–108. Newbury Park, Calif.: Sage, 1993.

Brinig, Margaret F. *The Contract and the Covenant: Beyond Law and Economics*. Cambridge: Harvard University Press, 2000.

———. "Rings and Promises." *Journal of Law Economics and Organization* 6 (1990): 203.

———. "Status, Contract, and Covenant" (review of Milton C. Regan, Jr.'s *Family Law and the Pursuit of Intimacy*). *Cornell Law Review* 79 (1994): 1573.

Brinig, Margaret F. and Frank H. Buckley. "No-Fault Laws and At-Fault People." *International Review of Law and Economics* 18 (1998): 325.

Brinig, Margaret F. and June Carbone. "The Reliance Interest in Marriage and Divorce." *Tulane Law Review* 62 (1988): 855–905.

Brinig, Margaret F. and Steven L. Nock. "Weak Men and Disorderly Women: Divorce and the Division of Labor." Unpublished manuscript on file with author.

Brown, Gene, ed. *The Great Contemporary Issues: The Family*. David J. Rothman and Sheila M. Rothman, Advisory Editors. New York: New York Times/Arno Press, 1979.

Brush, Lisa D. "Battering, Traumatic Stress, and Welfare-to-Work Transition" (forthcoming: accepted for publication in *Violence Against Women*).

Buchanan, Elizabeth. "The Constitutional Rights of Unwed Fathers Before and After *Lehr v. Robertson*." *Ohio State Law Journal* 45 (1984): 313.

Cahn, Naomi R. "Civil Images of Battered Women: The Impact of Domestic Violence on Child Custody Decisions." *Vanderbilt Law Review* 44 (1991): 1041–97.

Carbone, June. "Child Support Comes of Age: An Introduction to the Law of Child Support." In J. Thomas Oldham and Marygold Melli, eds., *Child Support: The Next Frontier*. Ann Arbor: University of Michigan Press, 1999.

———. "Economics, Feminism, and the Reinvention of Alimony: A Reply to Ira Ellman." *Vanderbilt Law Review* 43 (1990): 1463–1501.

———. "Equality and Difference: Reclaiming Motherhood as a Central Focus of Family Law." *Journal of Law and Social Inquiry* 17 (1992): 471.

Carbone, June and Margaret F. Brinig. "Rethinking Marriage: Feminist Ideology, Economic Change, and Divorce Reform." *Tulane Law Review* 65 (1991): 953–1010.

Cazenave, Noel A. and George H. Leon. "Men's Work and Family Roles and Characteristics." In Kimmel, ed., *Changing Men*, 244–62. Newbury Park, Calif.: Sage, 1987.

Chambers, David L. "Fathers, the Welfare System, and the Virtues and Perils of Child Support Enforcement." *Virginia Law Review* 81 (1995): 2575–2605.

———. *Making Fathers Pay*. Chicago: University of Chicago Press, 1979.

Cherlin, Andrew J., P. Lindsay Chase-Lansdale, and Christine McRae. "Effects of Parental Divorce of Mental Health Through the Life Course." *American Sociological Review* 63 (1998): 239–49.

Chodorow, Nancy. *The Reproduction of Mothering: Psychoanalysis and the Sociology of Gender*. Berkeley: University of California Press, 1978.

Coase, Ronald H. "The Problem of Social Cost." *Journal of Law and Economics* 3 (1960): 1–44.

Cohen, Lloyd. "Divorce and Quasi Rents: Or, I Gave Him the Best Years of My Life." *Journal of Legal Studies* 16 (1987): 267–303.

Cohn, D'Vera. "More Men Becoming Single Dads." *San Jose Mercury News*, December 11, 1998, 17A.

Coontz, Stephanie. *The Social Origins of Private Life: A History of American Families, 1600–1900*. London: Verso, 1988.

———. *The Way We Never Were: American Families and the Nostalgia Trap*. New York: Basic Books, 1992.

Cose, Ellis. *A Man's World*. New York: HarperCollins, 1995.

———. "Black Men and Black Women." *Newsweek*, June 5, 1995, 66.

Czapanskiy, Karen. "Child Support, Visitation, Shared Custody, and Split Custody." In Margaret Campbell Haynes, ed., *Child Support Guidelines: The Next Generation*, 43–50. Washington, D.C.: U.S. Department of Health and Human Services, April 1994.

———. "Volunteers and Draftees: The Struggle for Parental Equality." *UCLA Law Review* 38 (1991): 1415–81.

Deglar, Carl N. *At Odds: Women and the Family in America from the Revolution to the Present*. New York: Oxford University Press, 1980.

Deparle, Jason. "As Rules on Welfare Tighten, Its Recipients Gain in Stature." *New York Times*, September 11, 1997, A1.

Dolgin, Janet L. "The Fate of Childhood: Legal Models of Children and the Parent-Child Relationship." *Albany Law Review* 61 (1997): 345–431.

———. "Just a Gene: Judicial Assumptions About Parenthood." *UCLA Law Review* 40 (1993): 637–94.

Dowd, Nancy. *In Defense of Single-Parent Families.* New York: New York University Press, 1997.

Drake, St. Clair and Horace Cayton. *The Black Metropolis.* New York: Harcourt, Brace.

Du Bois, W. E. B. *The Philadelphia Negro: A Social Study* (1889). Rpt., New York: Schocken, 1967.

Duncan, Greg J. and Gretchen Caspary. "Welfare Dynamics and the 1996 Welfare Reform." *Notre Dame Journal of Law, Ethics, and Public Policy* 11 (1997): 605–32.

Early, Gerald. "Poverty and Race in America: A Look at the Historical Changes in Black Family Life." *Chicago Tribune,* June 1, 1997, 5.

Eekelaar, John. *Regulating Divorce.* Oxford: Clarendon Press, 1991.

Ellman, Ira. "The Theory of Alimony." *California Law Review* 77 (1989): 1–81.

Ellwood, David T. *Poor Support: Poverty and the American Family.* New York: Basic Books, 1988.

Elrod, Linda D. "Child Support Reassessed: Federalization of Enforcement Nears Completion." *University of Illinois Law Review* 14 (1997): 695–709.

Elrod, Linda D. and Robert G. Spector. "A Review of the Year in Family Law: Children's Issues Take Spotlight." *Family Law Quarterly* 29 (1996): 741, 771.

Engerman, Stanley L. "Black Fertility and Family Structure in the U.S., 1880–1940. *Journal of Family History* 1–2 (1977): 134.

Engels, Friedrich. *The Origin of the Family, Private Property, and the State* (1891). New York: International Publishers, 1964.

Eskridge, William N., Jr. *The Case for Same-Sex Marriage: From Sexual Liberty to Civilized Commitment.* New York: Free Press, 1996.

Estin, Ann Laquer. "Maintenance, Alimony, and the Rehabilitation of Family Care." *North Carolina Law Review* 71 (1993): 721–803.

Faludi, Susan. *Backlash: The Undeclared War Against American Women.* New York: Crown, 1991.

Fanshel, David. "A Study in Negro Adoption." *Child Welfare* (February 1959): 33.

Fennelly, John E. "Step Up or Step Out: Unwed Fathers' Parental Rights Post-Doe and E.A.W." *St. Thomas Law Review* 8 (1996): 259–311.

Fineman, Martha. *The Illusion of Equality.* Chicago: University of Chicago Press, 1991.

——. "Implementing Equality: Ideology, Contradiction, and Social Change." *Wisconsin Law Review* 1983 (1983): 789–886.

——. *The Neutered Mother, the Sexual Family, and Other Twentieth-Century Tragedies.* New York: Routledge, 1995.

Finnis, John M. "Law, Morality, and 'Sexual Orientation.'" *Notre Dame Law Review* 69 (1994): 1049.

Fisher, Helen E. *Anatomy of Love: The Natural History of Monogamy, Adultery, and Divorce.* New York: Norton, 1992.

Fogel, Robert W. and Stanley L. Engerman. *Time on a Cross: The Economics of American Negro Slavery.* Boston: Little Brown, 1974.

Folberg, Jay, ed. *Joint Custody and Shared Parenting*. Washington, D.C.: Bureau of National Affairs, Association of Family and Conciliations Courts, 1984.

Forman, Deborah L. "Unwed Fathers and Adoption: A Theoretical Analysis in Context." *Texas Law Review* 72 (1994): 967–1045.

Franklin, Donna. *Ensuring Inequality: The Structural Transformation of the African-American Family*. New York: Oxford University Press, 1997.

Frazier, E. Franklin. *The Negro Family in the United States* (1939). Rev. and abridged ed. Chicago: University of Chicago Press, 1966.

Friedman, David D. *Price Theory: An Intermediate Text*, 2d ed. Cincinnati, Ohio: South-Western, 1990.

Friedman, Lawrence. *The Republic of Choice: Law, Authority, and Culture*. Cambridge: Harvard University Press, 1990.

Friedman, Milton. *Essays in Positive Economics*. Chicago: University of Chicago Press, 1935.

Fuchs, Victor R. *Women's Quest for Economic Equality*. Cambridge: Harvard University Press, 1988.

Furstenberg, Jr., Frank F. and Andrew J. Cherlin. *The Family and Public Policy: What Happens to Children When Parents Part*. Cambridge: Harvard University Press, 1991.

Galston, William A. "A Liberal Democratic Case for the Two-Parent Family." *The Responsive Community* 1 (1990–91): 14, 23–25.

———. *Liberal Purposes: Goods, Virtues, and Diversity in the Liberal State*. Cambridge: Cambridge University Press, 1991.

Gardner, Marilyn. "When Marriage Ends, Should Partners Split Their Assets 50–50?" *Christian Science Monitor*, July 1, 1998, B8.

Gardner, Richard. *The Parental Alienation Syndrome: A Guide for Mental Health and Legal Professionals*. Cresskill, N.J.: Creative Therapeutics, 1992; 2d ed., 1998.

Garfinkel, Irwin and Sara S. McLanahan. *Single Mothers and Their Children: A New American Dilemma*. Washington, D.C.: Urban Institute, 1986.

Garfinkel, Irwin, Jennifer L. Hochschild, and Sara S. McLanahan. *Social Policies for Children*. Washington, D.C.: Brookings Institution, 1996.

Garfinkel, Irwin, Marygold S. Melli, and John G. Robertson. "Child Support Orders: A Perspective on Reform." *The Future of Children* 4 (1994): 84–100.

Garrison, Marsha. "Marriage: The Status of Contract." *University of Pennsylvania Law Review* 131 (1983): 1039.

Genovese, Eugene. *Roll, Jordan, Roll: The World the Slaves Made*. New York: Pantheon, 1974.

Gilligan, Carol. *In a Different Voice: Psychological Theory and Women's Development*. Cambridge: Harvard University Press, 1982.

Glazer, Nathan. "On the Gutman Thesis." *New York Times*, September 29, 1976. In Brown, ed., *The Great Contemporary Issues*, 361.

Glendon, Mary Ann. "Book Review: A Review of Liberal Purposes: Goods, Virtues, and Diversity in the Liberal State by William A. Galston." *George Washington Law Review* 61 (1993): 1955, 1957.

Goldstein, Joseph, Anna Freud, and Albert Solnit. *Beyond the Best Interests of the Child.* New York: Free Press, 1973.

Gordon, Linda. *PITIED But Not Entitled: Single Mothers and the History of Welfare, 1890–1935.* Cambridge: Harvard University Press, 1994.

Gordon, Michael, ed. *The American Family in Socio-Historical Perspective.* 2d ed. New York: St. Martin's, 1978.

Gorenberg, Carol A. "Fathers' Rights vs. Children's Best Interests: Establishing a Predictable Standard for California Adoption Disputes." *Family Law Quarterly* 31 (1997): 169.

Gottman, John M., James Coan, Sybil Carrere, and Catherine Swanson. "Predicting Marital Happiness and Stability from Newlywed Interactions." *Journal of Marriage and the Family* 60 (1998): 5–22.

Graves, Kay Williams. "Clarence Thomas' Sister Takes a Steady Step Up a Rocky Path." *Chicago Tribune*, August 4, 1991, 1.

Gregory, John. "Interdependency Theory: Old Sausage in a New Casing: A Response to Professor Czapanskiy." *Santa Clara Law Review* 39 (1999): 1037–51.

Grossbard-Shechtman, Shoshana. *On the Economics of Marriage: A Theory of Marriage, Labor, and Divorce.* Boulder: Westview, 1993.

Grossberg, Michael A. *Governing the Hearth: Law and the Family in Nineteenth-Century America.* Chapel Hill: University of North Carolina Press, 1985.

Gutman, Herbert G. *The Black Family in Slavery and Freedom.* New York: Pantheon, 1976.

——. "In the South and in Harlem, Tenacity." *New York Times*, September 24, 1976. In Brown, ed., *The Great Contemporary Issues*, 358–59.

——. "Long Together." *New York Times*, September 22, 1976. In Brown, ed., *The Great Contemporary Issues*, 360.

——. "Persistent Myths About the Afro-American Family." In Michael Gordon, ed., *The American Family in Socio-Historical Perspective*, 467–89.

Hamilton, Nigel. *JFK: Reckless Youth.* New York: Random House, 1992.

Harris, Leslie J., D. Dennis Waldrop, and Lori Rathbun Waldrop. "Making and Breaking Connections Between Parents' Duty to Support and Right to Control Their Children." *Oregon Law Review* 69 (1990): 689.

Heal, Felicity and Rosemary O'Day, eds. *Church and Society in England: Henry VIII to James I.* Hamden, Conn.: Archon Books, 1977.

Helminiak, Daniel A. *What the Bible Really Says About Homosexuality.* San Francisco: Alamo Square Press, 1994.

Herskovits, Melville J. *The Myth of the Negro Past.* Boston: Beacon Press, 1941.

Hetherington, E. Mavis and Margaret M. Stanley-Hagan. "The Effects of Divorce on Fathers and Their Children." In Michael E. Lamb, ed., *The Role of the Father in Child Development*, 3d ed. New York: Wiley, 1997.

Hirschman, Albert O. *Exit, Voice, and Loyalty: Response to Decline in Firms, Organizations, and States.* Cambridge: Harvard University Press, 1970.

Hirshman, Linda R. and Jane E. Larson. *Hard Bargains: The Politics of Sex.* New York: Oxford University Press, 1998.

Ives, Eric Williams. *Anne Boelyn.* Oxford: Blackwell, 1986.

Jencks, Christopher. *Rethinking Social Policy.* Cambridge: Harvard University Press, 1992.

Johnson, Charles S. *Shadow of the Plantation.* Chicago: University of Chicago Press, 1934.

Johnston, Janet R. "High Conflict Divorce." *The Future of Children: Children and Divorce* 4 (1994): 168.

Kalman, Laura. *The Strange Career of Legal Liberalism.* New Haven: Yale University Press, 1996.

Kant, Immanuel. *The Philosophy of Law* (1887; originally published as *The Philosophy of Law: An Exposition of the Fundamental Principles of Jurisprudence as the Science of Right*). Rpt., Clifton: Augustus M. Kelley, 1974.

Katzman, David. *Seven Days a Week.* New York: Oxford University Press, 1978.

Kay, Herma Hill. "Equality and Difference: A Perspective on No-Fault Divorce and Its Aftermath." *University of Cincinnati Law Review* 56 (1987): 1–90.

Kelly, Joan B. "The Determination of Child Custody." *The Future of Children: Children and Divorce* 4 (1994): 121–42.

Kimmel, Michael S., ed. *Changing Men.* Newbury Park, Calif.: Sage, 1987.

Kornhauser, Marjorie E. "Theory v. Reality: The Partnership Model of Marriage in Family and Tax Law." *Temple Law Review* 69 (1996): 1413.

Krause, Harry. "Child Support Reassessed: Limits of Private Responsibility and the Public Interest." *University of Illinois Law Review* 1989 (1989): 367–398.

Krauskopf, Joan. "Theories of Property Division/Spousal Support: Searching for Solutions to the Mystery." *Family Law Quarterly* 23 (1989): 253–78.

Kristol, William. "Women's Liberation: The Relevance of Tocqueville," in Ken Masugi, ed., *Interpreting Tocqueville's "Democracy in America."* Savage, Md.: Rowman and Littlefield, 1991.

Kurtzf, Lynne R. "Comment: Protecting New York's Children: An Argument for the Creation of a Rebuttable Presumption Against Awarding a Spouse Abuser Custody of a Child." *Albany Law Review* 60 (1997): 1345.

Lamb, Michael E., ed. *The Role of the Father in Child Development.* 3d ed. New York: Wiley, 1997.

Laslett, Peter. "Characteristics of the Western Family Considered Over Time." *Journal of Family History* 2 (1979): 98.

——. *Family Life and Illicit Love in Earlier Generations: Essays in Historical Sociology.* Cambridge: Cambridge University Press, 1977.

Laslett, Peter and Richard Wall. *Household and Family in Past Time.* Cambridge: Cambridge University Press, 1972.

Levit, Nancy. *The Gender Line: Men, Women, and the Law*. New York: New York University Press, 1998.

Luker, Kristin. *Dubious Conceptions: The Politics of Teenage Pregnancy*. Cambridge: Harvard University Press, 1996.

Maccoby, Eleanor E. and Robernt H. Mnookin. *Dividing the Child: Social and Legal Dilemmas of Custody*. Cambridge: Harvard University Press, 1992.

Machin, Theodore. *The Marital Sacrament*. New York: Pauline Press, 1989.

MacIntyre, Alasdair C. *After Virtue: A Study in Moral Theory*. London: Duckworth, 1981.

MacKinnon, Catharine A. *Toward a Feminist Theory of the State*. Cambridge: Harvard University Press, 1989.

Mahony, Rhona. *Kidding Ourselves: Breadwinning, Babies, and Bargaining Power*. New York: Basic Books, 1995.

Maine, Henry. *Ancient Law* (1861). Rpt., Boston: Beacon Press, 1963.

Marcosson, Samuel A. "The Lesson of the Same-Sex Marriage Trial: The Importance of Pushing Opponents of Lesbian and Gay Rights to Their 'Second Line of Defense.'" *Journal of Family Law* 35 (1996–97): 721–53.

Mare, Robert D. and Christopher Winship. "Socioeconomic Change and the Decline of Marriage for Whites and Blacks." In C. Jencks and P. E. Petersen, eds., *The Urban Underclass*, 175–202. Washington, D.C.: Brookings Institution, 1991.

Markert, Pamela. "Comment: Custody Relocation: More Questions Than Answers Result from High Court Opinions in California and New York." *Santa Clara Law Review* 38 (1998): 521–54.

Mason, Mary Ann. *The Custody Wars: Why Children Are Losing the Legal Battle and What We Can Do About It*. New York: Basic Books, 1999.

——. *From Father's Property to Children's Rights: The History of Child Custody in the United States*. New York: Columbia University Press, 1994.

McClain, Linda C. " 'Irresponsible' Reproduction." *Hastings Law Journal* 47 (1996): 339.

McInerney, Denis. "The Lawyer's Bookshelf: King of the Mountain; The Rise, Fall, and Redemption of Chief Judge Sol Wachtler." *New York Law Journal*, September 11, 1998, 2.

McLanahan, Sara S. and Gary Sandefur. *Growing Up with a Single Parent: What Helps, What Hurts*. Cambridge: Harvard University Press, 1994.

Meier, Joan. "Domestic Violence, Character, and Social Change in the Welfare Reform Debate." *Law and Policy* 19.2 (April 1997): 205.

Melli, Marygold S., Patricia R. Brown, and Maria Cancian. "Child Custody in a Changing World: A Study of Postdivorce Arrangements in Wisconsin." *University of Illinois Law Review* 1997 (1997): 773–800.

Mink, Gwendolyn. *Welfare's End*. Ithaca: Cornell University Press, 1998.

——. "Welfare Reform in Historical Perspective." *Connecticut Law Review* 26 (1994): 879–99.

Mintz, Steven and Susan Kellogg. *Domestic Revolutions: A Social History of American Family Life*. New York: Free Press, 1988.

Morgan, Lewis. *Ancient Society; Or, Researches in the Lines of Human Progress from Savagery through Barbarism to Civilization*. London: Macmillian, 1877.

Murray, Charles. "The Coming White Underclass." *Wall Street Journal*, October 29, 1993, A14.

Murphy, Jane C. "Legal Images of Motherhood: Conflicting Decisions from Welfare 'Reform,' Family, and Criminal Law." *Cornell Law Review* 83 (1998): 688.

O'Hare, William P., Kelvin M. Pollard, Taynia L. Mann, and Mary M. Kent. "African-Americans in the 1990's." In Rank and Kain, eds., *Diversity and Change in Families*, 85–95. Englewood Cliffs, N.J.: Prentice-Hall, 1995.

Okin, Susan Moller. *Justice, Gender, and the Family*. New York: Basic Books, 1989.

Oldham, J. Thomas. "The Appropriate Child Support Award When the Noncustodial Parent Earns Less Than the Custodial Parent." *Houston Law Review* 31 (1994): 585.

O'Neill, William. *Divorce in the Progressive Era*. New Haven: Yale University Press, 1967.

Patterson, Orlando. *Rituals of Blood: Consequences of Slavery in Two American Centuries*. Washington, D.C.: Civitas/Counterpoint, 1998.

Parrella, Fred J. "Same-Sex Marriage." November 6, 1998 (unpublished manuscript on file with author).

——. "Towards a Spirituality of the Family." *Communio* 9 (1992): 127–41.

Parkman, Allen M. *No-Fault Divorce: What Went Wrong?*. Boulder, Colo.: Westview, 1992.

Phillips, Roderick. *Untying the Knot: A Short History of Divorce*. Cambridge: Cambridge University Press, 1991.

Pleck, Elizabeth. "A Mother's Wages: Income Earning Among Married Italian and Black Women, 1896–1911." In Michael Gordon, ed., *The American Family in Socio-Historical Perspective*, 490–510.

Popenoe, David. *Disturbing the Nest: Family Change and Decline in Modern Societies*. New York: Aldine De Gruyter, 1989.

——. *Life Without Father*. New York: Free Press, 1996.

Posner, Richard A. *Economic Analysis of Law*. 5th ed. New York: Aspen, 1998.

——. "The Ethical Significance of Free Choice: A Reply to Professor West." *Harvard Law Review* 99 (1986): 1431–48.

——. *Sex and Reason*. Cambridge: Harvard University Press, 1992.

Prager, Susan Westerbrook. "The Persistence of Separate Property Concepts in California's Community Property System, 1849–1975." *UCLA Law Review* 24 (1976): 1–82.

Preston, Samuel, Suet Lim, and S. Phillip Morgan. "African-American Marriage in 1910: Beneath the Surface of Census Data." *Demography* 29 (February 1992): 13.

Rainwater, Lee and William L. Yancey. *The Moynihan Report and the Politics of Controversy*. Cambridge: MIT Press, 1967.

Rank, Mark Robert and Edward L. Kain, eds. *Diversity and Change in Families: Patterns, Prospects, and Policies.* Englewood Cliffs, N.J.: Prentice-Hall, 1995.

Rawls, John. *A Theory of Justice.* Cambridge: Harvard University Press, 1971.

Ray, Marilyn L. *New York State Child Support Standards Act: Evaluation Report, 1993.* Ithaca: The Finger Lakes Law and Social Policy Center, 1993 (prepared for the New York State Department of Social Services).

Regan, Milton C., Jr. *Family Law and the Pursuit of Intimacy.* New York: New York University Press, 1993.

Resnik, Scott A. "Seeking the Wisdom of Solomon." *Seton Hall Legislative Journal* 20 (1996): 363–430.

Reynolds, Suzanne. "The Relationship of Property Division and Alimony: The Division of Property to Address Need." *Fordham Law Review* 56 (1988): 827–916.

Rhodes, James. *History of the United States from the Compromise of 1850.* New York: Harper, 1893.

Ruggerio, Guido. *The Boundaries of Eros: Sex Crime and Sexuality in Renaissance Venice.* New York: Oxford University Press, 1985.

Russell, Sabin. "Teenage Pregnancy Rate Falls: Study Attributes 20-Year Low to Abstinence, Contraceptives." *San Francisco Chronicle*, October 15, 1998, A1.

Rutherford, Jane. "Duty in Divorce: Shared Income as a Path to Equality." *Fordham Law Review* 58 (1998): 539–92.

Sanger, Carol. "M Is for Many Things." *Review of Law and Women's Studies* 1 (1992): 1301, 1306.

———. "Separating from Children." *Columbia Law Review* 96 (1996): 375, 499.

Sault, Nicole. *Many Mirrors: Body Image and Social Relations.* New Brunswick, N.J.: Rutgers University Press, 1994.

Schneider, Carl E. "Marriage, Morals, and the Law: No-Fault Divorce and Moral Discourse." *Utah Law Review* (1994): 503.

———. "Moral Discourse and the Transforming of American Family Law." *Michigan Law Review* 83 (1985): 1803.

———. "Rethinking Alimony: Marital Decisions and Moral Discourse." *Brigham Young University Law Review* (1991): 197.

Schwartz, T. Paul. "Marital Status and Fertility in the United States: Welfare and Labor Market Effects." *Journal of Human Resources* 29 (March 22, 1994): 637–69.

Scott, Elizabeth S. and Robert E. Scott. "Parents as Fiduciaries." *Virginia Law Review* 81 (1995): 2401–2476.

Seltzer, Judith A. "Relationships Between Fathers and Children Who Live Apart: The Father's Role After Separation." *Journal of Marriage and the Family* 53 (1991): 79–101.

Seltzer, Judith A. and S. M. Bianchi. "Children's Contract with Absent Parents." *Journal of Marriage and the Family* 50 (1988): 663–77.

Service, Elman R. *A Century of Controversy: Ethnological Issues from 1860 to 1960.* Orlando, Fla.: Academic Press, 1985.

Shanley, Mary L. "Unwed Fathers' Rights, Adoption and Sex Equality: Gender Neutrality and the Perpetuation of Patriarchy." *Columbia Law Review* 95 (1995): 60–103.

Shorter, Edward. *The Making of the Modern Family*. New York: Basic Books, 1975.

Silberman, Charles E. *Crisis in Black and White*. New York: Random House, 1964.

Singer, Jana B. "Divorce Reform and Gender Justice." *North Carolina Law Review* (1989): 1103.

Solinger, Rickie. *Wake Up Little Suzie: Single Pregnancy Before Roe v. Wade*. New York: Routledge, 1992.

Stamp, Kenneth. *The Peculiar Institution: Slavery in the Ante-Bellum South*. New York: Knopf, 1956.

Staples, Robert and Leanor Boulin Johnson. *Black Families at the Crossroads: Challenges and Prospects*. San Francisco: Jossey-Bass, 1993.

Stark, Barbara. "Economic Rights in the United States and International Human Rights Law: Toward an 'Entirely New Strategy.'" *Hastings Law Journal* 44 (1992): 79.

——. "International Human Rights Law, Feminist Jurisprudence, and Nietzsche's 'Eternal Return': Turning the Wheel." *Harvard Women's Law Journal* 19 (1996): 169.

Stewart, James B. *Blood Sport: The President and His Adversaries*. New York: Simon and Schuster, 1996.

Stone, Lawrence. *The Family, Sex, and Marriage in England, 1500–1800*. London: Weidenfeld and Nicolson, 1977.

——. *The Family, Sex, and Marriage in England, 1500–1800*. New York: Harper and Row, abridged ed., 1979; paperback ed., Harper Torchbooks, 1979.

Strassberg, Maura. "Distinctions of Form or Substance: Monogamy, Polygamy, and Same-Sex Marriage." *North Carolina Law Review* 75 (1997): 1501–1624.

Sudarkasa, Niara. "Interpreting the African Heritage in Afro-American Family Organization." In Harriett Pipes McAdoo, ed., *Black Families*, 37–53. Beverly Hills, Calif.: Sage, 1981.

Sugrue, Thomas J. *The Origins of the Urban Crisis: Race and Inequality in Postwar Detroit*. Princeton: Princeton University Press, 1996.

Swidler, Arlene. *Homosexuality and World Religions*. Valley Forge, Penn.: Trinity Press International, 1993.

Taylor, Charles. *Sources of the Self: The Making of the Modern Identity*. Cambridge: Harvard University Press, 1989.

Trautman, Thomas R. *Lewis Henry Morgan and the Invention of Kinship*. Berkeley: University of California Press, 1987.

Thomson, Richard. "Profile: Economist of the Mind." *The Independent*, October 18, 1992, 11.

Waldron, Jeremy. *Liberal Rights: Collected Papers, 1981–1991*. New York and Cambridge: Cambridge University Press, 1993.

Wallace, Michelle. *Black Macho and the Myth of the Superwoman*. New York: Dial Press, 1979.

Wax, Amy L. "The Two-Parent Family in the Liberal State: The Case for Selective Subsidies." *Michigan Journal of Race and Law* 1 (1996): 491–550.

Weisberg, D. Kelly and Susan Frelich Appleton. *Modern Family Law: Cases and Materials*. New York: Aspen Law and Business, 1998.

Weitzman, Lenore J. *The Divorce Revolution: The Unexpected Social and Economic Consequences for Women and Children in America*. New York: Free Press, 1985; London: Collier Macmillan, 1985.

Wenig, Mary Moers. "The Marital Property Law of Connecticut, Past, Present, and Future." *Wisconsin Law Review* 1990 (1990): 807–79.

West, Robin. "Authority, Autonomy, and Choice: The Role of Consent in the Moral and Political Visions of Franz Kafka and Richard Posner." *Harvard Law Review* 99 (1985): 384–427.

Whitehead, Barbara Dafoe. *The Divorce Culture*. New York: Knopf, 1997.

Wilcox, Brian L., Jennifer K. Robbennolt, Janet E. O'Keeffe, and Marisa E. Pinchon. "Teen Nonmarital Childbearing and Welfare: The Gap Between Research and Political Discourse." *Journal of Social Issues* 52 (1996): 71–90.

Williams, Lucy A. "The Ideology of Division: Behavior Modification Welfare Reform Proposals." *Yale Law Journal* 102 (1992): 719–746.

Williams, Wendy W. "The Equality Crisis: Some Reflections on Culture, Courts, and Feminism." In Katharine T. Bartlett and Rosanne Kennedy, eds., *Feminist Legal Theory: Readings in Law and Gender*, 15–34. Boulder: Westview, 1991.

Wilson, William J. *The Truly Disadvantaged*. Chicago: Chicago University Press, 1987.

——. *When Work Disappears: The World of the New Urban Poor*. New York: Knopf, 1996.

Wood, Robert G. "Marriage Rates and Marriageable Men: A Test of the Wilson Hypothesis." *Journal of Human Resources* 30 (1995): 163–93.

Woodhouse, Barbara Bennett. "Hatching the Egg: A Child-Centered Perspective on Parent's Rights." *Cardozo Law Review* 14 (1993): 1747–1806.

——. "Who Owns the Child?: *Meyer* and *Pierce* and the Child as Property." *William and Mary Law Review* 33 (1992): 995–1122.

Woodson, Carter G. *The African Background Outlines*. Washington, D.C.: Association for the Study of Negro Life and History, 1936.

Wu, Larry. "Effects of Family Structure an Income on Risks of Premarital Birth." *American Sociological Review* 61 (1996): 386–406.

Yardley, Jim. "Executive, Once Spotlighted in a Divorce, to Wed Again." *New York Times*, August 16, 1998, 36.

Zielenziger, Michael. "Japanese Women Having Fewer Babies." *San Jose Mercury News*, July 9, 1996, 8A.

Zinman, Daniel C. "Father Knows Best: The Unwed Father's Right to Raise His Infant Surrendered for Adoption." *Fordham Law Review* 60 (1992): 971.

COPYRIGHT AND
PERMISSIONS ACKNOWLEDGMENTS

Chapter 1 (equation 1.1): Reprinted from *A Treatise on the Family, Enlarged Edition* by Gary S. Becker. Copyright © 1991 by the President and Fellows of Harvard College. Reprinted by permission of Harvard University Press.

Chapter 1 (figure 1.1, *Doonesbury* comic strip): December 21, 1989. DOONESBURY © 1989 G. B. Trudeau. Reprinted with permission of UNIVERSAL PRESS SYNDICATE. All rights reserved.

Chapter 2 (figure 2.1, *Doonesbury* comic strip): August 4, 1986. DOONESBURY © 1986 G. B. Trudeau. Reprinted with permission of UNIVERSAL PRESS SYNDICATE. All rights reserved.

Chapter 3 (figure 3.1, *Doonesbury* comic strip): March 17, 1982. DOONESBURY © 1982 G. B. Trudeau. Reprinted with permission of UNIVERSAL PRESS SYNDICATE. All rights reserved.

Chapter 5 (figure 5.1, *Doonesbury* comic strip): March 26, 1985. DOONESBURY © 1985 G. B. Trudeau. Reprinted with permission of UNIVERSAL PRESS SYNDICATE. All rights reserved.

Chapters 7 and 8: Portions of these chapters appeared in June Carbone, "The Tie That Binds: Fidelity to Children — Not to Spouses — May Be a New Way of Approaching Family Policy," *Issues in Ethics* 8 (1997): 20. Reprinted with permission of *Issues in Ethics*, the publication of the Markkula Center for Applied Ethics at Santa Clara University.

Chapter 10 (figure 10.1): "A brothel for the upper classes" (Stone's caption; artist's caption: "Charity Covereth a Multitude of Sins"). By T. Rowlandson, 1781. Copyright © The British Museum. Reprinted by permission.

Chapter 10 (figure 10.2): "A brothel for the lower classes" (Stone's caption; artist's caption: "Black, Brown, & Fair"). By T. Rowlandson, 1807. Courtesy the Metropolitan Museum of Art, The Elisha Whittelsey Collection, The Elisha Whittelsey Fund, 1959 (59.533.1386). Reprinted by permission.

Chapter 11 (figure 11.2): "Trends in Percentage of Total Births Delivered to Single

Comes of Age: An Introduction to the Law of Child Support," in J. Thomas Old-ham and Marygold Melli, eds., *Child Support: The Next Frontier* (Ann Arbor: University of Michigan Press, 1999). Reprinted with permission of the University of Michigan Press.

Chapters 18, 20, and 22 (Bontrager cartoons): Jessie Bontrager produced these original cartoons for this volume: "Child support" (ch. 18), "Parenting plans" (ch. 20), and "Children and the Internet" (ch. 22).

Chapter 19 (figure 19.1, *Doonesbury* comic strip): December 19, 1982. DOONESBURY © 1982 G. B. Trudeau. Reprinted with permission of UNIVERSAL PRESS SYNDICATE. All rights reserved.

Chapter 21 (figure 21.1, *Doonesbury* comic strip): September 13, 1994. DOONESBURY © 1994 G. B. Trudeau. Reprinted with permission of UNIVERSAL PRESS SYNDICATE. All rights reserved.

(Page numbers referring to illustrations appear in bold.)

birth control

Becker female employment

too low / social security

constitutional
equality

2 rev.

no fault
bright line

NyTimes

homosexuals

anti subordination priv.

women

sexual minorities